SOUND OF THE GUNS

Other Books by FAIRFAX DOWNEY

SOUND OF THE GUNS

The Story of American Artillery from the
Ancient and Honorable Company to the
Atom Cannon and Guided Missile

By FAIRFAX Davis DOWNEY

DAVID McKAY COMPANY, INC.
New York

The following material from military publications is reproduced by permission of the Association of the United States Army:

Colonel Jennings C. Wise, "Field Artillery in Rearguard Action," from the January, 1923, issue of *The Field Artillery Journal;* copyright, 1923, by U.S. Field Artillery Association (now Association of the United States Army).

Colonel Allen J. Greer, "The Roaring Guns from the Seven Days to Cold Harbor," from the January, 1936, issue of *The Field Artillery Journal;* copyright, 1936, by U.S. Field Artillery Association.

General Edmund L. Gruber, "The Caissons Go Rolling Along," from the July, 1926, issue of *The Field Artillery Journal;* copyright, 1926, by U.S. Field Artillery Association.

Fairfax Downey, "Over Hill," from the July, 1941, issue of *The Field Artillery Journal;* copyright, 1941, by U.S. Field Artillery Association.

Captain John F. Casey, Jr., pages 563-568, from the August, 1943, issue of *The Field Artillery Journal;* copyright, 1943, by U.S. Field Artillery Association.

Lieutenant Colonel S. L. A. Marshall, pages 13ff., from the January, 1945, issue of *The Field Artillery Journal;* copyright, 1945, by U.S. Field Artillery Association.

Lieutenant Colonel William R. Jesse, "Bastogne—An Artillery Classic," from the December, 1945, issue of *The Field Artillery Journal;* copyright, 1945, by U.S. Field Artillery Association.

Colonel Bernard S. Waterman, "The Battle of Okinawa, an Artillery Angle," from the September, 1945, issue of *The Field Artillery Journal;* copyright, 1945, by U.S. Field Artillery Association.

MANUFACTURED IN THE UNITED STATES OF AMERICA

VAN REES PRESS • NEW YORK

TO AMERICAN ARTILLERYMEN

Of the past, who built the arm's proud tradition; of the present, who carry it on; of the future, in the hope that they may find inspiration in this record of those who served the guns before them.

Acknowledgments

I T IS IMPOSSIBLE for the author fully to express his enduring gratitude to Colonel Harry C. Larter, Jr., Artillery, U.S.A., retired, who inspired this book and, chapter by chapter, encouraged its completion. Whatever competence it possesses is chiefly due to the guidance of his wide historical and technical knowledge; inadequacies are mine. Use of a number of Colonel Larter's stirring drawings of field artillery adds another debt.

Major Charles J. West not only compiled a list of illustrations for selection but ably served as a critic, along with Colonel Larter. My thanks go also to other fellow members of the Company of Military Collectors and Historians: Colonel Frederick P. Todd, curator of the West Point Museum; Jac Weller, expert on the ordnance of the Revolution and the Civil War; John Lewis Hathaway, maker of miniature cannon; Hampton P. Howell, Jr., collector of model cannon; Colonel John Bakeless, versed in guns of American frontier warfare.

General G. B. Barth and General J. F. Brittingham, a comrade-in-arms of the Twelfth Field Artillery; Colonel T. D. Stamps, Professor and Head of the Department of Military Art & Engineering, U.S.M.A.; Lieutenant Colonel William A. Knowlton, Associate Professor of Social Sciences, U.S.M.A.; Colonel C. H. M. Roberts, and Colonel George B. Dyer all provided highly useful material.

My appreciation goes to Colonel Jennings C. Wise for permission to quote extensively from *The Long Arm of Lee*; to Charles Scribner's Sons for the use of excerpts from Colonel John W. Thomason, Jr.'s *Fix Bayonets!*; to the Association of the United States Army and its publications: the discontinued *Field Artillery Journal* and the magazines succeeding it, *Army Combat Forces Journal*, now

Army. My indebtedness is also considerable to the *Journal* of the Company of Military Collectors and Historians, whose board of governors permitted use of its excellent and accurate plates. A number of them are the work of H. Charles McBarron, Jr., whose special permission was kindly given. Charles Morris Loxley and Charles E. Peterson allowed examination of the typescript of the autobiography of Benjamin Loxley, officer in the Revolutionary artillery. *The American Legion Magazine* permitted adaption of my article "Reilly's Battery." Other acknowledgments are made in text and footnotes. Helpful advice was given by Lieutenant Colonel James G. Chestnutt, chief of the Magazine and Book Branch, Public Information Division, Department of the Army.

Essential research was done at the Artillery and Guided Missile Center, Fort Sill, Oklahoma, through the courtesy of its commandant, Lieutenant General Edward T. Williams. Valuable help was given and many book loans made by Librarian O. Willard Holloway and Olen C. Jeffries, reference librarian. Thanks are also offered Master Sergeant Morris Swett, former librarian; Gillett Griswold, museum chief curator, and Captain William Stack of the visitors' bureau. Besides Fort Sill's, other most useful collections were consulted at Dartmouth and Bowdoin Colleges; Yale, Harvard, and Columbia Universities; the New York Public Library; The United States Military Academy, West Point; the University and Yale Clubs, New York City. With profit and pleasure I visited artillery shrines in addition to Fort Sill: the West Point and Fort Ticonderoga museums, General Knox's house in Thomaston, Maine; the Hall of Cannon in Copenhagen, Denmark.

Parts of chapters appeared in *American Heritage; The Army Combat Forces Journal* and *Army;* the *Journal of the Company of Military Collectors and Historians, Civil War History,* and *The Chronicle,* Middleburg, Virginia.

I am deeply grateful to Kennett L. Rawson, editor of the David McKay Company, and to Lelia B. Ryan for penetrating and painstaking editing; to my literary agent, Oliver G. Swan, of Paul R. Reynolds & Son, for unfailing service; to my wife, Mildred Adams Downey, for criticism and typing.

Finally a salute to those under whom I have had the honor to serve as an artilleryman: General Robert M. Danford, who commanded the Yale Batteries; my regimental commanders in the first World War, Manus McCloskey and the late Henry L. Stimson; Generals Edwin P. Parker, Jr., and Donald T. Cubbison, whose adjutant I was at the Field Artillery Replacement Center, Fort Bragg, in World War II. From them I learned the tenets and traditions of a gallant arm, which the following pages strive to set forth.

FAIRFAX DOWNEY

West Springfield, New Hampshire, 1956

Contents

Illustrations

Following page 114

Illustrations in the Text

Front End Paper: Gun Team, Number One Piece, Right Section, "Tidball's Horse Battery," A Battery, 2nd U.S. Artillery, 1861

Back End Paper: The "Alamo City Guards" of San Antonio, Edgar's Battery, First Texas Light Battery, C.S.A., 1862

Both end papers are by Colonel Harry C. Larter, Jr., and are reproduced by courtesy of the artist and the Company of Military Collectors and Historians. Both are copyright, 1955, by the Company of Military Collectors and Historians.

SOUND OF THE GUNS

The columns should always support each other, and therefore, unless they have received a specific mission, or are in conflict themselves, should march to the sound of the guns.

FURSE, *The Art of Marching*

As a general rule, the maxim of marching to the sound of the guns is a wise one.

JOMINI, *Précis Politique et Militaire de la Campagne de 1815*

CHAPTER 1

Storm of a Citadel

●——●——●

Fortified towns are hard nuts to crack, and your teeth are not accustomed to it. Taking strong places is a particular trade, which you have taken up without serving an apprenticeship to it. Armies and veterans need skillful engineers to direct them in their attack. Have you any? But some seem to think that forts are as easy taken as snuff.

> BENJAMIN FRANKLIN, A letter to his brother in Boston before the siege of Louisbourg.[1]

It may so happen that the heavy pieces cannot be carried through bad roads, as in America . . .

> JOHN MÜLLER, *Treatise of Artillery*

●——●——●

A GREAT mustering of cannon early took place in North America. The first guns came to the New World on the caravels of Columbus. Rapidly they increased in number and in size. Their muzzles peered over the ramparts of forts of the Spanish Main, defending the sea and land approaches. They guarded the ports and palisades of the English colonies. Between 1720 and 1755 the British army shipped across the Atlantic 649 pieces of ordnance, ranging from 3-pounders to 42's, with still more following.[2] In French Canada hundreds of powerful guns and mortars rendered the citadels of Louisbourg, Quebec, and Carillon (Ticonderoga) seemingly impregnable.

For many years these cannon remained coastbound or waterborne. The field guns of that era were too cumbersome for use in forest warfare against the Indians or other enemies. Yet, as for centuries on the battlefields of Europe and Asia, they were playing a vital part in shaping the destiny of a continent.

Privateersmen and merchant sailors began to build the great traditions of American naval gunnery. Land batteries were commanded by crusty old master gunners, mostly European professionals. They condescended to train husky recruits in the heavy work of loading and manhandling the pieces, and the youngsters were quick to learn. An officers' corps appeared with the foundation in 1638 of the Ancient and Honorable Artillery Company of Boston,[3] established by colonists from the London Company, chartered one hundred years earlier. As "scholars of great gunnes," members of that oldest military organization in America, still in existence with headquarters at Faneuil Hall, studied the art of the artillerist, gaining knowledge that would stand their country in good stead.

By 1745 cannon and crews to serve them were at hand for the first major action of American artillery.

Lines of hurrying men, volunteer militia from Massachusetts and her subprovince of Maine, loaded munitions and supplies on ships moored to the wharves of Boston in the spring of 1745. Artillerymen hoisted aboard cannon stripped from harbor defenses, and others borrowed from as far away as New York. Slings of round shot were lowered into holds, along with casks of powder, salt meat, hard bread, of water and of rum. Crammed with troops and cargo, vessels cast off and moved out to anchor in the bay. On March 24 a fleet of sixty sail, transports with an escort of a frigate and a few armed sloops, put to sea.

Off the Nova Scotian fishing village of Canso, they would make rendezvous with contingents from New Hampshire and Connecticut and sail on to lay siege to Louisbourg in French Acadia, one of the mightiest fortresses of the day.

The old struggle between Great Britain and France over North American colonies had flared up in a conflict spilled over from Europe—King George's War, declared in the past year. New Englanders were ready and willing to claim this quarrel of the second George for their own. To them Louisbourg, sea link with France and gateway to Quebec, which must some day be taken in its turn, was a stronghold of "popery, privateers, and pirates," a menacing and insolent rival of New England commerce and fisheries. Louisbourg must fall.

Neither British regulars nor the Royal Exchequer were asked to support this expedition, organized by Governor William Shirley of Massachusetts and commanded by William Pepperrell of Maine. A British fleet in the West Indies had been requested to co-operate, but its commodore, lacking orders, refused. In sublime disregard of the Royal Navy as unessential, the American flotilla sailed north. Had even one French ship of the line intercepted, she could have blown the few small American warships out of the water and sunk the transports at leisure.

It was a "mad scheme," this expedition, "a project of wild audacity." [4] Louisbourg was famed as the Gibraltar of the West. The fortress, after plans by the great French military engineer Vauban, had been twenty-five years in building. Its cost had mounted to thirty million livres, then equivalent to six million dollars. Two thousand regulars and Canadian militia garrisoned it. On the land side above an eight-foot moat rose walls thirty feet high and forty feet thick at the base, with jutting bastions and a citadel. Its seaward face was considered still more impregnable. Two formidable batteries protected the harbor entrance of its site on Cape Breton Island. Ramparts bristled with 250 cannon—powerful guns, mortars, and swivels. The third, small but murderous pieces, could ruin attempts at an escalade, sweeping storming parties from their ladders with deadly blasts of langrage—charges of nails, bolts, chain links, and other scrap iron.

To counter the fire of the French batteries and bombard and breach massive walls, the Americans carried only eight 22-pounders, ten 18's, twelve 9's, and four mortars, from 12- to 9-inch. A large proportion of the ammunition consisted of 42-pound cannon balls, almost twice too big for the caliber of the expedition's heaviest ordnance. Those, however, would exactly fit the bores of heavy cannon known to form a considerable part of the French armament. It would be necessary only to storm the Grand or the Island Battery, load captured 42's with balls foresightedly provided, open fire, and demolish the remainder of Louisbourg's defenses. Although such strategy, as Thomas Hutchinson, future Royal Governor of Massachusetts, caustically remarked, was "like selling the skin of a bear before catching him," few paid any more heed to him than to Ben Franklin's warning that fortified towns are not "as easy taken as snuff."

So with confidence as superb as it was foolhardy, an army of some four thousand farmers, fishermen, shopkeepers, and artisans, under command of a lumber merchant, set forth to assault and capture the great French stronghold.

Colonel Joseph Dwight and Lieutenant Colonel Richard Gridley of the artillery had mustered artificers to maintain and repair the guns. In addition, they could count upon the services of gunsmiths, blacksmiths, and armorers in other commands, such as Major Seth Pomeroy of one of the infantry regiments. (Pomeroy, who carried a musket of his own make, would come to the aid of the gunners at a critical moment with his smith's skill.) And in the rank and file of the army, many, though they might never have seen a cannon before, possessed the resourcefulness and handiness of pioneers. Show them how to put a piece in position, to load, aim, and fire, and they would manage.

Spirit and resolution were strong in these volunteers, who had flocked to enlist for the attack on Louisbourg at meager pay, though not without hopes of plunder. Booty, trade, and fishing rights aside, the campaign was hailed as a Protestant crusade against a New World Rome, a crusade proclaimed and sustained by the presence of a "goodly company of preachers." Chief of chaplains was the redoubtable Samuel Moody whose York, Maine, congregation endured its winter worship standing in an icy meetinghouse for his two-hour prayers, followed by sermons demanding equal fortitude; only the gift of a barrel of cider would induce the minister to show mercy. Chaplain Moses Coffin of Newbury—his life was later saved by a pocket Bible in which a bullet lodged—doubled as a drummer and was known as "the drum ecclesiastic." [5]

Not every regiment carried a parson on its rolls, but the artillery train took care to list its chaplain, Joseph Hawley. An aura of brimstone still lingered from the days when the secrets of the Gunners Guild were denounced as a compact with the Devil. Servers of cannon long were regarded with superstitious horror, and captured artillerymen in early European wars were likely to be tortured and mutilated

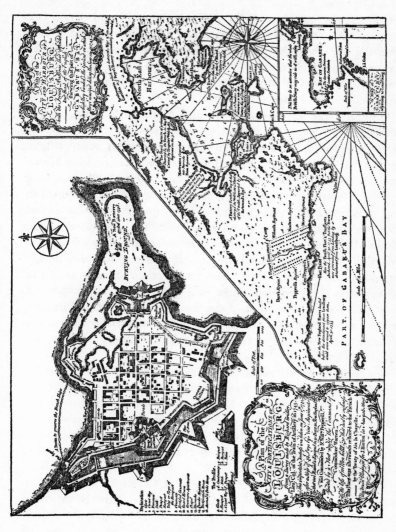

COLONEL RICHARD GRIDLEY'S MAP OF LOUISBURG (*courtesy of the Widener Library, Harvard University*)

before they were put to death. One pope saw fit to excommunicate all artillerymen.[6]

Chivalry had also branded artillery as the artifice of Satan. Don Quixote rails at its "devilish instruments" which enable "a base, cowardly hand to take the life of the bravest gentlemen." Shakespeare's Hotspur (*I Henry IV,* Act I, Scene 3) speaks of a lord who complained of "villainous salt-petre" and "vile guns," which had destroyed "many a good tall fellow."

Prejudice was not slow to cross the Atlantic. "Many a time it falleth out that most men employed for gunners are very negligent of the fear of God," declared a Puritan moralist, who added a fable about a wicked artilleryman, scathingly named "Christopher Slime" and claimed by the Devil for his own. The Ancient and Honorable Artillery Company, soon after its organization, prudently banned infernal associations by requesting some eminent divine to preach them an annual sermon. None other than the celebrated Cotton Mather had obligingly responded with redeeming discourses. "May this Artillery Company be a little Nursery of Renowned Souldiers," [7] he besought; then added the pious and appropriate sentiment that "Prayer was the great field-piece of Jehoshophat, and Luther was wont to style it the gun-shot of the soul." The profane and ungodly reputation of gunners may also have been mitigated by their seventeenth-century practice of timing a fuse's burning by repeating the Apostles' Creed.

But even the most fervent did not expect prayer to make a second Jericho of Louisbourg. Its walls would have to be scaled or battered down. By the time the Canso rendezvous was kept, no better plan had been evolved than a complicated night attack. Four divisions were to land separately, advance in "profound silence" (unlikely in view of the expected generous issue of rum), and launch an assault on the Grand Battery.

While the Provincial fleet was held at Canso by a report that Louisbourg harbor was ice-locked, five warships of the Royal Navy, led by the sixty-gun *Superbe,* arrived after all, Commodore Peter Warren having received orders. He could be relied on to beat off French attempts to relieve the fortress by sea. The expeditionary force sailed on, more confident than ever, its assurance echoed in a letter brought by a dispatch boat from Boston to one of its colonels:

"I hope this will find you at Louisbourg with a Bowl of Punch, a Pipe, and a P - - k of C - - ds in your hand and whatever else you desire [8] (I had forgot to mention a Pretty French Madammoselle)." [8]

A Massachusetts private was one of the few who realized such hopes. He recorded in his diary [9] that he and two companions downed four pints of wine in a Canadian inn, after which he "had thots of matching with a young French Lady: I went into her Company—Had But Littel Discource for could not understand one a nother." Future generations of Americans, campaigning in France, would, when faced with similar dilemmas, acquire *dictionnaires en peau.*

At first sight of hostile sails on April 30, signal cannon on the Louisbourg battlements boomed, and alarm bells called in all inhabitants living outside the town. Pepperrell wasted no time. Hardly had his transports anchored when boats were lowered, and infantry clambered down into them. Sturdy arms at the oars drove them through crashing surf past jagged rocks, pulling for Gabarus Bay, west of the harbor. A party from the garrison raced along the shore to repulse them. The boats were beached ahead of them, and cheering Americans poured out. There was a short, sharp clash. The French fled, leaving twenty dead. By nightfall two thousand troops had landed, followed by the rest of the force the next day. It was a neat amphibious operation, but the militiamen, huddled around their campfires, lost some of their confidence as they stared in awe toward the citadel of Louisbourg and its flanking batteries, looming high and forbidding above them.

Colonel William Vaughan, leading his regiment inland, came upon several undefended naval storehouses. Promptly he put the torch to them. Clouds of smoke, thick and black from tar, pitch, and oil, drifted down on the Grand or Royal Battery. The colonel and his troops, grinning over the coughing and eye-smarting to which they had treated the Frenchies, turned in for the night.

In the morning Vaughan advanced with thirteen men to reconnoiter. When they drew no fire from the battery, the colonel bribed an Indian of his detachment with a flask of brandy and sent him forward. Climbing up through an embrasure, the scout soon signaled them on with a whoop. They rushed in to find the works abandoned by their four-hundred-man garrison. The Grand Battery had been swept clean by a smoke screen with nothing behind it.

While a young soldier hoisted his scarlet coat on the staff to serve as a flag, and the guns of the citadel loosed an angry, futile salvo, Colonel Vaughan sent for reinforcements. Before they could arrive, four boatloads from Louisbourg sped in to attack and redeem the ignominious loss of the vital battery. The little party of Americans rushed down to the beach and blazed away until the French retreated before a regiment coming up at the double to clinch the victory.

In the Grand Battery were found large supplies of powder and shot and twenty heavy cannon. The French artillerymen had failed miserably and disgracefully to blow up the magazine and permanently disable their ordnance. They had hastily spiked the guns with iron rods hammered into their vents but neglected to knock off trunnions, supporting the barrels on carriages, and to burn or chop up the latter. Major Pomeroy [10] and twenty other gunsmiths, quickly summoned, handily drilled out the vents. By next morning the captured pieces were ready for action. Jubilant Yankee gunners shifted them, trained them on the town, and opened a thunderous bombardment. "The enemy," wrote the *Habitant de Louisbourg,* "saluted us with our own cannon and made a terrific fire, smashing everything within range." There was no need for the Americans to be sparing of the French ammunition, for most of the Grand Battery guns were 42's. The 42-pound cannon balls, so optimistically stowed at Boston, would shortly be available and serve admirably.

The Grand Battery, easy prize of panic, roared on, crushing outer works and riddling houses in the town. But its shot alone could not breach the principal defenses of the citadel nor even reach the Island Battery, which barred entrance to the harbor and supported the main fortress. Guns must be brought ashore from the fleet and put in commanding positions.

The achievement of that tremendous feat, by raw militia, never surpassed in all our wars, established a tradition for American artillery.

Flatboats were launched from the transports, tossing at anchor.

Down into those clumsy craft were lowered cannon, ammunition, and stores. Rowers plunged in sweeps and pulled with all their might through waves that broke over gunwales, threatening to swamp the entire flotilla. The flatboats, too big and heavily laden to clear rocky barriers offshore and be beached, had to be held in the shallows by force of arm and oar, while soldiers swung overside and waded waist-deep through the icy surf, unloading them. Tide and backwash wrenched at them as they struggled ashore, powder casks lifted high on head and shoulders. They risked the rocks to bring the cannon barges closer in and, for every gun landed, lost a boat, pounded to pulpwood. Drenched, exhausted men slept shelterless, many blanketless, through cold, foggy nights, and each morning limped stiffly back to their task until it was finished.

Worse still lay before them. Over rough and roadless terrain, without transport animals, the guns must be dragged more than two miles by man power. Inland rose a line of hills commanding the town and harbor. That high ground could be the key to Louisbourg, as the Plains of Abraham later were for Quebec, and Mount Defiance for Fort Ticonderoga.

Sand first—easy going considering what was to come. Brawny hands laid hold of long anchor cables, attached to gun and mortar carriages, and heaved away. On they rolled at a good pace. Rocks now, slowing them lest they break wheels. Long stretches of dense scrub and brush to push through or be hacked by axmen. Finally swamps confronted them, boulder-studded bogs deceptively carpeted with moss. Wheels mired, sank past hubs till carriages, then guns, went under, gulped down by sucking mud. Men hauled them out onto patches of firmer ground and halted in bafflement. There was no other approach to the heights except through the swamp. While the trekkers stood there, gunners in Louisbourg sighted them and opened fire with every piece that would bear, forcing them to take cover.

A man stepped forward to meet the crisis—Lieutenant Colonel Nathaniel Meserve of New Hampshire, a shipbuilder. He set lumbermen, farmers, and carpenters to constructing sledges six-feet-by-five, like the familiar stoneboats used to clear New England fields of rocks. A cannon was placed on each, and a team of two hundred men harnessed themselves in like horses with breast straps and rope traces. By night or in fog, to avoid the daylight hail of French shells, they hauled and tugged, staggering ahead, floundering through the clinging mud. No route could be used twice; the passage of a single sledge had churned each one into an impassable slough. Gun by gun, the teams won their way through the blackness and the haze to solid footing.

Earthworks and emplacements were waiting for them. Six pieces were sited on Green Hill, little more than a mile from the citadel, the King's Bastion. A week more of backbreaking toil, and another battery was in position: four 22's and ten of the small mortars called coehorns after the Dutch baron who invented them. At length five batteries were in action, the last consisting of five captured French 42-pounders, which had required teams of three hundred men to drag each one through the quagmire. Muzzles flamed, and iron fists knocked clangorously at the gates of Louisbourg.

Eager but inept crews swarmed around the smoke-wreathed guns and mortars. Instructions and commands were bellowed by officers of the Ancient and Honorable Company, aided by Chaplain Coffin, the "drum ecclesiastic," who surprisingly came forward with yet a third talent—gunnery. "Search your piece," they shouted, and matrosses [11] peered into dark bores, looking for burning powder particles or smoldering shreds of cloth—then swabbed with wet sponges on staffs to cool the barrels. Yet a spark might remain in the tube, and the next command, "Serve the vent," was a wise safety measure. Obeying, the gunner pressed down a thumb, protected by a leather shield, tightly against the vent. That kept the rush of air in loading from reviving any glowing bit to ignite the new charge. If the gunner neglected to perform that duty, the Number One whacked his pate lustily with the rammer staff. Such enthusiastic correction by its wielder was quite understandable. Number One was taking no chances on having his arms blown off.

Loose powder was then ladled in, or cartridges, and wads shoved down against the charge. "Regard your shot" (see to it that no dirt, a cause of premature bursts, clung to the ball). "Put home your shot gently," officers cautioned and bade loaders stand aside from the muzzle, for, as the old manual observed, "it is silly to run danger without reason." The order to fire—match to powder train—a thunderous discharge. Squat mortars rocked on their beds. Guns recoiled, their quoins—wooden wedges hammered under breeches to elevate them—flying in all directions.

"The first shot is for the Devil," ran a gunner's proverb, "the second for God, and only the third for the King." Veteran gun captains tried to ensure their first round would fall short so they could observe it, since overs were likely to be lost. Elevating for the second, they watched its impact and hoped to hit the target only with the third.

Big guns, aptly called battering pieces, pounded away at the walls, the heavy 42's with a range of 5,600 yards. It was the mortar shells, soaring over ramparts, that created the greatest havoc. Often they landed without exploding on impact and ricocheted among the defenders. Their effect was terrifying, as Müller, the artillery expert, described: "When they perceive the shells rolling along with their fuses burning, and expecting them to burst every moment, the bravest among them will hardly have the courage to wait for their coming near him."

Here and there a piece fell silent. Its barrel had grown too hot to be fired with safety, and it must be allowed to cool—must be "refreshed." Its fellows maintained the din of cannonading, drowning the rattle of musketry where the range was close. In reprisal the French ventured one halfhearted sortie, which was beaten back— then resumed the artillery duel. Between salvos their gunners drank toasts and leaned over the ramparts to make mocking offers of brimming cups of wine to the thirsty *"Bostonais."*

Gallic bravado soon was dissipated by converging fire from a semicircle of American batteries in the hills. They blasted away with captured ammunition and their own, landed from the fleet. Reckless cannoneers leaped out of trenches to retrieve rolling balls fired by the French and shoot them back.

The New Englanders suffered more from their own inexperience than from enemy retaliation. Stout Protestants, they neither knew nor would have followed a precaution the Catholic French inherited from early artillerymen. The wise and devout gunner, before firing that unreliable instrument, a cannon, crosses himself and invokes the patron saint of the artillery, lest the iron monster burst in his face. The rasher of Pepperrell's untaught crews had grave need of divine intercession. They overcharged and double-shotted their

guns, crammed their mortars full of powder. Then ensued the frightful blast, which even contemporary gunners dread, and few close to
it survive. Men, horribly mangled by jagged hunks of hurtling
metal, died around their guns. Since competent artillerists were too
few to prevent such accidents, Commodore Warren spared four
master gunners from his fleet to help instruct the overzealous ama-
teurs.

May wore into June. A month of constant combat, exhausting
labor, and exposure had taken toll. But in spite of losses from bursting pieces, French counterbattery fire, and a sick list of fifteen hundred, down with fever and dysentery, the bombardment of Louisbourg seldom slackened. American artillerymen, many barefoot and
in tatters now, kept the guns in action.

Round shot and shells raked the streets of the town, smashed
houses, and drove garrison and defenders to refuge in stifling casemates. Balls tore gaps in the stone walls of the citadel, yet those
were quickly repaired, and there was still no breach sufficiently practicable to permit a direct assault. Arrogantly the French boasted
that women alone could defend Louisbourg.

"But," as was written of a later siege, "the strongest fortress and
sternest virtue have weak points and require unremitting vigilance
to guard them: let warrior and dame take warning." [12]

Pepperrell and his council of war ordered the storming of the
Island Battery. Far from being a weak point, it was armed with
thirty heavy cannon, two mortars, and seven swivels, yet a surprise
night attack might well carry it if the French were caught off guard.
On a dark June midnight a party of three hundred volunteers paddled across the bay from the Grand Battery. They picked up a
hundred more men on Lighthouse Point and made a landing
through high surf on the shores of a narrow cove beneath the walls.
Twelve scaling ladders had been planted without detection when
a trooper with a bellyful of rum burst out with three loud and hearty
cheers. Alerted, the garrison sprang to arms. Guns, swivels, and
muskets poured down a withering fire from the ramparts. In a bloody
repulse, the Provincials lost 189 men, casualties and prisoners. An
assault that might have succeeded had been ruined by an undis-
ciplined sot.

Now the issue depended again upon the besiegers' guns. Lieutenant Colonel Gridley, acting as chief engineer as well as second in command of the artillery train, put cannon ashore on the rocks of almost inaccessible Lighthouse Point. Panting, sweating men hoisted them up a steep cliff and dragged them a mile and a quarter to a place of vantage. Soon a keen-eyed artilleryman, peering down into the water at low tide, spotted the dark bulk of ten heavy pieces, half buried by the sand. Sliding overboard when a ship was careened for barnacle scraping, the guns had lain there for ten years. All the French governors had known their location, but none had taken the trouble to fish them out. Elated New Englanders roped them and sent them up the cliff to join the rest of the armament.

Shot and shell rained down on the Island Battery. Bursting bombs shattered the casemates, and balls hurtled through embrasures, wrecking gun carriages. So fierce and effective was the bombardment that Frenchmen ran from the fort and dove into the sea to escape the storm of iron. Their cannon, unmanned or dismounted, stood useless.

American guns concentrated on the citadel. Fire from the inland emplacements and the Grand Battery redoubled. Great gaps yawned now in the citadel walls. Debris heaped higher, filling the moat. Pepperrell and Warren, whose reinforced fleet had been gathering in French prizes laden with food, molasses, and rum, made ready for a grand assault by land and sea.

It never was delivered. Suddenly a white flag of truce fluttered from the staff of the citadel. Louisbourg was surrendering.

Under terms of capitulation the garrison marched out, colors flying and drums beating, to be later embarked along with the towns-folk for France. They left behind them a shattered citadel, mauled by nine thousand balls and six hundred shells.

Chaplain Moody raged through the French churches, wielding an ax with bigoted zeal on altar and images; [13] mollified, he later astonished and delighted hungry diners at the victory banquet by the record brevity of his grace. "Lord," he prayed, "we have so many things to thank Thee for, that time would fail us to do it fully. We leave it, therefore, for the work of eternity." Knives and spoons clattered, the trenchermen immensely thankful that the parson, on this occasion at least, would not try to compete with eternity.

Spoils of war included a silver cross, which was presented to

Harvard College, but the army was bitterly disappointed in hopes of rich loot from Louisbourg. A clamoring rose, "a great Noys and hubbub," wrote one disgusted trooper, "a mongst ye Soldiers a bout ye Plunder; Som Cursing, som a Swarein." [14] It was the British Crown and Navy that drew huge dividends from the triumph: five million dollars worth of French prizes including a treasure ship from Peru, lured into the harbor by the fleur-de-lis banner flying over the citadel again in place of the English ensign. Sacks of cocoa in her hold concealed a fortune in coinage and gold and silver ingots. Not a cent of that vast windfall went to the New Englanders who had stormed Louisbourg, although the Royal Exchequer eventually reimbursed Massachusetts for her expenditure of two hundred thousand pounds sterling in financing the expedition. Pepperrell, who spent ten thousand pounds of his own funds on the campaign, was never repaid; he was rewarded with a knighthood and a colonelcy in the British Army.

Louisbourg's cost to its conquerors in blood and toil seemed vainly spent. Diplomats at the peace table traded away what soldiers had won, restoring the fortress to the French in exchange for Madras in India. It all had to be done over again. In 1758 a British expedition, without a Colonial contingent,[15] recaptured and thereafter held Louisbourg.

Yet the first siege, one of the most desperate and gallant exploits in the annals of warfare, an artillery epic, had been far from futile. Cannon had made and unmade kings before. At Louisbourg their thunder was the crack of doom for the empire of France in the New World. They helped shape the destiny of North America—of a nation-to-be, the United States. By storming the great fortress, against long odds and logical military expectation, Americans gained a confidence they would never lose. It was strong thirty years later at the outbreak of the Revolution, and its token and symbol were veterans of Louisbourg, old men in faded uniforms marching once more to the sound of the guns.

CHAPTER 2

Christening of the Cannon

•••

"The Hancock." Sacred to Liberty. This is one of the four cannon which constituted the whole train of Field Artillery possessed by the British Colonies of North America at the commencement of the war, on the 19th of April, 1775. This cannon and its fellow belonged to a number of citizens of Boston; were used in many engagements during the war. The other two, the property of the Commonwealth of Massachusetts, were taken by the enemy.

> Inscription placed by General Knox on a brass 3-pounder, preserved with its companion gun, "The Adams," in the Bunker Hill Monument

What the colours are to the infantryman, the gun is, or ought to be, to the artilleryman. It is our emblem, our standard. When I joined, the last honour to a gunner was the burial service "over the metal."

Times and habits may change, but the devotion to the gun must be inculcated into the heart of every gunner.

> Master Gunner F. M. Milne in *The Story of the Gun* by Lieut. A. W. Wilson, Royal Artillery

•••

Objectives of British and Provincial forces, campaigning to drive the French from the continent, were always fortified posts. In almost every case cannon were essential to reduce them, whether they were stone fortresses or stockaded, sod-roofed blockhouses, defensible against infantry and fire arrows.[16]

By waterways and through wildernesses, over appallingly difficult terrain, such as Pepperrell's men had encountered at Louisbourg, guns were transported to siege and battlefield. With them went the amazing amount of matériel, equipment, and stores demanded by the constantly more complicated arm of artillery—items that ran into the hundreds. Tarpaulins to cover guns in bad weather, aprons of lead to protect vent holes, tompions to stopper muzzles against moisture. Leather buckets for powder, wooden ones for water to cool bores hot from firing. Handspikes to shift trails, priming wires to clear vents and pierce cartridges, linstocks holding slow matches to ignite priming charges. Barrels of flints, iron-melting ladles and grates for heating shot. Lanterns and tallow candles, needles, pack-thread, rasps, and scales. Brass quadrants to measure the angle of fire for howitzers and mortars. Powder funnels and fuses for shells. Signal rockets, body and head armor, pioneer and artificer tools of many kinds. Traveling forges, powder carts and ammunition wagons, tumbrils to carry equipment, block carriages and sling carts for transporting heavy ordnance. Spare wheels, ropes, draft chains. Harness for horses and bricoles for men to haul the guns.[17]

Such stores, along with ammunition, filled the twenty-six wagons and carts of Braddock's artillery train when he led his ill-fated expedition west in 1754 to capture Fort Duquesne. French and Indians ambushed him on the Monongahela. Braddock died with many of his officers and men, and most of his guns were lost, but young Colonel Washington of Virginia, his coat riddled with bullets, survived to fight again.

Four years later British General Abercromby attempted to storm French Fort Carillon, ignoring his artillery, and suffered a shattering repulse. Lord Jeffrey Amherst did far better the following year. That able soldier of the King brought up his guns and forced the French to yield the stronghold. As the French retreated, they blew it up, but the British rebuilt and rearmed it, naming it Fort Ticonderoga.

The time had come for cannon, brought from Britain to blast out an empire in the New World, to be turned against the victors by men of their own blood, serving the cause of American independence. Yet most of those guns and the skill to use them still rested in

British hands in that momentous month of 1775 when the first shot of the Revolution was fired.

Two 6-pounders of the Royal Artillery rumbled along with Lord Percy's brigade when it marched out of Boston on the nineteenth of April, '75. Fifes shrilled "Yankee Doodle" in derision of upstart Colonials who dared defy the King, but drums beat the quickstep with increasing urgency. Ominous reports were coming in from another British force, sent out the night before to capture patriot leaders and military stores in the country towns. It was reeling back from Concord hard-pressed, sorely in need of rescue. Minute Men, turned out by midnight riders, hung on its flanks and rear, firing from behind stone walls and bushes, toppling the tall grenadiers and light infantrymen.

When Percy reached Lexington, he posted his cannon to command the approach from Concord. Routed redcoats of the first column stumbled back through his lines, and the guns boomed, covering their retreat. Americans, close on their heels, scattered wildly. Some took shelter behind the meetinghouse. Once more a gun slammed. Its round shot crashed through the church, and the Yankees ran again. "The balls went high over our heads," declared a fighting parson.[18] "But no cannon ever did more execution; such stories of their effect had been spread by the Tories through our troops, that, for this time, more went back than pursued."

These fighting men had stood under volleys of musketry and the threat of bayonets. Crumpled bodies in homespun, strewn from Lexington Green to Concord Bridge, were proof of their valor. But flaming cannon and the rushing wind of balls that could pierce a stout building were, as always, strange and terrifying to raw troops facing their first artillery fire.

Nevertheless they rallied and attacked fiercely, as the regulars formed up and countermarched toward Boston. Percy's flankers desperately fought them off, while his guns halted to blast back assaults on the rear guard where one harried regiment relieved another in bearing the brunt. On through the dangerous pass below Prospect Hill the 6-pounders stemmed the swelling tide of pursuit. Brought up from the rear, their fire held off Yankee reinforcements barring the way at Cambridge. There the scarlet column, burdened with its wounded, veered off and made its escape by way of Charlestown.

"The fear of the cannon," Allen French estimates in *The Day of Concord and Lexington*, "after all, won the day." [19] Rather, those two light pieces, with only the ammunition carried in their side boxes—twenty-four rounds per gun—saved a day nearly lost, one that cost the British 273 dead, wounded, and missing as compared to American casualties of 93. As vital as the effect of the enemy artillery in that first battle of the Revolution was the fact it demonstrated to colonies now in open rebellion. To conquer in the struggle before them they must match gun against gun.

A search for cannon and artillerymen, already begun by the Provincial Congress, was intensified. Guns were available, though mostly of small or moderate caliber; not a few of them were in poor condition, their bores pitted. Gunners were as scarce as powder was. Colonel Gridley [20] and other aging veterans of the French and Indian Wars were called back into service, and the members of companies in Boston, Philadelphia, and Charleston, South Carolina,[21] were mustered. Not until June, though earlier authorized by Congress, was the 1st Massachusetts Artillery organized under Gridley. Junior officers and most of its cannoneers were green, with no experience beyond drill and limited firing practice.

By great good fortune a commanding genius for the artillery of the army of the future United States was about to emerge—surprisingly from a Boston bookshop.

Henry Knox was a huge fellow. In young manhood his powerful six-foot-three frame packed two hundred and fifty pounds. Resolute and coolheaded, he had stepped into the mob scene called the Boston Massacre in a bold but vain attempt to prevent British troops from firing on rioting citizens. First as assistant, then proprietor of a successful bookstore, he supported his widowed mother and a younger brother. While he sold volumes of sermons, tomes on law and medicine, and popular novels, he dug deep into all the military history and tactics of his stock in trade; he learned Latin, French, and some German to read works not translated into English. Robins' *New Principles of Gunnery* and Müller's *Treatise of Artillery* [22] fascinated him. The latter would serve as a basic text for American artillerymen; the former was also highly regarded.

Knox took to the technicalities of Müller and Robins as avidly as youngsters did to the copies of *Robinson Crusoe* on his shelves, or women customers to the romantic passages in *Tom Jones* and *Tristram Shandy*. Likewise the lore, rights, and privileges of the artillery were at the big bookseller's finger tips. How Frederick the Great had decreed that a gunner's —

> monthly pay was reckoned anew from the day when a fortress was captured or siege repelled. No provost-marshal had the right to judge him; that was the prerogative only of his own superiors. His wife and child stayed with him, not with the general baggage train. When food was distributed, he did not have to stand in line with other soldiers, but need only raise his fire stick to be served immediately. He did not need to plunder, since by right all church bells of captured cities and all captured artillery belonged to him and must be purchased from him by his field marshal with money. When a foot soldier, chased by the military police, could gain the artillery train and lay his hand on a gun, his pursuers could not touch him, and his right of asylum lasted three days.[23]

At eighteen Knox joined the Boston militia. When he was twenty-two, his book knowledge and natural aptitude made him second in command of its artillery train. In his handsome uniform he looked the born soldier he was. His great bass bellow of a voice could be heard across the parade ground and above the bark of guns he handled so ably. British drill masters rated him highly, and as tension between Crown and colonies increased, Knox was pressed to accept a commission in the King's service but repeatedly declined. Although his shop was a fashionable gathering place for officers of the garrison and Tory ladies, the patriotic sentiments of the young bookseller and militiaman were steadfast. He preached them persuasively to a daughter of wealthy Loyalists, often in the shop and fond of books, particularly of books sold by Henry Knox. Lucy Flucker, tall and amply proportioned, though so light on her feet that she would become a favorite dancing partner of General Washington, may well have reminded her suitor of portrayals of the statuesque Barbara, patron saint of the artillery, by Rafael, Palma Vecchio, and other painters and sculptors.[24]

The legend of Barbara, a maiden of Heliopolis in Egypt, relates that her pagan sire shut her up in a tower after he discovered she had embraced Christianity. Baffled when the scourge with which he whipped her turned into a peacock feather, her father drew his sword and struck off her head. Whereupon "the dread artillery of Heaven flashed," and a lightning bolt scored a direct hit on the old heathen. It was a form of retribution that appealed some thirteen centuries later to pioneer gunners, manning their new, thunderous engines of war. They chose the martyred Barbara as their patron and wore her image, flanked by prison tower and lightning streak, on their caps. Gun crews invoked her to safeguard them against the all too frequent calamity of bursting cannon and to make their aim as true as that of the bolt which avenged her on her wicked father. She remains the gunners' saint, though St. Joan of Arc, a fine artillerist who sometimes aimed siege cannon herself, has been urged as a better choice.

Regardless of the fate of St. Barbara, Lucy Flucker was not in the least dismayed by the opposition of her father, Secretary of the Province, to Knox's courtship. By threatening to elope she won her parents' reluctant consent and married the young artilleryman.

After Concord and Lexington, Knox, proscribed as a rebel, was compelled to quit Boston to escape arrest. Lucy refused to be left behind, and the couple managed to slip out of town with Knox's sword sewn in the lining of his wife's cloak. Throughout the Revolution Lucy joined her husband whenever possible until it came to be said of her that she followed the army like the drum.

It was some months before Henry Knox buckled that sword on again as a soldier. Meanwhile he volunteered as a civilian engineer, helping to build the fortifications which began to ring Boston and place it under siege by assembling American forces.

Former Lieutenant Knox of the militia, decamping before British prison gates closed on him, had been forced to abandon the guns of his train: three brass 3-pounders, embossed with the arms of the Province of Massachusetts. Two of them recently had been given names in accordance with an old custom, which originated as a means of identifying pieces of the same caliber and was carried on by artillerymen, always fond of personifying the guns they serve.

Early types were named for serpents and birds of prey because of
the consternation caused by their fire: the falconet for the falcon,
the culverin from the Latin *coluber* (snake) and the basilisk for "the
serpent Basilicus who, as Livy writeth, killed Man or Beast with his
sight." Louis XII christened heavy cannon after the twelve peers
of France, while Charles V's "Twelve Apostles" appropriately bombarded the infidel Turk. A monstrous Russian piece, the largest
caliber gun on record, bore the title, "The Great Mortar of Moscow";
cast c. 1525, the diameter of its bore was thirty-six inches, its length
eighteen feet, and the weight of its stone projectile two thousand
pounds. Two 60-pounders in the Bremen Arsenal bore the telling
title, "Messengers of Bad News." Other individual names, embossed
on barrels along with decorative designs and coats of arms, included
"Thunder," "Fury," "The Organist," "The Pious One," "The Doctor." A bombard of noble proportions was named after Catherine
de' Medici by a courtly cannoneer who explained: "Madam, it is
because its caliber is larger and stouter than all the rest." Such inscriptions were sometimes added as: "I punish injustice," or "I am
called the Griffin. I serve my lord of Treves. Where he commands
me to exert my strength, I straightway throw down gates and walls."
The prowess of a 24-foot sixteenth-century fieldpiece, modestly
dubbed "Queen Elizabeth's Pocket Pistol," was etched on its barrel
in rhymes:

> Men call me a breaker of tower and wall.
> Through hill and dale I hurl my ball.
> Sponge me dry and keep me clean,
> And I'll fire a shot to Calais Green.

Even more poetic was the legend borne by "Zam-Zammah," the
first cannon cast in India: "... terrible as a dragon and huge as a
mountain; destroyer even of the strongholds of heaven, and a weapon
like a fire-raining monster." From "Dulle Griete," the giant 25-inch
bombard which fired a 700-pound granite ball, and from the Scots'
mighty 20-inch bombard "Mons Meg," known by the affectionate
diminutive of "Munce," the practice of naming guns extends through
artillery history to "Big Bertha" and "Atomic Annie."

Two of the three Massachusetts fieldpieces, once commanded by
Knox, were named for prominent rebel statesmen, John Hancock

and John Adams, but were not likely to keep their titles long. A British sentry mounted guard at the gunhouse on West Street where the guns were stored, and they were due at any moment to be taken over by Royal Artillery and Tories of the train.

Schoolmaster Abraham Holbrook, William Dawes, and four other young patriots acted first. They pried out planks in the rear wall of the gunhouse and squeezed through the gap. While the sentry, sleepy and heedless, walked his post, they removed the gun barrels from their carriages, which Yankee carpenters and wheelwrights could easily replace. The fine brass tubes, cast in England and still un-obtainable by colonial manufacture, were carried over to Holbrook's schoolhouse next door and concealed in the wood box. Dawes had ridden with Revere and Prescott to warn John Hancock and John Adams at Lexington of the British raid, and his part in the rescue of their namesake cannon was a fitting sequel.

British officers, who had inspected the gunhouse only half an hour earlier, were furious at the loss of the pieces, but the thorough search they ordered proved fruitless. The guns were soon spirited out of Boston by night and conveyed to the American lines.

Those three light guns, with a fourth shortly added, founded the American field artillery. They were its first and—until augmented by pieces from outlying towns, from outside Massachusetts, and by captures from British vessels—its only armament. Two were subse-quently lost in battle, but "Hancock" and "Adams" remained in action throughout the war and are today suitably enshrined in the Bunker Hill Monument.

The hill where that commemorative shaft was to rise was the first choice for an advanced American outpost threatening Boston. Breed's Hill, closer to the town across the Charles River, was fortified instead and there was fought the engagement which history, ignor-ing geography, calls the Battle of Bunker Hill.

Colonel Richard Gridley, the army's chief engineer and command-ing officer of the artillery, had designed the redoubt on Breed's Hill. Incredibly he, an experienced artilleryman, had failed to pro-vide gun platforms or to pierce walls for embrasures; when the gunners arrived, they were forced to blast gaps through the earth-works with their cannon to obtain fields of fire. The spirit and

leadership of the officer who had stormed Louisbourg's Island Battery had faded at sixty-five.[25] Morale was low in his regiment, in
which two of his sons had been commissioned. Major Scarborough
Gridley was constantly pressing his wavering father to make him
second in command. Captain Samuel Gridley would fail to meet the
test of combat. More than a few units, before and since the 1st Massachusetts Artillery, have been ruined by an overage commander or
by nepotism or other forms of favoritism.

When the dawn of June 17 revealed the new-built rebel redoubt,
British warships and a battery of 24's on Copp's Hill bombarded it
heavily but ineffectively. Yankee infantry under Putnam and Prescott
waited unshaken behind the ramparts for the direct assault the gunfire presaged. There Seth Pomeroy, carrying his Louisbourg musket,
joined them to be greeted with a roar by Old Put, "By God, Pomeroy, you here! A cannon-shot would waken you out of your grave!"
The veteran, who had been appointed brigadier general, paid no
heed to his rank. He had come to fight and he stood his ground to
the last. Then, musket shattered when he clubbed it to smash at an
enemy, he retreated, walking backward and muttering, "Pomeroy
must not be shot in the back." He died of pneumonia at seventy-one
on his way to join Washington's army in New Jersey.

Presently the Americans behind the earthworks sighted barge after
barge rowing across the river from Boston, barges crammed with
scarlet-uniformed troops—more than fifteen hundred men. Sun
glinted on the brass of cannon in the bows: mortars, 12's, and 6's.
Minute Men, who had scattered before Percy's fieldpieces at Lexington, squinted calmly at the glinting brass. They had stood their
baptism of artillery fire, and this time there were American guns to
answer: four at the redoubt and two, which Prescott had ordered
to support Knowlton and his Connecticut company and Stark and
his New Hampshire militia, manning the rail fence and stone wall
of the left flank down to the Mystic River.

The British landed, formed ranks, came marching up the slope
in a frontal assault. Picked men—the flank companies of every regiment in the Boston garrison—colors fluttering, officers with drawn
swords out in front, fifes and drums playing—it was a display of
martial splendor, beautiful precision, and courage no less superb
for its arrogance. Yankee marksmen, under strict orders to hold their

fire till the enemy advanced to within fifty yards, peered over musket barrels in awe and admiration.

Now was the moment, with the distance closed to artillery range, for the American cannon to open. Muzzles jutting through the redoubt embrasures barked once or twice, then withdrew. An infantry private stared, incredulous and disgusted, as the companies of Captains Callender and Gridley seized dragropes and hauled their four guns out of the fort in panicky haste.[26] They were out of ammunition, they shouted.

General Putnam met and halted the fleeing artillerymen, guns limbered, ready to flog their teams into a gallop and escape over Charlestown Neck. Listening skeptically to the yarn that their ammunition was gone, he flung open lids of side boxes to find them full of balls. At pistol point Old Put herded them back up the hill in angry scorn. No sooner was his back turned than they again deserted in the face of the approaching enemy.

Down at the rail fence Captain Sam Trevett's two guns stood fast. Word passed along the infantry lines from flank to redoubt. "Powder's scarce ..." "Fire low ..." "Aim at their waistbands..." "Wait till you see the whites of their eyes ..." "Pick off the officers." A bellowed command, and muskets and fowling pieces poured in a devastating blast of point-blank fire. Trevett's guns banged, plowing bloody lanes through the close-packed array. But it was the infantry's storm of lead that swept away almost all the redcoat officers in the forefront and mowed down the companies behind them as if a gigantic scythe had slashed through a field of poppies. Remnants of shattered regiments reeled back down the hill.

"Reload, stand by," the order was passed. "They'll be coming on again."

Fifteen minutes, and the shattered ranks, now reinforced, reformed and gallantly remounted the slope. British field guns, strangely silent until now, began to boom. They had failed to cover the first assault when some bogged down in swamps, and the side boxes of the 6's were found to be filled with 12-pound balls. Official explanations of that stupid blunder by Colonel Samuel Cleaveland, Chief of Artillery, could not compete with the story that he was too preoccupied dallying with a Boston schoolmaster's daughter to bother to check ammunition. Gossip buzzed that though he was getting on in years and no Samson, he must have his Delilah.[27] While Cleaveland escaped with a court of inquiry, his name became a laughingstock in both armies. A British artilleryman, deserting to the Americans, retaliated on his former commander with verse which, though mistaken on calibers, was fire for effect.

> But our conductor, he got broke,
>   For his misconduct, sure, sir;
> The shot he sent for twelve-pound guns
>   Were made for twenty-fours, sir.[28]

Generals Howe and Pigot led their men forward over ground dotted with their dead and wounded. This time they had support from their heavier guns, bombarding the American left at a range of nine hundred yards, while the 6's, discarding oversize round shot for grape, scoured out troublesome snipers sheltered in dips in the ground. But the same withering volleys of musketry, withheld till the last moment, again smashed the assault waves. What seemed to the British like an incessant sheet of fire streamed from the Continental lines. Shattered companies, some with only three or four survivors, staggered back down the hill.

The Americans' powder was almost exhausted, and Putnam was breaking open abandoned artillery cartridges and serving out their grains to musket men. Defenders watched the British rallying for a third try, ready to attack again with stubborn valor, though for all they knew the same terrible slaughter was awaiting them at the hilltop. They came on, converging on the redoubt. A final fusillade, flaming in their faces, dwindled to scattered shots, then to a shower of rocks. Grenadiers scaled the parapets, fired into the huddled men beneath, and leaped down with stabbing bayonets. The fort, which had cost so dearly, was won.

As the Royal Artillery raked a gap between the fort and the rail fence with grape, Knowlton's flank, enfiladed, caved in. His men and Stark's fell back, circling the captured redoubt. Captain Trevett was forced to leave one of his guns to the enemy but brought off the other and fought it to cover the retreat past burning Charlestown, set afire by red-hot shot from British warships. Old Colonel Gridley finally reached the field and was wounded while helping to serve the surviving fieldpiece.

Bunker Hill—a day of glory for the American infantry, a black one for the artillery. Five out of six guns lost, two out of three companies deeply disgraced. Their captains, John Callender and Samuel Gridley, were court-martialed. While the latter was acquitted, Callender was dismissed for disobedience of orders and cowardice, but re-enlisted as a private. Major Gridley, who at a safe distance from the battle had popped away futilely at British ships with 3-pounders, was also tried and deprived of his commission. Colonel Gridley's bravery could not disguise his incapacity. Although he was continued on duty as an engineer, the artillery was about to pass into the hands of a far more able commander who would redeem its honor.

General George Washington, who had ridden up from Virginia to take command of the Continental Army, received reports on the behavior of the artillery at Bunker Hill. It must have reminded him of the miserable handling and loss of Braddock's guns in the "massacre" on the Monongahela. Promptly he removed Gridley and offered the colonelcy to the two senior field officers. Both, Louisbourg veterans, declined on the ground that they, like their former commander, were too old. They generously recommended the former bookseller and militiaman now working as a volunteer engineer on the forts around Boston.

The husky young man, towering over even the tall Virginian, impressed the General with his forthright bearing, his knowledge of gunnery and of military tactics. Washington made one of those swift, unerring decisions of his.

Henry Knox at the age of twenty-six was nominated colonel, his commission dated November 17, 1775, to become the American Army's first chief of artillery.

All our wars repeat the story of a search for leaders, sometimes found early, sometimes developed late; of mustering and training troops—making soldiers out of civilians—at an hour so tardy that the lives of thousands of the partially trained are lost in battle; of supplying a critical dearth of arms and munitions. In the Revolution, when our army was of necessity built from scratch, the charge of military unpreparedness is not valid. But the cost of unpreparedness was comparably as great as in subsequent conflicts on through the intervention in Korea.

In the gun park at Cambridge and in the siege lines around Boston, officers uniformed in blue or black coats with facings of red, white breeches, and black tricorns, commanded ten companies of Massachusetts artillery, two of New York, and one of Rhode Island. They and the sergeants drilled sketchily-clad matrosses—drills which gunners of a later day were to call "dry runs." There was no powder to spare for firing practice, only enough for an occasional shot at the enemy. Civilian drivers and their teams were hired to haul the gun carriages and ammunition carts, as was still the practice in all armies.[29] It was by no means an efficient system. In 1800 Napoleon made drivers members of his batteries. The British organized their Gunner Driver Corps in 1801, and the Americans followed suit a few years later. As regular artillerymen, drivers were then trained to serve guns, replacing casualties, as well as to handle teams. Now the sturdy farm horses, some of the old Norman blood of the knights' chargers, were hitched in, and plunged and kicked at the strange vehicles rumbling behind them. When harness was broken, it was mended as often as could be, since saddlers could not keep up with the demand.

For powder the Americans had always depended upon England, where its export was now forbidden. Every colony was being scoured for the precious grains, and attempts made to purchase them in Bermuda, the West Indies, France, and Spain, but only driblets were coming in. While a few American mills had been started, they were thus far producing little. The powder which had repulsed two assaults at Bunker Hill and given out at the third had been seized by New Hampshire militia in a raid on Fort William and Mary, Portsmouth harbor. Washington's orders were strict against the waste of the little that had replaced it. Spears were being made and issued to infantrymen whose powder horns held charges enough for only a few rounds. Artillerymen were reduced to the point of kicking out burning fuses from British bombs as they rolled toward them, and salvaging the shells for their own guns. Yet there was seldom powder enough to shoot them back.

Even with ample ammunition the Americans' light pieces would have been of no avail against Boston. An infantry assault would prove disastrous without heavy cannon to breach the defenses and bombard the town and the warships in the bay, and siege ordnance was almost entirely lacking. The New Hampshire men, who had looted the Portsmouth powder, had also made off with the fort's smaller guns, but left forty-five of large caliber, ranging from 18's to 32's, to be repossessed by the British. Those cannon, transported by sea, were now ironically facing the Americans from the Boston defense lines.

In May a daring raid by Ethan Allen and Benedict Arnold surprised the British garrison at Fort Ticonderoga. On its ramparts were guns and to spare—one hundred and twenty pieces, many of them heavy ones. But three hundred miles of almost roadless wilderness, of broad rivers and mountains separated them from the army before Boston, in such grave need of them.

At last in November came a turn of better fortune. Captain John Manley of the young American Navy caught an unconvoyed British supply ship, the *Nancy*, and brought her into Cape Ann harbor. Her cargo contained two thousand muskets and bayonets, one hundred thousand flints, and other precious munitions.[30] Most jubilantly welcomed was a great 13-inch brass mortar, weighing twenty-seven hundred pounds, complete with its bed and three hundred filled carcasses (incendiary shells). Acclaimed "the noblest piece of ordnance ever landed in America," the pride of the Continental Army, it was taken to Cambridge where it was Americanized by chiseling off the second embossed initial of *G.R.* (for George Rex) and substituting a *W* for Washington. All the camp greeted it with wild huzzas, and General Putnam, using its capacious barrel as a punch bowl, poured it full of rum and christened it "Congress." A soldier-poet hymned it in a song that began:

> Tho' some folks may tell us, it is not clever
> To handle a musket in cold frosty weather;
> By yonder bright Congress, in spite of all such,
> I'll tarry this season, and take t'other touch.[31]

But "Congress" could not speak without powder to propel its shells, and the *Nancy*, otherwise so rich a prize, had afforded none. The big mortar, resting on its bed, gaped silently toward Boston.

While Yankee lack of munitions and British caution and inertia held the siege at stalemate, an American attack on Canada was launched, upon it hanging the fate of half a continent. For that expedition, gallantly led by General Richard Montgomery, who was later killed in action before Quebec, and Colonel Benedict Arnold, only a single company of New York artillery could be mustered.

Its commander was Captain John Lamb, then forty. Proud of his arm of the service, he emphatically informed the authorities that "artillery companies, in every country, are always looked upon in a superior light to other foot companies," and when they tried to merge his gunners with an infantry regiment, he wrathfully resigned. The only artillery officer available, he was persuaded to return on his own terms. Then he refused to march before he and his men were paid, so as not to leave their families destitute, and until his company had received its fair share of a clothing issue.

"Let the gunners alone. They are an obstinate lot." Napoleon's words would have fitted John Lamb. The independent captain's seniors put it another way: "Brave, intelligent, and active, but very turbulent and troublesome"—to all of which he lived up fully. He fought his guns through the campaign in which St. John and Montreal fell. It was late in the season and bitter weather when the invading army reached Quebec. Since the frost-hardened ground prevented the digging of earthworks, Lamb built an ice fort by heaping snow on logs and straw and pouring on water which quickly froze solid. Thence he bombarded the enemy with his five light pieces, none heavier than a 12-pounder, until opposing 32's and 42's blew the brittle walls to bits, killing and wounding some of his crews. In the final night assault on the town through a driving snow-storm, Lamb and his men dragged a gun forward on a sled until it stuck fast in deep drifts. Then they unslung their muskets and, acting as infantry after all, charged the barricades. In the fierce fire that shattered the American attack, part of Lamb's face was torn away by a blast of grapeshot, and he was taken prisoner with most of the survivors of his company. He later recovered and was exchanged. Serving through the remainder of the war, he was wounded a second time and rose to be a general.[32]

Failure at Quebec dashed Washington's hopes of obtaining powder and cannon from the Canadian stronghold for the storming of Boston. Winter was at hand, and the following spring would see new Royal armies, reinforced by Hessian, Brunswick, and other German mercenaries, crossing the Atlantic to raise the siege or to cut off Massachusetts and the rest of New England from the other colonies by the capture of New York and ports to the south. Unless Boston were taken in the meantime, it must be abandoned to the enemy, and the cause of American liberty suffer a severe blow.

There was one remaining source of siege artillery: Fort Ticonderoga, whose guns had stood useless on its stone walls since its taking by Allen and Arnold six months previously. It was Henry Knox who offered to bring the guns to Boston. Washington, promptly accepting the plan of his chief of artillery, issued orders declaring that the want of cannon was so great that "no trouble or expense must be spared to obtain them."

Winter, heightening the hardship of the undertaking, also gave it promise of success. Snow would pave the forest trails, and ice bridge the rivers.

Colonel Knox, traveling via New York and riding forty miles a day, reached Fort "Ti" in early December, 1775. To the young officer entering its sally port, the famous stronghold presented much the same appearance of martial might in a setting of scenic grandeur as it does today in its splendid reconstruction by the Pell family. Jutting bastions and demilunes of solid masonry surrounded the barracks and its *place d'armes,* while the pine- and fir-clad slopes of flanking Mounts Defiance and Independence—as they were later called—towered above, and the blue expanse of Lake Champlain spread beneath it. But surely it was the array of more than a hundred cannon on the ramparts that made Knox's gray eyes light up. Here, if he could transport them, were iron and bronze keys to the gates of Boston.

Leaving enough to defend the fort, Knox chose fifty-nine pieces: mortars ranging from three huge 13-inchers down to small coehorns; four iron howitzers which, like the mortars, would lob shells at a high angle of fire over earthworks or walls to burst in the midst of enemy sheltered behind them; iron and brass guns—one 24-pounder, a number of 18's, 12's, 9's, and light calibers. Knox, his detachment of artillerymen, and men of the garrison dismounted and loaded them, along with twenty-three boxes of lead and flints, on to block carriages and stoneboats. Horses and oxen hauled them over the neck of land to Lake George, the first stage of a tremendous trek which must move sixty tons of metal three hundred miles, must four times cross the Hudson and pass the barrier of the Berkshires.

They heaved and shoved the ordnance aboard "gundaloes," big flat-bottomed scows. Backbreaking toil on sweeps day after day sped them down the lake. Midway in the voyage a sudden squall struck them, tossing the heavy-laden craft about as if they were skiffs, dashing waves over the gunwales. Drenched, seasick gunners, bailing and rowing, strove to keep afloat. One scow was swamped and sank, but its crew was saved. At last they beached the boats at Fort George at the lake's southern tip and counted themselves lucky. The season of winter storms was upon them, and a little later it might have forbade passage until spring.

Now came the snow they needed, thick and heavy. They built "exceeding stout" sleds which were ready when drivers and teams arrived at this prearranged rendezvous. Far more than the horses it was the eighty yoke of oxen that were welcomed, strong, patient beasts of Dutch Holstein and English Devon strains, to drag the heavier loads. Spans were hitched in, teamsters shouted. Forty-two sleds creaking under their freight—several thousand pounds of metal apiece—glided forward on their runners.

Bitter, freezing weather, unremitting labor. Animals, hoofs balled with snow, slipped and fell, were helped to struggle back on their feet, pushed back in the traces, put in draft again. Cold bit through the mufflers artillerymen and drivers wound around their heads, through mittens and boots to numbed fingers and toes, through greatcoats to stiffened joints. Slowly, at the pace of the oxen, they put the miles behind them. They passed Fort Edward and came to Saratoga where a thaw halted them and they had to wait for another snowfall.

The going was even heavier now. Leading spans plunged into deep drifts, sank out of sight and had to be dug free. Steep grades forced the doubling of teams on each load, and every hard climb meant repeated relays. Sleds broke down under their burdens and had to be repaired or replaced. The lengthening train was divided into companies, often miles apart. Knox rode ahead to obtain fresh teams, or back along the column, directing, encouraging, and urging on his weary men.

Most of all it was the people of the settlements along the route who put heart into the expedition. They came from cabins and farmsteads to watch the column plod by, and in their eyes was wonder and pride. Here were guns going to General Washington, guns on their way to fight for liberty. Not content merely to wave and cheer, eager volunteers came forward to help, and offers of food and warming drafts of mulled cider and hot buttered rum were never wanting. Now and again Knox spared time to order one of the mortars taken from its sled and mounted on its bed. Squat and rotund, the weapon had been named "The Old Sow" by its crew. They ladled powder into her maw, rammed in wadding, and touched off the charge. To the delight of the audience "The Old Sow" uttered a mighty, reverberating grunt, a grand racket like that of the gun of "Yankee Doodle."

> And there we see a swampin' gun
> As big as a log of maple,
> Upon a deuced little cart,
> A load for father's cattle.
> And every time they shoot it off,
> It takes a horn of powder,
> And makes a noise like father's gun,
> Only a nation louder.

Crossing the Mohawk River at Half Moon, the present Waterford, they lost a 6-pounder through ice weakened by the weight of its predecessors.

The sunken cannon's story [33] is an extraordinary one. It lay on the bottom until 1835, when it was dredged up during the building of a power dam. Emplaced in the town square of Cohoes, it was annually fired by election winners. Poor losers one year threw it back into the river so it could not celebrate their defeat. In 1907 it was dragged out again and became a museum piece till World War II, when overzealous patriots sold it as scrap iron. After a long hunt searchers found it, smashed into three pieces, at the bottom of a junk pile. Skillfully reconstructed, it was returned and mounted on the ramparts of Fort Ticonderoga, 167 years after it crashed through the ice.

Three times the expedition faced crossings of the upper Hudson over a frozen surface not solid enough to bear the heavy loads. Knox ingeniously ordered holes cut in the ice. As the water bubbled through, freezing in another layer, the sleds passed over safely.

At Albany a "cruel thaw" in early January halted the trek for days. When Knox, harassed by the urgency of his mission, risked the Hudson ice a fourth time, the last sled in the train broke through, and the cannon on it, a long 18, was "drowned." Citizens rallied to help shivering soldiers grapple and raise the two thousand pounds of metal from the bottom. In gratitude to its rescuers the salvaged gun was christened "Albany."

They pushed on. Kinderhook, Claverack, Nobletown, and east into Massachusetts. Thirty handsome bronze plaques on granite monuments today mark the route.[34] Snow thinned, and extra teams were required to climb the Berkshires. At Springfield, New Yorkers turned over their task to drivers of their sister colony who met the train with strong, fresh animals badly needed, for now warmer weather had turned the roads into muddy bogs. But this was the last lap, and the pace was forced.

Fifty days after leaving Fort Ticonderoga, on January 24 in the memorable year of 1776, the advance section of the expedition dragged wearily into Cambridge. With pride, Colonel Knox presented what he justly termed "a noble train of artillery" to General Washington.[35]

Bringing guns to a battlefield was to be far more spectacularly performed in a later era, with horse artillery batteries galloping into action. But the winter march of ox-drawn cannon from Ticonderoga to the siege of Boston remains a feat of arms with few parallels.

Powder had been coming in, brought by ships running the British blockade and sent up from mills now in production as far south as Pennsylvania and Virginia. In the forts around Boston the guns from Fort Ticonderoga and other artillery were put in position. Washington gave the order for them to open fire on March 2 with the sudden shock of a night bombardment. The 18's boomed first, shattering the silence. Crews rolled them back from recoil to chalked lines which marked the position of wheels and trail on the platforms. Cannoneers with "worms," corkscrew-like affairs at the ends of staffs, cleared bores of cartridge shreds. Swabbers and loaders jumped forward. Gunners remeasured elevation with quadrants placed in muzzles. With a rush, mortar men bent to their task. They heaved up heavy shells, lowering them down through bores against charges. As crews leaped back holding their ears, gunners touched matches to the priming charges. Big 13-inchers bellowed mightily, their shells blazing crimson trails across the black sky. In Boston they burst with lurid flashes. Chimneys toppled, and the roof of a British regiment's barracks disintegrated under a roaring impact. While cheering Americans served their pieces, cannon in the enemy's lines furiously replied, but their balls fell short.

It was not the British guns, but lack of firing practice that took toll of the American artillery. Mortars, improperly bedded or over-charged by their green crews, split, the highly prized "Congress" being the first casualty. When smoke cleared from its third discharge, lantern light showed a disabling crack along the brass barrel. Out of action for the rest of the siege, the mortar was hauled away to a smithy where it was observed "hooped up with bands of iron in a most shocking manner, as if she had been ailing." Still serviceable, however, it was subsequently shipped to New York and mounted at the Battery. Removed to Fort Lee during the evacuation, it was there recaptured and restored to the Royal Artillery.

One of Knox's 13-inchers and three mortars of 10-inch caliber also split. Still there were guns aplenty for the task in hand. They boomed on for two ensuing nights, their shells raking the town and starting fires that sent columns of flame leaping up against the sky. Although the damage caused by such long-range bombardment was comparatively minor, it was serving a more important purpose: masking a strategic move long planned by Washington.

American artillery hurled 157 rounds at Boston and its defenses on the night of March 4, a heavy cannonade for the period, though minute beside the mighty barrages and concentrations of the World Wars. Its thunders, mingled with the din of the British reply, deaf-ened enemy ears to the noise of work parties fortifying Dorchester Heights. Next morning the besieged stared up confounded at Amer-ican breastworks on the crest of the peninsula that commanded the southern part of Boston and the anchorage of the fleet.

General Howe's only choice now was to storm the Heights he had neglected to seize, or to evacuate his garrison. Cannon on those hills could blast him out of the town and sink his warships and his own guns could not be elevated high enough to reach them. Hastily battalions were mustered and barges were massed at the wharves to ferry them across the channel to assault and carry the Heights next morning at all costs. It might be another Bunker Hill, but this time American powder would not fail, and every hour saw the works bristling with more artillery whose plunging fire could play havoc with the loaded boats and sweep the slopes with grape and canister. Under Knox, as the course of the war would give proof, artillerymen stood to their guns.

Howe's desperate venture went untried. That night a gale of close to hurricane force descended, mixed with torrential rain. It raged all through the next day and night, wrenching craft from their moorings and driving the drenched assault troops back to their barracks. Before the weather cleared the American forts had been made impregnable, and Washington was preparing to advance his guns to still closer ranges.

The end was at hand. To attempt to hold Boston longer was hopeless. Howe crammed his nine thousand troops and twelve hundred Tory refugees into frigates and transports, assured that Washington would hold fire and let them leave unscathed to spare the town further damage or retaliation.

Over the barrels of cannon from Fort Ti, gunners watched the British sail for Halifax.

CHAPTER 3

"No Artillery Better Served"

●—

...It is with peculiar pleasure...that the Commander in Chief can inform General Knox and the Officers of the Artillery that the enemy has done them the justice to acknowledge that no Artillery could be better served than ours.

> WASHINGTON: General Order, Head Quarters, Freehold (Monmouth County), June 29, 1778

...The same principles...forbid me to be silent on the Subject of General Knox, who is closely united with General Du Portail in the Merits of the Siege; being at the Head of the Artillery, which is the other principal Instrument in Conducting Attacks. The Resources of his Genius have supplied, on this and many other interesting Occasions, the Defect of Means; his distinguished Talents, and Services equally important and indefatigable entitle him to the same Marks of Approbation from Congress, as they may be pleased to grant the chief Engineer.

> WASHINGTON: To the President of Congress, Head Quarters near York, October 31, 1781

●—

AFTER the fall of Boston, the siege guns from Ticonderoga were shifted as rapidly as possible to another theater. Colonel Knox shipped them, including the "ailing" mortar "Congress," south to New York where the British were certain to attack. Fieldpieces rolled overland to the Connecticut shore for ferrying across the Sound.

Cannon were mounted at the Battery on Manhattan's tip. They peered from the embrasures of numerous redoubts along the East and Hudson rivers, laid to deny passage to enemy warships. Pick-and-shovel men made dirt fly on Brooklyn Heights, constructing strong forts. Heavily gunned, those works backed the army Washington marshaled on Long Island.

The array of American artillery was formidable indeed—121 guns, from 32's down, and 19 mortars.[36] To man them Knox, who still had mustered only some five hundred artillerymen in his regiment, resorted to drafts from the infantry. Two companies of New York gunners reinforced him, one commanded by an alert young captain not yet twenty, Alexander Hamilton. Later he served on Washington's staff, as colonel of an infantry regiment.

Under such able young commanders as Hamilton, Oswald, Moulder, Forrest, and Neil, the day of field artillery dawned in America. Guns had rolled on carriages since John Zizka originated that type of transportation in the Hussite Wars of Bohemia (1419-1424) by mounting his bronze pieces on carts for rapid maneuvering. Americans were now also following the tradition of Gustavus Adolphus, the great seventeenth-century king of Sweden, who carried on the development of light, fast-moving wheeled cannon. Drawn by one or two horses, manned by a crew of three, his copper-barreled 4-pounders, bound with iron and covered with varnished leather, fired faster than musketeers of the period. They used the first fixed ammunition—powder cartridges wired to cannon balls—so that separate loadings were not required. Frederick the Great of Prussia in the next century further increased field artillery efficiency. He supplanted cumbersome cannon which, once in position, were unable either to follow up a victory or to retreat before a rapidly advancing enemy, with light, mobile pieces; both gun carriages and ammunition carts were pulled by good teams.

American gunners before the Revolution owed most to British precept and instruction. Small English cannon had shared some of the glory of Crécy with the long bow, and the Royal Artillery in token of its far-flung service would later bear the proud motto, *Ubique*—Everywhere. But as at Louisbourg and Boston, Americans still depended largely on the big guns, and fieldpieces would not come into their own till the Battle of Trenton.

British cannon, tier on tier, stared out of gun ports when the fleet—towering ships of the line, frigates, and crowded transports—

was sighted at the end of June. Those guns covered a landing, as twenty thousand redcoat regulars and blue-clad Hessians, hired out by German princes to fight for King George, poured ashore unopposed on Staten and Long Islands.

Still there was no clash of the armies—no more than a few affairs of scouts and outposts. American guns, saving powder, stood silent during the celebration of momentous news from Philadelphia: that Congress on July 4 had declared the colonies to be free and independent states. Only when two British men-of-war sailed up the North River, hugging the Jersey shore, did the New York batteries open fire. Their round shot fell short, splashing harmlessly in the water. Although frustrated crews rammed in heavier charges and elevated their barrels, they still could not reach the enemy; one overloaded piece burst with a roar, killing six matrosses. Balls from the warships, however, crashed into the town, for the British fleet carried cannon as heavy as 64's and 74's, twice and more the weight of metal of the Americans' largest caliber.

All the defenses of Manhattan were outgunned by Admiral Howe, whose vessels could sail up the girding rivers to bombard the forts with impunity or cover the landing of troops. His brother, General Howe, on the night of August 26, 1776, moved forward on Long Island to sweep similarly around the flanks of Washington's army.

As Knox's too few fieldpieces went into action against the Hessians at the Battle of Long Island, Americans met Germans in combat for the first time.

The mercenaries from Hesse-Cassel advanced with colors flying and drums beating a burden to the weird, high notes of their hautboys. Above the music rose hoarse shouts of their battle cry, "Hoch! Hoch!" Big men in blue and yellow uniforms, they looked taller still because of the lofty brass-fronted caps they wore. Fierce jutting mustachios, darkened with shoeblacking, gave them an awesome, foreign look. Shot tore gaps in their ranks, and every one who fell increased King George's debt in blood money to their German rulers: thirty-five dollars for each soldier killed and twelve for a wound. The Hessians took their losses, closed up, and came on.

American guns, joined with the rattle of musketry, maintained a steady cannonade. The long hours of drill demanded by Knox were paying off. Crews of fourteen men per piece ran through their duties with precision. Gunner corporals sighted calmly along barrels, gave elevating screws a turn or two, motioned for trails to be shifted right or left, and stood clear. Officers shouted the order to fire, and the 6-pounders boomed and bucked backward. Matrosses, clinging to drag ropes attached to hooks on axles and trails, braked the recoiling cannon and rolled them back into battery. "Tend vent . . . sponge piece." Leather-covered thumbs pressed down on open touchholes to stopper the vents while the pieces were being loaded and rammed. "Handle cartridge." Ammunition passers bent over the side boxes unclamped from gun-carriage axles and placed beside trails— snatched out flannel bags of powder and round shot—ran to muzzles. "Charge piece . . . ram down cartridge." Rammer staffs shoved in loads, drove them home to the breech. "Prime." First gunners pierced the cartridge bags with vent picks, then thrust in priming tubes to which they laid a thin, gray-black train spilled from powder horns. "Take aim," and corporals sighted anew and jumped aside. Second gunners blew the slow matches on their linstocks to a red glow and stepped forward. "Fire!" Matches swept down to ignite the powder. While the sharp slams of the 6's beat against eardrums, clouds of choking smoke billowed around the hurrying crews.[37]

Not for long could the Yankee guns, scattered along the front, hold their ground. They and the infantry they supported were blanketed by the fire of three brigades of Royal Artillery and Hessian cannon, pulled into position by teams sold by Tory farmers of Long Island. Odds were too heavy—forty guns against six.[38] Hot-barreled American pieces limbered up and retreated, cannoneers following them at a panting run. Unlimbering, coming back into action, withdrawing again, they vainly strove to fight attacks which pressed them back on Brooklyn Heights. The enemy, flooding over the infantry, swept up to the gun positions. German bayonets flashed and stabbed. The Hessians, told by the British that Americans scalped and ate their foes as Indians did, were slaughtering wounded men and prisoners with the merciless brutality of Hitler's SS in the second World War.

Only once did an American artillery company come close to breaking. Dazed by a storm of shot that killed its officers, crews were about to abandon their guns when a private rallied them. John Callender, former gunner captain dismissed for cowardice at Bunker Hill and re-enlisted in the ranks, took command. He fought the guns, beating back one assault. A second, driving in from the flank, caught him ramming in a charge for a last shot. Bayonets, about to plunge into his back, were knocked aside by a British officer, who took him prisoner. General Washington ordered his court-martial sentence erased from the orderly book and when Callender was exchanged, his commission was restored with high praise for his valor.

Haslet's Delaware regiment battled like their gamecock mascots, the Blue Hen's chickens. Smallwood's Marylanders in fringed purple hunting shirts stood and fought and died. The stubborn bravery of an army outgeneraled, outflanked, and outnumbered, could not stem the rip tide of the enemy's advance. But Howe halted his pursuit short of the formidable Brooklyn forts, and his troops rested on their arms.

On the night of August 29, providentially black and foggy, Washington withdrew his beaten battalions and sent them marching down to the East River. Glover's fine regiment of Marblehead fishermen ferried them across to Manhattan. The remnant of the army—which had left hundreds of dead and wounded and a thousand prisoners on the stricken field of Long Island—was saved. So were most of its light guns. The heavy ones in the fortifications fell into the hands of the enemy.

Knox's New York batteries were no match for the twelve hundred cannon of the British fleet. Under blazing broadsides, redcoat troops stormed ashore. They made the island into a trap whose jaws almost clicked shut. Knox himself was nearly captured. It was a young officer named Aaron Burr who guided him out of an all but surrounded redoubt.

Gun after gun was lost—most of the heavy ordnance assembled with such difficulty. This was a blow from which the American artillery seemed unlikely ever to recover. Defeats at Harlem, White Plains. Fort Washington taken and with it 3,000 picked men and 114 cannon. Thirty-two more went with Fort Lee across the Hudson.

It was at Fort Washington that the first American artillerywoman won fame. Margaret or "Molly" Corbin (sometimes confused with "Molly Pitcher" of Monmouth), at twenty-five campaigned with her husband John, of Proctor's Pennsylvania Artillery, like the wives of other soldiers. War could still be a family affair as it was in the days of the Gunners Guild, when boys born in camp or in ammunition wagons on the march were dubbed "sons of guns." Margaret, useful as a cook and nurse, joined John in the desperate defense of Fort Washington. When a matross was killed, she grasped his rammer staff and went to work. Her husband did not live long to be proud of her. Under the fury of the bombardment he dropped with a mortal wound. Grimly his widow kept on serving the gun. Powder-grimed Margaret was not on her feet to see the Highlanders and Hessians scale the ramparts and overwhelm the fort. She lay bleeding on the ground, one arm nearly severed and a breast mangled by three grapeshot.

Margaret recovered, and was released on parole. She joined the Invalid Corps, that remarkable outfit of disabled veterans who did garrison, guard, and even riot duty, an organization that was revived in the Civil War. In 1779 Congress voted her a meager pension of half pay for life, plus clothes and rations. But when the liquor allowance was withheld because of her sex, she protested vehemently and forced the commanding general to restore her rum issue. "Captain Molly," as she liked to be called, wore an artillery coat and always accepted salutes as her due. She is buried at West Point beneath a stone with a bas relief depicting her gallantry as a gunner.

As the American Army retreated through New Jersey, Knox, now a brigadier general, labored to re-equip his depleted artillery. Slowly fieldpieces and ammunition came in from the French and from American foundries and forges, a flow which increased after the chief of artillery established Springfield Arsenal in Massachusetts. Companies began to be organized into regiments, with a reserve, the artillery park, under General Knox. Colonel Charles Harrison was named to command the 1st Continental, Lamb the 2nd, John Crane the 3rd, and Thomas Proctor the 4th. Ebenezer Stevens' "corps" operated in the north. There was a regiment of artificers under Benjamin Flower and various units scattered throughout the states, yet seldom men and guns enough until the great concentration at Yorktown, reinforced by cannon of our French allies.

But by Christmas night, 1776, Knox had mustered eighteen fieldpieces on the Pennsylvania shore of the Delaware River, and they would suffice for the valiant feat of arms that lay ahead.

Washington's spy, John Honeyman, reported that Trenton was held by a brigade of Hessians. Colonel Rall, commanding, had his own grenadiers, together with the Knyphausen and Lossberg regiments, Jaegers, and a detachment of British dragoons. They put out pickets but seldom bothered with patrols as far as the river. Their artillery, six brass 3-pounders, were lined up in single file in narrow King Street. A man could stand at the crossroads above town and roll balls down King and Queen Streets as if they were bowling greens; if the balls were cannon balls, they could tumble the 3's like ninepins. Snug in winter quarters, amply supplied with casks of rum, the Hessians would be celebrating Christmas Eve and Christmas Day with Teutonic joviality and thoroughness. Rall himself was capable of drinking the best topers on his staff under the table. If Washington's army could cross the Delaware, march the nine miles to Trenton and strike before dawn, a stunning surprise might be achieved. To fail would mean disaster, with the Hessians and other enemy garrisons in towns to the flanks catching the rebels with their backs to the river. General Washington's password, "Victory or Death," was well chosen.

Snow, sleet, and hail descended Christmas night. In fierce cold a bitter northeast wind whipped the water. Colonel Glover's Marbleheaders manned barge sweeps as they had after Long Island. Without those sturdy fishermen-soldiers, our first amphibious troops, the crossing of the dark river, where ice cakes swirled in the swift current, never could have been managed. Infantry groped their way into the long Durham boats and scows. Knox's great voice bellowed above the screech of the storm, repeating Washington's orders. Muffled matrosses manhandled cannon aboard, and drivers struggled to load their horses. The poor beasts, nervous at unsteady footing on bobbing craft, balked and kicked and had to be pulled and shoved forward with planks against their haunches.

The perilous passage was made without mishap. When the boat carrying the Philadelphia Light Horse Troop grounded offshore, that small body of cavalry jumped their horses into the river and swam them to the bank. But it was growing dangerously late, for the crossing had taken three hours. Dawn, creeping close, threatened betrayal and ruin. Sleet-soaked infantrymen forced the march. Behind them they left dark blotches on the snow—bloody prints of ill-shod feet, cut by ice crusts. Guns, spaced along the column, slithered behind their teams: Alexander Hamilton's of New York, Thomas Forrest's and Joseph Moulder's of Philadelphia, Daniel Neil's from New Jersey, a Massachusetts company [39] under Captain Winthrop Sargent, and others. Gunners harnessed themselves into bricoles, helping the horses. Captain Hamilton, like his men, was walking, now and then patting the barrel of one of his cannon as was his habit. His own mount was hitched in with a straining tandem.

Such wet weather as this was artillery weather. Infantrymen, in spite of rags wrapping the firelocks of their muskets, could not keep the powder in their priming pans from becoming sodden and flints too dampened to spark. Gunners, their flannel- or paper-covered cartridges dry in side boxes and ammunition chests, could load and shield primers until matches touched them off. This battle—its outset at least—would be an affair of cannon and bayonets.

Suddenly the sky was gray, then light. Up ahead a Hessian officer sauntering out of a farmhouse sighted the oncoming Americans and yelled for his men. They rushed out, fired a few scattered shots, and fled back toward Trenton before the threat of swooping bayonets. Ragged infantry charged after them, and gun teams took up the trot.

Hoarse shouting rose in the town. *"Der Feind! Heraus!"* "The enemy! Turn out!" Streets filled with German mercenaries, dulled with sleep and fuddled by rum, struggling into coats and equipment. Cursing officers shoved their men into ranks, trying to form line for volleys. The yellow metal fronts of grenadier caps reflected the early morning light. Uniforms splashed color against the snowy background—Rall's regiment and the Lossbergers both in blue, the former with facings of poppy color, the latter's of orange. In contrast showed the somber black trim worn by the Knyphausens. Here and there a flash of green with crimson trim identified the Jaegers, sons of German foresters and deadly shots with their short, heavy rifles.

American teams trotted up. Guns were unlimbered and put in position where the Trenton Battle Monument now stands. These were crack batteries, their pieces already loaded, balls wadded in to prevent their rolling out of muzzles. In less than a minute after trails hit the ground, crews had jerked off aprons that kept primings dry—sighted along barrels, taking aim—touched matches to vents. Pieces boomed and recoiled, as they spat round shot. The guns with their flat trajectories could not fire over the heads of advancing infantry, but they could clear the way for a charge. Shivering cannoneers warmed to their work—swabbing bores, running from side boxes with powder charges and shot, ramming them in. Now they were up to a rate of five or six rounds per minute—rapid fire.

Below them in the town, streets opened a field of fire like the bowling greens Honeyman had called them. Forrest's battery, reports sharp in the frosty air, raked crowded King Street where Hessian gunners struggled to hitch in their plunging horses. Now Hamilton was up and prepared for action, Knox himself bellowing the range. Brass 3-pounders flashed and roared, bowling shot down Queen Street.

Continental recruits, first with elation, then with fascinated horror, stared down at the carnage wrought by the hurtling cannon balls. They saw two horses of one enemy gun team, three of another, go down screaming and thrashing in the snow. Among them eight men of the crews lay mangled, still in death or writhing in agony. With the strength of desperation, survivors somehow freed the cannon from the mess and fired six shots from each at the American artillery pounding them from the hilltop. Soon only a Hessian lieutenant and one gunner were on their feet. They turned and shouted for help, but none came. A last round of grape, spattering short, and they fled, leaving the smoking guns to their fate.[40]

Cannon boomed from the other side of town where a second American column had launched its attack. Up at the crossroads Forrest's and Hamilton's guns ceased firing and limbered to follow the charging infantry. A Hessian bullet bored through both hands of Captain William Washington, destined to become a fine cavalry leader. Another thudded into the shoulder of Lieutenant James Monroe. Stoppering a spurting artery with a finger, he staggered forward; a future President of the United States would bear the scar of an honorable wound. Musketeers and riflemen forced their way into the houses. Under cover from the wet they chipped damp flakes from flints and reprimed. Lead spat from windows, mowing down the rallying Hessians. Colonel Rall, roused from his bed when the attack he had contemptuously discounted was already breaking his fine brigade, rode furiously through the disordered mass of fugitives, striving to stem the retreat. He had rallied them for a stand, and his grenadiers were advancing with band playing and colors flying when a fusillade drove them staggering back. Rall toppled from his horse mortally wounded. Stuffed unread in his pocket during a party was found a note, received Christmas night from a Tory, warning him that the Americans were crossing the Delaware to storm Trenton.

The Hessians, formidable still, made a fighting retreat to fields and orchards around the town. Lossberg gunners strained to extricate their two cannon, bogged down in a swamp, and reply to the Massachusetts battery firing on them from high ground to the south. Before they could succeed, American infantry closed in, and artillery moved forward to ring the trapped enemy with a deadly semicircle of loaded guns. A general shouted down: "Surrender, or we'll blow you to pieces!"

Proud silken standards of the German States were lowered to droop in the muddy snow. Arms thudded to the ground and officers, as a sign of submission, held up their hats on the points of their swords. Trenton was won, with almost a thousand prisoners, more than a hundred enemy casualties, six fine brass fieldpieces, and many other munitions and supplies—all at the cost of four American wounded.[41]

Washington left Trenton, then reoccupied it. Down on the town marched Lord Cornwallis, smarting under the sting of the first American victory since Boston, vowing "to bag the fox." The fox hunter from Virginia, annoyed by such metaphors and the "view halloo" enemy dragoons sounded tauntingly on their trumpets, stood and gave battle. With five thousand men and forty guns, outmatching the Royal Artillery, the Continentals fought His Majesty's regulars to a standstill.

That night Washington's army slipped away. Campfires were left brightly burning, orders given in whispers, wheels of the gun carriages muffled in rags. Even the artillery drivers, a noisy lot with their teams, kept silence, an accomplishment which veterans long remembered as extraordinary. Next morning the British woke to gape at empty fields. The Americans had skirted their left flank and were marching hard to strike their rear guard back at Princeton and their supply base at New Brunswick.

South of Princeton General Mercer's blue- and brown-clad vanguard fired on a picket of dragoons, drove them in, and moved against their infantry. The British commander, Lieutenant Colonel Charles Mawhood, of the 17th Foot, trotted up on a brown pony with two spaniels frisking at its heels, rallied his men, and led them forward. They came at the Americans with a dashing bayonet charge and broke them. Mercer and Colonel Haslet of the Delaware Blues, two of our bravest and ablest officers, strove vainly to halt the rout and fell fighting. Captain Neil and his Jersey artillerymen stood fast, and their two guns blazed away at forty yards with canister. Its leaden slugs, scattered from the metal can that gave the projectile its name, ripped into the oncoming British ranks. A surviving grenadier remembered how men hit "squealed horribly" under the canister's impact. The red line wavered and nearly broke but came charging on through the dense white smoke clouds. Neil and his crews, overrun, flailed away with rammer staffs and handspikes and died around their cannon under a storm of bullets and the thrusting bayonets of long Tower muskets.

Over on the American right Moulder's Pennsylvania battery also stood its ground, as infantry of its own state fled and left it unsupported. Although two British guns concentrated on it, they overshot, and Moulder and his men continued to serve their two long 4-pounders calmly. "Make your guns defend themselves," was a standing order to artillerymen, and the Pennsylvanians lived up to it. Officers carried swords and pistols, and matrosses were supposed to be issued muskets but seldom were. If the enemy rushed them, Moulder's men, like Neil's, had nothing to defend themselves with but staffs and spikes. They were loading with grapeshot, so called because its iron balls, bound around a rod on a disk base, resembled a cluster of grapes; deadlier than canister at long ranges, it could disable at almost nine hundred yards, or kill at that range if it struck a vital spot. Lethal sprays from the muzzles of Moulder's guns stripped a fence of redcoat light infantrymen clambering over to assault, then shifted fire to blast dragoons working around the flank. As the cavalry, gaps in its ranks, galloped off, more infantry converged on the battery. Their fire was too heavy for Moulder to bring up his teams for retreat. With all his men on the dragropes he got his guns clear. Even then he nearly lost them, for the dragoons were back and about to charge. The gallant little troop of Philadelphia Light Horse, only twenty-two men, formed in front of the retreating artillery and blocked off the pursuit.

Washington on his chestnut charger now galloped onto the field, stemming the rout. He rode up to within forty paces of the enemy, survived a point-blank volley unhit, and waved on his men. Hand's splendid riflemen and other regiments followed him on the double; Moulder's guns returned to mow down the enemy in rows. The British broke in their turn, running for their lives before Washington's exultant shout, "It's a fine fox chase, boys!"

It fell to Alexander Hamilton to stage an amusing epilogue to the Battle of Princeton. His battery, coming up with the main body, unlimbered in the town in front of Nassau Hall, a building of the College of New Jersey, subsequently Princeton University. Hamilton, a graduate of King's College (later Columbia), could not have been impressed by a rival institution. Besides, Nassau Hall was full of Britishers. The captain ordered a piece loaded, aimed it, and fired a fortuitous but telling round. It smashed through a window and neatly decapitated a portrait of George II on the wall within, a picture whose frame, unharmed, today holds a painting of Washington by Peale. Whereupon some two hundred of the troops of that monarch's grandson came pouring out to surrender. Their exit was spurred by a round from a second gun which thudded into the solid brick wall between the second and third stories; its dent has been preserved through all the reconstructions of Nassau Hall since that day. Before Hamilton attended King's College he had applied for acceptance by the College of New Jersey and been rejected. Now he had at least entered a cannon ball.

The American Army was too spent to march on to New Brunswick and lay hands on British pay chests crammed with seventy thousand pounds sterling, sorely needed. Hamilton, the future secretary of the treasury, must have sighed, though not for long. He was young and full of life. The fatal bullet from Burr's dueling pistol was still years away.

While the British Army, taking its ease, wintered in New York, Washington watched it from Morristown, New Jersey.

The spring and summer of 1777 saw short, sharp clashes, affairs of regiments or brigades, accompanied by a gun or two. Meanwhile Howe put his infantry and artillery, with 300 rounds per gun and a reserve of 6,000 shot and shell, aboard a fleet of 211 sail. He landed in Maryland and drove for the Continental capital, Philadelphia. On Brandywine Creek, September 11, the armies met in battle.

Trenton's and Princeton's glory were dimmed by an American defeat in which eleven cannon were lost, including two of the Hessian pieces taken at Trenton. Yet Knox could honestly praise the spirit of his artillerymen. "You stood to your guns even after our infantry supports were gone, even when you were surrounded by the enemy," he told them. "And still you fought on. This day my corps did me great honor."

Paoli—Anthony Wayne surprised and beaten. Germantown—at best a drawn battle. There General Knox scored one of his rare failures when he advised Washington to halt the advance and assault the stone Chew house. "Never leave a hedgehog in your rear, sir," Knox urged, speaking from his knowledge of the military classics. Balls from 3- and 6-pounders, the heaviest guns on hand, bounced off the stone walls like pellets from peashooters. Delay at the house, which should have been contained and by-passed, combined with a thick fog to ruin American hopes of victory.

Howe triumphantly captured Philadelphia. Twenty miles away, where the ragged, dispirited Americans made camp on the bleak and snowy fields of Valley Forge, bad news filtered down from the north. General Burgoyne, "Gentleman Johnny," bound for a junction with Howe, with an army of 8,000 regulars and Hessians, 142 cannon, 2,000 Canadians, and a thousand Indians, had taken Fort Ticonderoga.

That stronghold, athwart Lake Champlain's historic pathway of invasion, had again proved itself to be a potential key to the continent, as it would continue to be regarded on into the airplane age.[42] Its fall in 1777 is a story of artillery enterprise, both American and British—the former frustrated, the latter successful.

The threat of six-hundred-foot Mount Defiance, dominating the fort, had been ignored by all garrisons from the French on. An American major, John Trumbull (later a famous artist), warned that the height in enemy hands would prove fatal. Commanding officers ridiculed the idea. Thereupon Trumbull elevated a 12-pounder, aimed at the summit, and fired. The shot struck more than halfway up the hill. A 6-pounder, whose lighter projectile could carry about fourteen hundred yards, two hundred better than the 12's, threw a ball close to the top.[43] All very well, Trumbull's superiors responded, but the summit is inaccessible to enemy guns. Once again the Major staged a demonstration.

> Gen. Arnold, Col. Wayne, and several other active officers [he wrote [44]] accompanied me in the general's barge, which landed us at the foot of the hill, where it was most precipitous and rocky, and we clambered to the summit in a short time. The ascent was difficult and laborious, but not impracticable, and when we looked down upon the outlet of Lake George, it was obvious to all that there could be no difficulty in driving up a loaded carriage.

It was not obvious to General Arthur St. Clair and other closed minds until Colonel William Phillips, artillery chief of Burgoyne's advancing army, ordered a battery emplaced on Mount Defiance. "Where a goat can go, a man can go," Phillips declared, "and where a man can go he can drag a gun." [45] Up went the guns. The glint of sun on the brass barrels of the first 12-pounders to reach the crest, sighted through American field glasses, was as imperative as a trumpet sounding retreat. Those cannon up above could demolish Fort Ti with plunging fire. St. Clair did not wait for them to open. He evacuated the stronghold, and Burgoyne's way was clear.

The capture of Ticonderoga carried a curious consequence. To reduce the fort Burgoyne had brought his large train of artillery, with a good proportion of heavy pieces from 24-pounders down. As it chanced, they were not needed. The threat of the guns on Mount Defiance had been enough. For the rest of Burgoyne's march through that frontier country, with his cannon and ammunition wagons tied to such roads as there were, he was seriously encumbered. "Merely for his six- and three-pounders he carried over nine tons of projectiles alone, leaving out of account the projectiles for the other pieces and the powder charges for the whole. It was a bad business." [46] Gentleman Johnny's most useful weapons in such a theater were his 3's mounted on light carriages and capable also of being loaded on the backs of horses and mules. This pioneer pack artillery was the invention of the ingenious artillerist, Sir William Congreve, whose rockets would rout Americans in 1812.

But Burgoyne clung to his guns. They pre-empted transport needed for rations and other supplies, slowed his progress, gave the Americans time to close in on his flanks and rear. A British foraging column was soundly trounced by Stark of Bennington. Another American force, under the command of Gates but sparked by Arnold, closed in on Gentleman Johnny, still far from a junction with Howe, who had never received orders to march up and meet him. Neither did Clinton stir out of New York to help him. When the smoke of the hard-fought Battle of Saratoga cleared away, on October 17, 1777, Burgoyne was compelled to surrender his entire army.

Meanwhile Washington fortified his camp at Valley Forge and sought to keep the British cooped up in Philadelphia and to cut off their supplies by land and water.

As part of the blockade a young Maryland officer, Samuel Smith, held Fort Mifflin on Mud Island in the Delaware River. Not even the defense of McHenry, with which Sam Smith would later be concerned, ranks with his gallant stand in the stockades and blockhouses of ramshackle Mifflin. He had guns, French 8-pounders, some 18's, one 32, but only two gunners, so he made cannoneers of his two hundred infantrymen. Ammunition, provisions, and clothing were critically short, and soon "the stinking salt mud" of that unhealthy spot put many of the garrison on the sick list.

But Sam Smith was ready when the British attacked on October 10. He blasted back the assault and took its survivors prisoner. For five weeks enemy shore batteries and artillery on an adjacent island bombarded the little fort, pounding it into wreckage. On November 11 Lieutenant Colonel Smith sat down in his quarters, shaken by the concussion of shot and shell, to write a report:

This Morning the Enemy open'd their Battery in the Rear
of our N. West Block House about 500 yds. dist. from it of
6 pieces of Cannon & one Howitz & one other Howitz opposite
the Right of our Battery, they were so fortunate to strike one
of our 18 pr. in the two Gun Battery on the Muzzle by which
she is render'd unfit for service. The Shot from the Battery
rakes the Pallisades fronting the Meadow & Cuts down 4 or
5 at a time. They have laid open a great part of that side &
destroy'd all that Range of Barracks, they also keep up an
Incessant fire from their Hospital, they have dismounted 3
of our Block Houses & injur'd the Houses very much. . . . Gen.
Varnum has promis'd to prepare for us New Pallisades, we
will replace at Night such as are destroy'd in the Day & en-
deavour to keep the fort as long as in our power. . . . We are
determined to defend it to the last Extremity. . . .[47]

That was Sam Smith's last report from Mifflin. A ball crashed
through the stockade, barracks walls, two chimney stacks and, by
then luckily almost spent, buried the colonel under a mass of bricks.
Limp and battered, one wrist severely dislocated, he was evacuated
to Valley Forge. Fort Mifflin, a heap of ruins, lasted one week longer,
then surrendered. Washington offered the gallant Marylander a
place on his staff, which Smith declined, to return to his regiment.
Congress voted him the nation's thanks and a sword of honor.

A new American army was wrought in that bitter winter at Valley
Forge, a time of hunger and snow and ice, of disease, desertions, and
death. But Washington's nobility of character inspired the men,
tempered and strengthened their iron endurance. The new army
was hammered out on its cold forge by the mighty efforts of a superb
drillmaster, a Prussian veteran sent over by wise old Ben Franklin,
American ambassador to France—Baron Friedrich Wilhelm August
Heinrich Ferdinand von Steuben, to give him his full, his very full
name. Baron or not (some say his title was a prestige idea of Franklin's), he was a soldier and a great one. He trained the infantry with
strenuous thoroughness from manual of arms to battlefield maneuvers. Artillerymen, free for the moment from Knox's attentions,
grinned as they watched their comrades being marched about by

Steuben, shouting commands in broken English, French, and German. Not for long did the gunners escape. The drillmaster roared at them to the effect, "Und you, ver you vas ven die infantry she march? Die cannon mit die brigades alvays must go." He ordered them to man dragropes and join the column, to the vast delight of the foot troops.

To the band of Proctor's artillery regiment fell the honor of inaugurating the first public celebration of Washington's birthday.[48] Its tall drum major, marking tempo with his staff, led shrilling fifes and rolling drums through camp. On the flanks the fife major and the music master bent critical ears toward pupils who responded by doing them proud. Drummer boys in their early teens and under joyfully beat flams and flourishes. Fifers, despite cold-cramped fingers and blue lips, missed hardly a trill of the "Old Continental March." A mob of scarecrows tumbled out of huts to follow music that lifted hearts to the General's quarters where Washington, Mistress Martha at his side, smilingly received them and made a gift of hard money to the band.

Warmth of spring at last, more food. Then the splendid tidings that France had allied herself with the United States against her hereditary foe and was dispatching a fleet, an army, and supplies across the Atlantic. Chaplains preached sermons of thanksgiving, discourses cut off after half an hour by a cannon shot promptly fired by grinning gunners. At a grand review the artillery boomed out a thirteen-gun salute, followed by a running fire of musketry that rippled from man to man around a square of marshaled regiments.

Out of Philadelphia marched the British garrison to rejoin the army in New York; command of the seas no longer could be counted on, with a French fleet already on its way across the ocean and the young American navy daring to raid England's coast.

Washington broke camp at Valley Forge and pushed northward on the trail of the retreating enemy.

Even at dawn Sunday, June 28, 1778, was hot, and soon it grew torrid. Recruits emptied their canteens but veterans drank sparingly, refilling them at streams where artillery drivers let their thirsty teams dip their muzzles as they forded. Extra jugs of water weighted ammunition carts; much would be needed to cool bores on a day like this. From the sun alone gun barrels were already almost too hot to touch. Sweating soldiers ruefully remembered the Valley Forge winter, when they had sworn that no weather ever would be too warm for them again. It was mostly a shirt-sleeved army, coats shed, that pressed after the British rear guard, sweltering in heavy uniforms under full pack.

Major General Charles Lee, the former King's officer who had turned his coat and joined the Americans, rode by toward the van. Captured a few months previously by British dragoons, he had been exchanged—unfortunately for the patriot cause, which he would nearly succeed in betraying in the forthcoming battle. History, where his name is written black, reveals that he had given Howe a plan for the conquest of the United States. The surly-looking renegade drew no cheers as did the young redheaded French marquis, General Lafayette, from whom Lee had wheedled command of the advance.

Along the column fluttered occasional skirts. The wives and sweethearts of Continental soldiers were neither so numerous nor so bold and unruly as the camp followers from Philadelphia encumbering the British march. Like Molly Corbin of Fort Washington, another Molly trudged at the side of her husband, John Hays, once of the artillery but now with the foot. Mary Ludwig Hays (later McCauley by a second marriage) was a plain, ruddy-faced farm girl, as Pennsylvania Dutch as sauerkraut. She hiked along sturdily with her regiment and its accompanying cannon, which she had often watched her husband serve during his enlistment as an artilleryman.

Musketry rattled up ahead in the direction of Monmouth Court House, Freehold, New Jersey, where Lafayette's and Wayne's brigades struck Clinton's rear guard, which faced about and deployed to meet the assault. American infantry, splendidly trained by Steuben, poured steady, rapid volleys into the close-packed British ranks. Four pieces under Lieutenant Colonel Eleazer Oswald, marching with the vanguard, unlimbered and opened fire.

The battlefield, cut by ravines and strips of thick woods, was difficult terrain for artillery. Twice Oswald found himself without infantry support. Only rapid changes of position or the timely arrival of foot troops saved his guns from being cut off and captured. Yet they were well forward and blazing away to clear the way for a charge, when poised lines incredulously heard shouts of "Fall back!

Fall back!" as a staff officer galloped up with orders from General Lee. Raging, Lafayette and Wayne obeyed, drawing off their brigades in a stubborn fighting retreat.

The temperature was up in the nineties now and soaring close to a hundred degrees. Men gasped and dropped from sunstroke and heat prostration. Oswald's battery, with one gun knocked out and several matrosses and horses killed or wounded, began to suffer still more losses. Sweltering artillerymen, worn out from running beside the trotting teams, then serving their pieces at top speed, were keeling over across the trails. But the guns, reinforced by three others, managed to stay in action for a desperate stand with the infantry to fend off the British pursuit.

Across that bullet-swept ground a striped skirt fluttered. Molly Hays was earning her nickname by bringing pitcher after pitcher of cool spring water to parched, exhausted men. "Molly Pitcher" also tended the wounded and once, heaving a crippled soldier up on her strong young back, she carried him clear of a redcoat charge. On her next trip with water she found her ex-artilleryman husband back with the guns again, replacing a casualty. While she watched, Hays fell wounded. The piece, its crew now too depleted to serve it, was about to be withdrawn when Molly stepped forward and took the rammer staff from her fallen husband's hands. For a second time on an American battlefield a woman manned a gun. Expertly she ran through the familiar drill, staying at her post under heavy fire. Washington issued her a warrant as a noncommissioned officer, and the army hailed her admiringly as "Sergeant Molly."

All the rest of her life Molly remained an honored veteran. She smoked a pipe, chewed tobacco, downed her drams, and swore like a trooper on occasion. She loved to fight the war over and assured her grandson that if it had not been for her, Monmouth would have been lost. She would tell groups of girls, "You should have been with me at the Battle of Monmouth and learned how to load a cannon," and at militia drills she would remark with the bored superiority of an old regular, "This is nothing but a flea-bite to what I have seen." She died at the age of seventy-eight. A flagstaff and cannon flank her grave, and a sculpture on the Monmouth Battle Monument shows her manning her gun.

While Molly plied her rammer staff, Washington, urgently summoned, burst onto the field at a headlong gallop. He rode up to General Lee and demanded an explanation of the retreat. Lee's stuttering reply was drowned in a blast of language that "shook the leaves from the trees." That day, they said, Washington "swore like an angel." As he rallied cheering troops, the fortunes of battle swayed back and forth.

Batteries of all four regiments of Continental artillery came into action. At critical points Knox massed his guns in concentrations of eight or ten pieces. The cannonade rose in volume to become "the severest artillery fire ever heard in America." [49] Fresh batteries, ordered up from the reserve, galloped into position to spell dog-tired comrades. Their aim was so accurate that a round shot from one enfilading gun struck muskets from the hands of an entire British platoon. The big gunner general rode along the line shouting for all cannon to load with grape. At musket range the balls plunged into wavering enemy ranks like blasts of oversize buckshot.

Sundown and the darkening shadows broke off a battle that was the longest in the Revolution, a battle that was so nearly an American victory. That night Clinton slipped away and Washington's weary men were unable to follow.

At Monmouth "the American artillerist proved himself a match for the batteries of Britain." [50] And in Washington's orders praising the conduct of his troops, stood a proud citation for the gunners that "the enemy has done them the justice to acknowledge that no Artillery could be better served."

There was no major artillery action in the following campaigns until Yorktown. Wayne stormed Stony Point with the bayonet. Mounted riflemen won King's Mountain. Morgan's marksmen and William Washington's cavalry beat Tarleton at Cowpens; there two 3-pounders were in action against a small detachment of Royal Artillery. American guns in the defenses could not prevent the loss to the British of Savannah nor of Charleston with its five-thousand-man garrison. There was no need for the cannon at West Point to speak, since Arnold's treason and attempted betrayal of the citadel on the Hudson were discovered in time. But single guns and small batteries were well fought in Rhode Island and in the South, where General Green with brilliant strategy battled the superior forces of Lord Cornwallis, overrunning Georgia and the Carolinas.

At last, with a mighty massing of artillery, the war built up to its thunderous climax.

Six thousand elite French troops under the Count de Rochambeau landed at Newport, Rhode Island, on July 11, 1780. Some twenty heavy siege guns, ranging from 13-inch mortars to long 18's, were swung ashore, welcomed by salutes, fireworks, and bonfires. When the decision finally was taken to by-pass rather than attack New York and march south to Virginia where Lafayette's small force warily kept watch on Cornwallis, the French army joined the American in New Jersey. Washington as commander-in-chief led the two long columns southward.

Over rough and rutted roads that summer of 1781 flowed twin streams of metal. In the train of American artillery rolled twenty-three iron 24- and 18-pounders and twenty-one brass howitzers and mortars. Heavier calibers were mounted on strong traveling beds, drawn by four- and six-horse teams. Fifteen fieldpieces marched with the brigades. Here, combined with the French cannon, was marshaled such an array of ordnance as the New World had never seen save on the ramparts of such forts as Louisbourg, Quebec, and Ticonderoga. Washington and Rochambeau might have echoed the boast once made by Henry VIII: that the great bombards, culverins, falconets, and basilisks he mustered were "cannon enough to conquer Hell." The artillery of early European wars had marched with pomp and panoply, its huge cannon hauled by teams of as many as six hundred horses, its kettledrum chariots booming, and the carriage-borne standards of its flag guns boldly flaunted. To the village and farm folk along the route these long columns of American and French artillery were equally glorious emblems of victory to come.

Princeton, Trenton, Philadelphia saw the guns pass. It was no easy march. Carriages broke down under their weight of metal or overturned in ditches. Poles and traces snapped. Often weary gunners were forced to harness themselves into bricoles, with others straining at wheels, to help the struggling horses. Williamsburg, Virginia—then park was made in sight of the York River, flowing into Chesapeake Bay. The long, wearing march, averaging nearly fifteen miles a day, and one of the fastest in history for troops equipped with heavy siege trains, was over.

Yonder on a bluff on the south side of the river loomed the houses of Yorktown. Encircling it was a series of strong earthworks, built by two thousand Negro slaves. In ten redoubts were mounted sixty-five cannon: 18-pounders, ship guns, mortars, and fieldpieces. There Cornwallis and his seventy-five hundred veterans stood at bay. Only a few frigates lay anchored in the river. A British fleet, which had attempted to sail in to the aid of the garrison, had been driven off by the French Admiral De Grasse, who now kept the Chesapeake under blockade.

Cornwallis committed the folly of abandoning his outer works in favor of a tighter defense, confidently declaring that relief would arrive from New York. The allies promptly moved into those ready-made positions, reversing the parapets. In classic siege procedure, directed by Steuben and Knox, now a major general, entrenchments called parallels began to seal in the town. Infantry skirmishes and cavalry clashes ended in a British withdrawal behind their defenses.

It was time to bring up the big guns. Knox commandeered the mounts of all officers to help his tired teams.[51] When the heavies rolled up on their creaking sling carts, they were manhandled on to their platforms and trained on the enemy. On October 9, 1781, they opened the bombardment, Washington himself touching off the first American piece to fire. Its shell crashed into a house used as mess hall for the British staff, killed a commissary general and wounded three other officers. Another shot from the same battery sheared off the head of a major standing by Cornwallis's side.

All through the night and for day after day mortars, 18's, and 24's, French and American, roared away. They pounded houses into matchwood, or gutted them, blasting out their furniture to pile the streets of Yorktown deeply with debris. Cornwallis, shelled out of his comfortable quarters, took refuge in a tent under the riverbank. The Governor of Virginia, General Nelson, unhesitatingly directed fire on his own home.[52] Overwhelming the British batteries, the allies' mortars and howitzers lobbed shells into enemy works, smashing gun carriages and exploding magazines—flinging high cascades of earth and mangled bodies. A Hessian soldier wrote of that terrific cannonade, shuddering from its memory:

One could ... not avoid the horribly many cannon balls either inside or outside the city ... many were badly injured and mortally wounded by the fragments of bombs which exploded partly in the air and partly on the ground, their arms and legs severed or themselves struck dead ... One saw men lying everywhere who were mortally wounded ... I saw bombs fall into the water and lie there for 5, 6-8 and more minutes and then still explode ... fragments and pieces of these bombs flew back again and fell on the houses and buildings of the city and in our camp, where they still did much damage and robbed many a brave soldier of his life or struck off his arm and leg.[53]

French gunners found the range of the vessels at their river anchorage. Round shot, heated to a red glow, rained down on the frigate *Charon* and set her ablaze. Wrapped in a torrent of flame, she burned to the water line, along with two transports; a second warship, also hit, cut her cables and escaped. On the American front firing rose to a faster tempo, as powder-blackened crews swabbed, loaded, and fired without respite. General Lafayette, who had come to regard himself as an American, enthusiastically shouted above the din, "We fire faster than the French. Upon my honor I speak the truth. American artillery—one of the wonders of the Revolution!"

It was the infantry's turn now. Cannon signaled the assault, fell silent. American and French columns in a gallant night charge stormed the two strongest enemy redoubts and opened the way for the guns to move up to an advanced line. There, at the deadly range of four hundred yards, they poured a devastating stream of iron into the cramped and crowded enemy. It silenced the British guns one by one, until only a single mortar and a few coehorns still fired.

Doggedly Cornwallis held out. A fleet from New York, breaking the French blockade, could yet save him. He bought time by launching crack troops, the Royal Welch Fusiliers, in a desperate sortie to put the terrible enemy cannon out of action.

Tall grenadiers shouting, "Up the Fusiliers!" scaled the parapets. Close combat raged in the dark, crowded trenches. Before a rally drove out the invaders they succeeded in spiking four cannon with bayonets, but artificers drilled them out, and soon the cannon were firing again.

The end drew near. Cornwallis, his attempt to escape across the river a failure, sighted no sails of a rescue fleet. (It arrived three days too late.) A last, a hopeless council of war on October 17, and the British commander issued his fateful order.

Up on a battered parapet clambered a drummer boy. He stood there, a brave little figure in scarlet, sticks flailing away at his drumhead. In the thunder of the bombardment he might have been an actor in a pantomime. Then a sergeant climbed to his side and waved a white flag.

The sudden cessation of the sound of the guns, which had fired almost continuously since the ninth, was startling, memorable. It was a story veterans liked to tell—how in that breath-taking silence the drum beating the parley, parley that meant surrender, could be heard at last. Descendants of those soldiers of the Revolution, if the tale came down to them, must have understood their forebears' emotions as they stood back from hot guns in France at eleven o'clock on the eleventh day of November, 1918.

The British Army marched out of shattered Yorktown, bands playing but colors furled and sheathed. It filed between lines of its conquerors, drawn up opposite each other. Over the French regiments in gleaming white waved their varicolored regimental banners. The Stars and Stripes floated free above ranks in Continental blue and brown, uniforms often threadbare and ragged but worn proudly. As British fifes shrilled "The World Turned Upside Down," Lafayette was ready with an answer to leave King George's men no doubt about the cause of their upset world. He ordered American music to strike up "Yankee Doodle." Its lively strains, once defiant, now triumphant, heralded victory, independence won, although the war would not end until 1783 with the surrender of New York.

General Henry Knox was given the honor of leading the army into New York—Knox, Chief of Artillery, the resources of whose genius had, as his commander declared, supplied the deficiency of means. Founder of Springfield Arsenal, of the Order of the Cincinnati to keep alive the spirit of patriotism and loyalty, of the School of Instruction at West Point which became the United States Military Academy, Washington's first secretary of war—all these achievements and more stand on his record.[54] Fort Knox, Kentucky, site of the Armored School, and the Knox Trophy, for which batteries annually compete, today commemorate the artilleryman who brought the cannon from Fort Ticonderoga and fought his guns so ably at Trenton, Princeton, Monmouth, and Yorktown.

CHAPTER 4

The Rockets and the Bombs

•••

And the rocket's red glare, the bombs bursting in air,
Gave proof thro' the night that our flag was still there.
Oh, say, does that Star-Spangled Banner yet wave
O'er the land of the free and the home of the brave?

FRANCIS SCOTT KEY, "The Star-Spangled Banner"

God fights on the side with the best artillery.

NAPOLEON

•••

THE troops that won the Revolutionary War were rapidly disbanded, as happened again and again to the armies of the United States. Except for a small detachment at Fort Pitt, all that finally remained was Alexander Hamilton's old company of artillery. Those fifty-five men, guarding stores at West Point, maintaining a few 6- and 3-pounders and cutting the grass above the magazines, were now the entire United States Army, their commander, Captain John Doughty, its ranking officer. Hamilton's company, originally organized in 1776, by virtue of its survival through the drastic reduction of 1784 and its continuance through subsequent vicissitudes,[55] holds the distinction today of being the oldest unit in the Regular Army.

Continuity of existence, like battle honors blazoned on banners, means much to *esprit de corps*. Of such matters most of the young nation was as heedless as the Congress of 1784. With the memory of British oppression still vivid, it declared that "standing armies in time of peace are inconsistent with the principles of republican government, dangerous to the liberties of a free people, and generally converted into destructive engines for establishing despotism."

So there was no standing army, only those few artillerymen. Short-term militia were called up to meet the Indian menace on the frontier but proved unable to cope with it. That good soldier, Major General Anthony Wayne, formed and disciplined a "legion" and defeated the Miamis at the Battle of Fallen Timbers. In 1808 there was a brief but brilliant burgeoning of the gunners' arm, the first American light or horse artillery.

It sprang, like much of the contemporary organization, tactics, and matériel of American artillery, from the genius of two Frenchmen. In the late eighteenth century, the brilliant artillerist, Jean Baptiste Vaquette de Gribeauval, had introduced interchangeable parts, increased range and accuracy, reduced types, calibers, and weight, mounted the cannoneers, and made soldiers of drivers—reforms gradually effected. His improvements rendered Napoleon's superb handling of artillery possible. Napoleon, who launched his career as a young gunner lieutenant, won the nickname of "Corporal Cannon" and was now startling the world with his victories.

That first American horse artillery (all cannoneers on horseback), commanded by Captain George Peter, held high promise.[56] Peter staged a drill for Congress on July 4, 1808, greatly impressing that body. Galloping three miles, he dismounted, unlimbered, and fired a national salute; then returned to the starting point and fired a second salute—all in twenty-two minutes. He made a route march from Baltimore to Washington at better than six miles an hour—good time even by World War I standards and a remarkable rate over the plodding guns of the Revolution. Cheered by spectators, the battery paraded smartly down Pennsylvania Avenue, uniformed in blue coatees with red facings and yellow buttons, blue pantaloons, and leather caps with small visors and two wings, one of which was marked with brass letters, LA', for Light Artillery. Next the battery struck out for New Orleans, crossing the Alleghenies handily in midwinter, and finishing the journey by Mississippi flatboats. Then it was ignominiously stalled in the Louisiana mud when the new secretary of war, William Eustis, former contract surgeon and a small-minded politician, ordered its horses sold on the ground that

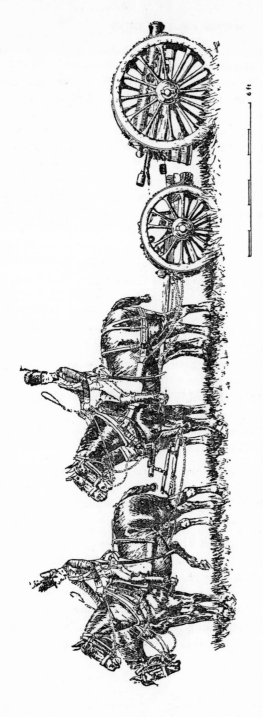

CAPTAIN GEORGE PETER'S LIGHT ARTILLERY, 1808–1809. THE GUN IS A CAST-IRON SIX-POUNDER. (From a drawing by Colonel Harry C. Larter, Jr., copyright, 1952, by the Company of Military Collectors and Historians, September, 1952)

forage was too expensive. Peter, his fine battery immobilized and ruined, resigned his commission in disgust.

Wars continued—the undeclared one with France at sea, engagements with the Barbary pirates. Fortunately there existed an American Navy—not considered, like a standing army, a threat to liberties —to fight them. In the approaching second war with Great Britain, the Navy would cover itself with glory on the Atlantic and the Great Lakes.

The outbreak of the War of 1812 found American artillerymen on the Indian frontier acting as infantry "in addition to their other duties." Coast defenses were well armed with 927 guns from 18's to 42's and on up to the new, big 50-pounder Columbiads. The last were the invention of an ordnance expert, Major George Bomford, who named them in honor of Joel Barlow's epic on Columbus which created a great stir in its day and has seldom since been read. The poem, in twelve long cantos, was an even heavier piece than its namesake cannon.

But the field artillery, dehorsed and neglected, was in sad case. It had manuals but no means for applying them: Kosciuszko's, translated by Jonathan Williams, and the "American Artillerist's Companion" by Louis de Tousard, a gallant French officer who, capturing a British gun on Rhode Island, was wounded in the right arm and had it amputated so he could more speedily return to duty.[57] Two artillery regiments were authorized in the emergency, but for long they were enrolled only on War Department lists.

> In time of war, ignorance of strategy and tactics demands a fearful cost in the lives of men. Unfortunately we do not seem to learn from history, for this was neither the first nor the last time that we drifted into war unprepared.[58]

A former lance corporal of Virginia horse was suddenly appointed captain of light artillery in 1808. Winfield Scott, tall and handsome, a huger man even than Knox, had yearned for a military career since the day a year before when he had charged into shallow water with his squad and temporarily captured a boat of the British warship *Leopard*, guilty of impressing American seamen. Two years after the outbreak of the War of 1812 he was a brigadier general.

"The best generals are those who have served in the artillery," Napoleon on St. Helena pronounced in retrospect. Scott made good the ex-Emperor's dictum in two wars. A third found him in command of the United States Army until old age and ill health forced his retirement.

He served his country most brilliantly in the chaos and confusion which marked the beginning of the second conflict with Great Britain. Scott, still a young field officer and an impressive figure with his six-foot-five height and 230-pound muscular frame, was the organizing genius who trained and disciplined a mob of raw troops and made them into an army to stem the British invasion which had burst over the Canadian border and taken Detroit. To his especial credit was the efficiency of the artillery battalion, some three hundred men under Major Jacob Hindman, which fought through the Niagara campaign. Its four companies, armed mostly with 12-pounders and commanded by able captains, Towson, Biddle, Ritchie, and Williams, wore gray as did a good part of the rest of the army, blue cloth being unobtainable. In honor of Scott's victory at Chippewa, West Point cadets were first uniformed in the gray they wear today.[59]

On July 5, 1814, the American army under hard-fighting Major General Jacob Brown struck the British position on the Chippewa River. Towson's 12's, their fire faster and more accurate than the enemy's, dueled with the Royal Artillery. Though one of his guns was knocked out, Towson retaliated by dropping a shot on an enemy caisson which exploded and disrupted the entire battery's service. Scott, galloping up, launched his brigade in a charge. A British general, who had soundly whipped troops in gray a year before, contemptuously scanned advancing ranks in the same color. In spite of losses, they came on so steadily, loading and firing, that he changed his tune and shouted in amazement, "Those are regulars, by God!" As the infantry plunged forward, bayonets fixed, American guns opened a murderous crossfire on the British lines. Both flanks, enfiladed, began to disintegrate. Scott saw with elation how they "mouldered away like a rope of sand." When the charge was driven home, the redcoats, their casualties more than twice as heavy as the Americans', beat a retreat that was close to a rout.

Beneath "Chippewa" the standard of the 2nd Artillery and the colors of old infantry regiments carry the legend *Lundy's Lane*. The

Battle of Lundy's Lane, fought close to Niagara Falls on July 25, was one of the bloodiest battle honors ever won.

While seven American 12's thundered, and the Royal Artillery replied, Scott's brigade assaulted strong enemy entrenchments on rising ground. "Scott came forward impetuously with his inferior force. It was seven o'clock on the July evening when he struck the British line like a tornado cast out from the near-by cataract. For two hours the deep roar of Niagara Falls was no more than a dull undercurrent to the fire of the muskets and the booming of the cannon in a battle that exceeded in fury and grimness any contest that had ever been fought on North American soil." [60] Two British 24's and five other pieces, served at top speed, poured a hail of iron into oncoming ranks. Too high and well emplaced to be reached by the American guns—this was a mission for howitzers or mortars—the battery and its supporting infantry hurled back repeated charges until Scott's command, decimated, fell back. Victory and even safe retreat were now impossible unless the British cannon were stormed. General Brown turned to James Miller, commanding the 21st:

"Colonel, those British guns on the hill must be taken! Can you do it?"

Miller's answer, perpetuated on his regiment's coat of arms, was, "I'll try, sir." The Colonel and his men, guided by Scott, advanced on the battery under cover of almost complete darkness, while another regiment made a diversionary attack. Rushing in, the 21st bayoneted the artillerymen in a short, fierce melee around their pieces. The British commander, both guns and position lost, strove desperately but vainly to regain them in a sanguinary combat in which both sides suffered heavily.

Now a novel artillery weapon swayed the battle's issue—the rocket. Although rockets had been fired from bamboo tubes by the Chinese in warfare with the Mongols at least as early as A.D. 1232, they had declined as cannon developed until the eighteenth century, when they were used in India against the British. There they aroused the interest of the inventive General Congreve. This recoilless weapon, he believed, would vitally affect military tactics, and he set to work improving it. More than twenty thousand of the type he devised were launched when Wellington besieged and burned Copenhagen in 1807 and they were effectively used in other sieges and battles.

Making its American debut at Lundy's Lane, a Congreve rocket struck General Brown, already wounded in the thigh by a musket ball, a violent blow in the side, disabling him. Scott—the third of the big chargers needed to carry his weight just had been shot under him—was hit both by a ricocheting cannon ball and a bullet. As both generals were carried from the field, Brown, badly hurt, made a decision he might not otherwise have taken. He withdrew his battered troops for rations and ammunition, ordering Major Hindman to retract his guns from the position they occupied on the captured hill.

Hindman limbered and pulled out, in the darkness taking a British piece instead of one of his own. When he returned for the rest of the enemy cannon, not having had enough horses to haul them on the first trip, it was too late. The British had reoccupied the hill and held the battlefield, and the Americans were no longer strong enough to dislodge them.

Desperate fighting again took place when British General Gordon Drummond attempted to storm Fort Erie on the shore of the lake. It was there that a phrase later telescoped into one word in a greater war is said to have been first used. "Give the damned Yankees no quarter," Drummond ordered angrily after repeated repulses. Curiously, it was applied to a brigade with many Southerners in its ranks.

When a column broke into the northeast bastion, a detachment of one hundred British artillerymen, redeeming the loss of their guns at Chippewa, held it for two hours of hand-to-hand combat. With comrades rushing to their aid, they might have won the whole fort but for the explosion of a large store of ammunition underneath the platform at the bastion's center. Some accounts call it accidental; others state it was the gallant deed of an American officer, who may have sacrificed his life in a flaming eruption of earth, splintered timbers, and mangled bodies. Remnants of the assault column abandoned the bastion, and Drummond, his losses 905 in killed and wounded to the Americans' 84, gave up and fell back.

The threat from the north was over, and the theater of warfare shifted southward.

Vice Admiral Sir Alexander Cockburn sailed into Chesapeake Bay in the summer of 1814 with orders "to destroy and lay waste such towns and districts upon the coast as you may find assailable." One such town, unfortified and eminently assailable, was Washington, capital of the United States. President Madison, Secretary of State Monroe, and Secretary of War John Armstrong compounded its confusion and unpreparedness. All Revolutionary veterans, they, particularly Monroe, could not refrain from interfering with the military command, and the results were disastrous.

Cockburn, unopposed, landed an army of forty-five hundred men under General John Ross after cornering Commodore Joshua Barney's thirty small gunboats in the Patuxent River. Barney, having put his ordnance ashore, burned his flotilla. In the battle ahead those guns would be served as gallantly as in any of the Commodore's sea fights.

Ross attacked the American force of between six and seven thousand men a few miles from Washington at Bladensburg, celebrated for its dueling ground. The Irish-born British general's infantry, veterans of Wellington's Peninsular campaign, was immensely superior in all but numbers. However, his scanty cannon, one 6-pounder and two 3's, were far outweighed by his adversary's: the twelve 6's of the Maryland and Washington militia, Barney's naval guns, and the new battery of Major Peter, returned to the service in the emergency. But Ross, like his compatriots in the north, was equipped with rockets.

Except for a few hundred regulars it was American militia that fought the battle on August 24, 1814. They were then more the nation's first line of defense than its second, these State troops. Many were uniformed in handsome regimentals, topped by shakos festooned with braided cords and tassels, or jauntily wearing cockaded beavers, and they made a dazzling spectacle in parades and reviews. Some of the citizen-soldiers, hastily mustered with only few desultory drills behind them—or none—broke in battle. Others, crack outfits like the 5th Maryland Infantry, along with the field batteries, gave a gallant account of themselves against Wellington's Invincibles during most of the fighting that followed. More than their inexperience and the battle-proven prowess of the enemy, it was inept command, hamstrung by the interference of civilian officials, that defeated them.

Where the turnpike from Baltimore crossed a bridge—to fork off to Washington and Georgetown farther on—two Maryland batteries and supporting infantry moved on that scorching morning to cover the span. "The guns came down the slope, the traces slack, the limbers crowding on the wheelers' heels, the cannoneers afoot to spare the weary horses," wrote Neil H. Swanson in his graphic descriptions of field artillery moving into action in *The Perilous Fight*. "Just past the southeast corner of the orchard, the drivers swung their teams. Fresh clouds of dust exploded. The guns jolted down into the ditch and up again and went bouncing, yawing, sliding sidewise downhill, across the open ground." They took position behind strong earthworks, already prepared. The pick-and-shovel men, who had constructed them, virtually had dug a grave for American hopes of victory that day. For down in pits made for heavy guns the 6-pounder crews found they could not clear the parapet. Even after they hastily whittled it down, muzzles had to be elevated, and point-blank fire was impossible. Furthermore, their fire must be oblique; it could not directly sweep the bridge. But it was comforting to be under cover, and the 6's stayed where they had been stationed.

A scarlet stream, the British vanguard, flowed through the village down toward the bridge. The Baltimore guns flamed and dammed that stream, its backwash surging against the houses along the street. Slowly it coagulated, built up a head, flowed forward again over a jetsam of bodies. Again the dull boom of guns, detonations half muffled in the pits. Balls thudded down, curveting in ricochets. The stream, split into twin rivulets, trickled along gutters or stagnated in red pools.

Suddenly a flash and a strange, roaring *whoosh* sprang from a warehouse yard.

The thing soared across the river, spitting sparks and trailing a blazing tail. To Americans on the hillside, gaping up at it, it looked like "a comet low in the sky." It cleared the treetops, seemed to hang there for an instant before it plunged downward in its fiery arc. A man couldn't see a bullet coming; if his number wasn't on it, he heard only the hum of its passing. But this swooping thing was dreadfully personal. It appeared to be darting directly at each watching soldier, making him shake in his boots, turning his knees to water. Only when he saw it strike the ground some distance in front could he believe it was not aimed straight at him. Even then the menace of the thing with a pointed iron head and a scorched eight-foot stick was not ended. Smoking and sputtering, it writhed through the grass like a serpent. Then a time fuse burst its black powder charge with a sharp report and a spurt of acrid smoke.

In the warehouse yard the British rocketeers touched matches to more of their missiles lying in launchers not unlike those used today for Fourth of July fireworks. Volleys of rockets with a range of more than two miles swelled into a barrage. Their targets "minds more than bodies," they were terrifying. The first flight was high, but a second, bearing down on the American lines, grazed heads. Three infantry regiments, stupidly placed on the slope in the open by ex-Colonel Secretary Monroe, broke in panic and raced for the rear. But riflemen and the Baltimore artillery stuck to their posts, and the guns shifted fire, driving the rocket troop to shelter.[61]

More guns were up now, and the cannonade rose to a crescendo, cutting through the crackle of rifles. Odds swung from British rockets to American batteries, with the fortunes of battle hanging in the balance.

Once more Wellington's veterans stormed the bridge. This time gunfire, elevated and oblique, could not stop them, could not even reach the brigade of eleven hundred men sweeping forward and around the flanks. Pull out or be lost. "The gun teams break from the edge of the orchard, the limbers crazily bounding, men clinging to bridles, wrestling the teams around, backing them up to the gun trails. One gun is hooked up. Whips cut at the horses' flanks. The wheel horses squat to the sudden dead weight of the gun, hoofs dig up the dirt in clouds, the horses scramble like cats and plunge into a maddened gallop." [62]

It was close to the finish. Rallies here and there could not stave off inevitable defeat. Neither could the fine charge of the 5th Maryland, shattered at last by musketry volleys and the terrible rockets. For a time Commodore Barney's five hundred flotilla men held the road to Washington against three thousand of Ross's regulars and rocketeers. Eighteens and 12's from the gunboats beat back assault after assault with round shot and grape, firing with the verve and accuracy which had won British acclaim for American naval gunnery on the Atlantic and Lake Erie. Major Peter's six lighter guns joined in with deadly cross fire, but the scarlet ranks still came on till the Commodore smashed them back with a bayonet charge of marines and sailors yelling, "Board 'em!" But with the rest of the American army routed and in flight, Barney could hold no longer. Against enemy onslaughts on his flanks and rear, he made a last stand. Then, severely wounded, with survivors of his flotilla men he was taken prisoner. The road to Washington was open.

Cockburn and Ross rode into the abandoned capital about sunset. A shot from a house dropped the General's horse. Torches which fired that building swept on through the streets. Soon the Capitol, the Arsenal, the Treasury, the War Office, and the White House were in flames, with ammunition exploding in the Navy Yard, set afire by the Americans to deny its use to the enemy. Finally a violent thunderstorm quenched the conflagration. While the nation stood in angered humiliation at the capture and destruction of its capital, the victorious British prepared to move against Baltimore.

Present at Bladensburg as a civilian aide had been a young lawyer and poet who had previously served as lieutenant quartermaster in Peter's first light battery. The United States was shortly to owe its anthem to that ex-artilleryman, Francis Scott Key.

Fort McHenry, on the tip of a peninsula, guarded Baltimore harbor. It was garrisoned by one thousand men commanded by a regular artillery officer, Major George Armistead. Above its ramparts floated the Stars and Stripes, so large a flag—thirty-two feet by twenty-nine—that the devoted women who made it had found space enough to cut and stitch it only in a brewery.

Early artillery had sounded the death knell of castles, and now the day of the strongest fortresses was waning. For a while longer they would half hold their own against wooden ships or siege cannon. The rifled guns and the ironclads of the Civil War would render them obsolescent, and most of the proud strongholds from Florida to Maine would be allowed to crumble into ruins, or become relics in national parks. However, many more years were to pass before the fact that they were antiquated was fully acknowledged. In World War I German artillery pounded the Belgian forts at Namur and Liége to bits, yet in the next war France based her defense on the concrete and steel Maginot Line, so easily by-passed.

Ultimately, bombs in the bays of planes proved to be the high explosive periods that wrote finis to fortresses.

But McHenry in 1814 was considered thoroughly modern. Upon its star-shaped bastions of masonry and earth was mounted a formidable armament of guns and howitzers, ranging through 18's, 24's, and 32's on to fifteen 42-pounders. The last, mighty weapons weighing three tons, had been borrowed from the French consul,[63] doubtless delighted to lend ordnance for use against Napoleon's enemy. Walls must withstand and guns match the might of the British Navy —shells from its five bomb ketches, missiles from its rocket ship, *Erebus*. Armistead, though the War Department had ignored his appeals to strengthen McHenry's earthworks and make its magazine bombproof, defended it to the utmost.

As for the rest of the defenses of Baltimore, they were also in capable hands. The veteran who had so stanchly held Fort Mifflin in the Revolution, Sam Smith, United States Senator from Maryland, was called back into service as a major general. Sixty-two but in full vigor, he barred the city's approaches with batteries and entrenchments. Citizens by thousands turned out with pick and shovel, as they had in New York, also expecting an attack by the British fleet.

General Smith, posting his troops, was ready when the British fleet of fifty sail anchored off North Point where the Patapsco River, waterway to the harbor, flows into Chesapeake Bay. When Ross landed a force of some five thousand men and eight cannon and marched rapidly inland, Sam Smith threw a brigade of thirty-two hundred—infantry, artillery, and cavalry—across his path.

Another Revolutionary veteran commanded that brigade: John Stricker, who as a Continental artilleryman still in his teens had manned guns from Trenton onward and ended captaining a battery. His orders were to fight a delaying action, and he obeyed them to the hilt. The spirited two-hour battle he waged began with the feat of two brave young riflemen, Daniel Wells and Henry McComas, who toppled General Ross from his horse with a mortal wound and paid for it with their lives. The British drive, though some of its impetus was spent, pushed on. Forward trotted the rocket troop, mounted now. An early type of pack artillery, its launchers were carried in leather buckets slung beside saddles, and spare ammunition in cases strapped on the backs of horses, with still more reserves in following tumbrils. Dismounting, eighty rocketeers brought their weapons into action within thirty seconds, each tube firing four times a minute. A volume of fire of 480 6-pound missiles in five minutes was "something that field artillerymen will not dream of for generations."

Guns and howitzers punctuated the morale-shattering rocket barrage. Then the Royal Artillery brought another novel projectile from its arsenal. Lieutenant Henry Shrapnel in 1784 had invented the spherical case shot which still bears his name, a shell loaded with balls whose time-fused bursting charge made it more devasting and longer-ranged than grape or canister. Americans under their first shrapnel fire ducked and shrank, as smoke puffs above them detonated with a clang, and iron hail pounded down, flattening whole ranks of infantry and strewing cannoneers around their pieces. Raw regiments panicked and ran.

Stricker's center still held, his guns still boomed. But the British columns, regulars and marines, marching and wheeling as if on parade, were not to be denied. They swept the field, then halted to tend their wounded and bury their dead, casualties heavier than the Americans'. Next morning they moved on, but stopped short of the Baltimore defenses. Let the fleet open the way. Its bombs should quickly demolish Fort McHenry.

Francis Scott Key, turned diplomat, had boarded the British fleet under a flag of truce. His mission was to obtain the release of Dr. William Beanes, a Maryland physician held under arrest aboard the flagship on the charge of having violated his parole when captured after Bladensburg. Admiral Cockburn granted the emissary's request but refused to put him and the doctor ashore until the surrender of Fort McHenry which, he boasted, would soon take place. On the morning of September 13, 1814, from the vantage of the vessel's deck Key watched the commencement of the bombardment.

Neither his peacetime service with Peter's light battery nor his experience at Bladensburg prepared him for the intensity of the hours-long cannonade he witnessed. Cockburn sent in his shallow-draft bomb ships: *Terror, Meteor, Aetna, Devastation,* and *Volcano.* Their ponderous mortars gaped skyward, coughed and spewed out

their 200-pound shells. Fuses sputtering, they soared up in lofty arcs
and swooped down on the fort.

Beneath the starry flag floating above the ramparts, Armistead's
cannoneers answered with the borrowed French guns, howitzers, and
land mortars—every piece that could be brought to bear. At two
miles, their targets, the small bomb ketches, were mere specks. Round
shot flung up waterspouts—short, far short. Gunners knocked quoins
from under breeches, raising barrels to maximum elevation, and
loaders, risking lives from premature bursts, crammed in powder
charges up to the safety limit and past it. Still short, they tried again
with the French 42's, now their only hope of making the range.
Stout-metaled barrels stayed intact under the heavy discharge, but
the cast-iron, ship gun-carriage wheels could not absorb the enor-
mous shock of the recoil. Three guns were dismounted, muzzles
tipped up at crazy angles. "Cease firing," Armistead ordered. There
was nothing to do but stand and take it.

Big mortars on the bomb ships, a good thousand yards closer in
than their extreme range, erupted like the flaming mountains that
gave two of the craft their names. Shells hurtled down on McHenry
at the rate of one a minute. Some burst above crews huddled around
their silent guns. Others, fuses smoking, plunged into the muddy
earthworks to dig a deep grave for themselves or to detonate and
fling up cascades of dirt mixed with jagged fragments of iron. One
knife-edged chunk sliced a soldier's wife in half. (Not all of the
families of the regular garrison, quartered in the fort, had obeyed
an order to evacuate.) A plunging black sphere scored a direct hit
on a 24-pounder, killing and wounding members of its crew. The
garrison crouched behind parapets and in casements, suffering the
artilleryman's toughest ordeal: enduring a punishing enemy bombardment without being able to reply. Only when one of the bomb
vessels ventured in closer did the American gunners find relief by
manning pieces and driving her off.

The rocket ship *Erebus* also came into action, spouting broadsides
of 32-pound incendiary missiles, their war heads packed with com-
bustibles—saltpeter, pitch, sulphur, corned powder. "She was reaching
out with fiery fingers for the houses in the forts, the ready ammunition in the batteries and bastions, the plank platforms and revet-
ments, and the gun-boats moored across the channel." [64] But the

fire from *Erebus* was inaccurate and largely ineffective. It was the crashing bombs that did damage. When one landed on the weak roof of the magazine, crushed it and stuck there, the doom of Mc-Henry was almost sealed. Miraculously the shell failed to explode. Major Armistead's orders rushed working parties to moving powder kegs and cartridges out of the fort into the open where they were spaced so that no single explosion could set off the lot.

All through the day and into the night, when the bombardment took on an awful grandeur, Key watched "the rocket's red glare, the bombs bursting in air." Darkness hid from him, as from the fort's sentinels, the approach of a British landing force of twelve hundred men in barges until rockets, sent up to light their debarkation, betrayed them. At last the artillerymen in McHenry had their chance. Forty guns opened up while those of other forts joined the thunderous chorus. One barge was sunk and some of its crew drowned; the rest rowed back in frantic haste. So Key by the dawn's early light beheld a glorious vision of red, white, and blue. "The flag was still there"—it yet waved "o'er the land of the free and the home of the brave." He sat down on a powder keg to write his immortal words on the back of an old letter.

Those words were printed on broadsides and passed around. They were sung in camps and towns to the tune of the old English drinking song, "Anacreon in Heaven," to which they were set. Though the "Star-Spangled Banner" was not recognized by Congress as our national anthem until 1931, it long before became so in fact.

At the peace table in Ghent, Belgium, British commissioners had presented demands as humiliating to the United States as the burning of Washington, which the terms reflected. Dispatches reporting the failure at Baltimore made all the difference. Now it was a treaty favorable to the United States. His Majesty's negotiators made no territorial claims and offered abandonment of the alleged rights of search, seizure, and impressment of American seamen. The treaty was signed December 24, 1814. Before the document could cross the Atlantic, the war had shifted southward again to a battle in which American artillery notably distinguished itself.

Spanish, then French, finally American by the Louisiana Purchase, the picturesque city of New Orleans was in a fair way to become British by capture. If it should fall to the army of eight thousand under Wellington's brother-in-law, Sir Edward Pakenham, which had been ferried from Jamaica by a fleet of fifty vessels, a second force, driving down from Canada, would co-operate in seizing complete control of the Mississippi. The great river would then form a barrier to the western expansion of the United States. A British victory at New Orleans might prompt a demand for revision of the Treaty of Ghent, still unpublished on this side of the Atlantic. With Napoleon defeated and in exile on Elba, Great Britain was now free to exert her full power.

The defense of New Orleans was entrusted to General Andrew Jackson, Indian-fighter and frontier lawyer. Taken prisoner at thirteen while serving as a dragoon orderly in the Revolutionary War, Jackson, in Gerald Johnson's vivid phrase,[65] came "reeling into history with a sabre cut on his head," a wound inflicted by a British officer whose boots he refused to polish. Now, thirty-four years later, an opportunity to even that score came to Old Hickory.

British warships, raking and boarding American gunboats on Lake Borgne, drove an entering wedge. Only a schooner and a sloop, the *Carolina* and the *Louisiana,* the latter still at her city dock unready for action, remained to bar the waterways. The invaders had to reckon with them both as floating batteries. When a British division was put ashore, pushed through the cypress swamps, and pitched camp near the levee on December 23, 1814, the *Carolina's* sweeps propelled her down the Mississippi to a point abreast the division. Crews under Master Commandant Daniel T. Patterson swept the camp with 12-pounder broadsides, as columns with two 6-pounders under Jackson and General John Coffee launched an attack. The British, their only artillery a pair of 3's and rockets, were beaten back through the gathering darkness in savage hand-to-hand fighting with clubbed muskets, knives, and fists, but rallied with their backs to an old levee which covered them from the *Carolina's* fire. Jackson, aware that the enemy's main body would soon advance, withdrew to his defense works. The schooner held the river until the British brought up heavy artillery, forcing her crew to abandon ship, and blew her up. But Patterson earlier had landed some of her guns and established a battery on the farther bank. Also under his command came the *Louisiana* whose seamen in small boats had towed her out of range of the hostile fire that destroyed her sister craft.

It was the *Louisiana's* stubby, big-bored carronades and the shore battery that almost alone broke up Pakenham's second thrust on New Orleans on December 28. When two redcoat columns drove on Jackson's position, the naval guns riddled the one nearer the river with scathing broadsides. As it deployed into line attack formation, the carronades and land-based 12's pounded it till it "fell apart like a broken string of beads." Fragments retreated, regrouped, and waited for the inland force, which pushed forward two fieldpieces to cover its advance. Patterson's sharpshooting gunners flattened them as soon as they came within range and shifted the line of metal so that their shot scoured the plain of infantry. The British commander called off an attack he now euphemistically described as a "reconnaissance in force." Heavy guns were ordered forward to pave the way for his next effort.

Battle lines drawn up before New Orleans presented such international arrays as Americans would not see again until the Boxer Rebellion and the World Wars. The British army facing them was composed of Englishmen, a regiment of Scottish Highlanders, and two of West Indian Negroes, supported by artillery, a rocket brigade, and sappers. In the ranks of the defenders, regulars and Tennessee and Mississippi riflemen stood shoulder to shoulder with colorfully uniformed Creole militia, who in turn were flanked by companies of "free men of color." A party of Choctaw Indians was stationed on the left. Patterson's scratch crews, recruited from the streets of New Orleans, were made up of every nationality except English. Jean Lafitte, who had refused a British bid for the services of his red-shirted Baratarians, pirates and smugglers of the Louisiana bayous, managed to persuade the reluctant Jackson to accept them, "hellish banditti" though Old Hickory branded them. As a result, one battery in the American line was manned by experienced freebooter gunners, captained by fierce little Dominique You. A second was commanded by General Garriques Flaugeac, a veteran artilleryman who had fought under Napoleon, then suffered exile on a charge of plotting against the Emperor. A third battery commander was a gunner corporal of the Regular Army; the chief of artillery a United States Army captain. Orders were given in French and

Spanish as well as English, and bands mingled the strains of "Hail Columbia" with *"La Marseillaise"* and *"Le Chant du Départ."*

The engagement on New Year's Day, 1815, has been called the Battle of the Bales and Hogsheads. Cotton bales barricaded the American guns in front of Jackson's main line along the dry Rodriguez Canal, while the British strengthened theirs with barrels of sugar. Such were the defenses—both ill-chosen as it developed —that supplemented the parapets of mud.

Up from the British fleet on Lake Borgne had plowed heavy ordnance, dragged by toiling sailors through the mire of cypress swamps. Emplaced under cover of night, the muzzles of twenty-four pieces—ten 18's, four 24-pounder carronades, ten field guns and howitzers—jutted out between sugar barrels. Confronting them besides Patterson's guns across the river, were four 24's, one 32, one 18, five 12's, three 6's, and one 6-inch howitzer, a weight of metal estimated as inferior to the British by some 300 pounds.[66]

In the shadows of the gun pits the crimson glow of slow matches illuminated the features of the ready crews of eight batteries. They made Dominique You—some said he had once been a gunner of Napoleon's—and his swarthy, bearded Baratarians fully look the part of "hellish banditti." General Flaugeac calmly checked the laying of his guns like the old soldier he was. What if he had led full divisions in Egypt against the Mamelukes and at Marengo? This was a good battery and it would be well served. The other battery commanders, from colonel to corporal, and their men stood to their guns in that tensity of nerves which is the prelude to battle.

They had to wait until the sun began to burn off the dawn's heavy mist. About eight o'clock a flight of swishing rockets opened a combat that proved to be almost entirely an artillery fire fight, gun against gun at the deadly range of seven hundred yards, with only one brief clash of infantry.

Red flashes stabbed through the shreds of fog, as the roaring of cannon rose to a steady drumfire. Picked gunners of the British Navy, veterans of Nelson's victories, drove General Jackson from his headquarters with a barrage of one hundred shells. American batteries, slower at first, warmed to their firing rhythm. Their "shot penetrated ... sugar-hogsheads as if they had been so many empty casks," confessed a British subaltern, "dismounting our guns and killing our artillery-men in the very center of their works." [67]

They were firing blind now through pungent clouds of smoke from their own cannon and burning cotton bales, hastily shoved aside as they ignited, but their pieces had been well laid, and round after round plunged into the enemy emplacements.

Battery and counterbattery, they pounded away at each other. As rockets swooped across among the enemy shells, Jackson strode along the line shouting, "Don't mind these rockets. They are mere toys to amuse children." His reassurance sounded hollow when the fiery missiles exploded two caissons with thunderous detonations and set more cotton bales ablaze. Three guns were dismounted, but the rest redoubled their fire.

British infantry, poised for an assault, were able to make only one sally, quickly repulsed by American riflemen. British artillery fire slackened, as gun after gun was silenced. After four hours of cannonading, three-fourths of the enemy's crews lay killed or wounded around their smoking pieces. Survivors abandoned the guns, and they were Jackson's for the taking, but he ventured no sortie against the enemy's infantry strength. Later recovered by the British, cannon still serviceable took part in the final battle that impended.

That day's combat had echoed Napoleon's cynical maxim that God fights on the side with the best artillery. Andrew Jackson recognized the superiority of his gunners in an order dictated at his battered headquarters:

> The Major General tenders to the troops he has the honor to command his good wishes for a happy new year, and especially to those officers and men at the pieces of Artillery.... Watch Word Fight on—The Contractor will issue half a gill of whiskey round.

That whisky issue, only a throat-moistener to the Baratarians, could have been no more than a faintly pleasant memory by January 8. At dawn that morning they were drinking Creole drip coffee when General Jackson inspected them in Battery Number Three and sniffed the fragrant brew.

"That smells like better coffee than we can get," Jackson remarked. "Smuggle it?" he asked Dominique You.

"Mebbe so, General," the little captain answered with a grin, and filled a cup for his commander.

Old Hickory grinned back at the raffish crew of artillerymen, recalling their gallant service on New Year's Day. "I wish I had five hundred such devils in the butts," he said.[68] It was a promotion for the "hellish banditti."

There was more ceremony in Jackson's inspection of General Flaugeac's guns, less at the other batteries; less still with the Tennessee riflemen, many of whom Old Hickory knew by name. All along the line infantry and artillery were ready. Alert also were troops on the right across the river, with Patterson's shore battery of nine heavy cannon, and the gunners of the *Louisiana*. Yet that flank was alarmingly weak, and Jackson had refused to reinforce it, believing that the main assault would be delivered on his position.

Distinctly unready was Sir Edward Pakenham. A good soldier, the British commander, but badly advised by the Navy and some undependable subordinates. He had intended to strike the American right first but let Admiral Sir Alexander Cochrane, with the arrogance of the senior service, goad him into making a simultaneous frontal attack. However, his left was late crossing the river; its leader had provided too few boats and underestimated the swiftness of the current which carried his troops far downstream. A poorly disciplined regiment in Pakenham's center, detailed to carry forward fascines to fill the dry canal and ladders to scale the ramparts, neglected its duty. So the frontal assault, planned to take place before dawn to escape the deadly rifle marksmanship of the frontiersmen —or the "Dirty Shirts," as the British called them—was launched while still no sounds of battle came from the column which should have been in action across the river, and with storming equipment still to be brought forward.

Two rockets soared to signal the assault, and with them, disastrously for the attackers, a concealing fog rose like a theater curtain to reveal the advancing ranks. "A heavy frost had embossed the cane stubble with silver. Across the shining carpet moved a field of red tunics latticed by white cross-belts, and a pulsing hedge of bayonets that gave an impression of infinity." [69] General Jackson ordered word passed to his riflemen to aim above the cross plates. They sighted along barrels resting on the parapet but held fire, for the enemy was still beyond effective rifle range—four hundred yards—as the cannonade crashed.

American guns fired furiously, heedless of British counterbattery. Their shot opened deep furrows in the oncoming ranks but could not halt them, and since smoke was blinding waiting riflemen, two batteries were ordered to cease firing. Within three hundred yards now, the enemy charge pressed on at the double.

The long orange flame of the first rifle volley outlined the parapet. Marksmen, stepping down to reload, were replaced by a second, then a third line, every man picking his target. Those rolling volleys, as rifleman spelled rifleman, were rapid fire that would stand unequaled until the advent of repeating weapons. Most of the horses of mounted officers, Pakenham's among them, were cut down. Red now carpeted the silvery field. "That leaden torrent no man on earth could face," an English lieutenant remembered.[70]

A second wave—tall, kilted Highlanders, every man six feet or more—swept forward. The rifles and the guns, blazing away with grape, mowed them down and heaped them high. Pakenham, remounted on his aide's pony, had taken a second wound but was still leading his men on when a grapeshot killed him. Another major general, taking over, died, while a third was severely wounded. A valiant remnant pushed on to storm the works. Two officers scaled the parapet; a major, who toppled dead into the trench, and a lieutenant, taken prisoner.

None followed them. The attack was shattered beyond hope of rallying. To Andrew Jackson, watching survivors struggling up to surrender from the windrows of British dead, came a "grand and awful idea of the resurrection." [71]

But on his right, across the river where the tardy onset had taken place at last, the tide of battle was flowing the other way. The enemy drove ahead, took his losses, and submerged the Americans' weak flank. Patterson, whose battery had fired over the water and helped break the earlier onslaught, spiked his guns before retreating. Undisabled, they could have been used to rake Jackson's lines from river to swamp, as Pakenham had originally intended. But nothing came of the British success on their left, for next day the column was recalled. Soon afterwards the beaten invading army, its losses 2,036 to the Americans' 71, embarked and sailed away.

New Orleans, regardless of the previously signed peace treaty, was a decisive battle. The artillery's triumph on the first, the riflemen's on the eighth, brought the war to a glorious climax. Combined with sea victories and fighting qualities displayed in the north and in the defense of Baltimore, they far more than redeemed the capture and burning of Washington. Together they won a powerful opponent's respect, upon which was founded friendship between the two nations, thereafter sometimes strained, but never broken.

A cannon, spiked in the fight on the west bank in the last conflict before New Orleans, could serve artillerymen as a fitting epilogue to the wars with Great Britain. It bore a plate inscribed, "Taken at the Surrender of Yorktown, 1781." [72] To that might well have been added, "Lost and Retaken at the Battle of New Orleans, 1815," and finally, *Requiescat in Pace*.

CHAPTER 5

The Flying Batteries

Our field artillery was excellent in personnel and material.

JUSTIN H. SMITH, *The War with Mexico*

Because the artillery rendered such signal service on the field yesterday [Palo Alto], Gen. Taylor was impressed with the idea that it was available for pursuit of cavalry in mountain passes, for storming entrenchments, or charging a line of battle.

SAMUEL G. FRENCH, *Two Wars*

The artillery of the Americans, much superior to ours, made horrid ravages in the ranks of the Mexican army. The soldiers yielded, not overwhelmed in combat in which they might deal out the death they received—not in the midst of excitement and gallantry which the ardor of battle brings forth, but in a fatal situation in which they were killed with impunity, and decimated in cold blood.

RAMÓN ALCARAZ, *The Other Side*

T HE light artilleryman of 1815, his felt shako recently replaced, was top-heavy under a weighty cylindrical leather cap with raised front piece; nor did his head lie much easier when the cap was sup-planted by a bell-crowned shako of jacked leather. His weary neck was supported by a lofty collar jutting up from his blue coat, a collar which regulations considerately provided should be "low enough in front to permit turning the head." He also wore a high, hot, leather stock whose exclusive use he would doubtless be happy to leave to the marines, along with their name, "Leathernecks." Gone were the bright scarlet facings of earlier years, but the traditional artillery color was carried on by the red-topped yellow pompons of light companies; those of the remaining eight units in each of the four regiments were all yellow, a hue they eventually relinquished to the cavalry. Trousers were blue for winter, white for summer.

Not many uniforms were required for the puny post-war regiments. The 1st, 2nd, 3rd, and 4th [73] were spread thin from Louisiana to Maine in forts whose guns they were too few to serve or even to maintain properly. Light batteries, light in name only since cannoneers were not mounted on horseback nor on carriages, were parceled out with the infantry, and generally gunners acted as infantry in the field. The period knew no irascible Captain John Lamb to make wrathful protest. Only on rare occasions did the artillery actually serve as such. In 1838 Company B of the 4th, complete with pieces, caissons, ammunition wagons, and traveling forge, campaigned against Indians in the South, "but the service . . . rendered was of little importance either against the enemy or in giving the officers practical experience as light artillerymen." [74]

Yet energetic officers accomplished all they could for their arm in the circumstances. A multiplicity of calibers was reduced to 24-, 18-, and 12-pound guns, and 6-pound howitzers, 10- and 8-inch mortars. In 1824, the first of our service schools, the Artillery School of Practice, was established at Fortress Monroe, Virginia, "an event of the highest importance." [75] French manuals were translated, one of them by the enterprising young Lieutenant Daniel Tyler, who had crossed the Atlantic to study French and English ordnance. He discovered that the latter had regained the lead in artillery design. As a result of his recommendations, the United States adopted the single- or stock-trail gun carriage; simpler and stronger than twin trails,[76] it carried through the Civil War. Another officer, sent abroad to bring back cannon and other equipment, made a fiasco of his mission by returning with only eight swords and belts.[77]

These were times, to paraphrase Thomas Paine, to try artillerymen's souls—or any other soldier's. "Less than 4,000 regular soldiers now guarded over 10,000 miles of seacoast and frontier for 15,000,000 people." [78] A private's pay of six dollars a month rose slowly to ten dollars with length of service. Promotion within regiments was so stagnant that there was small chance of a lieutenant's ever winning his captaincy. Miserable conditions in the outlying posts produced desertions, disease, despair, and drunkenness, punished by floggings and executions.

Disease, as it would continue to do for a century and a half still, killed far more troops than enemy action. Casualties in the 4th Artillery were especially appalling. Stationed in the South, in six years it lost 16 officers and 220 enlisted men, mostly to yellow fever —and then Congress dared question the expense of moving it to a healthier post in the North! During the Black Hawk War of 1832, the same regiment, moved eighteen hundred miles west from Philadelphia by rail, boat, and marches in eighteen days—a remarkable feat—but its strength was cut thirty per cent by Asiatic cholera, leaving it so weakened that it never reached combat with the Indians.[79]

In the Florida wars against the Seminoles and the Creeks, extending from 1812 past the middle fifties, wars in which artillery ordinarily served as infantry or mounted scouts, occurred a gallant, one-gun action. Half-forgotten, it stands out in its grim setting as a preview of the "massacre" of Custer's battalion of the 7th Cavalry.

Brevet Major Francis L. Dade, 4th Infantry, led a force of 112 men from Key West to Fort Brooke, Florida. Along with his infantrymen, Company C, 2nd Artillery and B of the 3rd marched beside their ox-drawn 6-pounder and ammunition cart. Vigilance was relaxed as the column drew nearer its destination, with no advanced guard and flankers out. Generally troops sweltered through Florida campaigns in winter uniforms, issued for all seasons, but heavy clothing was welcome that chilly morning of December 28, 1835. Men pulled on overcoats and buttoned them over their cartridge pouches.

Suddenly, at a range of thirty-five yards, a hail of lead poured from the pines, palmetto clumps, and high grass where Seminole warriors lay in ambush. Dade and half his command fell at the first volley. Survivors fired the one round in their muskets and tugged frantically at overcoat flaps to reach ammunition. The 6-pounder, blasting away with canister, alone held off the Indians while pines were hewn down to build a knee-high breastwork. Second Lieutenant R. Henderson, 2nd Artillery, his left arm shattered, helped load and fire the piece till he was killed. Its crew and replacements were whittled down by Seminole bullets, but Second Lieutenant W. E. Basinger of the 2nd kept the piece in action until the last gunner dropped and he himself was wounded. A charge swept over the barricade, tomahawks hacking, scalping knives ripping. Two cannoneers and an infantryman, all severely wounded, crawled off through the tall grass and escaped to tell of the disaster.

The day drew nigh when artillery would no longer depend upon transportation by oxen—except in the case of siege guns and ammunition wagons—and would to some extent be freed from service as foot troops. A top artilleryman, Brevet Major Samuel Ringgold, whose career was to be cut tragically short, led the way in modernizing the arm.[80] In 1845 he made an Americanized revision of Captain Robert Anderson's translation of the French *Instruction for Field Artillery, Horse and Foot*. His own company, the only horse artillery in the regular army (all cannoneers on horseback), wore dark blue forage caps with red bands, blue jackets trimmed with red worsted, sky-blue "overalls" striped with red, and boots. The uniforms of the three light companies (cannoneers riding on limbers and caissons) differed slightly, and those of the foot artillery resembled infantry's except for yellow trim.[81] Each outfit manned from four to six bronze pieces of improved casting: two or more 6's and usually one or two 12-pound howitzers. Side arms were pistols and sabers; sometimes musketoons were carried. Outstanding were the horse and light companies' speed and maneuverability behind their four- and six-horse teams, rapidity undreamed of in the Revolution, whose fastest moving piece was the galloper gun drawn by one horse in shafts. Peter's and other commands of 1812 foreshadowed these remarkable flying batteries of 1846 which would exert an effect far disproportionate to their number in the conflict to come.

Texas won her independence from Mexico and offered herself to the United States for annexation, an act which the nation to the south warned would be considered equivalent to a declaration of war. Congress, accepting the big new state, picked up the gauntlet, and President Polk ordered an army under General Zachary Taylor to the border.

A cavalry clash on April 25, 1846, opened hostilities in a war aptly termed "Rehearsal for Conflict." [82] It was a training ground for the great contest of the sixties, though the training was hard and bloodily earned against stubborn, courageous opposition.

Call the roll of American artillery officers of 1846–48, and a surprising number of ranking generals-to-be in the Civil War answer. That old artilleryman of 1812, Winfield Scott, Commander-in-Chief in Mexico, will retire in '61. Of the young captains and lieutenants who gallantly fight guns south of the border, nine will serve the Union as general officers: George H. Thomas, the "Rock of Chickamauga"; "Fighting Joe" Hooker, Henry J. Hunt, Chief of Artillery of the Army of the Potomac; John F. Reynolds, killed at Gettysburg; Thomas W. Sherman, Jesse Lee Reno, Fitzjohn Porter, Darius Couch, and Charles Kilburn. Armies, corps, and divisions of the Confederacy will be led by Thomas Jonathan "Stonewall" Jackson, "Prince" John B. Magruder, Braxton Bragg, D. H. Hill, Samuel G. French, and Robert S. Garnett. And the gunner's arm can lay claim by affiliation to the two foremost commanders in the War Between the States. Captain Robert E. Lee of the Engineers constructs and directs the fire of batteries that bombard Vera Cruz into submission and emplaces others at Cerro Gordo, Contreras, and Mexico City. Lieutenant Ulysses S. Grant, Infantry, blasts away with a mountain howitzer in a church steeple at the storming of Chapultepec. Both will know well when the time comes how to handle artillery for the Gray and the Blue.

It took Ringgold's battery, bound for Mexico, forty-six days to sail from Fort McHenry to Corpus Christi. Young Lieutenant Samuel G. French recorded in a diary later published as his memoirs [83] how the ship rolled in a tempest, and it seemed that the frightened horses below would kick the hold to pieces. He well remembers the march into the strange and vivid land of Mexico, and its abundant game, brought down by marksmen between shots at enemy lancers. He recalls luncheons served on the battlefield by the body servants of the other battery officers, with delicious meat and fish dishes, pastries, and sauces prepared by Major Ringgold's Negro chef, who would have graced Delmonico's or the Waldorf. He tells of a fine Mexican pony bought for fifteen dollars, a mount that loved the smell of gunpowder and would rub its nose against the wheel of a piece of action.

The flying batteries considered themselves a *corps d'élite* and were determined to prove it in combat. Sky-blue breeches with stripes of artillery red were worn with a swagger—stripes which gave them their nickname of "redlegs." Spectators admired their mounted drill, the exacting Captain Braxton Bragg's particularly, as a thing of beauty. However battered and powder-grimed they emerged from battle, they would gallop into action next time, uniform smart, guns, caissons, harness, and the hides of horses clean and shining. These four light batteries, plus the scant siege train, were far from sufficient artillery for the missions they would be called upon to accomplish, but by their splendid service they fulfilled them gloriously.

Palo Alto, "place of the tall timber," on May 8, 1846, resounded to the stirring drumbeat of the Long Roll, call to arms. Two heavy 18-pounders, hauled by oxen, moved up into line, followed by ammunition-laden, white-topped Conestogas, each with a twenty-ox team. Shouts by teamsters, urging on the big patient beasts with "Haw, Buck, Brindle! Whoa, Brandy!" struck Lieutenant French as highly unmilitary. The oxen were slow and lumbering; elephants, he reflected, would have been as fast and more picturesque. The light batteries sped past at a trot, a gallop, to confront the Mexican array, advancing with loud *vivas* and bands playing. One American gun piled up in a heap, caught by an enemy shell that pierced the lead pair and exploded, wounding three more horses, but other sections and batteries hurried forward to unlimber and open fire. Ringgold and James Duncan delivered cannonades that smothered the opposing artillery.

A wad from one of Duncan's guns set the dry grass blazing. Across the smoke-clouded battlefield charged squadrons of Mexican cavalry, lances leveled, red and green pennons whipping in the wind. Some blue-clad regiments formed British squares and beat off the horsemen with musketry volleys in the best tradition of Wellington's infantry, charged by Napoleon's cuirassiers. But none needed to resort to the bayonet, so rapid and well directed was the fire of the flying batteries. Frequently changing position as General Taylor shifted his troops behind the smoke screen, guns and howitzers smashed charges from the flank and enfiladed oncoming ranks. The

18's joined in, belching great blasts of canister at the dark masses of the foe and "driving them like sheep."

Toward sunset the Mexicans, who had had more than enough, withdrew. American victory was conclusive, yet among its cost was the life of the brilliant Major Ringgold. Struck by a shell as he sat his charger directing fire, both his legs were mangled. He would not let his men leave the guns to tend him, and a few days later he died of his wounds. The loss of the army's foremost light artillerist was a grave one, but there were other able officers to carry on.

Palo Alto had been primarily an artillery fight. The commanders had "maneuvered their batteries as if they were platoons of cavalry and fired them almost as if they were pocket pistols." [84] An observant infantry quartermaster, Lieutenant U. S. Grant, made notes on cannon fire power and its effect when massed, notes that would serve him well in the future. General Taylor, all of whose previous service had been as an infantry officer with few or no cannon available in his Indian campaigns, was deeply impressed. As French remarked, the General thereupon acquired the idea that field artillery could be used for pursuit of cavalry in mountain passes, for storming entrenchments, or for charging a line of battle. Though no such tactics were to be found in manuals, "Old Rough and Ready" proceeded to employ his guns in just such extraordinary fashions.

The Mexicans admitted the superiority of their adversary's artillery at Palo Alto and lamented the havoc it caused. Cannon that mowed them down at a distance seemed an unsportsmanlike and regrettable weapon. They preferred, they said, close combat, the shock of arms. [85] The dashing lancers of Mexico far outnumbered the American dragoons on most battlefields and, except for their lighter mounts, were highly formidable in direct cavalry clashes; but accurate, swiftly delivered gunfire often broke up their charges at the start. Mexican infantry, though they were mostly conscripts poorly rationed and long unpaid, fought with dogged courage; yet they, too, had been "killed with impunity and decimated in cold blood" by the Gringo guns. However, the Mexicans' own artillery, in spite of faulty powder whose propulsive power was so low that ricocheting round shot could be dodged, was not to be discounted, and it was to give a good account of itself in battles ahead.

One day after Palo Alto, combat was joined again. American artillery—Old Zach was using it as an advance guard now—moved down a road through the woods and chaparral to Resaca de la Palma. From an unseen battery up ahead a shot crashed through the treetops. Such fire would be far deadlier in later days of sensitive fuses detonated by branches; at present it served only as a summons to action.

"At the gallop, ho!" The guns dashed onward, unlimbered, and opened on smoke spurting up near the banks of a dry river. Manhandled farther forward, they closed the range. As they shot at the cannon smoke, lines of Mexican skirmishers debouched through the chaparral and attacked. The battery of Randolph Ridgely, who had taken over from Ringgold, engaged both enemy infantry and artillery singlehanded until its commander was forced to call for support. At length came the sound of pounding hoofs, and Captain Charles H. May trotted up with a squadron of dragoons in columns of fours. The tall, flamboyant cavalryman shouted over:

"Hello, Ridgely, where is that battery? I am ordered to charge it."

"Hold on, Charley, till I draw their fire, and you will soon see where they are," Ridgely called back.

As he blazed away, and the enemy guns flashed in reply, May was off at a mad gallop, long black hair and beard streaming. The dragoons thundered down on the battery, sabering gunners and bringing back General de la Vega as a prisoner. But most of the squadron overran and were half a mile past before they could turn their hardmouthed horses, nor were they able to control their mounts even then but galloped back through the battery to their own lines. Meanwhile Mexican artillerymen remanned their guns.

May's charge had been more like a runaway. Though it was he who offered De la Vega's sword to General Taylor, most authorities agree that the enemy commander's actual captor was a sergeant or a bugler.

Taylor merely glanced at the proffered weapon. He turned to the colonel of the 8th Infantry and snapped:

"Take those guns and, by God, keep them!" The regiment

promptly did so with the bayonet, while Duncan's guns staved off an attempt at rescue by lancers.

Lieutenant French, coming onto the field with a 12-pound howitzer, had ordered "Fire to the front!" when a Mexican volley emptied two saddles. Driverless pairs tangled, and wheels locked. Unlimbering in the face of an oncoming regiment, French sent a sergeant for canister. Before it arrived a gunner had loaded with shell. They rammed the canister down on top of it and touched it off. With a roar the howitzer leaped and bucked like a bronco, both wheels well off the ground, as the murderous charge tore into the foe's ranks. Two more shots were enough to break the advancing regiment, but men and horses still were falling under fire from other quarters. Ridgely, coming up with a gun whose lead driver had been killed, swung from his mount into the dead man's saddle, straightened out the team, and brought the piece into action.

More artillery, galloping out ahead of the cheering infantry and virtually charging the enemy, hastened his rout with shell fire. By late afternoon victory was won, many of the fleeing Mexicans being drowned as they sought to escape across the Rio Grande. Taylor, lacking enough fresh troops to pursue, camped on the battlefield.

Upon an eminence the old city of Monterey [86] stood girdled by three forts and strong earthworks, with the Black Fort and the Bishop's Palace as its citadels. Ramparts were defended by thirty-eight cannon and an army of nine thousand men. Taylor's decision to storm it struck his West Point officers as downright foolhardy. His force was only two-thirds of the Mexicans' and his siege train —two 24-pounders and a 10-inch mortar—woefully weak. In spite of all he asked of his light batteries, he could not expect them to breach stone walls. "His guns were so few and so small that the sight of them sent the regular infantry officers to bed that night with the sober thought that if they wanted an adequate artillery, they must take it from the enemy." [87] However, the General, whose strategy was limited to two precepts—attack and never retreat—issued orders for the assault.

Taylor dispatched the martial and energetic General William Jenkins Worth with a column on a wide detour to the south to cut off Monterey's supply route. Meanwhile, on September 20, 1846, light artillery pounded away futilely at the massive walls of the Black Fort. Next day while Worth attacked from the south, Taylor's infantry carried lesser works on the northeast and pushed into the city, followed by sections of Bragg's guns. Desperate street fighting ensued.

In 1791, French-born Major Pierre Charles L'Enfant, remembering the straight or twisting barricaded streets of eighteenth-century Paris, had laid out the city of Washington with plentiful circles where cannon could command the converging avenues. Old Monterey offered artillerymen no such advantage. Notwithstanding, gun teams pushed into its narrow thoroughfares, no more than alleys, with reckless abandon. Somehow crews managed to unlimber and open fire.

It was no place for muzzle-loading 6's and 12-pound howitzers. From roofs and windows Mexican snipers dropped men and horses. With a rain of bullets beating down on Lieutenant Thomas's pent-up section, he was ordered to withdraw, but the Civil War's "Rock of Chickamauga" paused for a parting shot. Then gunners lifted up and swung the piece around—the only way it could be done in those confines—and a fresh team was brought up to haul it clear. Hard by, Bragg, with other guns of the battery, was taking even severer punishment. Several of his men and more than a dozen horses were down in a street slippery with blood and foam. Bragg, in spite of the Mexican fire, insisted that harness be stripped from the dead and dying animals before the pieces were manhandled back with the aid of Maryland volunteers.

A crack artillerist but a strange man was Captain Braxton Bragg —"ambitious and of a saturnine disposition and morbid temperament"—a strict disciplinarian, even a martinet, careful to the point of being petty about equipment. Volunteers detested him as an arrogant regular. They were suspected of slipping under his cot the shell which exploded and riddled his blankets and tent walls but left him unharmed.

Now he sent French back to salvage the harness from the horses killed, but General Taylor, meeting the lieutenant and inquiring his errand, countermanded the order with a curt "Nonsense!". On another occasion Bragg directed his lieutenant to recover a dead driver's saber; when French handed it up, along with the man's knife, the captain refused the latter as not government property.[88]

As Bragg's canister broke a lancer charge said to have been led by a woman captain, in another part of the field Ridgely took his battery into the fight at a gallop, "his head bowed forward, face to the right, as if it were sleet instead of a hail of lead and iron that tore past him." [89] That gallant artilleryman did not long survive the battle. In spite of his expert horsemanship, he was killed by a fall from a stumbling mount soon after the fighting ceased.

More troops poured into the city. The infantry, drenched by a night rainstorm and rationless for thirty-six hours, fought with incomparable valor. Under heavy musketry and gunfire they scaled heights, climbing from rock to rock, and swept over ramparts without benefit of siege artillery. The big mortar, not solidly bedded, dug itself so deeply into the ground on its first recoil that it was long out of action while it was being excavated. Frustrated heavy artillerymen caught up muskets and joined the assault. They were on hand to man captured enemy cannon—some of them fine English 9- and 12-pounders dated 1842—and to trade rounds with the Mexican batteries defending the Bishop's Palace.

In the storming of that citadel, Texans raised a battle cry, rising from a low growl to a falsetto scream, that would become famous as the "Rebel Yell." Fire spurting from windows and battlements, the fort held out until a howitzer was brought up and battered in its main gate. Infantry, rushing forward to attack ranks of Mexicans barring the entrance, were suddenly halted by a shout from the gun crew: "Throw yourselves flat!" As they dropped, a double charge of canister roared over their heads. Like an iron broom it swept the way clear, and the Palace was won.

Street by street, from house to house, the blue-uniformed troops fought bitterly for the city. They pickaxed holes in soft stone and adobe walls and enlarged the gaps by jamming in 6-inch shells, 3-second fuses sputtering. Chiming in with explosions of that hand artillery, light batteries outside opened fire on barricades which blocked every street they entered. With bullets from walled, flat roofs rattling like hailstones on the paving, it was desperate work to unlimber and serve a gun.

Breech-loading cannon were years in the future and farther off still was the development of the gun shields and aprons which would afford crews some protection. Now it took sheer nerve for cannoneers to step out in front of muzzle-loaders, ram down powder and shot, stand clear for the discharge, then run back to swab and load again while lead from barricades and housetops spattered around them. Two loaders in French's section were hit, as that officer dismounted from the wounded pony tottering under him. He ordered his gun shoved back around a corner under cover. No man to quit, he adopted an unusual expedient:

> I now resorted to a device once practiced by a mob in the city of Philadelphia; two long ropes were made fast to the end of the trail. . . . The gun was now loaded, and leveled in safety, then pushed out, and pulled by the ropes until it pointed at the barricade, and then fired. The recoil sent the gun back, and the rope brought it around the corner to be reloaded. In this manner the gun was worked for two hours, and with all this protection, four out of the five gunners were killed or wounded. [90]

Slowly, grimly, bloodily, infantry and the guns of T. W. Sherman,[91] Reynolds, Bragg, and the rest cleared the streets and thrust back the Mexican Army into the plaza. Concentrated there, it was bombarded through the night by the 10-inch mortar, in action again after its inglorious debut. Fieldpieces took position to command all avenues of escape.

At dawn bugles in the plaza sounded a parley. The Mexican commander accepted Taylor's demand for the surrender of Monterey, agreeing to evacuate the city, provided that his troops be permitted to march out with the honors of war according to an ancient formula, "drums beating, colors flying, with arms and ammunition including one field battery, chests filled, ball in the mouth, and matches burning."

The Americans, marching up to the strains of "Yankee Doodle," marshaled ranks to watch the enemy's departure. They paid brave foemen the tribute of silence until a body of artillerymen in the uniform of Mexico filed by. Then jeers and hisses broke out.

Those gunners were deserters from the American army, organized as the San Patricio Battalion [92] by ex-Sergeant John Riley, 5th Infantry, an Irishman who was said to have previously deserted from the British Army in Canada and enlisted in the United States where he served as drillmaster at West Point before joining his regiment on the border. Riley, "going over the hill," was joined by some hundreds of other soldiers, as resentful as he of discipline, often harsh in various units,[93] and lured by Mexican promises of bounties and land. The infantry sergeant, a first-rate leader, along with the turncoat artillerymen, had trained the rest as gun crews. They had taken their baptism of fire at Monterey and had stood it well. Former comrades, who reviled their departure from the surrendered city, would meet the formidable San Patricios on other battlefields.

News of the victory set boys back home to singing:

> Old Zach's at Monterey.
> Bring on your Santa Anner;
> For every time we raise a gun,
> Down goes a Mexicaner.

But the city had been dearly bought at a price of 120 American dead and 368 wounded, with Mexican losses reported as totaling no more than 367. Don Antonio López de Santa Anna was back from exile now and in command as Mexico's dictator general. He advanced to Buena Vista with reinforcements to attack Taylor's army, most of its regulars having been drawn off to join Scott's expedition to Vera Cruz.

Meanwhile, during the last half of 1846 and the early months of 1847, New Mexico and California had been conquered by force of arms, though the United States subsequently paid Mexico fifteen million dollars for those territories.

Two field batteries comprised the artillery of the expedition which a veteran of the War of 1812, Colonel Stephen W. Kearny, shortly promoted to brigadier general, was ordered to march southwest from Fort Leavenworth, Kansas, to occupy the two Mexican provinces. The personnel of one battery were native-born Americans; that of the other German-Americans from St. Louis. Armed with sixteen bronze cannon, 6's and 12-pound howitzers, the battalion was led by a West Pointer, Major Meriwether Lewis Clark, son of the explorer. In the long ordeal ahead these volunteer artillerymen would prove themselves to be as good gunners as any that ever kept the caissons rolling along.

The Army of the West was played off in May, 1846, to the tune of "The Girl I Left Behind Me." Guns rumbled in a column of seventeen hundred men: Missouri riflemen commanded by tall, able Colonel Alexander W. Doniphan; other infantry, dragoons, and Indian scouts.

The artillery, smart in gray uniforms with yellow stripes along breeches, instead of the red proper for these light batteries, ran into trouble at first on the long marches of twenty to thirty miles a day. Green drivers overturned carriages crossing streams and cracked axles. On breaking camp, march order was slowly executed. Forthwith officers were assembled for a lecture by an old cavalryman, Colonel Kearny, whose regimental adjutant reported it with relish: [94]

> Inasmuch as they had no experience in managing horses on the prairie, he would say to them that in the dragoon service after getting into camp, the first thing every man should do was to strip his horse on the ground near where his tent was to be, and then take him to water and picket him out on the best grass. And after the men got their suppers, the stable call sounded, and every man went and groomed his horse and brought him near camp and picketed him down for the night. And the same way in the morning. Reveille blew at daylight; and a few minutes afterwards stable-call blew, when some of the men would remain to get breakfast while the others rubbed the horses down and took them to fresh grass.

Kearny sternly added that he would detail two of his own dragoon officers to the batteries to see that they cared for and handled their horses as well as cavalry did.

Thereafter when Stable Call was sounded, there was never any doubt in the artillerymen's minds that its traditional words meant what they said:

Oh, go to the stable,
All you who are able,
And give your poor horses some hay and some corn.
For if you don't do it,
The Colonel will know it,
And you'll catch the devil as sure as you're born.

March discipline promptly improved, and the guns were ready to roll each morning when the column struck out across the plains.

Kearny drove his army hard through long, waterless days when thirst, heat, and exhaustion took toll. So forced was the pace that one battery, in spite of its care, lost sixty of its hundred horses and had to resort to hitching in spare spans of oxen from the ammunition wagons. Even the dragoons, held up as an example, were compelled to exchange worn-out mounts for mules. With the foot-slogging infantry outmarching them all, they covered nearly nine hundred interminable miles. Their reward was the capture of Santa Fe without a fight.

From New Mexico General Kearny, with part of the army, marched on to California where the American Navy had hoisted the flag over Monterey a month earlier. The campaign secured for the United States a territory whose golden treasure awaited the Forty-niners.

Doniphan and his nine hundred Missouri riflemen, detached as a separate force, won a skirmish at El Brazito on Christmas Day and pushed on to take El Paso, where he ordered the artillery to join him from Santa Fe. They made it by a grueling march through snow, during which they nearly perished from hunger, then for a change were almost buried by a sandstorm. As they approached the town, the garrison decided they deserved a special welcome.

A cannon salute was decided upon as appropriate at the last moment. Hastily a captured Mexican piece was loaded with a blank charge of powder, but no wad could be found. Whereupon a public-spirited infantryman kicked off his boots, stripped off his socks, and magnanimously offered them as wadding. They were rammed in, and the gun touched off. As it roared in salute, the improvised wad hit a second soldier in the face. His wild yells died down for a moment when he discovered he was not hurt, then whooped louder than ever upon his being told what the missile was. Angrily he demanded the punishment of the saluting crew. He would rather have been shot with a solid ball, he shouted, than a pair of socks worn all the way from Leavenworth to El Paso for eight months without a change.[95]

Doniphan now invaded the province of Chihuahua, planning a junction with General John E. Wool of Taylor's army. At Sacramento on February 28, 1847, he fought a highly unusual battle.

When the towering Missouri colonel saw his advance was blocked by strong Mexican works and a hill fort manned by a force superior to his own, he marshaled his long wagon train, driven by trader volunteers, into four parallel columns of one hundred wagons each, with infantry and artillery in between—a formation reminiscent of the Mongols and the Hussite wagon-soldiers of the European religious wars.[96] Banners flying, the cavalcade of white-topped prairie schooners and troops made a stirring and redoubtable spectacle as it moved toward the defenses behind a cavalry screen. Abruptly it veered to the right. Down into a deep, sandy arroyo, deemed impassable, it plunged. Mules and horses tugging mightily, teamsters and artillery drivers shouting and whipping, soldiers heaving on the wheels, the swaying Conestogas and gun carriages were rushed up the other side of the gulch.

Major Lewis's trumpeter sounded Trot. Swinging out from between the masking wagons, the guns came smartly into position. "Form battery. Action front. Fire at will." At a range of half a mile shells burst over enemy lancers and infantry and pounded artillery whose round shot in reply was easily dodged; Mexican powder was of poor quality. The American guns limbered up and charged the fort. Though some pulled back before a counterattack, the rest stood their ground and blazed away with enfilading fire at fifty yards. Infantry swept in and took the fort in hand-to-hand combat against fierce resistance. A howitzer, knocking out a Mexican gun with a splendid shot at a range of 1,225 yards, helped turn a rally into a rout. The field was won at a cost of one American killed, one mortally and seven less seriously wounded. Doniphan estimated that the Mexicans suffered six hundred casualties.

After occupying Chihuahua City, the detachment was ordered back to Missouri for muster-out. The extraordinary march of Doniphan's one thousand, justly compared to Xenophon's Anabasis, covered thirty-six hundred miles.

A few days before Doniphan's engagement at Sacramento, Zachary Taylor, advancing from Monterey, Mexico, fought the last battle of the campaign in the north.

No battle ever epitomized the phrase "theater of warfare" so vividly as Buena Vista, its backdrop a range of lofty mountains, its stage a broad plateau cut by ravines—entrances from the wings. Late in the day a sudden unseasonable storm, with peals of rolling thunder and blinding flashes of lightning, added overwhelming sound effects to the roar of cannonading and the rattle of musketry.

The advance of Santa Anna's army of eighteen thousand through the pass, its descent of the slopes and deployment on the plain was pure drama. Martial pageantry of past centuries flourished again when, after a clash on February 22, 1847, the Mexican array was marshaled for battle on the following morning. Bugles blew fanfares, answering one another. Lancers, infantry, artillery formed. "All the colors of the rainbow—red, green, yellow, crimson, sky-blue, turkey-blue—clothed the troops. Even the horses appeared to be in uniform, for those of a corps were alike in color. Silken banners and plumes of many bright hues floated in the breeze. Handsomely dressed aides dashed from point to point. Tremendous *vivas* rolled in mighty echoes from the mountains." [97] Bands played sacred music, and incense, prelude to powder smoke, spiraled skyward, as priests in gorgeous vestments bestowed benedictions on kneeling soldiery. Horse and foot wheeled and countermarched in spectacular evolutions.

While a Mississippi rifleman muttered with a grin that the splendid lancers yonder looked "too pretty to shoot," General Taylor, in the nondescript civilian clothes he preferred to uniform, lounged in the saddle of Old Whitey and watched out the display. Then in nonchalant disregard of the Mexicans' considerably superior numbers he gave the order to attack.

A cannon boomed. Lieutenant John Paul Jones O'Brien of Washington's Battery, 4th Artillery, opened fire at fifteen hundred yards with the guns he called his "Bulldogs."

Out of the frigid mountains, through gullies of the plateau swept by chill winds, three columns of Mexican infantry moved forward to the assault. O'Brien deluged them with shrapnel. Bursts, beautifully timed, exploded over them, flattening whole platoons with each discharge while cheers rippled along the American front. Other sections of Washington's Battery, along with Thomas' and French's sections, poured in canister as fast as they could fire. But Santa Anna's spearheads came gallantly on and spread out into a wide semicircle, which tightened to envelop Taylor's left.

An Indiana regiment, confused by its colonel's orders, gave way and streamed to the rear. Jefferson Davis' Mississippi Rifles and Illinois men could not stem the oncoming tide, nor could the massed batteries. French, hit in the right thigh by a musket ball, still sat his horse, directing fire. Once down and left on the field, he knew he would be speared by lancers, merciless to American wounded. Across the plateau Sherman, Bragg, and Reynolds were in hot action. The volume of fire delivered by the American artillery this day would average 250 rounds per piece, a remarkable rate for muzzle-loaders.

To the flank and rear of the threatened point Thomas was working his guns rapidly. But it was O'Brien out in front who was bearing the brunt. He limbered and withdrew for a space with the retreating blue infantry, then halted and opened again.

Mexican 8-pounders had found the range and were throwing in a storm of iron, but the heaviest and most accurate fire came from a battery of 18's and 24's. Santa Anna had ordered the San Patricios forward. Under their banner blazoned with the arms of Mexico, a figure of St. Patrick, and a harp—though only a portion of the men was Irish—the deserters served their guns with smooth efficiency. These *Colorados* or "Red Company," as they also were called because many were redheaded, today and on a later field would account for the lives of many of their erstwhile comrades-in-arms.[98]

Under their shell fire and musketry volleys John Paul Jones O'Brien fought his three guns with the stubborn gallantry of the great sea captain whose name he bore. Enemy infantry pressed him so closely that he could not hold his ground. He retreated, but only by the distance his pieces recoiled after each discharge. As they rolled back, crews followed and flung themselves on them when they halted to load and fire again, blasting back the onslaught with double canister. Still the assault troops came on over the bodies of their dead. They took O'Brien's 4-pounder, as the last of its cannoneers fell.

One of the 6's, disabled, was withdrawn. Another, forwarded from reserve, replaced it. The two Bulldogs barked on, manned by powder-blackened skeleton crews, all that were left. Horses lay dead in their traces around the limbers, yet O'Brien might still have been able to bring his 6's off by hand. He "could have saved the guns," he told himself, "but in such case the day might, perhaps, have been lost." He stayed.

How he kept on firing with enemy infantry mere yards from the muzzles stands as one of the most heroic exploits in artillery annals. At last O'Brien, wounded, and the few surviving gunners limped and hobbled to the rear, abandoning the smoking pieces. Neither assurance that he had indeed saved the day nor the brevet as major he received for gallant and meritorious conduct diminished his sadness over the loss of his guns. His wound relegated him to quartermaster duty for the remainder of the war. A promising career as an artillerist, which might well have reached brilliance in the Civil War, was cut short by his untimely death in 1850 at the age of thirty-two.

A triumphant rush of men in gaudy uniforms seized the Bulldogs and sent them back to the rear. The Mexican artillery had acquired two new guns, guns the Americans would meet again six months later in the south.

Across the plateau Braxton Bragg's flying battery whirled at a headlong gallop, drivers whipping and spurring weary teams. Close to the spot where the capture of O'Brien's cannon had opened the way for a Mexican victory, it swung smartly from column into line. Cannoneers leaped from their mounts, turned them over to horse holders, swarmed around the spaced fieldpieces, loaded, aimed, touched matches to vents at Bragg's command, and poured shot into the Mexican masses. General Taylor rode up to the battery and calmly sat his target of a white horse while bullets whistled through his coat. It was then he gave his celebrated order.

Let the shade of Old Rough and Ready stand absolved from the mild "A little more grape, Captain Bragg" of history textbooks. The bluff old general's characteristic command, according to a member of his escort,[99] was: "Double-shot your guns and give 'em hell!"

Bragg's battery obeyed with enthusiasm. Mississippi infantry were back now, led by Davis, wounded but firm in his saddle. Their steady volleys were augmented by those of the Illinois regiment and the rallied Indianians. All along the line the guns flamed. Waves of an attack which had come so close to sweeping the field ebbed back into the ravines. Rifle and cannon fire from the front and the rims above slaughtered them. "The dead lay in the pent space body on body, a blending and interlacement of parts of men as defiant of the imagination as of the pen," Lew Wallace remembered.[100]

Santa Anna, "Old Wooden Leg" as the Gringos called him because of his peg leg, had been "licked up like salt." But it had been a near thing, with the fortunes of war hanging in delicate balance when the American left was enveloped and driven back. The sacrifice stand of O'Brien's Bulldogs and Bragg's battery galloping into action had saved the day. "Without our artillery," General Wool declared, "we could not have maintained our position for a single hour."

The Mexican Army beat a retreat to the south. Taylor, though enemy casualties—591 killed, 1,049 wounded, 1,854 missing—were twice as heavy as his, lacked sufficient strength to follow over the difficult terrain. From now on it was Scott's war.

Another aftermath occurred when a post with a large artillery range was established in North Carolina and in 1918 designated Fort Bragg in honor of the commander whose flying battery had reached a crucial spot of the battlefield at a critical moment. The War Department, however, took pains to explain that the post in Bragg's native state was named after him as a United States captain, not as a Confederate general.

Escorting a fleet of transports jammed with ten thousand men, the U.S. Navy cruised south through the Gulf of Mexico toward Vera Cruz. Northers whipped up high seas in which some forty of the smaller vessels carrying horses and mules were sunk. Field artillery, cavalry, and supply trains were rendered almost useless for the invasion ahead and would be forced to raid the countryside for remounts. But the first task belonged to the big guns.

The fleet hove to off the "city of the True Cross" in early March, 1847. Troops lining the bulwarks gaped at the mighty Castle of San Juan de Ulúa on the point of a long reef, guarding the mast-crested harbor. Eyes traveled on to the walled city and the nine forts that ringed it. Ramparts were known to be defended by four thousand men, with two hundred or more cannon. Doubtless General Scott, prominent on the bridge of the flagship, spyglass leveled, expected those strongholds to be taken by storm. Grim looks were exchanged between men on the thronged decks. It would mean a sizable "butcher's bill," and they would pay it. Nor would they put it past "Old Fuss and Feathers" yonder, an imposing façade of blue set off by glittering epaulets and a yellow sash around his midriff, to order the works assaulted with full dress as the uniform of the day.

If they managed to capture Vera Cruz, what next? Eyes rose to the massive barrier of the Cordilleras, surmounted by the snow-capped peak of lofty Orizaba. Beyond—many long miles of foot-slogging—lay Mexico City, the army's objective. Scott had probably already written marching orders, taking no account of whether there was a pass through those formidable mountains and a million Mexicans in the way.

Army bands on various vessels never more amply justified their existence than when, upon that first glimpse of awesome obstacles, they blared forth patriotic airs. Certainly it was the moment for martial and inspiring music.

But on March 9 when whaleboats, low in the water with loads of infantry, marines, and men of the 2nd and 3rd Artillery carrying muskets, sped ashore, the landing was virtually unopposed. Naval guns shelled lancers hovering in the background, and mountain howitzers and rockets of Captain G. H. Talcott's battery spurred the horsemen's flight. No sortie was made from the city to seize a golden opportunity to sweep invaders back into the sea. More troops were landed, and Captain Robert E. Lee, Engineers, commenced the construction of earthworks and gun emplacements seven hundred yards from the city walls.

Since the siege train had not yet arrived, General Scott—it came hard to an old artilleryman—was compelled to ask the Navy for heavy guns. He could have them, he was told, provided that they were manned by their own crews. Three long 32's and three huge 68's were ferried to the beachhead, hoisted up on improvised sling carts, and hauled to the emplacements, where Lee set grumbling sailors to shoveling to strengthen the earthworks further. Jealous artillerymen, watching the bluejackets station themselves at the breeches, were consoled when four 24's, two 8-inch howitzers, and seven 10-inch mortars were brought ashore and turned over to them.

General Scott's urgent offer to the garrison of Vera Cruz and its foreign consuls to permit the evacuation of women and children was summarily refused. He ordered the bombardment opened.

Roaring cannon, pounding the city and the castle, echoed the guns at Louisbourg, Boston, and Yorktown. As bands aboard ships played "The Star-Spangled Banner," and rockets spiraled into the city, the past lived again for veterans of 1812. Rocketeers were firing missiles improved from the Congreve model by William Hale with stabilizing sticks and three curved vanes which rotated them as rifling does a bullet and increased their accuracy. Two thousand had been manufactured. They would be fired also on other battlefields but discarded shortly after this war. The advent of rifled cannon and recoil mechanisms rendered them obsolete until more powerful charges and other new features restored them as a World War II weapon.

Mexican cannon boomed in counterbattery fire. While some were old pieces, beautifully embossed and inscribed, others were modern, including a number marked, ironically, *W.P.F.* (West Point Foundry) and sixteen long English '32's, which American artillery officers acclaimed as the finest ordnance they had ever seen. Shells whistled down on Lee's emplacements, screeching like northers. One of the first killed Captain John R. Vinton by the blast of its passage alone; it did not explode. (Charge drawn, it was sent home to mark his grave in Providence, Rhode Island.) Others detonated to blow holes in the sand, holes "big enough to bury a horse," or pulverized stone walls of a cemetery near a naval battery. The bluejacket commander, his crews unharmed, apologized to Captain Lee for complaining about all the dirt shoveling. Even though they weren't used to it on the deck of a ship, it had come in handy.

Only the long dead were victims of the shelling which smashed the cemetery's chapel, burst upon tombs, and scattered skulls and bones. Better directed fire achieved little more than ripping the sandbags and rawhide facings of the embrasures. Shells that fell within the position either failed to burst or when they did, caused few casualties.

The American cannonade told a different story. Steeple bells were set clanging as spires crashed. The earth quaked under the impact of projectiles from the ponderous 68's and big mortars. Supposedly bombproof roofs were no more than tissue paper to them. Domes and houses crumbled and flamed up in pyres. The face of Captain Lee, directing fire, was grave with pity. He knew that not only enemy troops but women and children, condemned by the arrogant refusal of the garrison commander to send them out of the city to safety, must be dying under that storm of iron.

Ramparts of Vera Cruz were illuminated like Fort McHenry's by "the rocket's red glare." Night and day the cannon thundered. Veterans of Monterey muttered against Scott's method of reducing a city with artillery; they had carried Monterey virtually without siege guns. Scott, who might have answered that he did not intend to pay such a price as they had except as a last resort, ordered heavier fire. A hurricane of shells, rising to a total of twenty-five hundred, had demolished most of the Mexican batteries and leveled all the southwest quarter of the city when a white flag was hoisted.

After three days and nights of bombardment, Vera Cruz surrendered August 29, won at cost of one hundred American casualties (nineteen killed). As the Stars and Stripes was hoisted above the Castle, the garrison filed out, laid down its arms, and was paroled. On April 8 Scott, in haste to avoid the impending yellow fever season of the coastal region, thrust into the interior, driving for Mexico City. So two centuries before Cortés had marched to storm the Halls of Montezuma and overthrow the Aztec Empire.

Santa Anna, vaunting Buena Vista as a victory, was down from the north. His heavily reinforced army of twelve thousand men barred Scott's advance, standing astride the National Road. Emplaced to rake it were thirty-five cannon, some on Cerro Gordo, the "big hill," some on a lesser height to its right, and some in between the two eminences, with more at the Mexican camp. Flanks were protected by the Rio del Plan, by unscalable cliffs and impassable ravines.

To dislodge defenders from so strong a position seemed an impossible task, but brilliant reconnaissances by several American officers found a possible route of attack which would avoid frontal assault. Captain Lee's daring scout took him behind the enemy lines where he barely avoided capture and probably death by hiding for hours behind a log with Mexican soldiers seated on it. Over the approach he had discovered around Santa Anna's left he guided a column of infantry and artillerymen. Wooded defiles masked them but afforded the toughest sort of going. Through oak forests, chaparral, and cactus, axmen hacked a path for the guns of Magruder's company of the 1st Artillery. It paused on the brink of slopes so steep that the strongest wheel horses, straining back against their breechings, could not have prevented carriages from overrunning them. Cannoneers fastened long ropes to axles, laid hold and eased the vehicles down behind the teams. Now ascents, some of them almost sheer cliffs, confronted them. Halt—unharness—ropes again. Crews at the top, heaving mightily, hoisted up guns and carriages while horses, climbing like mountain goats, were led up angled declivities. These were not light mountain howitzers being brought into action but three heavy 24-pounders.

It was a tremendous feat, which a report [101] thus modestly understated: "It may be proper to add that the difficulties of getting the artillery over the hills of Cerro Gordo were great."

The guns were in position and had opened fire when a premature attack by a blustering brigadier, Daniel E. Twiggs, carried two hills with losses that need not have been suffered if he had obeyed Scott's orders and waited for the general assault. However, though Santa Anna had been alerted to the threat on his flank, the main attack on April 18, 1847, swept forward steadily against the Mexican left and rear. During the night artillerymen had sweated their guns up still another summit, Atalaya, where a rocket battery joined them. Supporting bayonet charges, they pounded enemy infantry and gunners until they broke in frantic flight. Dragoons and Duncan's light battery galloped in pursuit of disorganized masses. A few salvos from the guns cleared a battlefield where three thousand prisoners, four thousand stands of small arms, and forty-three cannon were the fruits of victory.

The crippling of the Mexican Army at Cerro Gordo appeared to have opened the way to Mexico City. Puebla and its seventy-five thousand inhabitants fell an easy prey to the American advance, but there circumstances compelled a month's halt.

Time was almost up on twelve-month enlistments of seven volunteer regiments. Unpaid, miserable in tentless camps, many men were sick, hungry, and in rags. Foragers were caught by the lassos of Mexican irregulars, killed and mutilated. General Scott sent the volunteers back to the coast on their homeward way, though it whittled his army down to less than six thousand. Meanwhile Colonel Ethan Allen Hitchcock, of his staff, organized the highly useful Spy Company, composed of Mexicans under a bandit chieftain, Manuel Dominguez, and officered by Americans. Acting as couriers, and penetrating enemy lines and Mexico City itself, they brought back valuable information.

On the arrival of General Franklin Pierce with reinforcements, along with a siege battery, Scott, his strength raised to fourteen thousand—though many soldiers were still on the sick list—resumed his march.

Athwart Scott's line of advance to Mexico City lay not only the Mexican Army but a prehistoric barrier: a vast expanse of volcanic rock, lava anciently erupted by Popocatepetl, the "Blazing Star," which towered on the horizon eighteen thousand feet above the sea, and by its consort, Iztaccihuatl, the "Sleeping Woman." Its jagged edges would cut boots to shreds, and its treacherous fissures break horses' legs.

Reconnaissances by Lee and P. T. G. Beauregard found a mule path across that pedregal, as it was called, a path which pickaxes of pioneers widened into a road. But that avenue of approach was well guarded. A column moving along it was confronted by a fortified camp, garrisoned and flanked by masses of infantry and cavalry and covered by twenty-two guns.

For American artillery, coming into position under the slight protection of a transverse ledge, the pedregal proved a place of death and destruction. Magruder's 6-pounders, along with mountain howitzers and rocketeers, opened fire on August 19, 1847, and drew devastating blasts of counterbattery from the Mexican heavies, some of them 68's. The men in blue stood to their guns. "Prince John" Magruder, tall, blond, and handsome, was as tough a battery commander as the army ever saw. A star in amateur theatricals, he directed fire with the same dramatic intensity with which he played leads in camp shows. Well drilled crews responded with steady efficiency, two of the sections under command of Lieutenants Jackson, the future "Stonewall," and William L. Haskin, historian of the 1st Artillery, whose gallant performance on this day his pen would record. But the guns could not open the way for an assault. One cannoneer after another fell, until fifteen were killed and many wounded. An 18-pound shell smashed the axle of one piece, and soon a second was knocked out. For three bloody hours they maintained the unequal duel at nine hundred yards. Then all but put out of action, they withdrew in the gathering darkness.

The end of the first day of the Battle of Padierna, or Contreras, left Scott's army in almost as critical a situation as was Taylor's in the first phase of Buena Vista. Brought to a standstill, the Americans were far from their coastal base of supplies. They must keep that life line open by advancing, or retreat to defend it.

As at Cerro Gordo, a flanking movement furnished the key to victory. Cloaked by a black, rainy night and under covering fire by the half-crippled artillery, General Persifors Smith led a brigade through a ravine around the enemy's left. While the Mexicans were diverted by a feint at their front, Smith's infantry, followed by Captain Simon Drum's battery, 4th Artillery, burst out upon their rear. More blue troops rushed up from Padierna to catch defenders between two fires. Santa Anna's army disintegrated, its rout swelling to panic proportions, with lancers riding down a screaming mob of infantry, camp women, and laborers and herds of stampeding mules. Two Mexican 6-pounders, their gunners said to have been chained to their pieces,[102] alone held their ground and kept firing.

That pair of bronze cannon looked familiar to keen-eyed Captain Drum and his men closing in on them. Those pieces must be the two taken at Buena Vista from another battery of their own regiment—O'Brien's Bulldogs. Instantly Drum limbered up and signaled the gallop. In a hell-for-leather charge, the regimental standard streamed from its staff in the stirrup socket of its bearer, riding boot to boot with the driver of the lead pair of the first gun team. A volley of grapeshot swept the color-bearer out of his saddle, but Lieutenant Calvin Benjamin caught the flag as it fell. As the head of the column crashed into the Mexican position, Drum vaulted from his mount to lay hands on the trophies.

Word of the recovery of O'Brien's Bulldogs brought soldiers from every quarter to cheer with the artillerymen. General Scott himself rode up, joined in with hearty huzzas, and promised that the Buena Vista guns would be given to the 4th Artillery "in perpetual token of its achievement."

Their custodian for the regiment today is the Military Academy, West Point, where they flank the portal of the Administration Building, embedded in masonry. Upon a plaque with an eagle crest the muzzle-loaders are inscribed:

O'BRIEN
"Lost without
dishonor at the battle
of Buena Vista, by
a Company of the
4th Artillery.
Recaptured with
just pride and
exultation by the
same regiment at
Contreras."
Winfield Scott
DRUM

That morning's swift and spirited attack had won a tremendous triumph in only seventeen minutes. It netted twenty-two cannon, a large supply of invaluable ammunition, and many horses and mules. In the blue column, pushing forward on the last lap to Mexico City, rolled a new battery organized by Scott's order. Its guns were O'Brien's Bulldogs.

A hard core of veterans of the Mexican Army quickly rallied. At Churubusco they occupied a highly formidable position, a veritable "hedgehog." By-passing it appeared to be risky in view of Scott's tactical situation and the fact that he was still opposed by an enemy strength of sixteen thousand, estimated by him at a considerably higher figure. "To have taken the capital without first defeating such a force would have been a barren victory and perhaps a dangerous one." [103] Since Santa Anna was retiring with his main army,

Churubusco would prove to be a rear-guard action but a desperate one. The President General had ordered it held to the last to cover his retreat.

Access to the town was by a ditch-flanked causeway leading to a bridgehead which protected a stone span across a canalized river. An assault successful in carrying those cannon-swept approaches must still storm the massive walls of the Convent of San Pablo and those of a church and its garden. Churubusco, derived from an Aztec word meaning "place of the war god," now justified its name in a bloody battle where "the Mexicans fought as they had never fought before." And American troops displayed the headlong valor of Monterey.

Old regiments of regular infantry, adding to laurels of 1776 and 1812 by smashing attacks on the causeway, met volleys of musketry and a cannonade that drowned the music of a Mexican band. The withering shell fire that felled them was evidence that they were facing expert gunners. So also was the deadly accurate shooting that caught Duncan's light battery, trotting forward to support the drive by flanking fire. Sections, mired down in soft ground on both sides of the highway, were mercilessly pounded by a bombardment that exploded two caissons. As Francis E. Taylor's guns moved forward to support infantry in the cornfield, they were deluged by the severest shower of grape, canister, musketry, round shot, and shell the brigade commander, General Smith, had ever witnessed. Though two officers, twenty cannoneers, and fifteen horses were hit, pieces were served as if at drill. Taylor, shifting position to sweep sharpshooters from the roof and walls of the church, suffered further heavy losses.

There was no cover. Proved true that day was a maxim of later wars: "A battery seen is a battery lost." Yet the almost sacrificial gallantry of the gunners could not open the way for the infantry. "Even the artillery, backbone of the army, failed now." [104]

For the Americans, as at Buena Vista, were facing ex-Sergeant Riley's crack gun crews of the San Patricio Battalion. In their hands, as blue assault waves beat against the bridgehead, cannon became sniping weapons, with the deserters taking particular satisfaction in spotting their former officers and cutting them down with blasts of grape and canister. To the "Red Company's" guns was attributed a large portion of the considerable American losses: 137 killed, 879 wounded, 40 missing.

At last the defense of the approaches collapsed. Fieldpieces were manhandled up into the infantry lines and shelled the town from the bridgehead. On the highway two of Duncan's guns, coming into action against the convent, "fired with a judgement, rapidity, and accuracy that delighted onlookers." [105] But that stronghold was defended with the utmost desperation by the San Patricio renegades, aided by an elite Mexican regiment. There was no thought of surrender among the American deserters, who could feel the hangman's noose around their necks. Thrice they shot or sabered native comrades who attempted to raise a white flag.

Scott's Mexican Spy Company, joining the final rush, flung themselves on the San Patricios in a hand-to-hand melee. Such was the ferocity of that conflict that it was remembered above all the bitter battling as evidence of "the odium attached to treachery, even among traitors." [106] Finally Riley and his remaining men, their ammunition exhausted, were overpowered. Seventy-five survived out of a battalion of 260; the rest, except for some who escaped, lay dead in the uniform of Mexico. "Give me a few hundred more men like Riley's," Santa Anna said, "and I would have won the victory."

The deserters were tried by a court-martial with scrupulous fairness. Some were acquitted as having been legitimately captured and forced into the ranks but refusing to fight. Riley and others, who deserted before the commencement of hostilities, were sentenced to lashing and branding. Fifty were condemned to be hanged as deserters in time of war.

Riley, bound to a post, took his fifty lashes, savagely laid on by Mexican muleteers since he was not deemed worthy of being whipped by Americans—took them without a moan. But when he was branded with a *D* for deserter on the cheekbone, according to regulations "near the eye but without jeopardizing the sight," he cried out under the agony of the red-hot iron, inflicted twice, since the letter was first seared on upside down. He would labor as a convict as long as the army remained in Mexico. Then, head shaven, buttons stripped from the uniform he had once worn with honor, he would be drummed out of camp to the derisive fifing of "The Rogue's March."

> Poor old soldier, poor old soldier,
> Tarred and feathered and sent to hell,
> Because he wouldn't soldier well.

Meanwhile he was forced to dig graves for his comrades who were to be executed. One group, hands pinioned and nooses around their necks, were placed in carts, driven out from under gallows erected at San Angel. The carrying out of the death sentence for the remainder was reserved for an anticipated occasion.

In San Angel, suburb of Mexico City, stands a cross in memory of the San Patricio Battalion. It is fittingly marked with a gamecock, dice, and a skull and crossbones. John Riley, having escaped burial there, indulged in a final roll of the dice in 1849 at Cincinnati, where he had the supreme gall to sue the Government for damages received through his flogging and branding. The jury ruled against him and assessed him costs of the court action.

Before his desertion Riley had been recommended for a commission. His leadership and ability as an artillery commander might have carried him far in the United States Army.

Mexico City in its gorgeous setting of broad valley, sparkling lakes, and towering mountains spread before the invaders as the final, most tempting prize of a long, hard-fought drive. Swiftly admiration gave way to grim forebodings. Monterey, Vera Cruz, and Churubusco had presented no obstacles comparable to the redoubtable defenses of the capital. Artillery officers scanned them through spyglasses, choosing positions, estimating ranges. Molino del Rey, reported to be an arsenal and cannon foundry and rumored the first objective, showed clear in the field of vision. It would take heavy guns to breach its thick masonry. Those causeways, highways, and aqueducts, offering avenues of attack, were certain to be swept by shell fire and musketry. Passage would mean a bloody toll of infantry, and batteries galloping into action would lose men and horses. Yonder, upon a ridge rising two hundred feet above the city, loomed the mighty Castle of Chapultepec. Plunging fire from its embrasures on troops struggling up to assault was unpleasant to contemplate. Each of the city's close-packed houses was a potential fortress, and rooftops and church steeples vantage points for sharp-

Major General Henry Knox, by Gilbert Stuart
Courtesy of the City of Boston and the Museum of Fine Arts

Santa Barbara.

St. Barbara, Patron of Artillery,
by Palma Vecchio

The First Muster, Ancient and Honorable Artillery Company, Painting in Faneuil Hall, Boston

Courtesy of the Ancient and Honorable Artillery Company

Knox Brings the Guns from Fort Ticonderoga, by Tom Lovell

Courtesy of the Joseph Dixon Crucible Company

Washington Fires the First Gun at Yorktown, by Comte J. Onfroy
de Breville (from *Washington, Man of Action,* by Frederick Trevor Hill,
published by Appleton-Century-Crofts, Inc.)

"Merry Christmas, 1776." The Guns at Trenton, by H. Charles McBarron, Jr.

Courtesy of the Department of the Army

Captain Peter's Battery, First American Light Artillery, 1808–1809, by Colonel Harry C. Larter, Jr. *From the collection of Major Charles West, courtesy of the artist and Major West*

Artillery Regiments, 1825–1832 (above); First U.S. Artillery Regiment, 1834–1851 (right). By H. Charles McBarron, Jr. *Courtesy of the artist and the Company of Military Collectors and Historians. Copyright, 1949, 1952, by the Company of Military Collectors and Historians.*

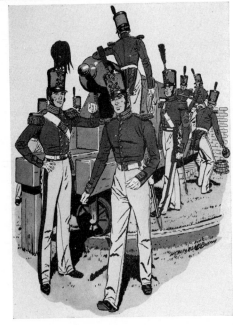

Battle of Buena Vista (above) and Siege of Vera Cruz (below), by Carl
Nebel (from *The War Between the United States and Mexico*, by George
Wilkins Kendall and Carl Nebel, in the collection of Major Charles West)

Wilkeson's Battery at Gettysburg (from *Battles and Leaders of the Civil War*)

New York Artillery Galloping into Action at Gettysburg, by Paul Dominique Philippoteaux (from the Gettysburg Cyclorama)

Courtesy of the National Park Service

Through the Wilderness, by Edwin Forbes (from *Life Studies of the Great Army*)

"Rodney," Famed Artillery Wheel Horse

Courtesy of the National Archives.

General Maxwell Taylor at the Grave of "Pat,"
Fort Sam Houston

U.S. Army Photograph

Gatlings to the Assault, San Juan Hill, Cuba, by H. Charles McBarron, Jr.

Courtesy of the Department of the Army

Refugees from the Château-Thierry Sector, by Captain Harry Townsend

Courtesy of the Department of the Army

"Order in Flank Column," Platoon Commander and First Section Piece, Battery A, 16th Field Artillery, 1935, by Colonel Harry C. Larter, Jr.

Courtesy of the artist and the Journal of the Company of Military Collectors and Historians

This Gun of the 90th Field Artillery Battalion Was Dubbed "The Little Professor" in Korea, August, 1950

A Night Harassing Mission by a Battery of the 937th Field Artillery Battalion, Korea, May, 1951

Atom Cannon and Bursting Shell, 1953 Test

Courtesy of the Department of the Army

shooters covering the streets. Dominating all rose the crenelated walls of the citadel where once stood the storied Halls of Montezuma. Some three hundred years before, Cortés had held, then yielded them to Aztec siege and, retreating over a causeway with his little band of horse and foot, suffered the grievous slaughter of the *Noche Triste*. If the forthcoming assault failed, a Night of Sorrow might also befall the Americans.

Before the opening of the battle on September 8, 1847, many a soldier in Scott's army sat down to write a letter home that would prove to be a last one.

For the bombardment of Molino del Rey, Robert E. Lee, Corps of Engineers, sited the gun positions as well as any regular artilleryman could ask. Twenty-four-pounders boomed above the bark of the Bulldogs, now Drum's by right of recapture. Terrific converging fire smashed them back. The Mexican artillery, though it had lost one of its top outfits in the San Patricios, was still excellently served. Nevertheless storming infantry dashed forward, with Drum, back in action, supporting them until their advance masked his fire. Deep ditches filled with dead, but the mill was carried, and enemy guns were turned on their fleeing crews.

Now 8- and 10-inch shells from howitzers and mortars, again placed by Lee, burst over Chapultepec in a fourteen-hour cannonade. They failed to silence either the castle's heavy ordnance or a fieldpiece which joined it to decimate an infantry regiment advancing over a causeway. A courier on a lathered mount dashed back to Magruder's battery with an urgent request for support. "Prince John" snapped an order to one of his lieutenants. Mr. Jackson, he directed, would take his section and clear the way.

The young officer mounted up and rode forward toward a brevet for gallantry. From the minute his galloping guns came within range he ran a gantlet of fire from the castle artillery and the fieldpieces slamming away from behind a sandbag barricade. He dared not leave the road—mud would mire his carriages hub-deep. He kept on until shells blasted him off, one gun smashed, drivers and teams tangled in a struggling, bloody welter. Surviving cannoneers hit the ditch except for one sergeant. Jackson and the noncom ran to the remaining gun and opened fire.

Cadets of the Virginia Military Institute, sitting in class before their professor of artillery and military tactics a decade later, would strive to imagine that stirring scene. It was hard to visualize dour, religious old Major Jackson as that dashing young lieutenant. Picturing it would come far easier to artillerymen of the Confederate Army of the Shenandoah. General Jackson, they knew, expected as much of them as he had demanded of himself that day on the causeway.

Under the enemy's massed fire, Jackson and his sergeant stood to their gun. If Lieutenant Barnard Bee of the infantry, fighting in another part of the field, had been near the road, he might then have bestowed his nickname "Stonewall" of the first Bull Run. An order from General Worth to withdraw drew the cool reply from Jackson: Give him fifty men and he would capture the barricade.

Up galloped Magruder with the rest of the battery. His horse was shot under him, but he swung clear as it fell, and brought his guns into roaring action, joining Jackson's and its rallied crew. As their shells deluged the Mexican piece, infantry stormed the breastwork, and the way was open.

Assault troops, rushing across a mine field before it could be touched off, drove ahead. A column under Worth, and Quitman's division of infantry and marines closed in on the Castle of Chapultepec. Artillery fired over their heads as they climbed the rocky slopes. Drum and Benjamin abandoned their beloved Buena Vista guns for heavier ones, an 8-inch howitzer and 16-pounder, to breach the walls. Infantrymen poured through the gap, while others planted scaling ladders. Shoved back, toppling with their loads of men, raised again, the ladders were held steady at last. A freshet of blue surged up them and over the parapets. Bullets and bayonets broke the final fierce defense of brave young cadets of the castle's military school and other remnants of the garrison.

As the eagle and snake banner of Mexico was lowered from Chapultepec's tower, a moment of high drama was enacted on the hill of Mixcoac, commanding a full view of the city. There on a gallows was stationed the remaining group of the condemned San Patricios. They watched the Stars and Stripes soar aloft and flutter from the castle staff. Just before the traps were sprung, with their last breath in a shout that was heard across the valley, the deserters cheered the flag they had betrayed.

Thrusting into the city, in close support of the infantry, artillery toppled walls and blasted barricades apart. Jackson battered down the San Cosme Gate. Bayonets paced the guns through streets whose defenders obeyed Santa Anna's furious orders to resist to the last. Several of the heaviest dams were burst by two officers who were not artillerymen. U. S. Grant and Rafael Semmes, later a daring raider in the Confederate Navy, mustered crews to manhandle mountain howitzers up into belfries. The deadly fire they poured down on rooftop snipers and enemy massed behind barriers cleared a passage that could otherwise have been won only with severe loss.

The ramparts of the citadel, still to be taken, were a ring of flame. Its cannon thundered at the blue tide which lapped its base, smashing a redoubt. Along with the onrush of infantry stormers, Lieutenant Hunt galloped his light gun over the last 150 yards. Though almost every man and horse was hit as he unlimbered, he and cannoneers still on their feet shoved the piece forward until it was muzzle to muzzle with a Mexican gun in an embrasure. The future Chief of Artillery of the Army of the Potomac fired first and blew the enemy weapon and its crew to bits.

A white flag. Muskets clattering to the ground. Cannon stilled to sullen silence. Santa Anna, declaring that honor had been satisfied, withdrew from the city. It was the end.

Further fighting took place at Puebla and elsewhere, and a peace treaty was not confirmed by the Senate until March, 1848, but the war was virtually over on that morning of September 14, 1847, when the American Army fully occupied Mexico City. Scott's entry into the Halls of Montezuma was as triumphal as it deserved to be. In full dress uniform, the grand old soldier rode up on his big bay charger, preceded by a cavalry escort with flashing sabers and a mounted band, kettledrums booming and horns blaring "Hail Columbia," "Washington's March," "Yankee Doodle," and finally "Hail to the Chief." Gallant infantry and marines presented arms, and artillerymen stood at attention beside the guns they had served so well.

CHAPTER 6

Guns of the Blue and the Gray

●•

In 1861 artillery was an arm consisting of so many individual batteries.

COLONEL JENNINGS C. WISE, *The Long Arm of Lee*

The artillery, like the other arms, must be collected in mass, if one wishes to attain a decisive result.

NAPOLEON

It has been well said that "a battery carries with it all that goes to make up a civilization." It requires many mechanics with their tools and stores, and also what are called "handy men," intelligent and self-reliant, for no two men at a gun do the same work. No country furnishes better men for the artillery proper than our Northern, and particularly our New England States, and if, as in other armies, the best fitted for this service were assigned to it, we would lead the world in this arm.

GENERAL HENRY J. HUNT

●•

A HERD of rambunctious mules, corraled in Texas in the spring of 1851, lent a touch of slapstick comedy to the perennial pattern of interludes between our wars. They became long-eared chargers for artillerymen converted into cavalry to prevent Indian raiders from running cattle across the Mexican border. It required a squad of redlegs to wrestle a saddle and bridle on each protesting beast, snorting, kicking, and trying to rear, though it was snubbed to a fence post. Riders climbed aboard and cast loose. In seconds the air was filled with bucked-off gunners, literally a flying battery. But the ludicrous scene was essentially tragic, for this was Battery B, 4th Artillery, whose guns under O'Brien had made the supremely gallant stand at Buena Vista. To such a pass had postwar economy reduced it.

The commanding general agreed that more time was needed for breaking mounts and pack animals. In the eight days allowed, the battery paraded, hailed by grinning infantrymen, "Why, that's the jackass cavalry!" The lead pack mule went on a rampage, scattered its load of pots and pans, and disrupted the entire cavalcade. Finally the artillerymen took the field, armed with flintlock pistols and sabers; the latter at least, an officer consolingly observed, were never known to miss fire.[107]

All the fine light batteries that distingushed themselves in the Mexican War were dehorsed except Bragg's of the 3rd Artillery and Taylor's of the 1st. Serving as foot troops, cavalry, mounted riflemen, or fort garrisons, they were scattered across the country. They fought hard and usually successful actions against Indians in Florida, the West, and on the Pacific coast. The luck of "B" of the 4th turned, and it became artillery again, trading mules for horses in such ample supply that it could be particular about color. Sections matched their teams—bays for the right, the center blacks, the left sorrels (chestnuts), with grays for the battery wagon and forge. It took part in Indian campaigns and in the expedition which forced the Mormons of Utah to obey federal laws and cease bloody clashes with other settlers.

Emphasis was placed on siege and mountain artillery as a result of experience in the war with Mexico. Drill regulations were issued for heavy howitzers, for mortars from coehorns to 13-inchers, for the 12-pound pack howitzer, its gun, carriage, and ammunition carried by three mules. Light guns would be called for by the terrain of most Civil War battlefields, but it continued to be the military policy of the United States to fight the next war with the weapons and tactics of the last. Foresighted planners were discouraged or ignored.

Such was the lot of Captain Robert Parker Parrott, 3rd Artillery, who invented a rifled iron cannon, strengthened by a hoop shrunken on its breech, the point of maximum strain. A wrought-iron ring cast on its shell rotated it as the powder charge propelled it through the grooved bore, and a contact fuse on the shell's nose detonated it. Although tests demonstrated accuracy and range far surpassing the smoothbores, a government board rejected it. Not so Major Thomas Jonathan Jackson, instructor in artillery at Virginia Military Institute, who tried it out with cadet crews in 1860 and highly approved. On his recommendation Virginia placed an order for which good use would soon be found by the Confederacy. Belatedly the North would follow suit.

The work of another inventor fared somewhat better. Captain Thomas Jackson Rodman, Ordnance Corps, devised a method of casting guns on a hollow core, cooling the inner surface by a flow of water so that each successive layer of metal was compressed by the shrinkage of the outer ones. His fieldpieces were made by bending a sheet of iron around a mandrel and welding the side. From light calibers to a big 15-incher, they passed successful tests. Rodman guns with their strength and range proved such formidable armament for Federal coast defenses that they served as a weighty argument against the threat of foreign intervention on the side of the South. The 3- and 4½-inch wrought-iron rifles he invented also bore his name.

Breechloaders, English Whitworths, Armstrongs, and Blakelys, would be imported and employed in the coming struggle, but the heyday of those weapons did not arrive until the invention of a recoil mechanism and a better breechblock. Muzzle-loaders, rolling back on their wheels in recoil, still were simpler and quicker to reload.

Remarkably, it was a muzzle-loading smoothbore that emerged as the foremost fieldpiece of the Civil War: a French 12-pounder developed under the auspices of Napoleon III and named after him. A gun-howitzer, capable of the longer range of the former and the higher-angled fire of the latter, it fired solid shot, shell, spherical case (shrapnel), canister, grape, and chain shot—the last for very short ranges. Batteries of Napoleons were almost as mobile as horse artillery. For the close fighting of the War Between the States, Napoleons were first-rate cannon.

At war strength the field batteries moved into action with six pieces: four 12-pounder guns and two 24-pound howitzers for a

12-pounder battery; six 12-pounder guns for a light battery; six 6-pounder guns for a battery named for that caliber. Each piece and each of the twelve caissons per battery was drawn by a six-horse team, with three drivers mounted on the near horses of the lead, swing, and wheel pairs. Three cannoneers rode on the limber chests and on the forward chest of the caissons. The total ammunition load carried in the chests varied from 1,112 rounds for a 6-pounder battery to 1,218 for a 12-pounder battery and 1,344 for a light battery. Each unit's complement included a traveling forge, drawn by six horses, and a wagon for stores and spare parts. Such light artillery was capable of traveling long distances across country under reasonably good conditions at a good pace, and of negotiating tough going more slowly.

The red glare of molten metal lit Northern foundries casting the 7,892 cannon issued from 1861 to 1865. Richmond's Tredegar Works, the Confederacy's principal and for some time its sole ordnance manufactory—reason enough for holding the city at all costs—flamed and rang with activity. The South augmented its artillery by importations from abroad until blockade shut off that source, by seizure of Federal arsenals and by battlefield captures. Hard-pressed by shortages, it was forced to piece out its metal supply by scouring the countryside for house piping and window weights, for hearth irons, brass candlesticks, and church and plantation bells. The Second Baptist Church of Richmond gave its bells and also raised funds to buy metal enough to cast six guns for a unit to be called the Second Baptist Battery. Cloth came to supplement leather for bridles. Yet in many an engagement Gray batteries faced Blue on equal terms.

However, artillery, so often dominant in Mexico, now bowed to infantry. In the Civil War the shoulder rifle, able to kill at a thousand yards, was pre-eminent. It fired the French invention, the Minié bullet. Sharpshooters used telescopic sights with deadly effect. Ordinary marksmen at the usual battle ranges of two hundred or three hundred yards often cut down gun crews with "minnie balls" before the artillery was able to fire more than a few rounds.

The rifled fieldpieces were accurate and had plenty of sustained velocity even at two miles but they couldn't produce enough casualties. The old balance was upset. . . . The number of guns per 1,000 foot soldiers remained practically constant in the Napoleonic Wars, the Civil War, and World War I, yet the percentage of casualties caused by the field artillery was far less in the Civil War, particularly in the first two years, than in the other two. . . . Experience taught the infantry that when the enemy's guns were too far away to be fired at successfully with their rifles, the guns weren't really dangerous. If a battery was close enough to do damage and in the open, it could be quickly put out of action by infantry fire.[108]

American artillery nevertheless maintained its glorious traditions. It fought in the line, gunners shoulder to shoulder with infantrymen. It charged, unlimbered, and opened at pistol range. At Fredericksburg a single gun of Pelham's Gray horse battery held up Burnside's advance for almost an hour. There were sacrifices as gallant as O'Brien's and swift maneuvers as dashing as Ringgold's and Bragg's. Massed fire at Malvern Hill, Gettysburg, and Petersburg carried on standards set by Knox at Yorktown and Scott at Vera Cruz toward the volume and fury of the concentrations of 1918 and the 1940's. And it was an artilleryman who fired the first shot in defense of the Union.

History's spotlight beat on Fort Sumter on its island in the harbor of Charleston, South Carolina. Only an outwork, it was, as its small Federal garrison was well aware, at the mercy of fourteen mainland batteries bearing on it—batteries mounting thirty heavy guns and seventeen mortars. Mustered to man them and launch an assault were three thousand troops, with four thousand more in reserve, rebels against the authority of the United States since December 4, 1860, when South Carolina seceded from the Union. Early next year their guns opened fire, twice hit and drove away an unarmed steamer, *Star of the West,* approaching with supplies for Sumter.

The march of events quickened. More southern states seceded, and Jefferson Davis was chosen to head their confederacy. A little more than a month after Abraham Lincoln had been inaugurated President of the United States, Charleston artillerymen loaded cannon trained on Sumter. The fort's commander, Major Robert

Anderson, refused a demand to surrender. Confederate gunners—
the Morris Island Battery, manned by cadets of the Southern military school, The Citadel, opened first—jerked lanyards, and shells
burst over Sumter, April 9, 1861. Captain Abner Doubleday, U.S.
Artillery, fired the first round in reply.

Rebel mortars knocked out the guns of the barbette tier, forcing
gunners to take cover in casemates. Barracks blazed up, flamed
luridly through the night. More fires compelled the magazine to be
sealed off, and all but four barrels of the powder still available had
to be thrown into the sea to save the fort from being blown up by
its own explosives. Provisions were almost exhausted. A Rebel round
carried away the flagstaff.

Major Anderson's colors had been struck for him. He had no
need of his Mexican War service or the books he wrote on gunnery
to tell him his case was hopeless. His surrender was accepted on
terms he stipulated, and he marched out his garrison of six officers
and seventy-six enlisted men of the 1st Artillery with the honors of
war. Surprisingly, not until then were casualties suffered: one private killed and another seriously wounded by an ammunition explosion when the Major's guns saluted the flag he sought vainly to
defend.

Tread of marching feet, clatter of hoofs, rumble of gun wheels.
Far-flung batteries of regular artillery were summoned, one half of
them under urgent orders to rush to the defense of Washington.
While the new 5th Regiment was being organized, units of the 4th
were brought from Utah, of the 3rd from Washington Territory,
and of the 1st from enemy-held Gulf states. Rebels let the gunners
of the 1st go, *noblesse oblige,* as the United States permitted Southern officers to resign and transfer their allegiance.

Heavy batteries of the 2nd Artillery had been taking their turn
at manning the eastern seaboard forts, a soft detail. They rejoiced
in extra blankets, civilian-type bedsteads, stoves, libraries, well con-
ducted messes, and private pig herds to furnish frequent pork roasts.
It was too good to last. Soon they found themselves foot-slogging it
in the field minus their big cannon, jeered at as "heavy infantry."
One artilleryman, rashly asking a command of dismounted cavalry
where its horses were, drew the retort: "Gone to fetch your heavy
guns." [109]

More martial were the light batteries that rolled into Washington. "Old Regulars" they proudly called themselves. They wore their blue forage caps, adapted from the French kepi, at a jaunty angle; short, brass-buttoned blue jackets belted above their sky-blue breeches; their side arms sabers and perhaps pistols. A captain and two or three lieutenants rode at the head and on the flanks of a battery's column of four to six guns and a varying number of caissons, followed by a forge and a supply wagon. At their posts were two staff sergeants (orderly and quartermaster), six line sergeants (chiefs of piece), twelve corporals (gunners and chiefs of caisson), five artificers, and two buglers. Boot to boot with the lead driver of the first gun team rode the guidon-bearer. In his right stirrup socket rested the butt of the staff of his small standard, once a sergeant's scarlet sash fastened to a rammer staff to mark the gun line for the battery when it formed front. The red guidon was emblazoned in gold with the artillery's insignia: crossed cannon, regimental numeral above them, battery letter beneath. Sometimes the guidon was a small silk swallow-tailed Stars and Stripes. Cannoneers and drivers raised the personnel to 152, if the battery was at full war strength.

Soon most of the officers were promoted to command of regiments, brigades, divisions; the artillery suffered for lack of trained field officers. Sergeants were commissioned to take over the batteries, and ranks filled with recruits. For President Lincoln had called for volunteers. This war, like its predecessors, could not be fought without them. The Old Regulars, the veterans, the West Pointers, were only a leavening and a scant one. States mustered their regiments in armories and camps, but those, too, must fill their ranks with untrained men. From farms, sawmills, shops, and factories volunteers flocked to the recruiting stations. "We are coming Father Abraham, three hundred thousand strong," sang the young fellows, older men, and drummers and buglers who were only boys. There were the makings of artillerymen in many of them—especially the mechanics, who could keep guns in action, and the farmers, who as drivers learned to keep the guns and caissons rolling along at a pace unknown to plow or stoneboat.

Camps were scenes of confusion and waste motion, seemingly inevitable when the United States prepared for war. Precious weeks were spent on showy drill for the battery mounted, with no time given to route marches through clinging mud or woods, such marches as must bring the guns on to most battlefields. Of target practice there was little or none. One intelligent young recruit, who would never fire a shot until he faced the enemy, confided his discouragement and apprehension to a veteran gunner corporal and drew a gloomy reply:

My boy, you are just beginning to discover the artillery humbug. You serve in what should be the most efficient arm of the service; an arm where men and horses and guns should be wasted as water, where tons of ammunition should be expended in target practice, because if a gunner cannot hit the object he fires at he had better not fire at all, as to miss excites the contempt of the enemy. I have served for two years in this army, and there is not a general officer in it who understands how to use artillery, not one. Wait until you get into the field and your heart will be broken.[110]

Despite the pessimism of old soldiers, artillery met the eventual test of battle, though its commanders had first to learn the principle of massed fire which Napoleon Bonaparte had taught fifty years before.

South of the Mason-Dixon Line artillerymen were as green and untried. Yet such organizations as the Washington Artillery of New Orleans and the Richmond Howitzers furnished cadres to build on, and Jackson's V.M.I. cadets strenuously drilled volunteers to handle the rifled Parrotts. Johnny Reb as a cannoneer was less handy with machinery than Billy Yank, but the former was a better horseman. The Confederate horse artillery, like the cavalry it supported, would win glory on many a field.

Rumbling guns rolled toward the front, the disputed ground between Washington and Richmond. Blue and Gray armies met head on at the first Battle of Bull Run, which the South called Manassas.

The confusion of first combat was capped at Bull Run by a motley of uniforms. Regiments in both armies wore the blue jackets and baggy red trousers of French Zouaves. Federal units appeared in cadet gray, indistinguishable from the Confederacy's chosen color. A number of Rebel officers had not yet discarded their U.S.

blue. Even the battle flags became emblems of doubt. The Stars and Bars then carried, with its two broad stripes of red and one of white and its circle of seven stars on a blue canton, looked like an abbreviated version of the Stars and Stripes. At one point Southern reinforcements, assumed to be Northern troops, were almost shot down by their comrades. A mistaken identification on the other side proved fatal. It crippled two fine batteries and led to a Union disaster.

As artillery opened fire in the early morning of July 21, 1861, Mexican War veterans in blue or gray sniffed the familiar, acrid tang of powder. Ladies and gentlemen, who had driven out from Washington with picnic lunches to watch the gladiators from colosseum tiers of Virginia hills, thrilled to the swelling cannonade. Standing on carriage seats, they gaped at Rhode Island, New York, and two regular batteries galloping into action. The rapid, steady service of the pieces of the latter, Captain J. B. Ricketts' unit and Captain Charles Griffin's West Point Battery, so called because it had been organized and trained at the Military Academy, was an admirable sight. Their shells burst over a Confederate brigade and sent it reeling back. General Bee, rallying it, pointed to the commander of a rock-firm Gray line in reserve and shouted, "Look, men! There is Jackson standing like a stone wall!" A good soldier, who died on this field, had widened his niche in history by naming a better one.

Stonewall Jackson's guns, sited with an old artilleryman's skill, answered the Union cannon. He had placed them so that their recoil ran them back behind their hill-crest position for reloading. Manhandled up into battery again, they blazed away furiously. Imboden's red-shirted Virginia gun crews joined them in dueling with the Federals and held their ground until most of their pieces were disabled by Griffin's and Ricketts' concentrated shelling, more than half their horses killed, and their captain, directing fire close beside a muzzle, deafened and flung twenty feet by the gun blast.

Rifled Parrotts and smoothbores thundered above the rattling musketry, as battle lines surged forward or bent and broke. The battery of Captain Henry J. Hunt had reached Washington only on July 14, but that veteran of Mexico had used his week's grace well to equip and drill his recruits. Now, keeping his horses under cover and running his guns forward by hand, he smashed a Rebel charge on the left with shrapnel and canister, firing so fast that no time was allowed to swab bores between rounds. It was worth the risk, he judged—"Minutes were more valuable than arms." When hard pressed, Hunt protested but obeyed an order to retreat and brought off his battery with the loss of only a bridle.

On through a brutally hot afternoon the conflict raged. Griffin and Ricketts, ordered to close range, limbered up and galloped ahead. They stood and slugged it out like infighting prize fighters, with guns massed by Jackson on Henry House Hill. From the windows of the house Confederate sharpshooters began to pick off the cannoneers. The blue-clad regulars shifted fire, scouring them out. Old bedridden Mrs. Henry, hemmed in her home by the conflict centering around it, died under shell fragments with the riflemen. Unaware that they had taken a civilian life, artillerymen jerked lanyards and plied rammer staffs at an ever increasing tempo.

They won an enemy's tribute, those regular gunners, and none is more highly prized. "The batteries of Ricketts and Griffin," declared a Confederate officer,[111] "by their fine discipline, wonderful daring, and matchless skill, were the prime features of the fight. The battle was not lost until they were lost." Now approached the moment of sacrifice for which they might have given the Washington spectators lining the route to action the gladiators' hail, *"Morituri salutamus."*

Jeb Stuart's cavalry and a Gray reserve battery overlapped and drove in the Union right. The Blue artillery's support, taken in the flank, melted away. Still the regulars stood firm, their cannon rolling out drumfire. Then on Griffin's right a regiment of infantry emerged from the woods. He swung his guns to meet it and was about to open point-blank with a blizzard of canister, but Major William F. Barry, Artillery, yelled to him to hold fire—that the oncoming troops were Federals. That mistake was tragically corrected when the newcomers, Virginians, blasted out a volley at seventy yards. Gunners dropped across trails, and drivers slumped in the saddles of screaming horses. Ricketts, desperately wounded, his first lieutenant killed, lay amidst the wreckage of his battery, flooded over by the Confederate assault. In seconds Griffin, also wounded, lost forty men and seventy-five horses but managed to drag off three pieces. The remaining nine guns of the two batteries were captured.

That was the turning point of the battle. The toll of ordnance fallen into Rebel hands mounted to twenty-seven cannon, including a 30-pounder Parrott, thirty-seven caissons and other carriages, sixty-four horses, much harness, and five thousand rounds of ammunition. Retreat merged into rout and panic, as a well-aimed shot from a Confederate gun smashed a wagon on the stone bridge spanning Bull Run and jammed it with a struggling mass of men and animals. Soldiers cut the traces of artillery horses and galloped back to Washington in a turbulent jetsam of defeat.

Out of that wreckage and an inchoate mass of recruits General George B. McClellan molded the Army of the Potomac. He turned troops who had panicked at Bull Run and new regiments thronging to the defense of the Union into a first-rate fighting machine. Subsequent defeats they met were usually due to failures by the high command, including "Little Mac's" own, and to the superior Confederate generalship of the earlier years of the war.

McClellan's reorganization of the artillery was an extraordinary accomplishment. It was carried out largely along lines suggested by his chief of that arm, General Barry, who as a major had made the tragic misidentification at Bull Run. The new regulations took batteries away from brigade commanders, generally incapable of directing them, and gave them to divisions. A reserve of all types and a siege train were established. The amount of ammunition to accompany field batteries was specified at not less than four hundred rounds per gun. In July of '61 McClellan inherited nine incomplete batteries—30 guns, 650 men.

> By the first of the following March, the force created . . . consisted of 92 batteries of 520 guns, 12,500 men, and 11,000 horses, all fully equipped and ready for the field. Of these batteries, 30 were regulars and 62 volunteers. All this great work of organization, equipment, and instruction was accomplished at camps in and about Washington and in the incredibly short period of seven months, including the severe winter of 1861-2.[112]

"Little Mac" demanded the discipline, training, and hardening that make an army. Enforcement, properly strict but humane, degenerated in some commands into cruel punishments condoned in that more callous day. Insubordinate artillerymen were tied on the spare wheel at the rear of a caisson, arms and legs spread-eagled, for five or six hours. If the offense was graver, the wheel was given a quarter turn so that the culprit hung horizontal, cords cutting into his limbs. Some fainted; others, jaws set, endured silently. If they cried out they were gagged. Rare, and, as a rule, inflicted only for such a heinous crime as a murderous assault on a superior, was the brutal practice of "tying on the rack." The mutinous soldier was roped to the back of a battery wagon with his weight pressing against the sharp edge of the forage rack. Usually he lost consciousness in ten minutes; sometimes he was crippled.[113] But the great majority of those who manned the smoking guns, Blue or Gray, willingly and honorably served a cause.

When McClellan invaded Virginia by the Peninsula in the spring of 1862, his field artillery for the expedition comprised 49 batteries, 299 guns. His siege train boasted a formidable armament of seventy-one heavy cannon, including nine 200-pounder Parrott rifles, five 100-pounders, and a number of 13-inch mortars. Yorktown was the first objective. Manning that historic town's defenses, "Prince John" Magruder, C.S.A., did not repeat the futile resistance of Cornwallis in 1781. His service as an artilleryman in Mexico told him that he was hopelessly outgunned, and he evacuated the works. His rain-swept retreat, like the Yankee pursuit, was a grueling mud march. Road-bound guns, carriages, and wagons were dragged through sloughs by animals which sank in to their bellies or at times disappeared completely, emerging covered with slime. When a horse stuck in the mire so that he could not move, he was unhitched, a prolonge tied around his body and the rest of the team hooked to that rope to pull him out. Infantrymen waded in to help cannoneers straining at the wheels. Rear-guard cavalry fought off Federals, closing to capture stalled pieces. During one such stand, a British volunteer with a monocle and an Oxford accent rode up to his troop commander and asked:

"I beg pahdon, Capting, but may I enquire why we are staying here so long?"

"To save this gun," the Captain replied.

"What, that damn thing?" the trooper persisted in a puzzled manner.

"Certainly. We can't afford to leave it."

"Pahdon me again," begged the monocled one, "if I ask how much it is worth."

"I suppose about a thousand dollars."

The Englishman deliberately readjusted his eye-glass, regarded the enemy advancing and now firing on the troop and made a nonchalant offer to his commander:

"Well, Capting, let's move on. I'll give you my check for it at once." [114]

The campaign saw the establishment by an artilleryman of a hallowed custom when a cannoneer of Battery A, 2nd Artillery, U.S.A., died of wounds. At his burial the battery commander, John C. Tidball, dared not risk the usual three volleys over the grave. The Confederate lines were near, and the firing might precipitate an attack. Instead he ordered the sounding of a new bugle call, composed a few months previously by General Daniel Butterfield. The slow, sweet strains of Taps, then first played at a military funeral, have ever since served as a soldier's farewell.

Magruder halted in his fighting retreat and built a chain of redoubts across the Yankees' path. How desperately his men struggled to hold them is instanced by the gallantry of a Gray cannoneer. The story was vividly told by Robert Stiles, of the Richmond Howitzers, who never learned the other gunner's name:

At the crisis of the battle we were stationed in Fort Magruder . . . , the key to our position. I was standing, sponge-staff in hand, awaiting the firing of my gun, the next piece to the left being a gun of the Fayette Artillery. As my eye fell upon it No. 1 was sponging out, the No. 3 of course having his thumbstall pressed upon the vent. Suddenly I saw No. 3 stoop, clap his right hand upon his leg below the knee; and then I saw him topple slowly forward, never, however, lifting his thumb from the vent, but pressing it down close and hard—his elbow straining upward as his body sank forward and downward. The heroic fellow had been first shot in the calf of the leg, and as he bent to feel that wound a bullet crashed through his skull; his last effort was to save No. 1 the loss of his hands by premature explosion as was rammed home the next charge. I have never witnessed more sublime faithfulness unto death than was exhibited by the downward pressure of that thumb, as it was literally dragged from the hole of the piece by the weight of the sinking body of the noble cannoneer.[115]

Blue assaults broke the redoubt chain and pressed on toward Richmond, but that city was not to fall to McClellan. Confederate General Joseph E. Johnstone, whom he had driven back steadily, was severely wounded at Fair Oaks, or Seven Pines. Robert E. Lee was given command of the Army of Northern Virginia. Only to Ulysses S. Grant would he finally yield the capital.

That same spring a bloody and confused combat was waged in the West. Union forces had stormed Forts Henry and Donelson and were clearing the upper Mississippi, finally to meet Admiral Farragut's gunboats, battering their way up from New Orleans. On April 6 and 7, 1862, Blue and Gray armies collided at Shiloh.

In spite of the heavily wooded nature of the battlefield, which made maneuvering difficult, artillery played an important part at Shiloh. On both sides guns were lost and retaken. It was an affair of individual batteries, unco-ordinated, on their own, until toward the end of the first day a strong Confederate attack rolled over the Federal lines to the verge of victory. Then twenty Union batteries were hastily collected and put in position near Pittsburgh Landing. Their massed fire, aided by the heavy pieces of two gunboats in the Tennessee River, beat down on the oncoming ranks and shattered them. All but one battery stood firm under the Rebel cannonade that strove to dislodge them. When an enemy shell blew up a caisson, the men of the 13th Ohio Light Artillery stampeded and abandoned their guns. Its name was blotted out on Ohio's roster, and its place remained blank throughout the war.[116]

The second day's conflict resulted in a final Rebel repulse and retreat. Grant failed to pursue. But Shiloh was a milestone for him

toward command of the Army of the Potomac and his rendezvous
with Lee and the Army of Northern Virginia.

The Seven Days' Battle around Richmond saw the first American
use of railroad artillery, suggested by General Lee. At Savage Station
a 32-pounder rifle was mounted on a flatcar of the York River Railway and armored with iron plates.[117] Its effective fire contributed
to McClellan's repulse. His losses heavy in men and guns, he fell
back to prepare for one more drive on the Confederate capital.

Malvern Hill, July 1, 1862, last engagement of the Seven Days,
stands as an artillery classic. The Union position, naturally strong,
was located on a commanding plateau, with flanks well protected.
An arc of 340 guns, tier on tier, crowned its summit, strong infantry
support guarding their rear, a line of skirmishers out to the front.
The splendid field of fire of the lighter pieces swept the approaches,
including an open space from three hundred to four hundred yards
wide over which an assault most likely would be delivered. Heavy
cannon behind the crest could also flail the wheat fields of the
slopes with fire and range into the thickly wooded swamp ground
beyond, ground "passable at but a few places and difficult at those."

The posting of those massed guns in anticipation of the battle
was the work of Colonel Hunt, who had risen from battery command at Bull Run to head McClellan's artillery reserve. In the
forthcoming combat he would emerge as the gunner genius of the
Civil War without a peer on either side. His superb handling of
the guns at Malvern Hill, repeated at Gettysburg the next year,
earned him high rank among artillery immortals.

That bristling hilltop was a challenge to Lee's skilled maneuvering. A thrust from a flank might find a crevice and crack those formidable defenses. He chose instead to blanket and enfilade its guns
with counterbattery fire and, once they were silenced, to assault
frontally.

His purpose was frustrated by poor staff work and equally bad
reconnaissance which sapped the strength of the powerful Confederate artillery. One good position, a knoll on the right, was occupied,
but the too few guns placed there were no match for the Union
array. Others were battered back and forced to withdraw into the
woods which enveloped them and masked their fire. Four bat-

talions of the reserve, containing the best pieces, took no part in the engagement. Lee did not consult his artillery chief, General William N. Pendleton, nor did the latter, more able as an organizer than as a tactician, seek out his superior to offer advice or to ask for orders.

In the face of the failure of counterbattery on Malvern, an attack was close to being abandoned. Then Lee, misled by a shifting of Union troops on the height, mistook it for a withdrawal and gave the order to attack. With magnificent *élan* the Gray columns debouched from the woods and began the ascent of those fatal slopes. Cheering men, rifles at port or trail, bent their backs and climbed upward.

Smoke and flame rippled around the arc of the batteries above, as the Union cannon opened with a defiant roar. Colonel Hunt brought every gun in line into action. In a masterpiece of fire direction he controlled a group of sixty cannon as if they were one huge battery—as if he were an organist pulling the stops for the instrument's mightiest diapason. The thunder of the guns rose in a deafening crescendo. Shrapnel burst to spray deadly cones of balls down on the Rebel infantry. Divisions, brigade by brigade, were broken and leveled, dead heaped on wounded in an amphitheater of carnage. Three-quarters of a mile to the rear of Hunt's front-line battery positions, the big siege guns erupted shells that shattered enemy ranks advancing in support.

Without intermission the furious cannonade continued. When a battery ran low on ammunition—one six-gun battery alone expended thirteen hundred rounds that day—a fresh one from the reserve moved up and took over its field of fire. Desperately the troops in gray and butternut-brown listened for the sound of their own artillery to cover their charge and silence those terrible, tiered cannon above. They heard only a few shells whistling over their heads toward the crest. For as supporting batteries pressed singly through the thickets, each had scarcely unlimbered and gone into action before it was smothered by an avalanche of iron. Upon them Colonel Hunt converged the sheaf of fire of those sixty guns under his immediate control, knocking out one group, then shifting to blast the next that appeared. The effect of that terrible concentration was described by a Rebel gunner fortunate enough to live through it:

I never conceived anything approximating the shower and storm of projectiles and the overwhelming cataclysm of destruction which were at once turned upon our pitiful little popguns. In the short time they existed as effective pieces they were several times fired by fragments of Federal shell striking them after the lanyard was stretched and before it was pulled; and in almost less time than it takes to tell it the carriages were completely crushed, smashed and splintered and the guns themselves so injured and defaced that we were compelled to send them to Richmond after the battle to be remolded.[118]

Attacking infantry reeled back down the hill. "Valor could not conquer those perfectly served batteries on the crest, nor could fortitude long endure the fire that seemed to sweep every foot of the open ground." [119]

That night men of a Massachusetts regiment around their campfires slowly sang Julia Ward Howe's words, set to the tune of "John Brown's Body." The majestic lines of the first stanza of "The Battle Hymn of the Republic," particularly the third line, seemed to have been written for the tremendous bombardment by the cannon on Malvern Hill, witnessed a few hours before.

Mine eyes have seen the glory of the coming of the Lord;
He is trampling out the vintage where the grapes of wrath
    are stored;
He hath loosed the fateful lightning of His terrible, swift
    sword; . . .

The battle cost the Confederates five thousand killed and wounded, the Federals about a third as many. But next day McClellan retreated as he had after every preceding operation. "Seeking glory at the cannon's mouth," he had found it at Malvern and let it slip. It was not in him to win victories, only to create armies capable of winning them when a stronger hand grasped the baton.

On August 29-30, 1862, the armies met again, and the cycle of Union defeat found completion on an old battlefield.

Second Bull Run lifted Southern arms higher still in a rising tide of triumph. There as Lee with forty-seven thousand men crushed bungling General John Pope's army of sixty-five thousand, Confederate artillery redeemed its disaster at Malvern Hill. It brought into action 175 guns against the North's 125, which, however, included some 20-pounder rifled Parrotts with superiority in range over the South's pieces. But there was no Hunt present to mass and direct the fire of the Blue cannon, while those of the Gray were masterfully handled except for the reserves, which as at Malvern were permitted to lag twenty miles behind the advance and never reached the field.

Even without reserves, the second Bull Run, or Manassas, again proved the maxim that the god of battles favors the better-served artillery. Now it was the Confederate guns that were at the right place at the right time. Stonewall Jackson's divisional artillery ably supported him until it could no longer bear on a rapidly advancing Federal attack without hitting its own infantry. Stapleton Crutchfield's and Stephen D. Lee's groups on the right then shifted aim to open on the enemy reserves. But Jackson's line bent under the weight of strong and valiantly led Blue columns, and infantry reinforcements from Longstreet were called for. The latter saw a quicker means of aiding his hard-pressed colleague. A galloping aide carried an order that sent two batteries, limbered and ready in anticipation, dashing into position with foam-flecked teams. With devastating volleys they raked the Union left rear. The attack, enfiladed and hamstrung, collapsed as Jackson slashed it with a charge, and Longstreet's whole line swept forward and drove the enemy across Bull Run.

Among the guns that broke the Union attacks and scourged the retreat were those of Captain William Johnston Pegram, one of the South's finest young artillerymen. It was no new experience for Pope to retire under the whistle of Pegram's shells. At Cedar Mountain earlier in August the General and his staff had scurried for cover when the gunner officer showered them with a salvo. On that same field Pegram galloped up to within a hundred yards of a strange column, identified it as Yankee, waved his hat as a signal for his guns to open, and rode back unscathed. There as at Mechanicsville he held critical ground for hours in close-range duels with Union batteries, the odds heavy against him, until his pieces finally were disabled. From the beginning of the war he fought through most of the general engagements in Virginia on to the trenches of Petersburg.

Let a Confederate cannoneer speak the epilogue for Second Manassas. His unit, the Rockbridge Battery, had galloped into action with Longstreet's artillery when it poured in its telling fire on the Union flank. The guns, having done their work, had fallen silent, and Number One of one of them was leaning wearily on his sponge staff as General Lee rode up and reined in fifteen feet away. Eyes alight, the cannoneer identified himself to a staff officer and asked permission to greet the Commander. The staffer smiled, led him forward and said:

"General, here is someone who wants to speak to you."

The bearded man on "Traveller" looked down at the artilleryman, face powder-blackened, uniform ragged and clay-stained, and inquired:

"Well, my man, what can I do for you?"

"Why, General," the young soldier asked, "don't you know me?"

Not until then did the General recognize his youngest son, Artillery Private Robert E. Lee, Jr.[120]

CHAPTER 7

Artillery Hell

••

The gun is the rallying point of the detachment, its point of honor, its flag, its banner. It is that to which the men look, by which they stand, with and for which they fight, by and for which they fall. As long as the gun is theirs they are unconquered, victorious; when the gun is lost, all is lost. It is their religion to fight it until the enemy is out of range, or until the gun itself is withdrawn, or until both it and the detachment are in the hands of the foe. An infantryman in flight often flings away his musket. I do not recall ever having heard of a Confederate artillery detachment abandoning its gun without orders. Nor were the Federal artillerymen one whit behind in this loyal devotion to their pieces.

MAJOR ROBERT STILES, *Four Years Under Marse Robert*

No higher ambition can come to the gunner than to merit the full confidence of his sister arm. It should be his one desire, as it is his duty, to relieve the infantry of so much of the shock of battle as he can divert to himself, even if he succumb under the blow.

COLONEL JENNINGS C. WISE, *The Long Arm of Lee* 121

••

THE old custom of christening cannon was carried on in the War Between the States. "The men," wrote Thomas Nelson Page, "from admiration of their guns grew to have first a pride in, and then an affection for, them, and gave them nicknames as they did their comrades." His story, "Burial of the Guns," tells of a Confederate battery whose four Napoleons were dubbed "The Evangelists": Matthew, Mark, Luke, and John, while of its two rifles one was called "The Eagle," because of its scream and the swoop of its shells, and the other "The Cat" because when it became hot from fast firing, it jumped like a cat. Union artillery boasted "The Swamp Angel," a 200-pounder Parrott emplaced in the South Carolina marshes to bombard Charleston, and "The Dictator," a mammoth of a mortar that held sway during the siege of Petersburg.

Field artillerymen of the period, even with smooth-bore muzzle-loaders, achieved amazing accuracy and reached a rate of fire as rapid as three or four rounds per minute. Range finders, traversing gear, and recoil mechanisms were still to be invented. Officers or gunners sighted along barrels, estimated distances and elevated or depressed the barrel by a wheel screw beneath the breech. If shells were being used, they called for the fuse to be cut at the mark in seconds timed to burst the projectile in front of or above the target. By hand motions they directed cannoneers to shift the trail right or left. On target, crews stood clear. "Fire!" and the lanyard was jerked. Then the smoking piece, rolling back in recoil, was manhandled forward into battery to be swabbed, loaded, sighted and fired again. Procedure had changed little since the advent of field artillery, but well-drilled crews, Blue or Gray, were expert and served the guns swiftly and steadily in the hottest actions.

Crack battery commanders were alert for what the artillery calls targets of opportunity. John Pelham, Jeb Stuart's incomparable horse artilleryman, with one round at a range of eight hundred yards, struck down a color-bearer on whom a Union regiment was rallying. Pegram's salvo that flushed and scattered Pope and his staff has been mentioned. At Antietam General D. H. Hill, rashly exposing himself in a mounted reconnaissance, was spotted by a Blue gunner; a round shot carried away the forelegs of the General's charger. Confederate cannon, opening on Hooker's headquarters at Chancellorsville, toppled a pillar whose bricks stunned "Fighting Joe." At Spotsylvania General Lee, who had just been dissuaded from leading a charge, almost fell victim to the Federal artillery when long-range batteries opened a heavy, accurate cannonade on the Bloody Angle. Traveller, excited by the shelling, reared on his hind legs. The moment the horse rose up, a shot hurtled beneath his girth only a few inches from his rider's stirrups. On the North

Anna a Federal battery commander sighted an officer in gray on a porch, and a round shot thudded into the door frame within a few feet of the seated figure. The target, General Lee, calmly finished the buttermilk he was drinking, thanked his host, and rode away. There are numerous other instances of first-rate gunnery, of cannon sharpshooting, by both sides, the more remarkable in the Confederate case because of the inferiority of their ammunition, particularly the shell fuses. Many projectiles which would have caused considerable casualties had they burst failed to detonate—in the language of a later day were "duds." [122]

Drivers matched the efficiency of gunners. Gray and Blue horse artillery and light batteries were worthy heirs to Mexican War traditions of speed and mobility. Galloping teams, drivers bent low over their necks, brought guns onto the field, and as the pieces, caissons beside them, were unlimbered and prepared for action, the horses were swung around, dashed back and took position in rear of the guns or under such cover as could be found. As prompt to return when a battery was forced to change position or withdraw, they limbered up under fire. Sometimes all but two of a six-horse team were knocked out. Traces of dead or disabled animals then were cut, and the surviving pair pulled the gun out, or if all the horses had been killed, drivers and cannoneers on ropes and at wheels hauled and heaved to save the piece from capture. As battle losses drained the South's horse supply,[123] the Confederate artillery resorted to a daring expedient. Certain picked teams were stationed well to the front during close engagements. When their drivers sighted the sleek horses of a Union battery, they rushed forward and in a whooping roundup herded them back into the Gray lines. "This method was often successful and caused the drivers of a battery to become as active in combat as their gunners." [124]

The North's horse artillery, like its cavalry, was overshadowed by the South's in the first years of the war. Exploits of the latter under its spirited young commanders stand among the most stirring annals of the gunner's arm. Supporting Stuart's and Ashby's horsemen on raids and in battle, the horse batteries frequently charged with the cavalrymen. In the Valley campaign Robert Preston Chew galloped his guns forward behind a thin line of cavalry in an onslaught upon enemy horse massed on a turnpike. As the screen fanned off to the flanks, Chew unlimbered and went into action at one hundred yards, turning the stone-walled road into a veritable slaughter pen. Pelham, greatest horse artilleryman of them all, led a hell-for-leather charge of his own at Fleetwood, Virginia, in 1862. Putting a howitzer in a concealed position on a hill in advance of his cavalry supports, he routed Union horsemen in the valley below with rapid fire. Then he swept down on the fugitives with his mounted cannoneers in a headlong gallop and captured a standard, prisoners, arms, and horses.

Stonewall Jackson raided Harper's Ferry September 15, 1862. That old artilleryman placed seventy guns on the hills commanding the town. Their fire bought him seventy-three enemy cannon, some of them sorely needed rifles, when he captured the Federal arsenal. For his expenditure of ammunition it was an excellent trade, even without the bonus he collected; eleven thousand prisoners and thirteen thousand stands of arms.

Two days later Lee, invading Maryland, fought McClellan at Antietam (Sharpsburg).

It was the bloodiest battle of the war, with Union losses reaching 12,400 and the Confederates' more than 8,000. Twice during forty-eight desperate hours of attack and counterattack, battery and counterbattery, general and staff officers served guns whose crews were wiped out or reduced to one or two men.

Cannon in the facing hills thundered and battered away at each other, shells screaming high above Antietam Creek. Every wall in the town of Sharpsburg echoed to their roar. Forward into action galloped the light artillery in close support of advancing infantry. Batteries from New Hampshire, New York, Rhode Island, Pennsylvania, regulars, and others, kept a rendezvous with the guns of Pelham, Pegram, and Stephen Lee. Guidons snapping in the wind, drivers whipping lathered horses, cannoneers clinging for dear life to their seats on bounding limbers and ammunition chests, they swung into the battle lines. Infantry charged, eager to take them. At pistol range the muzzles of Napoleons, the equivalent of huge sawed-off shotguns, belched canister. Rank after rank was swept out of existence. No wonder Gatlings and other newly developed machine guns saw little service in this war of terrible infighting. Point-blank canister was "murderous beyond belief." Yet at Antietam, as on many another field, heroic infantrymen came on over the bodies of their slain. Cannoneers stood them off or pulled out. If the charge had driven in too close to let them load and fire again or to limber and escape, they died around their guns under a leaden hail of minnie balls or stabbing bayonets.

Battery B, 4th U.S. Artillery, would long remember Antietam. Hotly engaged with sharpshooters in a cornfield, it lost nine killed and thirty-one wounded, including its captain, out of a complement of one hundred. It was still holding its ground when an incident took place that gave the battery a cherished tradition. Its former commander, John Gibbon, now a brigadier general of Volunteers, galloped up and vaulted out of his saddle to help man a piece whose crew had been whittled down to a point where it could no longer be served. In full uniform, a conspicuous target for enemy riflemen, he took the places of both the fallen gunner and Number One. When the battery was finally forced to withdraw, it retreated without the loss of a gun or caisson, though several carriages had only two horses left.

In another part of the field a Confederate battery was in similar straits. Most of its cannoneers and drivers casualties, it stood helpless in the face of an oncoming attack, with the place and moment critical. As opportunely as Gibbon, General Longstreet and his staff arrived. While "Old Pete" acted as horse-holder, his officers ran to the silent guns. The fire of the two they were able to man, together with the bayonets of a regiment whose cartridge boxes were empty, beat off the assault and held the line.

McClellan sent division after division to be shattered by the deadly fire of Rebel riflemen entrenched in a sunken road called the Bloody Lane. Piecemeal attacks, gallant though they were, could not break Lee's center. But the Confederate commander's attempt to turn the Union right failed as signally, blasted back by fifteen Union batteries in line in the north wood and the fire of the heavy guns across the creek. For a third time the tide of battle was reversed when a Blue rush on Sharpsburg was repulsed by the advance guard of Jackson's troops, rejoining after the Harper's Ferry raid.

Hot guns cooled as the cannonading dwindled to defiant parting shots of a battle which Union artillerymen must have regarded with mixed emotions. The odds had been on their side: 273 pieces with longer range and heavier metal against the Confederates' 200. Yet they had failed to give adequate aid to their infantry by concentrating on the points of attack and, with certain exceptions, to advance field guns in close support as had their opponents. On the other hand, their overwhelming fire on counterattacks had staved off defeat, and their magnificent counterbattery had punished the enemy so terribly that it won a tribute from one of his best gunners. "Sharpsburg," declared Colonel Stephen Lee, "was Artillery Hell."

Gray ranks, no longer singing "Maryland, My Maryland," recrossed the Potomac unpursued. So much and no more could McClellan claim—he had fought a drawn battle, and the foe was in retreat. As Commander of the Army of the Potomac Little Mac was through; nothing remained but his futile attempt at self-justification by running against Abraham Lincoln for the Presidency. He had lost too many battles, too many men, too many guns. As his military epitaph, the ingenuous remark of a North Carolinian captured at Antietam can aptly serve.

While the prisoner was being marched to the rear, he paused to stare curiously at the *U.S.* marking on the barrels of Yankee cannon he passed. Finally he turned to his escort and drawled:

"Mister, you-all has got as many of these 'U.S.' guns as we-uns has."

Odds again strongly favored the North at Fredericksburg, December 13, 1862: 100,000 men versus 70,000, 321 cannon against 250. But in generalship the scales were again weighted more heavily on the side of the South. General Ambrose Burnside, taking over from McClellan, fell far shorter than his predecessor of being a match for Robert E. Lee.

It was Lee of the Mexican War, the engineer with a flair for artillery, who ruled the battle on the banks of the Rappahannock that cold winter's day. Marye's Hill crowned by his batteries was another Malvern, plus a sunken road at its base—a natural breastwork before which thousands of storm troops in blue would die. Pick-and-shovel men dug the Gray guns into the frozen ground, guns under Lee's strict orders not to duel with the longer-range Federal ordnance but to remain silent in their concealed positions until Burnside's infantry attacked.

Bridge the river, cross and assault, Burnside directed, disregarding upper fords by which Lee's flank might have been turned. The artillery must cover the pontoon crews and the army's crossing.

On Stafford Heights Henry Hunt massed his reserve artillery, begging more batteries from division commanders to fulfill his mission. They were lent reluctantly and only on his promise to return them immediately after the crossing was made. Covering the bridges, 149 rifled cannon on the high ground bellowed in a bombardment that drove a Rebel brigade from the town. Fire lifted to sweep the southern bank. Slowly, link by link, pontoons thrust out into the river until five boat spans were completed. Troops and rumbling batteries poured across them.

John Pelham took two Napoleons of his horse artillery and galloped down on a spearhead of three Union divisions advancing through the valley. Ravines and underbrush masked his coming. With the dash and verve for which he was celebrated he wheeled into position on the Union left flank and opened rapid fire at four hundred yards. Meade's and Doubleday's divisions halted and recoiled, facing left to meet the threat.

Stonewall Jackson, chary of praise, once had declared, "With a Pelham on each flank, I believe I could whip the world." This day a Pelham on one flank was enough to paralyze the whole Yankee advance with blasting volleys of canister. Six Union light batteries, joined by the heavies back on the heights, concentrated on the two pieces. One of Pelham's crews was composed of cannoneers of French descent from Mobile. Today, as they always did under the heaviest fire, they joked and sang "La Marseillaise" while they served their gun. Though counterbattery knocked out one of the Napoleons, Pelham kept the other in action, constantly shifting position when the enemy found the range. Twice Jeb Stuart's orders to his horse artilleryman to retire were answered: "Tell the General I can hold my ground." The third time Stuart made it peremptory. "Get back from destruction, you infernal, gallant fool, John Pelham!" Then and then only Pelham, his ammunition exhausted, obeyed. In one of the greatest artillery stands of all time he had held ten thousand men at bay for almost an hour, for most of it with one light gun.

The Confederacy suffered an irreparable loss when the twenty-four-year-old commander was killed the following March while taking part in a cavalry charge.

As Burnside launched a massed assault on Marye's Hill, Lee's concealed, entrenched batteries broke their silence. Cannon, from 12-pounders to 30-pounder Parrotts—"Long Toms"—lanced and leveled the blue ranks. Hunt's long-range guns on Stafford Heights, their fire now masked by their own infantry, could not help. Still the Union attack drove forward with superb valor under overwhelming shell fire from above and deadly musketry from the sunken road until the last of fourteen charges was shattered, and the fields beneath Marye's strewn with sixty-three hundred dead and wounded. Federal artillery covered the retreat across the river. The Union had lost another battle, a battle which never should have been fought on the lines Burnside chose, a defeat owing in large measure to the skilled employment of the enemy's inferior artillery.

Another campaign, another Yankee general. "Fighting Joe" Hooker led his army, 130,000 strong, toward the woods of Chancellorsville early in May of 1863. Cannon covered the crossing of the Rappahannock. Green woods swallowed column after column as Hooker flung four corps forward to strike the left flank of Lee's army of 60,000, a fifth to turn his right. Scouts, lines of skirmishers, long ranks broken by the trees and underbrush, pushed ahead. Nerves tautened with the sensation of hunting, prelude to battle in a forest, a lethal sport where the game is as deadly as the hunter. Eyes strained for the glint of gray and butternut-brown through the foliage, and ears for crackling rifle fire to shatter tense silence into bits.

Along with the infantry, the wilderness gulped guns of the divisions, guns that were only a portion of the mighty array of 404 pieces brought to Chancellorsville to oppose the Confederates' 224. Many had been left behind on the north bank of the river without the knowledge of Henry Hunt, chief of artillery.[125] Hooker had relegated him to administrative duties in the rear once the crossing had been made, and not until the second day of the battle was control restored to him. Meanwhile the mere five field officers of artillery available vainly strove with their green staffs to direct and mass the guns against the ably handled batteries of Pendleton and E. P.

Alexander. On the record of Joe Hooker, who had worn crossed cannon insignia with honor in Mexico, stands a damning indictment:

> If Hooker were open to criticism as a general in no other respect, the gross mismanagement of his artillery, the Federal arm *par excellence,* already famous the world over for the superiority of its material and the high efficiency of its officers and men, would appear to be inexcusable.[126]

Blue batteries entered another sort of artillery hell that day, when they forced their way over woodland trails and through dense growths of scrub oak and pine—drivers cursing the branches that lashed their faces like bullwhips, horses stumbling and falling, cannoneers struggling to unlimber in the narrow aisles and manhandle pieces through thickets. So limited were fields of fire that most of the battle was fought with canister at close ranges. Seldom were guns massed.

Behind the brow of a hill two pieces of the Richmond Howitzers prepared for action. Number Six of one crew opened the lid of an ammunition chest. One hand grabbed fuses to serve out; the other lifted from a shell compartment the battery's tiny mascot dog named "Stonewall." As the guns boomed, the little fellow capered around them, barking shrilly and keeping the spirits of the grinning cannoneers high with his antics. Shells fell on Yankee artillery, emerging into a clearing, and exploded one of its caissons. The wilderness echoed to the muffled roar of combat. Lee, staving off Hooker with two divisions, sent Jackson around the Union right in a daring and brilliant maneuver that won the day, though it cost the life of the great Stonewall, mortally wounded by his own troops, who mistook him and his staff for enemy cavalry.

Against the dark background of surprise, rout, and defeat shine the exploits of a half-forgotten captain of Union artillery.

"Leatherbreeches," they called him. Hubert Dilger was too old a horseman to wear the issue cloth that wore through after days in the saddle. At the outset of the war he had resigned from the German horse artillery and come to America to fight for the Union. Given command of an Ohio battery, he made it into the best in the XIth Corps. With his guns in position on the Federal right, he was making a reconnaissance well forward when Jackson's "foot cavalry" came boiling down the turnpike. Dilger, recognizing the gravity of the threat to the flank, instantly wheeled his mount and galloped back to Hooker's headquarters. They laughed off his report as a "yarn." The XIth Corps reprimanded him for spreading rumors. He rode back to fight his guns.

At his sharp order, cannoneers shifted trails, and the muzzles of his pieces swung northwest like six pointing fingers. Elevated to clear their infantry, they opened at half a mile on the leading Gray brigade. Two other batteries joined the cannonade, but there was no stemming the steady advance that swept back Blue regiments, caught utterly unprepared. Dilger, changing position to command the turnpike and bordering fields, soon found himself barring the approach alone. Infantry had fled, and both the other batteries were out of action, one forced to withdraw by exhaustion of its ammunition, the second's guns overrun and captured.

Jackson's cannon thundered, one bowling a bounding 6-pound round shot two thousand yards down the turnpike. Still Dilger stood fast. "There, for more than thirty minutes, singlehanded, he maintained his position, changing from shell to double charges of canister as the enemy filtered closer and closer through the scrub thickets in his front." [127] Then counterbattery and point-blank musketry forced him to order five of his guns to retire. He and the crew of the sixth piece, which had been unhorsed, dueled on with Rebel artillery on the pike, Dilger directing fire until his horse was hit and fell on him, injuring his leg. Now enemy riflemen swarmed over the gun, and Dilger ran, limping painfully down the road after his retreating crew, pursuers hot after him shouting for him to surrender. He was close to being overtaken when his orderly, young Private Ackley, galloped back, heaved his lamed captain up on his horse, sprang up behind him, and made good their escape.

Leatherbreeches was not through fighting. Rejoining his battery, he supported infantry in rifle pits, first with all five surviving pieces; then, sending four under his lieutenant back to a better position, with a lone gun again—he himself helping to serve it—he held the line.

With flanks caving in, that single gun, the sole piece of all the Federal artillery on the right still in action, checked Jackson's victorious assault for precious minutes. Its rapid blasts of canister swept back enemy horse batteries galloping up the turnpike. Blue infantry rallied on it, then streamed back, leaving it isolated. Not until Dilger and his gunners were almost cut off did they pull back their smoking weapon. Halting to load and fire again, making one determined stand after another, they covered the retreat of broken divisions. For the second time that day Dilger fought as gallant a rear-guard action as artillery annals record, a feat of arms surpassed neither by O'Brien at Buena Vista nor Pelham at Fredericksburg. He yielded the way, limbered and retired only after four Union regiments had established a firm line of resistance, supported by a strong force of reserve guns on Fairview Heights. There he reassembled his battery and continued in action through the night's desperate fighting.

The South cherishes the memory of its fine artillerymen. In bitter contrast, glaring example of the ingratitude of republics, stands the North's treatment of Hubert Dilger. Because he was foreign-born and a member of the XIth Corps, several times routed, that splendid battery commander remained a captain to the end of the war, though repeatedly recommended for promotion.[128]

Sedgwick's resolute drive to reach Lee's rear failed. Hooker had long since lost the battle when a round from a Confederate cannon thudded into the Chancellor house and stunned him with a brick. Casualties of his crushing defeat, seventeen thousand against the foe's twelve thousand, would have risen still higher if Hunt, freed at last to reach the field, had not shielded the retreat with his guns.

As an aftermath of Chancellorsville, authority was tardily given the Union chief of artillery to reorganize his disrupted arm.[129] Batteries were grouped in battalions, battalions in brigades. Horse artillery was increased. Efforts were made to repair the shortage of field officers, and gaps in the commissioned personnel of batteries were filled by transfer of officers from other branches. Fire power and the ability to wield it would tell heavily in July on the ridges around the little Pennsylvania town of Gettysburg.

Cannon stand today among the monuments of the peaceful park that was the battlefield of Gettysburg [130]—cannon to which less than a hundred years have lent an aspect of antiquity. It is not easy to picture them in the blazing action of those first few days of July, 1863, except during the rolling reverberations and lightning flashes of a summer thunderstorm. Then can be re-created their crashing discharges, flame-jetting muzzles, and crews in blue or gray busy with powder, shot, and rammer staff—whistling shells of counterbattery, roar of exploding caissons—infantry in assault and humming minnie balls—dead around the still-served guns—drivers, teams, and limbers in iron-shredded woods to the rear waiting command to gallop forward. As postlude, in the silence of the storm's end, like the cessation of the clamor of a cannonade, forever echo at Gettysburg Lincoln's majestic words. "The brave men, living and dead, who struggled here, have consecrated it far above our poor power to add or detract. The world will little note, nor long remember, what we say here, but it can never forget what they did here."

When General Lee marched north, he rehorsed his artillery from farms of the invaded countryside, for the South's supply of animal transport had begun to dwindle. With his three corps rolled 103 3-inch rifles, 107 Napoleons, 30 12-pound howitzers, some Parrott rifles, 4 6-inch Whitworth breechloaders—62 batteries, 248 guns. Arsenals of the Confederacy were able to provide him with no more than 150 rounds of ammunition per gun, not a little of it of poor quality. Those shortages and defects, with their bearing on the coming battle, were beyond Lee's remedy, but he had won other fields despite them. At Gettysburg some of his corps commanders and other subordinates failed him, letting artillery stand idle at crucial moments.

Lee's opponent at Gettysburg, George Gordon Meade, had, like Hooker whom he superseded, been an artilleryman. Unlike his predecessor, Meade understood the value of that arm, competently directed. He was the first Union general since McClellan to place in Henry Hunt the confidence he deserved. Under the artillery chief's able control 370 guns, mostly of caliber similar to the Confederates' but including heavier pieces, rumbled over the roads to Gettysburg. An innovation was the detail to each brigade of five hundred heavy artillerymen, armed as infantry, to guard transport and perform camp duties. Another was the assignment by every battery of a mounted orderly to brigade headquarters for liaison. Hunt furnished an average of 270 rounds for each gun and saw to it that

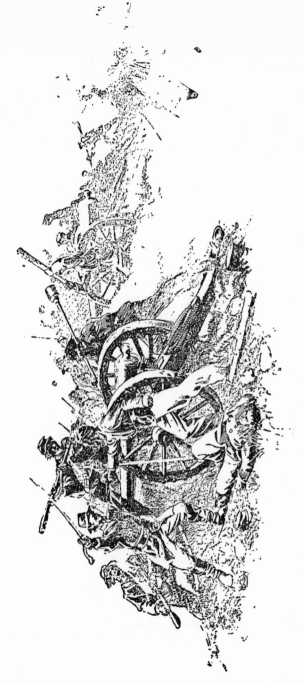

HAND-TO-HAND FIGHT FOR THE GUNS ON THE SECOND DAY OF GETTYSBURG (from *Battles and Leaders of the Civil War*, Vol. III)

dumps were accessible for replenishing caissons. In the three days' fighting 32,781 rounds, about 100 per gun, would be expended.[131] While Hunt demanded that ammunition not be wasted, he never went to the lengths of a corps artillery chief, who in the heat of combat when a battery commander asked for more shells, sternly admonished, "Young man, are you aware that every round you fire costs two dollars and sixty-seven cents?" Bearded General Hunt of eagle eye and firm-chiseled nose, thoroughly versed in his profession, a fine organizer and handler of guns in battle and of utmost coolness in action—he of the point-blank cannon duel at Chapultepec. Hunt has been called the greatest American artilleryman, and his was a large share of the glory of Gettysburg.[132]

Powder smoke billowed in the arena of Seminary and Cemetery Ridges and the commanding hills, Culp's and the Round Tops. It drifted through Devil's Den, the Peach Orchard, the cornfields, and along roads which led into the little town. On the Union right, nineteen-year-old Lieutenant Bayard Wilkeson with the fire of his Battery G, 4th U.S. Artillery, blocked the advance of a Confederate division until its commander ordered two batteries to concentrate on the mounted officer. Wilkeson fell mortally wounded, his horse killed; his guns retreated.

Battery B of the same regiment watched the tips of Rebel color staffs coming over the low ridge to its front, then bayonet points, then the Johnnies themselves. Remembering honors won at Buena Vista and at Antietam, it stood to its guns, facing them at obliques in two half-batteries in defense of the Cashtown Pike against enveloping Gray waves. Orders came, quick and sharp. "Load—canister—double!" Rammer heads thumped in bores. "Ready. By piece—at will—fire!" An officer ran from piece to piece, cheering on the crews, yelling, "Feed it to 'em, God damn 'em, feed it to 'em!" The very guns seemed to a young cannoneer, "Cub" Buell, to become things of life—not implements, but comrades.[133] Blasting charges from the muzzles of Napoleons and bullets of supporting infantry raked the road. In the rapid tempo of the firing, water in buckets turned black as ink from swabbing powder-fouled bores, and leather thumbstalls, stoppering scorching vents, burned to crisps. Steadily "B" served its guns, though murderous musketry from three sides splintered carriage wheels, drove horses mad with wounds and terror, and cut

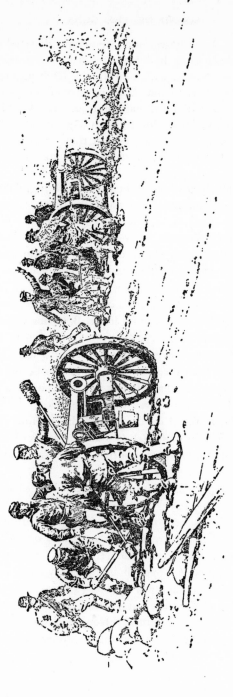

UNION GUNS IN ACTION (from *Battles and Leaders of the Civil War*, Vol. II)

down cannoneers. A badly wounded lieutenant directed the fire of a smoothbore whose crew had been reduced to its corporal and Numbers One and Three, with two drivers fetching ammunition. When at last the battery could hold its ground no longer, teams trotted up under a redoubled hail of lead. "Hook on!" and the pieces were limbered. Horses dropped and were cut out of traces, drivers were shot from their saddles, but they saved all their guns. Captain Stewart, last to leave, blazed back at pursuers with his revolver.

During the night following the first day's fighting, General Hunt ordered up guns and ammunition from his artillery reserve. Forward moved the fine brigade of Colonel Freeman McGilvery with four batteries from Massachusetts, New York, and Pennsylvania. Hunt personally posted many of the guns of the first line and reserve, often without the aid of staff officer or a flag-bearer to mark his presence for messengers. Once, after a reconnaissance on foot, he had to force his way through a gulch full of panic-stricken horned cattle, stampeded by shell fire, to regain his horse. Batteries, occupying positions he chose, performed marvelous feats of driving in the passage of chasms and ascents of steep, rocky hills. Guns were heaved and lifted by hand over final yards. Some, hemmed in by boulders, must stay where they were and fight it out in the event of a sudden assault, but their fields of fire were worth the risk.

Desperate fighting raged on the second day around the bases of the Round Tops and in the Peach Orchard, as Lee's divisions thrust ahead. Lines of Blue infantry stubbornly resisted, and cannon smoke swirled through the fruit trees.

John Bigelow's 9th Massachusetts Battery had marched fifteen miles from the artillery reserve to reach the field. When Bugler Reed blew assembly, drivers were mounted within five minutes, and the battery moved at a lively trot toward the sound of the guns. Near the Trostle house, about two hundred yards back of the Peach Orchard, it unlimbered and opened, immediately under heavy enemy fire—artillery and sharpshooters. The 9th's shrapnel blew up two limber chests and silenced the guns of two opposing batteries, then swung to spray oncoming infantry. Sweeping salvos cleared the battery's front, but its flanks soon were left without support. Bigelow did not realize he was completely isolated until the brigade commander rode up.

"All of Sickles' men have withdrawn," Colonel McGilvery called out. "You're alone on the field without supports of any kind. Limber up and get out."

Bigelow answered, "If I do that, sharpshooters on my left front will shoot us all down. I'll have to retire by prolonge and firing."

Quick hands fastened prolonge ropes to pintles of limbers and to gun trails. Cannoneers hauling hard, they made a four-hundred-yard fighting retreat, halting at intervals to batter back a battle line of Mississippians with solid shot and stave off sharpshooters with canister. Like O'Brien at Buena Vista they retired by recoil, with the ropes keeping the guns in alignment. They were far enough back to limber when McGilvery ordered them to make another stand. There was a gap of fifteen hundred yards in the line, he said, with no reserves. The 9th must hold it at all hazards until he could find some infantry and form a second line of artillery.

Far out in front, without supports of any kind, the gallant survivors of the Massachusetts battery held firm. At one piece the gunner was hit as he was about to fire. Another man, jumping to replace him, dropped, then a third—a fourth jerked the lanyard. Lieutenant Erickson, a bullet through his lungs, his mouth frothing blood, but refusing to leave the guns, was shot through the head. Cannoneers beat off Rebel charges, braining assailants with rammer staff and handspike. Ammunition chests were almost empty, and casualties were mounting toward their appalling total of one officer killed, one mortally and one seriously wounded out of four present; six out of seven sergeants killed or wounded; twenty-eight out of sixty cannoneers lost; eighty of eighty-eight horses killed or disabled.

Bigelow still was keeping four guns in action when six sharpshooters took deliberate aim at him. He stopped two bullets, his horse two. As he slipped from his saddle and his orderly ran to help him, he "saw the Confederates swarming in on our right flank, some standing on the limber chests and firing at the gunners, who were still serving their pieces; the horses were all down; overhead the air was alive with missiles from batteries, which the enemy had now placed on the Emmetsburg Road, and, glancing anxiously to the rear, I saw the longed-for batteries just coming into position on the high ground, 500 yards away. I then gave orders for the small remnant of the four gun detachments to fall back. My battery had delayed the enemy 30 precious minutes, from 6 to 6:30 P.M., and its sacrifice had not been in vain." [134] The wounded captain, held on his horse, was slowly escorted from the field under heavy fire by Bugler Reed, who received a Medal of Honor.

Now to Colonel E. P. Alexander, Longstreet's artillery chief, came a stirring moment such as few of the gunners' arm have known. As Gray infantry flooded through the Peach Orchard, he ordered his six batteries limbered to the front and led the full battalion in a charge.

"For 500 yards the foaming horses dashed forward, under whip and spur, the guns in perfect alignment, and the carriages bounding over the fields," runs Colonel Wise's eloquent description in *The Long Arm of Lee*.[135] "Every officer and non-commissioned officer rode at his post, and not a team swerved from the line, except those which were struck down by a blizzard of Federal shell. Fortunately most of the enemy's projectiles overshot their mark, and as the great line of six batteries with over 400 horses reached the position abandoned by the enemy, 'action front' was executed as if by a single piece. Hardly had the teams wheeled, and the trails of the pieces cleared the pintle-hooks when again a sheet of flame burst from the 24 guns of Alexander's magnificent battalion.

"Small wonder then that Alexander cherished no regret at having declined the command of a brigade of infantry. Surely there was glory enough to be found at the head of such a command as he led across the fields and into action in front of Little Round Top!"

But at sunset Blue infantry and guns still held the high ground. Back ebbed the Gray assaults, and the sounds of battle faded. Pickets out, the two armies mustered their forces for decision on the morrow. In the artillery lines both sides devoted the night to repairs, replenishment of ammunition, and reorganization of batteries that had lost heavily in men and horses.

The third day. General Lee resolved to attack Cemetery Hill, which might have been taken the first day if one of his corps commanders had followed orders to press forward and storm it, "if practicable." Because Lieutenant General Richard S. Ewell had then considered an assault impracticable, the hill was now about to justify

ALEXANDER'S BATTALION GALLOPING INTO POSITION AT GETTYSBURG (from *Battles and Leaders of the Civil War*, Vol. III)

its name as an open sepulcher for many Confederate dead. The Union guns would blanket its green slopes with bodies in gray and butternut brown.

Those guns were ready when daylight revealed to their chief, General Hunt, masses of enemy artillery going into position, forming a two-mile line planted thick with cannon. He issued orders to his gunners: Concentrate on one battery at a time until you silence it—fire deliberately—waste no ammunition—save rounds to meet the assault. Those orders had just been personally given to the last battery on Little Round Top when a signal gun loosed the Confederate cannonade, and the Union guns boomed in answer.

> Looking up the valley toward Gettysburg, the hills on either side were capped with crowns of flame and smoke, as 300 guns, about equally divided between the two ridges, vomited their iron hail upon each other [a witness remembered].[136] Dense clouds of smoke settled over the valley, through which the shells went hissing and screaming on their errand of death. Numbers of these from opposite directions exploded midway over the valley, apparently with venomous impatience, as they met each other in mid-air, lighting up the clouds with their snake-like flashes.

At noon the artillery fire swelled into the greatest volume ever heard on this continent. One hundred and sixty-six Union guns on Cemetery Ridge, soon to be increased to 220 by Hunt with pieces from the reserve, traced the half-rim of a gigantic, blazing wheel. Its spokes were the paths of projectiles from 172 Confederate cannon replying. Many of them were not properly sited to deliver vital cross fire. Fifty-six guns of the reserve were almost completely inactive, while battalions of the three Confederate corps failed in co-ordinating and concentrating their counterbattery. These were blunders that brought fatal consequences, "baring the breast of the infantry assault to the guns of the defenders." [137] The Southern batteries' fire preparation for the attack was nevertheless tremendous.

Thunder and lightning of battery and counterbattery. A young lieutenant of Union infantry, Frank Aretas Haskell, General Gibbon's aide, later described those cataclysmic hours in glowing prose that was martial poetry.[138] He wrote of a storm of shells, "incessant, all-pervading, in the air above our heads, on the ground at our feet, remote, near, deafening, ear-piercing, astounding; and these hailstones are massy iron charged with exploding fire. ... [Our] guns are great infuriate demons, not of the earth, whose mouths blaze with snaky tongues of living fire, and whose murky breath, sulphur-laden, rolls around us and along the ground, the smoke of Hades. These grimy men, rushing, shouting, their souls in frenzy, plying the dusky globes and the igniting spark, are in their league, and but their willing ministers. The projectiles shriek long and sharp. They hiss, they scream, they growl, they sputter,—all sounds of life and rage; and each has its different note and all are discordant. Was ever such a chaos of sound before?"

As cannoneers in blue increased the fury of their fire, Haskell watched them stand to their guns under enemy retaliation.

We see the solid shot strike axle, or pole, or wheel, and the tough iron and heart of oak snap and fly like straws. The great oaks there by Woodruff's guns heave down their massy branches with a crash, as if the lightning had smote them. The shells swoop down among the battery horses, standing apart; a half dozen horses start, they tremble, their legs stiffen, their vitals and blood smear the ground. And these shells have no respect for men either. We see the poor fellows hobbling back from the crest, or unable to do so, pale and weak, lying on the ground, with the mangled stump of an arm or leg dripping their life blood away, or with a cheek torn open or shoulder smashed. And many, alas! hear not the roar as they stretch upon the ground with upturned faces and open eyes, though a shell should burst at their very ears. ...

Only a few yards off a shell exploded over an open limber box of Cushing's battery, and almost at the same instant a shell over a neighboring box. In both boxes the ammunition blew up with an explosion that shook the ground, throwing fire and splinters and shells far into the air all around, and destroying several men.

Incoming shells seemed to Haskell to hang suspended for long moments in the air above before they burst. "Their blind fury shattered ambulances full of wounded men, riddled hospitals and strewed the ground around the house that was Meade's headquarters with dead horses of officers and orderlies."

Taking punishment, inflicting it in full measure, the Union gun crews served their pieces with the steadiness of the veterans they were. "Sponge—thumb the vent—ram—correct the aim—trail right—trail left." Each command was smoothly and steadily executed. A lieutenant watched one of his gunners lying—

> stretched along the trail, setting off his elevations by 1, 2 and 3 finger breadths, just as he measured his whiskey, in happier days, and checking every move of his cannoneers. Suddenly a round shot carried away the head of No. 1, and his body fell across the gun breech—blood and brains spattering and splashing the gunner from head to waist. Deliberately, the gunner wiped the ugly mess from his face, cleared his eyes, lifted the corpse from the gun, laid it on the sod, resumed his post and continued operations with scarcely the loss of a count.

The lieutenant, in after years when he commanded a regiment, was to tell his young officers, "That was discipline—the discipline that every man must acquire before he can call himself a field artilleryman." [139]

Gray storm troops assembled in the woods for the final fling of the gage of battle. As Pickett's men made ready for their historic charge, Longstreet, in grave doubt that the assault ordered by Lee could succeed, shifted heavy responsibility onto the shoulders of his artillery chief. Alexander, judging from the effect of his preparatory fire, was to "advise" Pickett whether to attack, then to tell him "when the moment offers." Reluctantly the artilleryman finally replied, "General, when our artillery fire is at its best, I shall order Pickett to charge." It had to be touch and go. Ammunition would not last long.

Crashing salvos swelling into drumfire, sweeping the crest. Diminuendo by Yankee guns, seemingly silenced. Alexander's urgent message to Pickett: "For God's sake, come quick . . . or my ammunition won't let me support you properly." Brigades and following batteries clear-

CANNON SCOURGED THE RETREAT (from *Battles and Leaders of the Civil War*)

ing the woods and marching steadily forward in a charge over five hundred yards of open ground that was valor's self.

Once more smoke and flame leaped along the opposite crest where Union artillery reopened with a roar, joined by fresh batteries from the reserve. Round shot and bursting shell were iron flails, wielded under Hunt's eye, beating down rank on rank. Red and blue battle flags fell, rose again, slanted forward in the face of the storm. Sun flashed on bayonet and upswept sword. Over rail fence, stone wall, and mounting dead, the superbly gallant charge came on. Deadly cross fire raked it until cannon on the Union right fell silent, long-range ammunition too soon spent by a corps commander's order, contrary to those of Hunt, who believed all his life that the assault would have been crushed in mid-career if his directions had not been countermanded.

Still the charge struggled on, veering to the left, shredded by canister. Its spearhead pierced the stone wall in a last desperate thrust. Rebel riflemen flung themselves on the smoking cannon, firing point-blank, bayonets stabbing, taking vengeance. Battery commanders and their crews died around their guns. Lieutenant Alonzo H. Cushing, Battery A, 4th Artillery, fell with a bullet through his head as he fired a charge of canister from his last surviving gun. Then the Blue infantry closed in. Short, furious combat, and Pickett's spent remnants ebbed back. All along the front Gray troops, who had done their utmost, reeled back down the hill, back from "the high watermark of the Confederacy." In their bloody recessional, cannon scourged them, exacting a still costlier toll of the retreat than of the advance. Lee retraced his course southward, and Meade slowly followed.

"Thus they fought along that fiery line at Gettysburg." [140]

CHAPTER 8

Field and Siege Piece

●●●

Infantry and cavalry require the aid of artillery for specific purposes: to destroy walls, earthworks, and other means of cover; to set fire to, or render untenable, farm buildings, villages, woods and other lodgements, etc. Its presence alone, if known to be powerful, often prevents an enemy from resorting to such defenses. Thus set free for its primary objectives, the artillery is used in the open field to commence battles, to prepare the way and aid in attacks, to protect the movement of our own troops, and to hinder those of the enemy, to pursue and prevent the enemy from rallying, or to cover our own retreat.

> GENERAL HENRY J. HUNT, *Journal of the Military Service Institution of the U.S.*[141]

When a couple of batteries are attached to a division, every infantryman in that division regards the guns of those batteries as his personal estate or private property. He may not care a continental about the artillerymen who work those guns. But the guns themselves have been placed in his care; he has been made their guardian; he knows that if the enemy tries to take them, the Cannoneers themselves can do but little to defend them, and that, therefore, it is the infantryman who must always protect the guns of the artillery, or, failing to do so, must incur the reproach for losing them.

> AUGUSTUS BUELL, *The Cannoneer* [142]

●●

Heavy artillerymen manned the big guns in the defenses of Washington and the coastal forts north to Maine where it was deemed necessary in 1861 to build granite Fort Popham to protect the Kennebec River against Confederate Navy raiders.[143] Those gunners missed the lively action seen by their Southern counterparts in the batteries of Gulf and Atlantic ports, covering the swift steamers which ran their invaluable cargoes through the Union blockade.

Yet the Federal heavies came into their own at Vicksburg. There the fire of their mortars, up to 13-inchers, 10-inch Columbiads, and 32- and 42-pounders, many borrowed from the Navy, was tremendous in volume and effect. They counterbatteried large-caliber pieces in the Vicksburg works such as "Whistling Dick," so called from the sound made by its projectiles in flight,[144] and paved the way for the storming of the stronghold, long and stoutly defended by General John Pemberton. When General Grant's assault columns and Admiral Porter's gunboats finally reduced the town on the high bluff on July 4, 1863, and opened the Mississippi, 30,600 men, 172 cannon, and 60,000 stands of arms were surrendered.

In the attack on Charleston, South Carolina, later that month Union crews fired a mighty 300-pound Parrott whose shells all but demolished Fort Sumter. Artillery companies achieved a notable engineering feat when they put a second big rifle, a 200-pounder (8-inch), into position to fire into the city at a range of five miles. Two and a half miles of railroad track were laid through the marshes, and a pine log platform was built on piling. There "The Swamp Angel," as her crew christened her, was emplaced and barricaded by thirteen thousand sandbags. Twenty-pound powder charges flung her shells, some of them incendiary, into Charleston where an uproar of bells and whistles, followed by indignant protests against "barbarity," acknowledged hits. Though "The Swamp Angel" was disabled by the premature explosion of her thirty-sixth round, she had fulfilled her mission by damaging morale and drawing considerable enemy fire. Charleston, however, held out despite the capture of Battery Wagner and the shattering of Sumter.

Elsewhere heavy artillerymen were embittered by inglorious inactivity. Train guard and camp fatigue at Gettysburg were at least field duty, but most unwelcome to the 1st Maine Heavy Artillery, among others, was the soft detail to the Washington forts. Only the "coffee-coolers" in the battery were content with the luxury of three square meals a day, good beds, and nothing to do but parade and stand to at silent guns. Most of the officers and the rank and file

chafed under it. They had not " 'listed to get kilt," but they had
joined up to fight and risk it. For months they fretted, sulked, and
cursed their lot. Like other heavies, the men of the 1st Maine
cheered when they were finally ordered to the front where they took
a tough ribbing, as they marched up in their neat, fresh uniforms,
some with two knapsacks strapped to their backs.

"Brought your trunks along?" combat troops jibed at them. "Got
a full supply of paper collars? There's plenty of fortifications for
you boys to man yonder in the brush."

While the heavies, brass shoulder-scales gleaming, marched singing
behind their bands, light artillerymen joined the foot troops in
taunting them. "Why, dearest, did you leave your earthworks behind you?" Wounded showed them bloody gashes, shattered limbs,
and dead men lying in the fence corners, and called out derisively:
"That's what you will catch up yonder in the woods!" Blanched,
sober-faced, the heavies, armed as infantry, marched on into battle.

Soon the men from the forts made the scoffers swallow their sneers.
"They fought with a steadiness and determination that could not
be excelled," a light gunner, who had himself pitched in with a
rifle, acknowledged. "The whole army honored them." The Maine
battery went in at Spotsylvania 147 strong; after a month of fighting
only seven answered roll call. Recruited back up to a strength of 900,
in a charge at Petersburg it took the most severe losses of any regiment in a single engagement of the entire war—632 killed and
wounded in less than half an hour. In the Wilderness, at Spotsylvania, and at Cold Harbor the 6th, 7th, and 15th New York Heavy
Artillery also proved their fighting quality and suffered considerable
casualties. True enough they manned fortifications, but those were
Rebel earthworks, taken at the bayonet point.[145]

The Wilderness, old battleground of Chancellorsville, held grim
memories for the Army of the Potomac, but Lee maneuvered Grant
into facing him there (May 5-7, 1864), as he had Hooker. Grue-
some testimony for new troops dotted the fields and clearings: thousands of bleached skulls and bones of the hastily buried.

There was savage infighting again over thousands of acres of
tangled scrub forest and interlaced underbrush, a North American
version of the clutching vines and knife-sharp grasses of Bataan and

New Guinea descendants of these troops in blue or gray would en-
counter in wars to come—country difficult for infantry but far worse
for cavalry and artillery. General Grant, believing he had more
cannon than could be effectively employed on such terrain, made
a decision in accordance with general practice in such circumstances.

> Artillery is a very burdensome luxury where it cannot be
> used [he wrote]. Before leaving Spotsylvania, therefore, I sent
> back to the defense of Washington over 100 pieces of artil-
> lery, with the horses and caissons. This relieved the road
> over which we were to march of more than 200 six-horse
> teams, and still left us more artillery than could be advan-
> tageously used.[146]

Furthermore, he reduced the pieces of batteries he kept from six
to four, and his guns on hand were not wholly utilized, either in the
Wilderness or in the two following conflicts. "Fewer were engaged
in any one battle than remained idle, and this in spite of Hunt
with his skill and ability." [147] Grant, who had manhandled a mountain howitzer up into a belfry to rake the streets of Mexico City,
neither showed nor encouraged such artillery enterprise in the Virginia woods. It was the southerners who carried on the tradition
of Louisbourg, Trenton, and Cerro Gordo. James Warner Bellah
voiced it in The Valiant Virginians: "Never say a cliff's inaccessible;
just say difficult for horse artillery." Gunners in gray forced their
Napoleons and rifled pieces through choked trails and up hills
bristling with trees and brush. They brought them into action where
they were most needed, as in the instance of Colonel William T.
Poague's great stand, first with a single gun, then with his entire
battalion, to beat back a Federal charge.

In sullen frustration the Army of the Potomac recoiled from a
stricken field of blazing brush where, flames driving back attempts
at rescue, hundreds of wounded burned to death. Grant marched
by the flank, threatening Richmond. Lee, sideslipping, confronted
him at Spotsylvania Court House. Again they fought in wooded
country, but here trees were larger; mighty oaks, twenty-two inches
thick, were hewn down by bullets of the furious fusillades around
the Bloody Angle. Once Union troops were close to victory, for
Rebel divisional artillery in that salient had been withdrawn by

night on Lee's order to prepare for a sudden movement planned
for the next day. Hancock's surprise attack through a dawn fog
bit into the Angle, caught enemy batteries in column hastening
back into position, and swept over them and captured twenty guns.
But the Gray infantry rallied, was reinforced, and held.

Spotsylvania cost Grant seventeen thousand casualties; Lee lost
only eight thousand. Among the fallen was Lieutenant Thomas
Goodman, a replacement in Battery B, 4th U.S. Artillery, who met
a death as appropriate to an artilleryman as that of a cavalryman
killed in a galloping charge. While directing the fire of his section,
shrapnel burst above him, and a ball drove the crossed cannon insignia on his cap into his head, inflicting a mortal wound.[148] Not
long afterward another unusual incident occurred when the Richmond Howitzers began shelling a house sheltering Yankee sharpshooters. Two women, one carrying a baby and leading a child,
emerged from the building. Adjutant Stiles of the Howitzers rushed
forward and hurried them back to his lines, taking the infant from
its mother's arms. As he passed his battery, he halted to order
firing resumed and remained to conduct it. The baby, cooing and
enjoying the racket, pulled at his beard, and Stiles had almost forgotten his burden when a laughing cannoneer called his attention
to it, and he left the guns to return the little artilleryman to his
mother.[149]

Marching and maneuvering, clashing in battle, the generals
played their deadly chess, with Richmond as the prize. Grant, the
Charles Martel of his day, hammered away, suffering heavy losses
the North could endure, exacting a lesser toll the South could not
afford. At Cold Harbor, June 3, 1864, he lost fifty-six hundred men
in a futile frontal assault on entrenchments, mostly from the deadly
cross fire of Alexander's cannon. Meanwhile two stirring artillery
actions took place, a rear-guard fight and a charge. While they were
only moves by pawns in the game of grand tactics and strategy, they
upheld the highest tenets of the gunners' arm.

At the Battle of New Market, May 15, 1864, where the young
cadets of Virginia Military Institute made their valiant assault,
Federal General Franz Sigel's line was broken. Part of his army
fled in rout along the Valley Pike, Rebel regiments pressing forward
to catch the disorganized mass jammed in the bottleneck of a stone

bridge across the Shenandoah River. With nothing barring the pursuit, heavy casualties and captures appeared inevitable.

First Lieutenant Henry A. Du Pont, graduated at the head of his class at West Point in '61, commanded Battery B, 5th U.S. Artillery, in reserve that afternoon. In the sultry heat he had unharnessed and watered his thirsty teams, then harnessed and hitched and was standing by. When the Blue ranks gave way in disorder and confusion, orders sent the battery galloping to the front. Du Pont, disregarding contradictory directions from excited staff officers, took matters in his own hands and posted his guns. He stationed them in three platoons of two pieces each, under his lieutenants and first sergeant, in echelon, at intervals along the turnpike. They held a comparatively narrow defile, their right flank protected by the Shenandoah curving down toward the bridge, their left by Smith's Creek.

As Du Pont's forward pair of guns took position and were prepared for action, he poured their fire into the low-lying haze of battle smoke that marked the advancing enemy. The crimson flare of bursting shells rent the white curtain and rocked back the pursuit in sudden check. While the scattered column rallied on a crest and waited for reinforcement, one of its officers watched with admiration the smooth precision and accurate firing of the gun crews below; he would remember and praise them when he met Du Pont by chance years later.

The advance regained momentum, red rifle streaks stabbing downward. B Battery's first platoon limbered and galloped back to a post in rear of the third. Its second took over the defense, Du Pont directing its gun-laying until it, too, was forced to retire. Now it was the third's turn, then the first's again. Successively each platoon, with beautifully adjusted fire, built a barrier of exploding shrapnel in front of the oncoming infantry and brought to a standstill two light batteries, four guns of horse artillery, and two pieces of the cadet battery, which had been rushed forward to bombard the mass at the bridge. Balked in that objective, they concentrated on the Yankee gunners but failed to hit the fleeting target of the rapidly shifting platoons. For four hours Du Pont's battery, singlehanded, held the pass, a Virginia Thermopylae. At dusk it retreated over the Shenandoah span, destroyed it, and rejoined the army it had saved.

Lieutenant Du Pont's bravery and that of his men was not the prime feature of that memorable rear-guard combat. "Courageous action is expected of a battery commander." [150] Later at Cedar Creek he would be awarded a Medal of Honor for individual heroism. Most notable were his quick decision, ability to estimate situation and terrain, initiative, and judgment in risking only two guns at a time. Displaying those qualities, he had fulfilled artillery missions specified by General Hunt: ". . . to protect the movement of our own troops, and to hinder those of the enemy . . . to cover our own retreat."

Another Battery B, that of the 4th U.S. Artillery, veteran of Antietam and Gettysburg, made the gallant charge at Bethesda Church, June 2, 1864. [151]

General Charles Griffin, who had fought so splendidly at First Bull Run as an artillery captain, watched a Rebel battery wheel into position in a clearing and open fire on his infantry. He beckoned to Stewart, B's commander. The latter, turning his horse to ride over, called out to his men waiting beside their pieces in column.

"This means us, boys. Drivers, mount! Cannoneers, mount! Attention!"

Griffin asked, "James, can you go into battery under that fire?"

"Yes, sir. Where shall I unlimber?"

"Suit yourself about that, but keep an eye on your supports. I would like to see that battery silenced."

"I will shut it up, sir."

A choice of two positions confronted Stewart. One near the church would necessitate firing over his own infantrymen at a range of half a mile. The second demanded a dash right up into the skirmish line and going into action a matter of hundreds of feet from the muzzles of the enemy guns. Stewart never hesitated. He spurred back to the head of his column, drew his saber, flourished it in a moulinet, and shouted:

"Forward, ho! Trot! Gallop!"

Straight down the pike toward the front line the battery thundered. Swishing case and canister cut into its dust cloud. Stewart, five or six yards ahead, roared back through the tumult, "Come on, boys! Follow me! Charge!!!!" There was no such command in the light artillery manual, but they knew what it meant. They charged, every driver low over his horse's neck, whipping and yelling—every cannoneer clinging desperately to handles of limber chests and bouncing six inches high as wheels hit ruts.

Slow up now. Yonder lay the ground. "The Old Man" volleyed orders. "Action front! Right section load solid shot and case alternately. No. 1 gun, left section, load common shell. Cut fuses one second. 'Old Bess' [that was the left gun], give 'em double canister. Fire by piece! Sock it to 'em!" Veteran crews handled their 12-pounder Napoleons like horse pistols. Skirmishers on both flanks cheered the blazing cannon, and the crackle of their musketry redoubled.

The battery, unscathed by shelling on the road, began to suffer. Eleven men dropped during the first minute of unlimbering and loading. The count rose to fourteen men and a dozen horses, but survivors served the guns fast. Though enveloped in dense smoke, they had the direction, marked by the track of wheels in recoil, and the range, twelve hundred feet, had been estimated perfectly. In three minutes they felt the enemy's fire slacken. Eight or ten more, and it ceased entirely. Lifting of the smoke cloud revealed the Rebel battery standing dismantled and deserted, bodies strewn about the pieces. Captain Stewart, his promise to shut them up kept, begged the General to be allowed to capture them. "If you will advance your skirmish line to cover me," he said, "by God I'll take some of my teams and haul them in myself with my men." Griffin refused, since no general forward movement had been ordered, and the cost in lives would have been heavy. Under cover of night the battered guns were withdrawn. But "B" of the 4th had added another battle honor to the long list begun at Buena Vista.

Transported by waterways, a siege train of 188 pieces converged on Petersburg, Virginia, as Grant drove toward Richmond from the south in the summer of 1864. Sturdy, hard-hitting 4½-inch Rodmans, 6-inch howitzers, 100-pounder Parrotts. An array of mortars presided over by a 13-inch, 17,000-pound monster, which would be mounted on a railroad flatcar; the thunderous flight and tremendous impact of its 200-pound projectiles, fired at a range of two and one-half miles, would win it the name of "The Dictator" or "Petersburg Express." With each big gun traveled one thousand rounds of ammunition—two hundred for a mortar—spare carriages, sling carts, battery wagons, forges. Landed, reserve artillery and quartermaster teams hauled them into position where they replaced fieldpieces.[152]

It was "shovel and shoot" now for artillerymen, with the long hard labor of the former a prerequisite. Along ten miles of breastworks emplacements for fifty-five batteries were constructed. Classic terms for fortifications were revived as troops toiled to make gabions (wicker frames filled with earth), the rows of sharpened stakes called "fraises" or "chevaux-de-frise," the interlaced branches of an abatis, mantelets of coiled rope, timbered palisades, barricades of thousands of sandbags, shelters known as "bombproofs." Back of the lines, ammunition, rations, forage, and all sorts of war materials (to be envied by hungry, short-supplied Confederates) heaped high. Huts, corrals, bakeries, even a steepled church were built. Signal towers rose, invaluable to Union gunners as observation posts.

Southerners paralleled the long lines of entrenchments and emplacements. The months-long siege of Petersburg, junction of strategic railways and gateway to Richmond, began as Grant's assaults were flung back, and he concluded he could not storm the enemy's works until the defense was worn down.

Sound of the guns day and night. Twenty-four soaring mortar bombs could often be counted in the air at one time. Through the roar of cannon cut the sharp *ping* of sharpshooters' bullets, dropping members of working parties, drilling men between the eyes who rashly exposed themselves in gaps or embrasures. Grandsons of these soldiers would see just such grim service in the trenches of France. In July Grant resorted to that expedient of a stubborn siege, a mining operation. Coal miners of the 48th Pennsylvania dug, timbered, and ventilated a tunnel which extended 586 feet to a point beneath a battery in a Confederate salient. They charged it with four tons of black powder and spliced two fuses in a 98-foot line to the magazine.

While four divisions were mustered to burst through the great aperture the explosion would tear, artillery spotters in the towers plotted the location of nearly every gun in the Rebel batteries. Eighty-one heavy cannon and mortars were laid on them, along with as many fieldpieces brought forward for a mighty bombardment to cover the assault. But observers had overlooked a sixteen-gun battalion in a sunken road, which was under strict orders from General Alexander to remain silent, its cannoneers to lie low. The muffled noises of Federal tunneling had been reported, and though countermines had been started, the able artillery chief had foresightedly determined to hold the strategically placed battalion in reserve for an emergency.

Early in the morning of July 30 the mine's fuse, timed to burn fifteen minutes, was lit. Those tense minutes passed, ticked on into an hour. Assault troops with fixed bayonets, gunners with lanyards taut, waited in suspense for the eruption. The enemy breastworks still stood, solid and forbidding. Then two supremely courageous soldiers, Lieutenant Jacob Douty and Sergeant Harry Rees of the 48th Pennsylvania, crawled into the tunnel, groped along its utter blackness, and found the fuse burned out at the splice. They relighted it and scrambled back to safety.

Eleven minutes, and the ground heaved up in volcanic fury. The awesome spectacle of the explosion burned itself into the memory of every witness. A Confederate artillery captain, William Gordon McCabe, thus vividly described it: [153]

> A slight tremor of the earth for a second, then the rocking as of an earthquake, and with a tremendous burst which rent the sleeping hills beyond, a vast column of earth and smoke shoots upward to a great height, its dark sides flashing out sparks of fire, hangs poised for a moment in mid-air, and then hurtling downward with a roaring sound, showers of stone, broken timbers, and blackened human limbs, subsides—the gloomy pall of darkening smoke flushing to an angry crimson as it floats away to meet the morning sun.

At least 278 men were killed or wounded. Two guns of the salient's battery were flung high into the air. In the defense lines gaped a crater 170 feet long, 60 to 80 feet wide, 30 deep.

A crashing cannonade caught up the echoes of the blast, sustained and carried them on in a continuous roar. Blue regiments rushed forward, down into the fuming breech. Few were destined to charge on up its slope. At the right, left, and rear of the yawning gap Gray riflemen rallied. For moments no artillery seconded them, since Union counterbattery was smothering opposition all along the front. Several guns close to the crater stood deserted, ordered abandoned by their young commander, his nerve broken by the explosion. Virginians manned one that could be brought to bear and poured its fire downward. Now Alexander's battalion, hidden in the sunken road, opened with deadly effect, beating back reinforcements for troops in the crater. Vainly General Hunt's big mortars searched for the battalion to silence it. Its sixteen guns under Colonel John C. Haskell flamed on in furious action. Sharpshooters, whittling down their crews, forced all but six to pull back. That half dozen, all served by volunteers, stood fast; their "cannoneers labored at their pieces like fiends." Now Haskell brought forward two mortar detachments and their weapons, so close to the chasm that charges of a few ounces of powder were sufficient to hurl their shells in arcs that dropped them into the huddled masses in the bloody excavation. While the leader of one of the storm divisions cowered in a bombproof, rifles and cannon of the defense turned the crater into an abattoir. The cost of the "miserable failure," as Grant styled it, was five thousand Union dead, wounded, and captured.

Grant hammered on, striking at flanks, cutting railroads, but Petersburg held out through a winter of stalemate. In the spring of '65 Lee assaulted Fort Stedman, took it, then lost it, his final attack shattered by the massed fire of the guns of Tidball's brigade. Petersburg fell at last. Listening to the final shots, a Confederate major of artillery,[154] risen from the ranks, read with his surviving men "The Soldier's Psalm," the Ninety-first. "Thou shall not be afraid for the terror by night . . . nor for the destruction that wasteth at noonday." On through Richmond retreated the Army of Northern Virginia, exodus lighted by burning warehouses, supply depots, and bridges. It was near the end.

Battling in the Valley, in the West, in the South. Sherman driving through to Atlanta and the sea, marching north and cutting a swath of devastation. Sheridan's cavalry, horse and field artillery, and infantry closing the cordon. A harvest of Gray cannon at Five Forks. Grant taking the surrender of Lee and his army at Appomattox Court House April 9, 1865.

A number of Confederate batteries had escaped the encirclement.

Some destroyed their guns, others buried theirs by the roadside. Many artillery horses, claimed by officers and men, were allowed to be kept under Grant's generous terms. Sixty-three of General Alexander's guns, their caissons, and exhausted, starving teams stood in a mile-long column at Appomattox, a melancholy symbol of defeat.

For the Army of the Potomac [155] in May, 1865, and for Sherman's Army of the West in June came days of glory: the grand reviews in Washington. Pennsylvania Avenue from the Capitol to the White House echoed to the blare of bands and flourishes of massed bugles, tread of marching feet, clatter of hoofs, and rumble of wheels, the cheers of spectators. Grief watched with Triumph. Eyes dimmed with tears for the many fallen in battle, for Abraham Lincoln, dead of an assassin's bullet. The long blue column, tattered banners flaunting, streamed down the avenue. Headquarters, the cavalry corps, the provost marshal's brigade, engineers with lumbering pontoons, regiment on regiment of veteran infantry, ambulances, artillery with cannon burnished and horse hides and harness gleaming.

An infantry officer in the reviewing stand, General Chamberlain, recognized passing batteries. Those were guns which had valiantly supported his regiment at Gettysburg. In surging memory he heard their cannonade once more above the cheers of the crowd and paid them tribute. "Roar on, ye throngs around and far away; there are voices in my ear out-thundering yours!" [156]

CHAPTER 9

Black Powder

●●

Our infantry thought well of us, our enemy feared us—could gunners ask more?

> GENERAL E. D. SCOTT, "Gunner in Luzon" [157]

Over hill, over dale, we have hit the dusty trail,
    And those caissons go rolling along.
"Counter march, right about!" hear those wagon soldiers shout,
    While those caissons go rolling along.
For it's hi! hi! hee! In the Field Artillery.
    Call off your numbers loud and strong! (*Call off!*)
And where'er we go, you will always know
That those caissons are rolling along; (*Keep 'em rolling!*)
That those caissons are rolling along. Batt'ry halt!

> GENERAL EDMUND L. GRUBER, "The Caissons Go Rolling Along." Written for the 5th Artillery in the Philippine Islands, 1908 [158]

Gentlemen, there must never be anything to explain in the Battery.

> CAPTAIN HENRY J. REILLY, Light Battery F, 5th Artillery

●●

Lᴇᴛ us have peace," General Grant proclaimed, and between states rent by disunion for four bloody years there was peace. In the West, where settlers, railroad builders, buffalo hunters, and miners invaded the lands of the Indian tribes, fighting, which had continued through the great conflict, flared higher. Bugles blew the call to arms, and drums rattled in the long roll. Once more the United

States Army took the field, but a familiar sound usually was missing as the blue-clad columns marched. The rumble of gun carriages seldom mingled with the tread of infantry and the clatter of cavalry.

The fine state and volunteer batteries of the Civil War were mustered out, their pieces stored in arsenals and armories or parked in city squares and village greens, their standards and guidons glass-cased in capitols. Only the regular artillery remained—the five regiments that had fought through the war—and each had been reorganized into ten heavy or foot units and two of field, armed with Napoleons and 3-inch Rodmans. Famed light batteries turned in their guns and teams and manned coastal ordnance or shouldered rifles. Vanished was the fast-moving horse artillery, which had ably supported Sheridan's troopers and might have served well with cavalry against the Sioux and Cheyennes. Pack artillery was shelved. Even General George Crook, a master of pack mule transportation, made no use of mountain guns and admitted to only one instance— a campaign in Idaho in 1867—when he could have employed cannon to advantage against the Indians.

That artillery played so little part in the Indian wars from 1865 to 1890 seems incomprehensible. The Great Plains and the deserts gave it scope that had been denied by the eastern forests and the swamps of Florida. Kearny's and Doniphan's artillerymen and the batteries of the war with Mexico had brought guns into telling action on the same or similar terrain. Nevertheless the red guidon and crossed cannon were emblems rarely seen in the long series of combats that won the West.

Colonel Henry B. Carrington was one of the few officers to demand the arm he had seen served so well through the Civil War. When he advanced into the Powder River country to build and garrison Fort Phil Kearny in 1867, he providentially took several howitzers along. During the stronghold's defense, more than once desperate, in a long, close siege by hordes of Sioux, Cheyennes, and Arapahoes, those cannon repeatedly saved details, sallying out of the stockade to cut wood or hay. Their covering fire shattered savage attacks. The Plains Indians, incomparable horsemen, who preferred to fight our cavalry rather than infantry, dreaded shell fire far above saber, revolver, or rifle.

No artillery accompanied one foray which rashly rode too far away from the post in disobedience of orders. Chief Crazy Horse ambushed it and massacred three officers and seventy-nine men. Later on in the siege one of Carrington's invaluable howitzers took part in the relief of the gallant wood-cutting party of thirty-two riflemen who, barricaded behind wagon boxes, had beaten off charges by fifteen hundred warriors.

After Fort Phil Kearny was abandoned by treaty, artillery was forgotten until the Modoc outbreak of 1872-1873. Armed with good rifles, the Modocs entrenched themselves in the lava beds of northeastern California, a natural fortress which the Army soon grimly dubbed "Hell with the Fire Out." There, without loss, 75 warriors, burdened by 150 women and children, bloodily repulsed assaults by 400 troops. A few mortars, unused since the Civil War, were brought up, but they were manned by pick-up crews, not trained artillerymen, and their blind, fog-shrouded fire was ineffective. Another attack was about to be mounted against the triumphant, unyielding defense when Washington called a peace parley. Conducting it, General Canby and other commissioners were treacherously murdered by Captain Jack, the Modoc chieftain, and several tribesmen. A fight to the finish now was the only recourse.

Again the mortars, little coehorns with 30-inch-long barrels, came into action in trench warfare, 1873 style. This time they were better served by gunners of the 4th Artillery. For two days and nights they boomed incessantly. Their shells soared aloft in steep arcs and descended to burst in the jagged fissures of volcanic stone that sheltered the enemy. One that failed to detonate was pounced on by an Indian, who tried to pull out its fuse with his teeth. It exploded, killing him and two companions. Defenders were blasted out and slowly forced back despite their fierce counterattacks.

In a reconnaissance to locate new mortar positions Captain Evan Thomas, 4th Artillery, with a detachment of eighty-five men of his own regiment and some infantrymen, was trapped in a dark gorge. Under a hail of Modoc bullets more than half the soldiers, many of them recent recruits, fled in cowardly panic. Captain Thomas died rallying men who stood fast. Though the mortars helped clear the lava beds and bring about the tribe's surrender, a distinguished artillery regiment had incurred a blot on its record, a stain for which a government which sent untrained recruits into battle must bear the major blame.

A striking, little-remarked instance of the neglect of artillery occurred in 1876. It involved the Gatling gun, then regarded as artillery equipment, not as the infantry weapon later types of machine guns became. Invented in 1861 by Dr. Richard Jordon Gatling but little used in the Civil War, it had been adopted in Europe in 1872 and favored over the French mitrailleuse. Its ten parallel barrels, rotated and fired by turning a crank, could spit 350 shots per minute. It was mounted on a wheeled, horse-drawn carriage.

When Lieutenant Colonel George Armstrong Custer kept a rendezvous with Generals Terry and Gibbon before leading his 7th Cavalry to the fateful field of the Little Big Horn, he was offered three Gatlings. He refused them because their teams were condemned cavalry horses (another shameful government economy); also because he believed, having cut loose from his wagon train, that wheeled vehicles might not be able to negotiate the broken country ahead. What might have happened if he had dismounted and left behind a few troopers, put their good horses in Gatling traces, and risked rugged going is only speculation. Yet the fire of three machine guns—1,050 shots a minute—when from 3,000 to 3,500 Sioux and Cheyennes fought the regiment's 600, divided into three battalions, might have told a different story than the Little Big Horn's tragic toll of Custer and 264 dead and 52 wounded.

In the subsequent campaign it was artillery that saved Colonel Nelson Miles's command when masses of Sitting Bull's warriors surrounded it and forced him to form a hollow square. Shell fire broke the assault, and cavalry in a countercharge routed the hostiles. Again Miles made skillful use of his guns when in 1877 he attacked a thousand Sioux under Crazy Horse on the snowy cliffs of Wolf Mountain.

> In careless defiance, Crazy Horse and his warriors, rifles ready, let the soldiers come on. Then out of the train turned two slightly different wagons. Canvas tops and their supporting bows were stripped off. Two field guns stood revealed, knots of cannoneers busy behind them elevating their muzzles and loading. Lanyards jerked, and shells soared screeching to

burst on the cliff tops. In consternation and terror, the Sioux ducked behind the rocks, close to flight. But the fighting spirit of Crazy Horse rallied and held them.[159]

It took a charge by infantry, covered by the cannon, to clear the high ground.

The close artillery combat of the Civil War was revived in 1877 during the magnificent retreat of Chief Joseph and his Nez Percés for more than sixteen hundred miles through Oregon toward the Canadian border, an epic in which the tribe engaged ten separate commands of the United States Army in thirteen battles and skirmishes and fought them to a standstill for eleven weeks. Howitzers and Gatlings, manned by the 4th Artillery, failed to overawe the valiant Nez Percés. Joseph and his horsemen charged, captured them and rolled them back into their own lines. At daybreak next morning Lieutenant C. F. Humphrey of the 4th led a dash of eleven men to recover the guns. It cost three killed, and four were wounded, including the officer, but the heroic sortie brought back all the pieces along with the dead and disabled. Shells and a stream of lead from the Gatlings compelled the Indians to resume their retreat. Later Joseph again took a howitzer despite a stout defense by some of its crew and crippled it by removing the wheels and hiding them. But field guns accompanied a relentless pursuit by Miles and shelled the encampment where the surviving Nez Percés finally surrendered.

In the last pitched battle with the Indians eighteen Medals of Honor [160] were won, four of them by artillerymen.

Through the West and Southwest the Sioux and other tribes were dancing the ghost dance, praying for a messiah to deliver them from the thralldom of their white conquerors. Bereft of their hunting grounds, herded on reservations, they were victimized by corrupt agents, one of whom cleared a graft of sixty thousand dollars in two years. In the winter of 1890 the Sioux nation, cheated, cold, and half-starved, sold their government rations, bought rifles, and went on the warpath. Again the Army was called on to suppress a revolt for which it was blameless.

Old Sitting Bull, fanning the uprising, died in a fight at the hands of Indian scouts. Cavalry rounded up Chief Big Foot's band of 120 warriors and 320 women and children, seeking a last refuge in the Bad Lands of the Dakotas. The chief surrendered and he and his people were escorted to a camp on Wounded Knee Creek near the Pine Ridge Agency in Nebraska. There on December 29 when the camp was searched for arms, squaws handed rifles, hidden under their blankets, to the bucks, and the madness bred by the ghost dance surged up into sanguinary combat.

Soldiers and Indians stood face to face and shot it out. The Sioux blazed away with repeaters, but the single-shot Springfields, cracking steadily while the enemy fumbled to reload, were more accurate and deadly. Women and children inevitably were killed by the storm of bullets, though officers kept shouting to their men to spare noncombatants. Red rushes broke through the blue lines, and battle spread over the prairie.

In position on a knoll were the four 1.65 Hotchkiss mountain guns of Light Battery E, 1st Artillery. They went into action as the smoke and confusion in the camp dissolved. Shells burst among Sioux snipers in the tepees and silenced them. Then Lieutenant Harry L. Hawthorne swung his guns around and blasted back warriors trying to recapture their pony herd. At ranges of from four hundred to twenty-five hundred yards the little 2-pounders shelled groups of the fleeing foe.

Half a mile away in a ravine a party of hostiles made a stand, beating back attacking troopers of the 7th Cavalry. Up to the battery galloped an orderly with a call for artillery support. Hawthorne limbered a Hotchkiss and dashed forward. As he was about to open fire, he was gravely wounded. Gunner Corporal Paul H. Weinert sent one of his two cannoneers to carry the officer from the field. With the other he manhandled the piece straight into the ravine's entrance and commenced firing. Bullets riddled the gun carriage. One knocked a shell from the corporal's hands as he was loading. He kept shooting until the Indians were dislodged.

The battle smoke of the Indian wars cleared away. It was and continued to be for some years the smoke of black powder. Its dense white clouds, betraying the position of gunners and riflemen, was to cost American lives in the next war.

Smokeless powder had been produced for the Prussian artillery in 1865. When the French developed a far more efficient compound in 1884, European nations promptly adopted it, discarding black after a reign of six hundred years. As important as the lower visibility of smokeless powder was the increased power and hence longer range produced by its slower burning grains. About the same time appeared melanite, the pioneer high explosive later developed into TNT. Such was the striking force given heavy artillery by the new HE, coupled with smokeless, that stronger fortifications had to be built. Even they would not be able to withstand it, as the bombardment of Belgian forts by big German howitzers in World War I demonstrated.

However, most of the United States Army, as well as the Navy, under the dictates of "economy" would be provided with nothing but black powder until stocks on hand were exhausted.

Elsewhere than in explosives, American artillery matériel, after a long period of decadence, commenced to advance, stimulated by inventions proved in foreign wars. Steel carriages began to appear, equipped with pneumatic or hydraulic recoil brakes, at first for seacoast armament only, later for mobile artillery. Elevating, traversing, and sighting mechanisms were invaluable innovations. Rifled guns supplanted all the old smoothbores that had lingered on so long. For cannon as for small arms, breech-loading superseded muzzle-loading. Ammunition now was fixed (projectile and propelling charge in one piece) or semi-fixed (bagged powder charges inserted in a brass case and the shell superimposed) for light pieces; heavies still used separate loading. Time and impact fuses were improved.

With new gun-sighting apparatus came indirect laying, which had been crudely employed in a few instances during the Civil War. It permits artillerymen to fire from concealed and protected positions on targets unseen by the men at the guns. The sight of one gun of a battery, the base piece, is laid on some well-defined aiming point such as a stake or the center of a tree trunk or steeple. Then the angle between that point and the target, an angle measured by a forward observer or on a map, is set off on the sight dial. The base piece and other guns, allowing for intervals, are then traversed degrees requisite to bring them to bear on the target. Range is estimated and adjusted by observation of fire; if shells burst to the right or left of the target, deflection is similarly corrected. Indirect laying, replacing except on rare occasions the old direct or point-blank fire, is a triumph of modern artillery.

Now given a fourfold increase in range, considerably greater accuracy and rapidity of fire, and superior mobility, the gunner's arm built on its ancient heritage and came into its own.

The French 75-mm. gun, which we would come to know so well in the first World War, had been invented in 1897. Its splendid hydropneumatic recoil system, making all other cannon obsolete, forced other nations to redesign their ordnance as soon as its closely guarded secret could be penetrated. However, in the United States service the 3.2 gun (later reduced to 3-inch caliber) remained the standard fieldpiece until 1917. Gatlings were supplemented by the heavier 37-mm. Hotchkiss automatically loaded, revolving cannon of five barrels, which were fired and the shell cases ejected by turning a crank. A dynamite gun, which threw a projectile filled with that explosive by pneumatic propulsion, was briefly experimented with, but its range was too limited.

The American artilleryman of the era was the same type of soldier who had fought gallantly in our battles from Louisbourg on. For twenty-five years after the Civil War his undress uniform continued to be the same dark blue sack coat or jacket and sky-blue trousers. In the 1870's he blossomed out into full dress inspired by the uniform of the Prussian victors in the war with France: a helmet, scarlet-plumed for light batteries and spiked for heavies; pipings, trouser stripes, and chevrons also of the artillery color over the traditional blue. The forage cap was replaced in the late nineties by a pillbox affair, described as "a cross between the cap of a sleeping car porter and that now worn by naval officers, a most unmartial looking head-piece more suitable for bicycle riders." [161] Cork summer helmets were adopted for all ranks and persisted until World War I.

A light battery on war footing consisted of six guns and nine caissons with limbers for each, a combined battery wagon and field forge, and one relatively light artillery wagon. Five officers, one hundred and seventy-five enlisted men, and one hundred and forty-four horses made up the complete war complement.[162]

In 1907 field and coast artillery would be separated and reorganized into permanent regiments and battalions. Meanwhile light batteries, isolated at inland garrisons, were on their own. A captain took pains in—

> jealously guarding the age-old prerogative of exemption from post guard and fatigue duty and successfully resisting all attempts of post commanders and other superior leaders to engage his battery in exercises with other troops, setting up a little kingdom of his own with his officers and men as loyal retainers, his stables and parking area as his castle, and his battery carriages and equipment as the royal exchequer. No wheel ever turned in those days, come hell, high water, or commanding generals, except "by order of the Captain." [163]

Such clannish independence of course made impossible the infantry-artillery teamwork so splendidly displayed during the Civil War; it would have to be relearned. Even if the ten scattered light batteries had been assembled, they could have achieved little in massed fire. That, in the forthcoming war, would be left to the United States Navy.

Black powder stands as a symbol of the war with Spain, and its use by the United States blots pages of our annals as dark as its hue. Ironically the enemy, their great days as a nation past, were equipped with smokeless.

Government supplies of the modern explosive were sufficient only for the regular infantry. The artillery, all the volunteer forces, and the Navy were provided with nothing but black. The handicap of its billowing white clouds was overcome in the Navy's case by superior gunnery, ships, and crews, and aggressive tactics, which won overwhelming victories over Spanish fleets at Manila and Santiago Bay. On land it was a different story.

When the battleship *Maine* was blown up in Havana harbor February 15, 1898, with a loss of 260 lives, freeing Cuba from the yoke of Spanish oppression became incidental to vengeance. To the stirring strains of Sousa's "The Stars and Stripes Forever" the United States girded for war. Familiar scenes were re-enacted: a mustering of untrained troops, a rush to arms which did not exist in adequate quantities or were outdated, belated appropriations. The fifty million dollars Congress tardily voted remedied such neglected matters as the nearly empty magazines of seacoast forts. No more than from twelve to twenty rounds per gun had been on hand in any of them.[164]

Mobilization gave the regular artillery two new regiments, the 6th and 7th. Eight batteries of heavy and sixteen battalions of light artillery, Volunteers, were called into Federal service. Among them was a battery, complete with guns, equipment, and ammunition, imported from abroad and presented by John Jacob Astor. As the gift of a patriotic citizen, the Astor Battery, which saw service in the Philippines, was in pointed contrast to government "economy."

Strenuous efforts assembled a complement of artillery for the expeditionary force to Cuba. It comprised four light batteries of four guns each, one Hotchkiss revolving cannon, one pneumatic dynamite gun, four Gatlings, four 5-inch siege rifles, four 7-inch howitzers, eight 3.6-inch mortars, and their animal transport. Mr. Dooley, spoofing the nation's exaggerated ideas of its martial prowess, hoisted count and calibers a bit. "Last Choosday," he remarked, "an advance ar-my iv wan hundherd an' twinty thousand men landed fr'm th' Gussy, with tin thousand cannons hurlin' projick-tyles weighin' eight hundred pounds sivinteen miles."[165]

Guns were landed from the convoy by lighter at Daiquiri, Cuba, without enemy opposition. Animals were shoved overside to swim ashore; one contrary horse paddled five miles out to sea before a boat crew in an amphibious roundup headed him back. Finally harnessed and hitched, the artillery struggled forward over narrow trails, leaving most of its ammunition behind on the beach for lack of transport. As it pushed on to support attacks on Spanish defense lines on San Juan Hill and at El Caney, roads, churned into muddy pits, became almost impassable. How "Rodney," the famous wheel horse of Captain George S. Grimes' Light Battery A, 2nd Artillery, pulled out all his own and another battery's mired guns, unaided except by his teammate, is told in the following chapter.

Grimes reached the front and opened on the enemy's blockhouses and entrenchments on San Juan at twenty-five hundred yards, too long a range for effective fire. The white smoke of black powder marked the position of each of his four guns like an advertising billboard. The Spaniards let him have it. Their artillery was scant and some of it obsolete—two 3-inch, rapid-fire Krupp mountain howitzers were their best weapons—but it was well served. Because they were using smokeless, their batteries went unspotted and their gun-laying unhampered. They pounded Grimes' crews and in forty-five minutes drove surviving cannoneers from their pieces. Then they raked attacking infantry, similarly outlined by smoke. Black powder, along with the yellow fever mosquito and "embalmed" beef, contributed handsomely to American casualty lists.

Captain Allyn Capron's Battery E, 1st Artillery, backing up the assault on El Caney, wasted shells, like Grimes, at too long a range. Only when it advanced to within a thousand yards of the Spanish lines did its fire help an infantry charge carry them. Two other batteries were uselessly held in reserve though greatly needed.

It was Lieutenant John H. Parker's Gatlings that upheld the gunners' honor and won the praise of other arms. Four of them, each carrying ten thousand rounds of ammunition on its carriage and pulled by a pair of mules, went into action against the Spanish blockhouses on San Juan at from six hundred to eight hundred yards. The little "woodpeckers" hammered away, cranking out five hundred shots a minute, sweeping the ridge. Though men and mules dropped under a heavy bombardment, their fire never slackened. For a time a sergeant, pointing and operating his gun alone, kept it spitting bullets. As it emptied, a feeder ran up with a fresh belt. Now with Negro troopers of the 10th Cavalry and Teddy Roosevelt's Rough Riders whooping forward in a charge, the Gatlings flushed the Spaniards from their trenches, riddled them and strewed the ground with figures in white tropical uniforms. Parker ceased fire and limbered. Cutting barbed wire, he forged ahead and swung his guns to catch six hundred Spaniards escaping from El Caney. All but forty of them fell under the deadly stream of lead. Before the Gatlings were allowed to cool that day they had sprayed sharpshooters out of trees and silenced enemy cannon at two thousand yards. Although other fieldpieces served competently at Santiago and in Puerto Rico, none equaled the gallant action of the Gatlings at San Juan.

In the Philippines, once Admiral Dewey had sunk the Spanish fleet, hostilities broke out between the American troops of occupation and the natives, denied immediate independence. During the insurrection led by Aguinaldo, our artillery took part in trench, open, and even amphibious warfare, the last when the Utah Battery on a steamboat blasted open a river passage. There were scores of small-scale but hard-fought actions, demanding close support by the guns while the infantry "civilized 'em with a Krag." Filipino Mausers cracked in reply, with bamboo joints, pierced by bullets, exploding and redoubling the racket of the fusillade. Spanish stone churches became citadels, snipers in the belfries.

The Old Army, given character by veterans of the Civil and Indian wars, fought this campaign. Artillerymen admired the coolness in action of Charles King, West Point 1866, the soldier-author, as he stood beside the guns in complete disregard of the fire of Filipino sharpshooters. King, retired because of wounds, had returned to active duty as a brigadier general, U.S.V. He was one of five general officers of his family to have served his country, beginning at Louisbourg in 1745.

Artillerymen of the 5th and 6th regulars and the Volunteers, wearing creased campaign hats, khaki breeches, and blue flannel shirts, which showed up conspicuously against the green foliage, worked 3.2-inch fieldpieces and mountain guns. Although the guns were breech-loaders, they were not equipped with recoil mechanisms, and a shot per minute was regarded as extremely fast work. Lacking caissons, a box of shells was slung under the limber and one of shrapnel carried on each gun-axle seat. When a battery had to move rapidly, most of the ammunition was dropped, and cannoneers mounted carriage seats and off mules; following wagons or carts picked up the rounds. Communication was by runner or signal flag; field telephones were not yet issued. Transportation was catch-as-can. Officers mounted the rugged little Philippine ponies. When no full-size draft horses could be obtained, one battery commander refused six-pony teams in disdain and ordered his men to haul the guns. After an exhausting hike through sand, Lieutenant E. D.

Scott on his own authority hired carabaos and Chinese drivers. With the animals hitched in tandem, he made two miles an hour and reached the front in time to support an infantry attack. Later mules replaced the lumbering bovine teams.

Scott and other able young artillery officers were equal to their duty. They and their well-trained crews brought their pieces into action through canebrakes and rice paddies and stood to them, unprotected by gun shields or aprons, under the fire of the *Insurrectos'* modern rifles. They smashed shells through church doors to burst among defenders and raked stoutly held trenches with shrapnel. Shooting over the heads of their own infantry, so closely sometimes that the doughboys complained that "the blankety-blank artillerymen kept our noses in the dirt," they opened the way for charges. Indirect fire was employed with bamboo aiming posts. Since the foe possessed only a few obsolete cannon, counterbattery was rarely faced. On one occasion a Philippine fieldpiece began to fire effectively under command of a deserter from the California Volunteers, an echo of the San Patricio Battalion of the Mexican War. Quickly it was shelled by an American mountain howitzer, which silenced it with two rounds, the second bursting within four feet of the target.

They served with credit, those U.S. artillerymen on Luzon. Captain William E. Birkhimer, the artillery historian, whose detail as judge advocate kept him away from the guns, nevertheless succeeded in breaking free and getting into the fighting. He led a charge of twenty men to rout three hundred Filipinos and won a Medal of Honor.

Out of the Philippines, though not until 1908, came a song artillerymen cherish as dearly as vivid battle memories. How "The Caissons Go Rolling Along" was composed is best told in the words of its author, then Lieutenant Edmund L. Gruber: [166]

> In April 1908, the First Battalion, Fifth Field Artillery, came over to the Philippine Islands to relieve the Second Battalion. It was the first time that the regiment had been together since organization. All officers and men felt a great pride in the regiment and were anxious to see it get a good start. We thought the best booster for regimental morale

would be a regimental song. By common consent I was told to write one.

. In searching for a good catchy title for the song, an incident which took place during a difficult march made by the Second Battalion in 1907 across the Zambales Mountains from Stotsenburg to Iba on the China Sea, recurred to me. On that march I was ahead with a detachment to select the route and make the necessary repairs to the numerous streams' crossings. We were well in advance of the battalion which during the afternoon was slowed down considerably by the difficulties encountered on the mountain road. Accompanied by the scout sergeant I proceeded to a high peak not far from the road in order to get a better view of the terrain which lay before us and, if possible, to see what progress the battalion in rear was making. From our observation post we could see the rolling country for miles. Here and there we caught glimpses of the mountain road, but not a sign of the battalion. Listening closely, we soon heard the distant rumble of the carriages which gradually increased and was punctuated at intervals by shouts and commands echoing up the valleys as the men urged their teams along. The sergeant turned to me and said: "They'll be all right, Lieutenant, if they keep 'em rolling."

After a hard march the battalion finally crossed the divide and made for camp on the other side. We rejoined as it was approaching camp. In passing the leading sections we again heard one of the chiefs of section call out to his drivers: "Come on, keep 'em rolling." That expression, which was frequently used by officers and men of the battalion, made quite an impression on me and seemed to characterize the spirit and determination of the battalion to push on in spite of obstacles.

Now Gruber had his theme. With a friend strumming a guitar, he developed a lively, lilting melody. Other officers helped with the first verse; the author later added subsequent ones. So was born a song of a battery marching in a distant land ... "morning dew on the hills and dales of Pampoanga valley—the beckoning road—

the good companion, boot-to-boot—a bugle call ahead—behind the guidon whipping in the dust churned by the wheels of the rolling caissons." [167] Sousa incorporated it in his "Artillery March." Radio advertisers, despite indignant protests, would make crass use of it, until a belated copyright protected it.

Today the song belongs to the arm for which it was written and to all who pledge love and loyalty to it. It matters not that there are no longer any caissons—that the ammunition they once carried is stowed in trucks that pull the guns, or in self-propelled mounts. Sung or played, the song lives. When Gruber died in 1941, another artilleryman strove to pay a deserved tribute:

"OVER HILL"
To Brigadier General E. L. Gruber

A last salute, sir, from all us who've sung
That song you made those years ago as young
Lieutenant in the Philippines. We sang
To keep the caissons rolling. How it rang
On "dusty trail," in dugouts, hall. And though
Men songless into modern battle go,
That song of yours could not be set apart,
For many a one still heard it in his heart.

The guidon glows as red as setting sun.
On the parade ground booms the final gun.
The flag-draped caisson, as your song forecast,
Rolls for the field artilleryman at last.
"Taps" in farewell, three echoing volleys shot.
But you, good soldier, will not be forgot
By gallant arm you loved and served so long,
Catching its spirit in a stirring song.[168]

Across the China Sea from the newly annexed Philippines, a single battery inscribed a stirring saga on the annals of the artillery.[169]

Although the United States had not engaged in the partition of China with other great powers, our involvement was forced by the bloody uprising of the Chinese Boxers in May, 1900. That secret "Society of Harmonious Fists," covertly encouraged by the Empress

Dowager, slaughtered hundreds of missionaries and other foreigners and thousands of native Christians. Murdering the German minister in Peking, the fanatical Boxers laid siege to the city's foreign legations, including the American. Guards and diplomatic personnel, defending themselves and their families against massacre, slipped an urgent appeal for rescue through the enemy lines. An expedition was rushed from the Philippines to join the Allied relief column: three regiments of infantry, a detachment of marines, a troop of cavalry, and Light Battery F, 5th Artillery.

Reilly's Battery, they called it after its commander, Captain Henry J. Reilly, in the manner of the Old Army. A neat, straight, soldierly man of medium height, pince-nez glasses over his steel-blue eyes and an intellectual forehead gave him a scholarly appearance. His mustache and close-trimmed beard were streaked with the gray of thirty-nine years in the service; he had fought up the Mississippi on a Union gunboat in '61. "F" was a crack outfit, the work of his hands, and no excuses for failure accepted. His picked officers, Lieutenants Charles P. Summerall, Louis P. Burgess, and Manus McCloskey, were well aware of the Captain's dictum: "Gentlemen, there must never be anything to explain in the Battery."

Six weeks at sea, most of them stormy and with a fire smoldering in the coal bunkers beneath ten thousand rounds of ammunition, and the transport carrying Reilly's Battery at last hove to off Taku, China. The Captain got the horses safely ashore, but the barge carrying the six guns wallowed helplessly in choppy water when a hawser snapped, and the towing tug vanished in the night. It was a recruit who saved them, a scrawny little stowaway hauled out of the hold and enlisted by Summerall on the hunch that he might come in handy. In this sudden emergency he emphatically did. A former sailor, he rigged sails and a rudder and kept the barge afloat. At dawn a pilot brought them in.

Guns of the American expedition's sole artillery, which had come so close to rusting at the bottom of the Gulf of Prihi, reported to the impatient Captain Reilly. The battery entrained in shell-torn Tongku, bombarded by the allied navies, rattled through the night and unloaded at Tientsin, wrested from the Boxers at the cost of heavy casualties to open the way to Peking. It took its place in the relief column, Reilly at its head on the charger he always groomed himself and little First Sergeant Follinsby on a big horse bringing up the rear. Under command of a German field marshal, the allies, eighteen thousand strong, a United Nations preview, moved out —twenty-five hundred Americans, eight thousand Japanese, three thousand British, forty-five hundred Russians, eight hundred French. Other troops, including the German, were left in reserve, protecting the base and coast concessions.

Dire urgency forced the march. The last message from the besieged legations, received ten days ago, reported the defenders desperate; guards and civilians holding the compound walls were dwindling under the fury of Boxer attacks. Reilly's drivers, by the "Old Man's" orders not riding but leading their pairs to spare them, walked them out at a good pace.

Rifle fire crackled up ahead. The Japanese advance guard was in action, but the columns pushed steadily on. Soon the action became general and the wounded and dead among the Japanese told of the severity of the assault on the Psi-Tsong lines. Good little *soldados,* the Japs. Reilly's Battery approved, and wondered when they were going to get in the show themselves. Before long, they guessed, knowing Reilly, and shortly the sound of their guns was added to the din of the battle.

Again, the guess worked out the next day as the American and British columns side by side attacked up the Pei-ho River. Captain Reilly galloped back from one of his characteristically thorough reconnaissances. A sharp order and the battery trotted front into line; another, and the limbers galloped to the road in the beautiful maneuver of action front, leaving the guns and their caissons preparing for action. Six gunners sighted on the parapets of a fort behind which yellow men swarmed with rifles, pikes, and strange triangular banners, and guns threw their shell against the Americans. A few quiet-spoken words from the battery commander, and shrapnel began to sweep the wall tops. The cannoneers could hear the screams of surprise of the scattering Boxers, who had been persuaded their bodies were invulnerable. Charging, the American infantry took the village. The battery limbered up and followed.

The day was sizzling hot, so hot it parched the skin. There was no water, and men's tongues became so swollen they could scarcely speak. These khaki-clad troops from the Philippines thought they had known heat, and they had—enough to leave them enervated. Now the Chinese sun beat down upon them and men gasped and toppled over sun-struck into the shimmering millet fields. But the attack drove on, the 14th Infantry as its spearhead, Reilly's Battery supporting. Old side-kicks in the Islands, these two. They had a saying in the 14th that no gun of Reilly's ever would be lost as long as there was a squad of the 14th left, and the 14th would never go under as long as Reilly had a gun and a round of ammunition.

From position to position the battery galloped, guns spraying shrapnel wherever the enemy massed or attempted to make a stand in a village, blasting away anything that stopped the infantry and getting their guns where they could do it.

At last the scorching sun went down, and men and horses halted in exhaustion. The muddy waters of the Pei-ho, putrid with hundreds of floating bodies, quenched their thirst. Dawn broke camp and the columns of the allies took up the race to Peking again. Reilly's redlegs, hiking along beside their horses and carriage wheels, admired the advance guard of picturesque Bengal lancers riding forward through the millet fields. Sputtering enemy rifles drove the turbaned horsemen back on the main body. As the infantry deployed, the battery rumbled forward, while the rising sun turned the corpse-filled river a ghastly red. Then action again, the 3.2's speaking in salvos and volleys. And always the close contact which the infantry that had fought with Reilly in the Islands confidently expected—had expected ever since they had seen him run his guns up to within seventy-five yards of the rifle pits of the *insurrectos* at Putal Bridge and open fire.

The battery trotted up to a bridge where the river must be crossed, and pulled down to a halt. A column of Russian infantry had commenced to move across. Riding to the officer in command, Captain Reilly in his courteous way requested permission to pass through. The watching artillerymen saw the Russian officer shake his head and refuse. "Must be loot in the next village," a caisson corporal grunted. The "Old Man" stiffened ominously as he stared across the river where doughboys were in action. He turned in his saddle, ripped out an order, and the battery smashed through, scattering Russians right and left. "To hell with diplomacy!" the caisson corporal chuckled, shoving a soldier of the Czar into the parapet with his horse's shoulder. On the other side of the river the battery caught up with its infantry.

March, fight, march, fight. The precious days rushed by. The expedition which had started August 5 might with luck reach Peking in eight or nine days, and there the great walls enclosing the city would hold it longer from the relief of the legations—if relief were not already too late. And how, barring its further progress on the road, the Boxers and Imperial troops had massed by the thousands in front of the town of Yangtsun.

Over the crooked, devil-baffling roads and through the fields nearing harvest, the columns of the nations converged on the town. Skirmishers felt the strength of the enemy and recoiled, and assaults were held back as the artillery which the Boxers had brought up opened fire. British and Japanese cannon replied. Reilly's Battery ploughed ahead through head-high grain.

Summerall's platoon unlimbered, masked by millet stacks. From a caisson a fifteen-foot observation ladder was unstrapped and erected. Summerall climbed it until he could see the target and calmly began to call down firing data. The target idea worked two ways. Every Chinese rifleman in the vicinity concentrated his fire on the foolish foreign devil, perched up above the grain. But they missed and were still missing when shrapnel commenced bursting among them. In another part of the field, McCloskey stood on the top of a caisson, similarly exposed, and directed the fire of his platoon. The enemy's batteries were silenced, and the American infantry pushed in with the bayonet.

While Captain Reilly, always making certain of the extent of an advance, ordered cease firing, British batteries, not so well informed, continued to fire, causing casualties in the 14th Infantry. Yet the advance carried on with the fierce sun peeling skin from men's lips and choking them with a thirst that was tantalized by the poisoned wells that must be passed. The Chinese fell back steadily, defiantly planting by the roadside pikes on which heads of native Christians were set.

Now the weary forces of the allies had pierced to within striking distance of Peking. Russian Lieutenant General Linivitch proposed that a concerted attack be delivered August 14, and it was so agreed.

But as Reilly's Battery huddled under its gun carriages and pup tents beneath a heavy storm on the night of the thirteenth, they heard heavy firing in the direction of Peking. Was it a last assault on the legations? Every man was standing to horse or at his post by the carriage wheels before daybreak when Captain Reilly returned from Headquarters, where he had learned that the Russians had slipped out of camp during the night. By daylight the battery was rolling rapidly down the Grand Canal Road, and the great walled city was looming ahead.

Nobly as always, the artillery horses played their part. How "Putnam," near wheeler of a gun section, alone saved the piece and the rest of the team from crashing down a steep bank, is told in the next chapter. The guns were pulled through and laid on target—Peking. On a knoll the right platoon under Lieutenant Burgess prepared for action. With a grin—for it is not every day that an artilleryman gets a chance to shoot at a pagoda—he gave the range as thirty-two hundred yards. His two 3.2s threw twenty shells into that great tower of the Tartar City, and it burst into flames.

With the abandon of men who fear they may be too late, with the anger of troops who have been tricked, the Americans flung themselves on Peking. Displaying high valor that would win him a Medal of Honor, Bugler Calvin P. Titus scaled the city's thirty-foot outer wall by footholds on loose bricks. His own and another company of the 14th Infantry clambered up after him, and under heavy rifle and shell fire the Stars and Stripes was planted, first of all the allied banners, on the ramparts.

Reilly's Battery rolled toward a gate, its route marked by Russian dead. The dead led to the living, a column of the Czar's infantry and artillery helplessly stuck in a sally port, peppered by Chinese riflemen and unable to advance or retreat. The Russians had jumped the gun but they had not won the race into the city.

Captain Reilly waited to ask no permission this time. Through the mass of bottled-up Russians he pushed two unlimbered guns until a house blocked their path. Reilly motioned the gun crews to come up. "Tear this house down," he ordered.

The cannoneers fell upon that Chinese shack with their bare hands and wrecked it. Muzzles peered over its debris and spouted flame. The crash of shells against the pagoda which dominated the sally port opened a morning of heavy fighting through the streets of Peking, the American infantry and artillery thrusting in hot haste toward the heart of the city and the compounds of the beleaguered legations, now so near to rescue.

Against street barricades, gates, and bridges, the three platoons of the battery went into action, separated to support the storming infantry companies to which each was assigned, Captain Reilly controlling them all. Summerall's guns advanced to sweep the south and east walls of the Tartar City. Burgess pushed through to the Chien gate fronting the Imperial City. McCloskey's fire blew up the portcullis of the Ha-ta gate of the Tartar City. Chinese sharpshooters tumbled, balconies of pagodas splintered beneath them, or scuttled out of flaming huts. Shells screamed down narrow streets and burst apart high-piled barriers.

Americans, converging on the legations, found the British had won the honor of relieving them first. A warm welcome awaited the troops from the Philippines from their countrymen—marines of the guard, diplomats who had fought at their side, the pale, thin women and children who had run the messes and hospitals. Sixty-five defenders had been killed, 135 wounded. They had made their last stand in the British compound, its walls newly mined by the foe, and relief had come only just in time.

But the battle was far from over. Now the allied armies closed in to assault the innermost citadel, the Forbidden City.

Near the Chien gate, the left platoon of Reilly's Battery waited in marching order while its fellow guns thundered on the wall above. An orderly galloped up with a call for support. Lieutenant Summerall snapped an order, and the platoon was off on a dead run at his horse's heels.

In front of the first gate of the Imperial City, the clattering teams circled and left two drab-painted guns squatting in the open. Allied observers saw the figures of the cannoneers, clad in the khaki blouses which Reilly made them wear instead of the more visible shirts of army blue, fling themselves upon those guns and prepare them for action. Bullets from the walls kicked up spurts of dust beside the wheels, but the gunners at their unshielded posts squinted over their sights, and the muzzles rose and glared.

Then the observers watched the artillery lieutenant walk forward calmly to the gate. Summerall carefully examined the strong eight-inch timber of its construction and peered through a crack at the heavy crossbeams, secured by ponderous Chinese locks. Pulling a piece of chalk from his pocket, he marked the location of the bar and walked back to the guns.

Cannoneers sprang to trails and wheels, rolling a piece to within twelve feet of the gate.

"Load with thorite," Lieutenant Summerall commanded Number One gun. A cannoneer gingerly shoved a shell of that previously untried explosive into the breech.

Summerall pointed to the chalk mark he had made.

"Right thar, sir?" asked Gunner Smith of Tennessee, sighting.

"Right there," Summerall answered.

The gun crew stood clear. The 3.2 roared and rolled back out of battery with the force of its recoil. A splintering smash, a creak of ancient hinges, and the gate swung open. Americans were staring into the Imperial City of Peking through the first gap in a centuries-old stronghold.

From the second wall the fire of the Chinese rose in an angry crescendo. The foreign devils were threatening their holy of holies. Four walls still barred their way. Not another must fall.

But the hot fire of the sharpshooters of the 14th Infantry replied from the top of the captured first wall, and the artillery platoon opened from the archway at seven hundred yards, as fast as they could load and fire.

White dust of shattered battlements again replaced the smoke of Chinese rifles. Again the advance rolled forward. Again Summerall carefully drew his chalk X on the great beams in front of the crossbar, while breathless observers stared at the pagoda that towered above him and waited for a torrent of boiling oil to hiss down on his head. He returned to the guns unharmed, nodded. Gunner Smith asked once more, "Right thar, sir?" A brief pause, and again a thorite shell played key to a gate of the Imperial City.

Four more gates were burst open by Summerall's guns. As the Lieutenant, pieces laid on the portals of the last gate, held fire under orders of the allied command, a sergeant spoke quietly to him. "Sir, they say the Captain's been killed." It was true. Captain Reilly, observing the fire of his battery from the wall, had been mortally wounded by a bullet ricocheting from the masonry. He died in Sergeant Follinsby's arms.

Soon after the fall of Peking an army reorganization changed the designation of Reilly's Battery, and its insignia passed to another unit. Yet the memory of its gallantry and his will live as long as the red guidons of the artillery flaunt unfurled.

CHAPTER 10

They Also Served

•━•

From Rhine to Rio Grande we two
    Have taken battle in our stride.
The prairie sun, the ocean blue,
    Have tanned and toughened up our hide.
    Hunger and fear and wounds have tried
All of our courage and our will.
    We lose a comrade from our side—
You take the last long road to Sill.

COLONEL JOHN N. GREELEY, "Ballade." On the occasion of
the motorization of the 12th Field Artillery and the turning in of its horses, sent to Fort Sill, Oklahoma.[170]

I'd rather be a soldier
    With a mule and mountain gun
Than a knight of old with spurs of gold,
    Of Roman, Greek, or Hun.
For when there's trouble brewing,
    They always send for me
To start the fun with a mountain gun
    From a mountain battery.

COLONEL GERALD E. GRIFFIN, "The Mountain Battery"[171]

•━•

A LONG cavalcade marches through the past of American artillery: single horses in the shafts of galloper guns and the tandems
and pairs of the Continental regiments; those swift teams of the
flying batteries in Mexico which remind one of Homeric chariot
steeds on the plains of Troy; lead, swing, and wheel pairs whose
drivers wore blue or gray, straining at traces to drag Napoleons and

Parrotts in mud, snow, and wilderness; mounts of officers, sergeants, corporals, horse artillerymen; strong, sure-footed pack mules, mountain howitzers on their backs, climbing heights or thrusting into canebrakes; horses that hauled the guns in foreign lands—horses by the hundreds, then by the hundred thousands of the first World War.

The procession dwindles, disappears. Hoofbeats give way to clatter of tractors and trucks, to the rumbling treads of self-propelled gun mounts. Cannon jut from the moving steel fortresses called tanks, fly in planes, drop from the skies by parachute. Artillery horses vanish except for a team to draw a caisson and its flag-draped burdens in military funerals.

They yielded to the efficiency of the age of motors, and even surviving artillerymen of the horse-drawn days, who knew the thrill of a battery galloping into action, are resigned, content to cherish the memories of four-footed companions that served them so gallantly and so well. Too often they saw the faithful creatures killed in battle, suffering from wounds, gassed, or dying from the exhaustion they could not be spared.

Many an artillery animal, single mount or team member, was a true scion of Job's war horse, going on to meet the armed men, mocking at fear and not affrighted. But, as a Confederate veteran remarked,[172] Job's horse did not have to face artillery fire. Though mortally afraid under cannonading, the sensitive creatures displayed heroism equal to their masters'.

> I have seen the poor brutes when the shells were flying low and close above their backs, squat until their bellies almost touched the ground. They would be perfectly satisfied during battle, or at least entirely quiet, if their drivers remained with them, especially on their backs; and when the men were compelled to absent themselves for a time and return again to their teams, I have heard the horses welcome them with whinnies of satisfaction and content, and have seen them, under fire, rub their heads against their drivers with confiding and appealing affection.
>
> And the poor animals loved not only their drivers but each other. I have heard and seen a horse whose mate was killed at his side utter an agonized and terrified neigh, meanwhile

shuddering violently, and have known a horse so bereaved persistently refuse to eat, and pine away and die.

In the Civil War, Union horse losses reached five hundred a day in eight months of 1864; the Army of the Potomac alone used up forty thousand. The North's remount supply was ample, but the South's inability to replace wastage of draft animals and cavalry mounts was one of the causes of defeat. A glowing epitaph for them appeared in the *Richmond Examiner:* "Tens of thousands of them have fallen and died and gone to the eternal pastures of the horse heaven that we trust is in reserve for all good, loyal horses and mules that have discharged their burdens and duty in this world." And General Lee, reading it, added: " 'Eternal pastures'—a 'horse heaven'? I wonder. I would like to believe there are such. Poor creatures! They suffered and died in our service."

Horse casualties in World War I were still more appalling, with some organizations losing 65 per cent. In the summer of 1918 the average life of an artillery horse at the front was ten days.

Let them rest and may they ever be remembered.

There is a dearth of accounts of artillery horses of our earlier wars. After the Revolution, drivers, hitching old Tom and Jerry to the plow again, must have boasted how they helped pull a 6-pounder through the snow to Trenton and endured the scorching heat of Monmouth. Favorite pairs, cut down by Mexican bullets when O'Brien and his Bulldogs made their stand at Buena Vista, surely were mourned by the men who had driven them. Yet stories told around campfires or at hearthsides were not set down on paper. In the War Between the States it was such generals' chargers as Lee's "Traveller" and Sheridan's "Winchester" that were celebrated, along with cavalry horses. However, a tale of an artilleryman's mount survives.[173]

Adventures and battle scars lay ahead of "Tartar" when as a four-year-old he entered the service at Fort Leavenworth, Kansas, in 1857 and was branded *U.S.* Assigned to Sergeant James Stewart, he marched with Battery B, 4th Artillery, on the Utah expedition, until he fell sick with a malignant type of distemper near Salt Lake. He could no longer keep up, and the battery must push on. Since

he might recover and join a wild herd, his rider did not shoot him
but sadly turned him loose to shift for himself.

Next spring Indians, tempted by a reward of thirty dollars for any
horse or mule with a goverment brand, brought him into camp.
After finding him abandoned, they had used him all winter to haul
tepee poles, but he was in better condition than other horses that
had remained with the outfit. Stewart rode him on through the
summer of 1860 when the battery, acting as cavalry and often covering forty or fifty miles a day, kept open the mail, emigrant, and pony
express routes.

In '61 Tartar and his master entrained for Washington and went
to war with the artillery of the Army of the Potomac. At the second
Bull Run the horse was struck by a shell which carried away his
tail and wounded him in both hams. Stewart, doing all he could for
his hurts, was once more forced to bid his beloved mount farewell.
Next morning as the battery rolled away, Tartar neighed shrilly
from the farmyard field where he had been left. Then he switched
his stump of a tail, cleared the fence with a fine leap, and trotted
after the guns.

Through most of the rest of the war Stewart, rising from the ranks
to the command of Battery B, regularly rode the fine animal. In
front of Fredericksburg, Tartar was honored by an interview with
President Lincoln.

> After I had passed in review, riding Tartar [Stewart wrote],
> I was sent for, to allow the President to look at the horse's
> wound. As soon as Mr. Lincoln saw it, he said to the general
> officers about him: "This reminds me of a tale!" which he
> proceeded to relate to their great amusement, but I was not
> near enough to hear what it was. But his little son, "Tad,"
> mounted on a pony, followed me and insisted on trading
> horses. I told him I could not do that, but he persisted in
> telling me that his papa was the President, and would give
> me any horse I wanted in trade for Tartar. I had a hard time
> to get away from the little fellow.

Tartar was wounded again at Fredericksburg, and thereafter he
was gun-shy under musketry fire, but still carried his master well.
The day before the battery arrived at Gettysburg he was lamed by

a nail in one forefoot and did not go into battle, nor was he able to march in pursuit of Lee's retreating army. There was a third sad parting, the horse being entrusted to a farmer's care.

A month later Stewart heard his mount had been seen on the picket line of a cavalry division. If there was an argument over his ownership, the artillery won it. "I went over and got him," Stewart said simply. Horse and rider served on together until Stewart was promoted again and transferred to the infantry. Tartar, in the tenth year of his honorable and distinguished career, remained with the battery.

"Rodney," the most famous horse of the U.S. Field Artillery, was a near-wheeler. Ridden by the driver of the rearmost pair of a six-horse team, his was the most important post. It was his duty and his mate's to furnish part of the draft, to swing the pole, or to hold back in the breeching, aided by cannoneers at the brakes, when the limber and gun behind them descended a downgrade. When he joined the service in 1896, he was eight years old, an unusually good-looking light bay with dark points, of Thoroughbred and Clydesdale blood, 15.3 hands high, weight 1,250 pounds. He was named after Caesar Rodney of Delaware, who made a noted ride to Philadelphia to affix his decisive signature to the Declaration of Independence; or, as some say, he was the namesake of Colonel George B. Rodney, a Civil War artilleryman.

Rodney was the pet of every driver who sat him and the pride of every battery with which he served. He was never sick and never refused a feed or a task. Intelligent, strong, and willing, he pulled so hard that he sometimes broke his harness. His great moment came at El Poso, Cuba, in 1898, as mentioned in an earlier chapter. When the guns of Light Battery A, 2nd Artillery, badly needed on the firing line, became mired in a churned-up, almost impassable slough, Captain George S. Grimes ordered all teams unhitched. Rodney and his teammate "Shaw" alone were kept in draft. Urged by their driver, that mighty pair, belly-deep in mud, threw their weight into their collars, tugged for dear life at traces, and hauled limber and gun out onto firm ground. Then they extricated all the rest of the stalled carriages, and the battery galloped forward into action. The same day they rescued another bogged-down outfit, much to its chagrin, and later, before Santiago, repeated their feat. After the Cuban campaign Rodney made many a long route march, including one of seven hundred miles, averaging twenty-one a day, and in maneuvers always outlasted his fellows.

As a veteran, he hazed rookie horses for a week or so, then let them alone if they took it in good part; otherwise he continued to be tough. In Rodney's time the morale of Battery D, 3rd Field Artillery, never lacked a lift. He was camera-shy, and soldiers used to point cameras at him for the fun of watching him gallop away in the corral. Once he adopted a mare and a colt (a platonic friendship, since he was a gelding), and the three were known on the post as "The Rodney Family." Every Christmas fond redlegs decorated his stall.

When years began to tell on him, he was retired on the understanding that he would not be discarded and sold to pull a huckster's cart, dray, or dump wagon, but in 1916, without the knowledge of the battery, he was inspected, condemned, and put up at auction. Just in time his friends in the ranks got word and rushed to the sale, where against the competition of a mean-spirited dealer, who bid up the price, the artillerymen in heart-warming loyalty pooled their money to buy him for $107. A plea by the battery through military channels required nineteen endorsements but resulted in orders that at government expense Rodney would be provided stable, forage, and care "wherever he may be for the rest of his life." He lived it out doing light work, hoisting hay and grain to a loft, but playing hookey to graze whenever disposed. At the ripe old age of thirty his legs failed him, and he was mercifully put to sleep.

Rodney's saga was finely told by an artilleryman, Colonel Leonard Nason, in a short story,[174] often reprinted in anthologies, and made into a motion picture.

"Putnam," another near-wheeler, namesake of General Israel Putnam, is second only to Rodney in the hall of fame of artillery horses. One of his admirers, General Charles P. Summerall, described him as a large, handsome dark bay of Percheron and Thoroughbred strains, perfectly proportioned, intelligent, responsive, and a great favorite. He stood sixteen hands high and weighed sixteen hundred pounds. None of his teammates could outpull him.

In 1898 he served in Cuba. After the war with Spain he was the first horse chosen for Reilly's Battery, F, of the 5th Artillery, which was limited to twenty-four animals when it sailed to the Philippines in 1899. There he saw a year of campaigning. With each carriage hauled by two horses and two mules, "Old Put" pulled lustily, bringing his gun through the muck of rice paddies into action against the *insurrectos*. In 1900 he suffered severely during the rough weather of the voyage to China for the Boxer Rebellion, but his driver took tender care of him, and no creature could have shown his appreciation more plainly.

Putnam was in fettle again in time for the ninety-mile fighting march to Peking. When the allied force had battered through the Boxers' fanatical opposition to within a few miles of the city, Reilly's guns were urgently called for to blast a way through the enemy, making a last stand before the walls. The commander signaled his battery to turn out of a steeply banked sunken road and take position on higher ground above. The team of the first piece hit the grade. Lead, swing, and wheel pairs had scrambled up and over when a trace spring snapped just as the limber wheels reached the top. Five horses out of the six quit pulling and began to slide back. Old Put alone dug in his hoofs and kept the remaining trace taut. Then without a word from his driver he virtually crawled up the slippery slope. Unaided, the splendid wheeler hoisted the carriages on to the level plain, averting a crash which would have disabled both gun and team.

That fine performance and his service in the storming of the city won the horse the new name of "Peking." Following the relief of the legations, he was returned to the Philippines where he spent the rest of his career. He was retired in his old age, with forage authorized for his lifetime by an order signed by Brigadier General John J. Pershing. At all ceremonies the grand old horse was led behind the battery. When he died, he was honored with a military funeral and buried from a flag-draped caisson while a band played a dirge and a bugler sounded Taps. No less was due a gallant veteran.

"Foxhall," joining up in 1886, was shipped to Cuba in 1898 with "F" of the 5th Artillery. Shoved overside close offshore to swim to the beach with other horses and mules, he paddled five miles out to sea before being herded back to duty by a boat crew. He served through both the Cuban and Puerto Rican campaigns. In old age he was assigned to the bread cart and, driverless, would pull it to the commissary, draw the battery's rations, and take them to the kitchen. After receiving his share—four loaves—he would gallop back to the stables to be unhitched. Until near his death at forty, there was plenty of life in him, and he would buck off every soldier who tried to ride him bareback.

To "D" of the 1st Field Artillery belonged "Jumbo," a big eighteen-hundred-pounder that could pull a gun out of the deepest mud hole. He spent his spare time stamping the life out of scores of Fort Sill's rattlesnakes, no more to him than horned toads. Acting as an equine top sergeant, he disciplined remounts, sinking his teeth in the necks of any that loafed and shaking them until they did their share in draft. Once when a stubborn balker was unhitched by disgusted drivers, Jumbo half killed him in punishment. It was no wonder that at feed time the rest of the horses in the corral respectfully stood aside, opening a path for Jumbo to enter the stable first. He, like Rodney, was bought with battery funds when an inspector condemned him as unfit. For the remainder of his long life he grazed on post lawns with impunity and munched frequent treats of apples and sugar until death turned him out "in fenceless pastures that are always green."

A remarkable individual mount of the first World War was "Jeanne d'Arc," a mare ridden by a sergeant of Battery D, 15th Field Artillery. After serving through the regiment's hard fighting, she won many jumping events in the horse shows of the Army of Occupation in Germany. She was bought by an officer and taken back to the United States where she was bred and produced two fine foals.[175]

The artillery knew well the horse's cousin, that offspring of mare and jackass—the mule. For packing mountain howitzers and pulling supply wagons he had no equal. In emergencies he served in gun teams, but that was not the forte of the long-eared hybrid, which would stand fire with utmost nonchalance but objected to galloping into battle. He was castigated as "unapproached in devilment, fathomless in cunning, born old in crime, of disreputable paternity and incapable of posterity, stolid, imperturbable, with no love for anything but the perpetration of tricks, no dexterity in aught save the flinging of his heels, no desire for anything but rations, and no affection at all." Yet he was justly prized as the king of toiling beasts, and one of his nicknames is carried on from the days of the Old Army. When bumptious mule recruits joined up, their manes were roached and their tails shaved to distinguish them from better-behaved old-timers. Their sobriquet, "shavetails," is still applied to new, know-it-all second lieutenants.

Under pack and in the traces of supply wagons the long-eared fellows were incomparable. Only in emergencies were they used in artillery teams; they balked at being driven into action in the face of enemy cannon and rifle fire. Otherwise they were extraordinarily stolid in bombardments. Wagon train mules of the 19th British Division in the first World War, calm under heavy shelling, panicked only when they met the division's tame mascot lion "Poilu" wandering loose around the front.

Mules carried packs and mountain guns into action in Mexico and in the Philippines in 1900. Fifty-eight thousand American and foreign mules served us in World War I. Leaving them home in the second World War proved to be a mistake; it became imperative to improvise pack trains of native animals for the campaigns in mountainous Italy. Later the 10th Mountain Division, with a contingent of packers and pack artillerymen and their mules, played a major part in breaking the German defense of the heights. Mules plunged through Burmese jungles that defied jeep or tractor. Korea saw a very considerable use of animal transport by the enemy. One hardy American mule, which had survived the Chinese Revolution, was taken over by the Communists and pressed into service in Korea. His U.S. Army brand still on his flank, he was captured by an American sergeant and put to work.[176]

The mountain battery and pack mule have outlasted the artillery horse. Two organizations, the 4th Field Artillery Battalion and the 35th Quartermaster Pack Company, stationed at Fort Carson, Colorado, still stretch picket lines for braying "jugheads." Sturdy backs are saddled with aparejos, cinched tight on rounded bellies. Disassembled 75-mm. pack howitzers—tubes, trails, wheels, and so on—

are each apportioned between seven animals, with others carrying ammunition and various equipment. Loads for the strong gun mules range from 199 to 248 pounds. Officers and sergeants swing aboard their easy-gaited riding mules. The battery commander's right arm sweeps forward, drivers lead out—and they climb mountains up to and including Pike's Peak. High up in some dominating, almost inaccessible position, the guns are unpacked and assembled and open fire in twenty minutes. Neither gasoline nor wheels nor treads, nor even the helicopter—highly vulnerable to pursuit planes and artillery fire, as demonstrated in Korea—have yet relegated the mule and mountain battery to military limbo.

Mule celebrities include the musical animal which recognized all the bugle calls and kept his long ears slanted for the notes of Recall; the minute he heard it he bolted for the stables. Artillerymen named him after the labor leader, Samuel Gompers, because he always knew how long a day's work should be. "Verdun," foaled under shell fire in World War I, became the mascot of Battery E, 15th Field Artillery. After the war he returned with the regiment to Fort Sam Houston, Texas, where, caparisoned in a red blanket embroidered with insignia and service stripes, he graced parades. Granddaddy of them all was "Mexique," whose record showed an extraordinary span of army service from the 1820's into the 1880's. When at last he was ordered branded "I.C." (inspected and condemned), old friends, from General Sherman to men in the ranks, rallied to his rescue and obtained a government pension for the rest of his life. The patriarch was "turned out never to be harnessed again, to roll at his own sweet will and to be furnished a full ration till time with him shall be no more."

For the artillery horse the first World War marked a zenith.

From its outbreak belligerent powers scoured the world for draft animals and mounts. It was the United States, a mighty reservoir of horses and mules, that principally supplied them. American exports to Europe, reaching 22,776 in 1914, soared upward despite slackening of cavalry needs due to trench warfare. The amazing quota filled in 1916 was 357,553.[177] Heaviest demand was for light draft horses for artillery, and they were the greatest American contribution. The British called them "Yanks" and prized them highly, as did the French.[178]

Perhaps it was an American horse far from home, tugging away in the traces to pull a French 75 into action, that inspired a moving appeal by Captain de Condenbove of the French Army, "The Artillery Horse's Prayer."

> To thee, my master, I offer my prayer.
>
> Treat me as a living being, not as a machine.
>
> Feed me, water and care for me, and when the day's work is done, groom me carefully so that my circulation may act well, for remember: a good grooming is equivalent to half a feed. Clean my feet and legs and keep them in good condition, for they are the most important parts of my body.
>
> Pet me sometimes, be always gentle to me so that I may serve you the more gladly and learn to love you.
>
> Do not jerk the reins, do not whip me when I am going up-hill. Do not force me out of the regular gait or you will not have my strength when you want it. Never strike, beat or kick me when I do not understand what you mean, but give me a chance to understand you. Watch me, and if I fail to do your bidding, see if something is not wrong with my harness or feet.
>
> Don't draw the straps too tight: give me freedom to move my head. Don't make my load too heavy, and oh! I pray thee, have me well shod every month.
>
> Examine my teeth when I do not eat; I may have some teeth too long or I may have an ulcerated tooth and that, you know, is very painful. Do not tie my head in an unnatural position or take away my best defence against flies and mosquitoes by cutting off my tail.
>
> I cannot, alas, tell you when I am thirsty, so give me pure cold water frequently. Do all you can to protect me from the sun; and throw a cover over me—not when I am working, but when I am standing in the cold.
>
> I always try to do cheerfully the work you require of me: and day and night I stand for hours patiently waiting for you.
>
> In this war, like any other soldier, I will do my best with-

out hope of any war-cross, content to serve my country and you, and, if need be, I will die calm and dignified on the battlefield; therefore, oh! my master, treat me in the kindest way and your God will reward you here and hereafter.

I am not irreverent if I ask this, my prayer, in the name of Him who was born in a stable.

It spoke for all artillerymen and lovers of horses. American gunners heeded it as best they could when the United States entered the war and they sailed to France with still more horses from their native land. In battle their teams gave them devoted service unto death like Kipling's "Snarleyow" which, fearfully mangled by a round shot, dragged his gun into position and not until then, " 'is 'ead between 'is 'eels," did he totter and fall.[179]

Although after American entrance into the war thousands of horses were shipped to the A.E.F., they fell far short of filling needs. About 104,000 were purchased from the French at an average price of $450 a head and sold back after the armistice at a fraction of their cost. Fifty-six thousand of the artillery animals remaining in the States were ultimately sold as surplus.[180] Their old drivers could only hope that the faithful creatures, in future years of pulling carts, drays, or plows, abroad or at home, received the humane treatment they had known when they kept the caissons rolling along.

A few American horses and mules came home with the A.E.F. Most of the survivors stayed abroad to pull plows and carts instead of limbers. General Pershing placed a bronze tablet in the old War Department Building in Washington to pay tribute to the sixty-eight thousand horses and mules that died in the service of their country.

Armistice Day, 1918, signaled the beginning of the end of war horses. Finis had been written for them by tanks, trucks, tractors, and planes which would serve artillery in their turn, though a few horsed units were still in existence on the eve of World War II; and in that conflict horse-drawn artillery and cavalry saw action with foreign armies.[181]

Meanwhile the efficient U.S. Remount Service, established in 1920, achieved much in restoring the drained horse supply and improving it with a careful breeding program. Its blooded stallions of Thoroughbred, Arab, and Morgan lines sired fine colts to horse the field artillery regiments of the peacetime army and helped meet civilian needs. Many a farmer, lumberman, cattleman, and pleasure rider still has reason to be grateful for its accomplishments. Although its stations had been transferred to the Department of Agriculture by 1948, it continues to function to provide animals still required by the Army.

The last years of the artillery horse were years of glory—of hard duty well done—maneuvers and five-hundred-mile hikes; of perfected achievement; of pomp and circumstance. Batteries competed hotly for the cherished Knox Trophy, and in its winning, teams and individual mounts played a splendid part. For long the National Horse Show's most stirring spectacle was the mounted drill of one of the Regular Army's firing batteries, red guidon streaming, bugler sounding, as it performed intricate evolutions in the arena at a full gallop. In the riding hall at Fort Myer, Virginia, were staged similar exhibitions of driving skill along with simulated firing demonstrations. Batteries, their horses color-matched, hides and harness gleaming, red-blanketed, hoofs blackened, strove to outdo one another. At night shows the hall was darkened, and drivers, switching on small red electric lights on the crown pieces of their pairs, guided them in dashes between burning stakes. A shouted order, "Action front!," and guns unlimbered and opened fire with blanks at miniature tanks moving across a panorama. The 16th Field Artillery revived the past by uniforming its men as artillerymen of the Revolution and the Mexican War. Immaculate, burnished teams drew the funeral caissons for burials in Arlington National Cemetery, as they still do today.

At last, inevitably, came the order: turn them in. The artillery was to be motorized.

Wryly a former officer of the horse-drawn era wrote a parody of "The Caisson Song":

> Over hill, over dale, motorized from head to tail,
>   With the caissons and hosses all gone.
> Stop to fix up a flat, or to get the captain's hat,
>   Motor trucks with the pieces hooked on.

Then it's high, high see! the Field Artillery.
Sound off your Klaxon loud and strong!
No more we'll go, with a team in low,
If our motors keep buzzin' along.[182]

Probably the old stable sergeants took it hardest of all. They
frowned down at the horse heads on their chevrons, doomed insignia. They would have to convert themselves into motor sergeants
now, if they could manage the shift, and most of them did so
handily. But it was like the family coachman learning to drive the
brassy, sputtering Pope-Toledo that replaced the spanking pair of
high-stepping bays in the barn, become a garage. Sergeant Mike
and his counterparts grumbled bitterly to this effect:

'Tis truck-drawn we'll be from this day on. We'll be feed-
ing and watering at gas stations—when iny is convanient.
We'll be picketing at tourist camps. We'll go into action—
if we can foind parking space. If the inemy shows a red
traffic light, we'll stop dead. Wurra, wurra, I hope we breaks
down, and little bhoys hollers at us, "Git a horse!" [183]

Regiments bidding their beloved animals good-by made it into
an occasion, for horsemen are sentimental fellows. Certainly trucks
were faster and more serviceable. They carried all the cannoneers
along with ammunition once contained in caissons, and each pulled
a rubber-tired gun. But for the old-timers part of the glory and
glamor of field artillery—and part of their hearts—was departing with
the horses.

At Fort Sam Houston the men of the 12th Field Artillery, organized in the first World War, wore solemn faces when Assembly
sounded one December day in 1938. They were about to relinquish
their teams to the 18th, which would march them over a 450-mile
route to Fort Sill and use them for a while before being motorized
in its turn.[184] Sergeants, caisson corporals, and drivers of the Fort
Sam regiment had had photographs taken of themselves with their
mounts and pairs to keep as precious mementos; also they had presented their commanding officer with a large picture of the heads of
all the horses they were losing.

Officers and enlisted men of the 12th lined the route to watch the

horsed column of the 18th march past. For them there was one con-
solation. Old "Pat" had been retired and would stay with them.
Foaled in 1908, he had joined the army as an officer's mount when
he was a four-year-old and as a battery horse served in France
through the first World War, returning afterward to the States.
In retirement he would wear a scarlet blanket bearing his name,
regimental insignia, and eleven service stripes. When he died, he
would be buried with honors at Fort Sam beneath a granite shaft
on which, above his record, his noble head with "the look of eagles"
is portrayed. His grave is decorated each Memorial Day.

But on this day of 1938 Pat was still vigorous enough to play his
part. They hitched him in front of the lead pair of the departing
cavalcade, to be taken back to his stall after the review. When the
guidon-bearer started forward, Pat put his weight against his breast
strap and pulled as never before—as if he knew this was his last
parade in harness. Bands of the 9th and 23rd Infantry regiments,
with which the 12th had served in France in the famed 2nd Division,
struck up "The Caisson Song." Redlegs along the roadside saw all
the horses' ears prick up. Surely they recognized that music. They
seemed to be keeping step to it. Guns of one of the new motor-
drawn batteries fired a salute of four salvos. Then the bands played
"Auld Lang Syne." That was almost too much. The Texas sun
glistened on moisture in the corners of eyes, and throats gulped to
swallow sudden lumps. Dust dropped a curtain behind the receding
column. Hail and farewell!

CHAPTER 11

Arms and the Artilleryman

●••

The proud privilege of being able to say, "I once commanded a BATTERY!"

> BRIGADIER GENERAL GEORGE D. WAHL in *Field Artillery
> Journal*

The American artillery, trained and commanded by such
chiefs as Generals Hinds, McGlachlin, and Lassiter, always com-
ported itself in a manner deserving all praise and earning the
admiration of those French artillerymen who were privileged
to find themselves by its side in combat.

The quickness of its evolutions, taking up battery positions,
and changes of firing objectives, the care and vigor in the
preparation and execution of fire, gave it at once a marked
superiority over the German artillery, and this the enemy himself was compelled to acknowledge on several occasions. A
German document... states that their troops feared American
artillery on account of "the power and accuracy of its fire."

> COLONEL J. H. DE CHAMBRUN, *The American Army in the
> European Conflict*

●••

FROM 1900 to 1916 the U.S. Artillery, along with all branches and
services, perforce rested on its arms. Neither the efforts of a few
forward-looking statesmen nor of military men with a knowledge of
history and pride in their profession could disturb that traditional
repose, the will of the nation. The conflict raging in Europe and
threatening American involvement caused no more than uneasy
stirrings. Secretary of State William J. Bryan, on the very day that

Austria broke relations with Serbia, had announced that the treaties he had negotiated "ought to make war impossible." If war should come to the United States, the time to prepare for it was, he insisted, after it was declared; then, if necessary, "a million boys would spring to arms between dawn and sunset." Whereupon Theodore Roosevelt snorted, "To whose, or what arms?" [185]

At least a forward step had been taken toward instructing soldiers how to handle what arms there might be after they sprang to them. The School of Fire for Field Artillery was established in 1911 at Fort Sill, Oklahoma, an old post of the Indian wars. A succession of able commandants, slowly overcoming grave shortages in personnel, quarters, and classrooms, gradually developed it into the present efficient and extensive Artillery and Guided Missile Center. On the broad ranges of Sill, justly termed the American artilleryman's Mecca, many a gunner has learned his art.

A little less than a year before the United States' entry into the World War, Mexico once more provided the stage of a "rehearsal for conflict," though on a much smaller scale than in 1847. When Mexican revolutionists raided across the border, a punitive expedition was organized, under John J. Pershing, promoted brigadier general from captain of cavalry. The future Commander in Chief of the American Expeditionary Force led a small, fast-moving force, including units of the 4th and 6th Field Artillery, into Mexico in pursuit of Villa, a campaign of hot, thirsty marches and sporadic combat. President Woodrow Wilson ordered a partial mobilization which sent National Guard regiments to the border or to camps elsewhere. Among them was the forerunner of the Reserve Officers Training Corps, the Yale Batteries, formed at the university a year earlier and mustered into federal service as the 10th Connecticut Field Artillery. Along with General Leonard Wood's "summer soldiers," attending Plattsburg and other volunteer training centers, these guardsmen became a reservoir of officer material. Toughening training they underwent soon would stand them and their country in good stead.

So through the action of bands of Mexican raiders the United States fortuitously achieved some measure of preparedness for an approaching ordeal.

Nevertheless when we declared war on Germany, April 6, 1917, "the condition of the Field Artillery as regards its organization, its equipment, its training, and the control of its commissioned personnel was nothing short of deplorable and chaotic." [186] It could muster no more than six hundred 3-inch guns, subsequently discarded except for training purposes in favor of the French 75-mm. Heavier guns and howitzers were far scantier. In spite of the extraordinary expansion of American cannon foundries, they would not be able to meet the demand in time; none manufacturing heavy ordnance reached quantity production before the armistice.[187] Larger weapons were borrowed from seacoast forts and the Navy as makeshifts. Purchases were made from private dealers in military antiques and supplies, and frantic procurement efforts only stopped short of raiding relics in museums and on village greens.

Gun carriages, limbers, and caissons were an equally pressing problem. Horses to pull them would be forthcoming at home and abroad, as related in the previous chapter, but supply of the tractors and trucks, beginning to replace equine draft, was difficult. Heaped upon that were new requirements for mobile artillery: caterpillar tread mounts and that innovation, the tank; also the massive apparatus of railway guns. Shortages in such vital fire control instruments as battery commander's telescopes, aiming circles, range finders, and prismatic compasses—the "brains" of a gun—were appalling. Small wonder the hair of officers charged with providing ammunition turned gray when they checked records of expenditures by the British artillery. All the shells fired at Gettysburg would have lasted only a few minutes of the tremendous bombardments on the battlefields of Flanders.[188]

Among glaring organization deficiencies was the lack of ammunition trains or trench mortar batteries, essential elements for the conflict ahead. General William J. Snow, who had reactivated the School of Fire at Sill, closed during the border troubles, was appointed chief of field artillery, the first since Henry Hunt. Backed by the Army Chief of Staff General Peyton C. March, also an artilleryman, Snow under seemingly insuperable difficulties set in motion the tremendous expansion of the arm, toiling against time while our hard-pressed Allies held the line in France.

Artillerymen in training matched the broomsticks of the infantry with wooden guns called "Bryan howitzers," or stovepipes in default of cannon. They swung astride flour barrels with stilt legs for riding lessons until the picket lines filled with real horses. Drivers, many meeting these strange creatures for the first time, managed to stay on the back of the near horse and drive them off. Through team-work of lead, swing, and wheel pairs, they came to know the thrill of a battery galloping into action. Cannoneers, finally manning actual pieces, stirred to the click of the breechblock against a live round—the "Set!" of Number One, leaving the range dial to grasp the lanyard—the "Ready!" of the gunner, his deflection and site bubbles leveled—upraised arms of the chief of section and execu-tive officer sweeping downward with the latter's command, "Fire!" At his observation post the battery commander watched through his binoculars the white bursts of shrapnel or the gray of high explo-sive. Adjustments telephoned back to the guns brought a sensing of "Target!" and fire for effect. So must the battery serve its pieces in France.

Beside the men at the guns and on the teams stood the signal and reconnaissance details, mechanics, stable sergeants, horseshoers, sad-dlers—those specialists General Snow was striving so hard to obtain, since 62 per cent of field artillery personnel must now meet that classification. Thousands with such skills and crafts were needed. Only for one vital post, that of first sergeant, could the chief find no corresponding civilian occupation. When he quoted the army adage that a good first sergeant is "the noblest handiwork of God," the classifying committee replied that it knew of no such position in civil life unless it were a clergyman.[189]

The ranks filled—men in olive drab with cords of artillery scarlet around their campaign hats. Nine old regiments, relinquishing some of their noncoms to form cadres for new units, expanded into twenty-one. Eight regiments of rueful cavalrymen were converted into field artillery for this conflict in which trench warfare and the ma-chine gun were tolling the horseman's knell. Elite National Guard regiments of horse met the same fate, to bring that component up to an authorized strength of fifty-one artillery regiments, with the same number for the National Army.

It was our allies who would furnish the guns for them to man, answering at last Mr. Roosevelt's question, "To whose, or what arms?" France alone, in exchange for metals and materials, provided the woefully under-gunned American artillery with 3,834 field-pieces and trench mortars and 10,000,000 rounds of ammunition during the course of the war.[190] Only about 100 of the cannon used in action by the A.E.F. were of American manufacture.[191]

Regiments of artillery, first a few, then many, loaded aboard transports for England and France, standards cased, bands silent in secret embarkations. Unarmed except for Colt .45 automatic pistols or revolvers, and unhorsed, they must wait till they reached their destination to be issued strange cannon and stranger horses, which seemed to understand only French. The cannoneer of 1917-18 soon became familiar with and fond of the gun he served. Like the long line before him he named it, often as inelegantly as "The Old Sow" Knox brought from Fort Ti. A 75 painted olive drab, for instance, might be dubbed and lettered—if the battery commander was not unduly fussy—"The O.D. Bitch." A driver might christen his big wheel pair "Pete and Repeat."

France, the battleground. These artillerymen came to know it both as a land of sunny loveliness and as a sea of mud, devastation, and death. Landing regiments crammed into toylike boxcars labeled *Hommes 40, Chevaux 8,* their capacity for men or horses. One red-leg, as he wedged himself in, remarked: "Well, in the next war I'm going to be one of these here chevaux. I see where only eight of them goes in a car." [192] The legend on the "side door Pullman" drew this comment from another passenger: "I don't know either team, but it must have been a rotten game."

At training cantonments provided by the French Army, most regiments were issued 75's, France's famous *soixante-quinze,* rugged but light, possessing the grace of simplicity. Crews, firing it at all ranges up to its maximum of six thousand yards, warmed to their work and soon were reaching its remarkably high rate of fire of twenty or as many as thirty rounds per minute. Artillerymen trained also on machine guns for close defense of battery positions; on 37-mms. and light and heavy trench mortars whose crews dubbed themselves Suicide Clubs; on hard-hitting 155-mm. howitzers, on antiaircraft guns, and on long-range heavy artillery up to 400-mm. railway ordnance. In the spring they heard of the German "Big Berthas" bombarding Paris at ranges up to seventy-five miles, but they would never man such monster cannon.[193]

Officers and enlisted men buckled down to learning manifold phases of their trade. Firing by night and by map. Camouflage— it was more certain than ever now that "a battery seen is a battery lost." Observation and direction of fire from dugouts sunken in hill-sides, from planes and balloons. Determination of the meteoro-logical data Robins had outlined in 1747—barometric pressure, temperature, wind speed and bearing—become vastly important for their influence on the flight of long-range projectiles. Target prac-tice seemed prodigal to regulars, used to scant ammunition allow-ances, but this conflict already had been proved to be a war of fire power, the defense grown so strong that no advance could be made without a tremendous superiority of artillery to blast open a path for an offensive with shells.[194]

Training completed, divisions one by one took over quiet sectors of the front—the 1st, 42nd, 26th, and 2nd as the vanguard of a host to follow. To Battery C, 6th Field Artillery, 1st Division, went the honor of firing the first American shot—shrapnel directed at a Ger-man battery—on October 23, 1917.

Batteries moved up into the line through the blackness of night, on toward the distant rumble of cannon. Yonder a glare like sheet lightning lit the sky, or a shell burst luridly on a crossroad. It was an adventure those young artillerymen would remember all their lives; some like Jefferson Feigl, of the 7th Field, the first U.S. artil-lery officer killed in action,[195] would not have long to hold the mem-ory. Responsibility weighed heavily on every man, pressing more ponderously than the steel helmet on his head, the gas mask on his chest, the .45 on his hip. He must not fail his regiment, his country, the people at home who were proud of him, the infantry his guns must support.

Thud of hoofs and slither of wheels, and the columns turned off the highway to grope through a forest trail to positions vacated by the French. Guns were manhandled into their emplacements onto platforms, muzzles jutting toward the enemy, while flashlights showed guarded beams, for a hostile plane might be hovering over-head. A whispered order, and the first sergeant guided teams and limbers back to the echelon. Quickly gunners laid their pieces on the slit of a hooded aiming light and set off firing data for a barrage on their sights and scales.

Dawn revealed the marvels wrought by French artillerymen in these quiet sector positions during months of the stalemate of trench warfare. The roofs of emplacements were sodded and timbered, with a deep dugout hewn in rock for reserve ammunition. Other dugouts in whose tiers of bunks Americans had slept were roomy and comfortable, their walls decorated with drawings of unclad mademoiselles from the pages of La Vie Parisienne. One battery discovered a wine cellar, albeit empty, and off in the woods a tiny chapel. Paths were covered over by camouflage netting against air observation. Wires to the switchboard in the telephone dugout were well buried for protection during bombardment of the position.

Then came the night when the lookout sighted a soaring rocket that scattered four green balls—the battery's signal—a call for help from the infantry. The Germans were staging a raid. Shout of "Barrage!" and clang of alarms—empty shell cases or cowbells. A guard seized a ready-fused shell lying on a gun trail, shoved it into the breech, closed the block, jerked the lanyard. Deafening crash of the gun, and the first, all-important shell screamed off to burst in front of the American lines. Crews rushed from dugouts to man all guns and swing into the steady rhythm of the barrage. The cannoneers knew—and it still seemed miraculous—that some two or three miles away in front of the trenches of their infantry, where machine guns and rifles were cracking, a shield of high explosive was being upraised, that six shells per gun per minute, spaced along a registered line, were a barrier of rending steel before the German raiders.

Now the detonations of German counterbattery fire cut ominously through the banging of the 75's—seeking to silence the American guns—explosions that sent steel fragments hurtling at emplacements, or the worse-dreaded dull *plops* that meant gas shells—deadly phosgene or searing mustard.[196] Cannoneers kept the barrage thundering while they struggled into cramping gas masks. The fear of death was on them, yet training and resolution steadied them. At length "Cease firing," and stillness and darkness again. In the morning arrived a message of thanks from the infantry for quick action, music to artillerymen's ears.

Thus they held the line in the *secteurs tranquilles,* though raids were not always handily repulsed. At Seicheprey the 26th Division took 634 casualties in beating off an onslaught by veteran German storm troops.

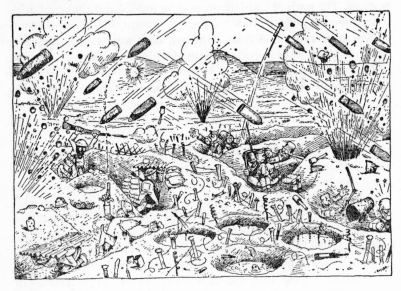

AN ARTILLERY DUEL

This illustration and those on pages 220 and 226 are from *"Happy Days!"* by Captain Alban B. Butler, Jr. By permission of Lieutenant General C. R. Huebner, President, Society of the First Division.

It was not until the end of May, when American troops had been in France eleven months, that the French high command permitted them to undertake an offensive action. Then the 1st Division, its artillery laying down a neat box barrage, stormed and took the village of Cantigny and held it against seven counterattacks. Here was proof that the soldiers from overseas, somewhat doubted because of the long, slow build-up, could deliver a combat punch and keep ground they won. The surprise and delight of French observers was depicted in one of the cartoons drawn by Captain Alban B. Butler, Jr., aide to General Charles P. Summerall, commanding the artillery brigade. Efficient and exacting, Summerall was more dreaded than the Germans by officers and men of his brigade and later of the division. An unfortunate, smarting under one of "Sitting Bull's" blistering reprimands, could find some solace in a comical Butler cartoon which might take the very occasion as its subject.[197]

Stabilized trench fighting seemed to have assumed a permanent aspect, but when American troops were relieved from the line and sent to rest areas, General Pershing insisted that they be trained in open warfare. An imminent event proved that to be one of the wisest decisions of a great soldier.

Irresistibly the Kaiser's armies struck in their mighty spring offensive of 1918. They shattered the French on the Chemin des Dames, swept across the Aisne River to the Vesle and on to the Marne—within forty miles of Paris. In this dire emergency there could be no withholding United States forces, whether little tried or untried. Eleven additional American divisions were now in France, some without their artillery, but only two were within reach to help block the drive: the 3rd, without even quiet sector experience, and the more experienced 2nd. The French high command threw them in. While the 3rd, notably its valiant machine gun companies, balked German attempts to cross the Marne at Château-Thierry, the 2nd pushed forward to stand astride the Paris Road, "trail of empire across Europe for many centuries... trod by the armies of Caesar, Attila, Turenne, and Napoleon." [198]

Following the infantry, the artillery marched toward the sound of the guns. Advancing horsed columns met hundreds of refugees, their homes abandoned, once more streaming rearward in pitiful recessional to escape the relentless invader. Decrepit nags, oxen, or cows pulled wagons piled high with household goods, little children and the very aged perched atop them. Women and old men—all the young men were at the front—trudged wearily, tugging heavily loaded handcarts. To watch them wrung a soldier's heart, then made him grit his teeth, fighting-mad. His homeland might behold such tragic scenes if the Germans won the war here and carried it overseas.

An urgent message from the French. The German mailed fist had smashed a gap in the line four kilometers wide. The 2nd must seal it.

Machine gun and rifle fire sputtered in the fields of wheat and poppies where the infantry and marine brigades and combat engineers faced oncoming Germans and stood them off. The hard-surfaced highway lined with Lombardy poplars rang to hoof and wheel, as the artillery hurried forward. Regulars of the Old Army still with the colors, like Colonel Manus McCloskey of the 12th Field Artillery, who as a young second lieutenant had ridden with Reilly to Peking, thrilled to a stirring sight out of their past—batteries galloping into action. They passed French guns, which unlimbered by the roadside, fired a round or two and resumed retreat, but the American guns pressed onward, found such cover as they could, and opened fire.

ONE IN THE GUN—THREE IN THE AIR

No more well-protected emplacements, nothing better than hastily dug gun pits—often no time even for them. Barrels of 75's and 155's grew hot, were swabbed cool, heated again. Fuse shells, slam them into the breech, check sights, fire on. Sometimes German artillery found an American battery and began to bracket it. A salvo burst beyond it, a second short. The next rounds would narrow that bracket, then a volley would split it, crashing down on the target. Time to move and move fast. Battery commanders called up teams, limbered in hot haste, pulled out at a gallop for a new position. "Action front!"—column swinging into line—cannoneers unlimbering, setting trail spades, taking posts—sharp commands, and the cannonade swelling again. This was war in the open, as the forefathers of these artillerymen had fought it. From Valhalla the shades of Hamilton, of Ringgold and O'Brien, of Pelham and Pegram, of Dilger, Bigelow, and Du Pont, must have watched pridefully. Shell cases heaped higher around the smoking fieldpieces. Now and then the flashing roar of an enemy round wrecked a gun and knocked out its crew; the others blasted on. Horse lines were targets, too, and picketed animals, torn by high explosives, screamed and died. Yet every night the caissons, replenished by the ammunition train, brought the batteries more shells, galloping like the ration carts through perilous crossroads between the methodically timed bursts of German interdiction fire.

So the 2nd stood, blunting the spearhead of the German drive, and then began the attack.

Athwart its path lay the Bois de Belleau, flanked by villages. That little wood, where once noblemen of France had disported themselves in a pleasure pavilion or stalked the stag, was full of other game now. Its rocky depths, thick with shrubbery, were studded by German machine gun nests with interlocking fire lanes. That strong point, from which the enemy could launch his drive anew, must be stormed.

Marines assaulted across the open, spending lives with superb élan. Supporting field artillery could help them little. Barrages fired on those hidden machine gunners in their natural citadels of rock and underbrush would fall on the close-pressing attack waves as well. The tide of assault ebbed in bloody spume, swept forward again, at last flooded into the southern tip of the miniature wilderness. Savage infighting by men willing to die, marines and engineers, carried it on bitter yards farther till it was dammed.

Pull back to the edge of the wood, came the order. As the thinned forest-green and olive-drab line withdrew sullenly, a mass of metal clanged and roared down on the boulder-strewn ground relinquished—HE-shells from all the divisional artillery and heavier stuff from French and American guns, which had been rushed up the

Paris Road to join battle. From south and east they raked the Bois de Belleau, rolling barrages crisscrossing as they swept through it. After them the foot troops surged inward again, caught unwounded German gunners before they could man their weapons, and pushed on till half the wood was won.

> Belleau Wood had become a place of horror. Splintered and torn by shell fire, reeking with gas, stinking with high explosive fumes, its gaunt leafless trees seemed to have died. There was little opportunity to bury the dead on either side and that most awful of all the odors of the front was heavy in the warm June air.[199]

Two more weeks of attacking and beating off counterattacks, and then the wood was captured at last from the hard-fighting veterans who had defended it with such resolute bravery. Marines reached the northern tip where a beautiful memorial chapel now stands, surrounded by white crosses and Stars of David marking graves of the fallen.

Vaux, a solidly built village southeast of the wood, was stormed by the infantry brigade in an operation which, small though it was, is notable for the skilled precision of the artillery preparation. From the village mason, who had escaped the German advance, was obtained an exact location and description of every house. Each battery was assigned one house as its target. Light artillery and heavy guns far to the rear registered with a few rounds, their fire seemingly casual. When all was ready, a tornado of thousands of shells burst on Vaux. Roofs and walls erupted into the air and descended as flattened ruins. The infantry, briefed with similar minuteness down to squad leaders, rushed in and bayoneted enemy survivors emerging from their deepest dugouts, then charged on to take the slopes beyond and hold them against counterattacks.

The last great German drive on Paris had been halted, and a beginning made in rolling it back. French and American divisions on the flanks of the break-through had played their part as well as the 2nd, and Marshal Foch had been massing his remaining reserves. It could not be claimed that the division of the Indian head emblem singly had stopped the foe.

But in a sense broader than the strictly strategic—in that sense which explains the sudden stirring of a new spirit in armies and in nations, the sense which more than strategy explains victory in war—the service of the 2nd Division was almost as momentous as if it alone had brought to an end the German advance.[200]

CHAPTER 12

Fire Power

But neither he [the field commander] nor the artillery should fall into the error of attempting to *shoot a way to victory.* The field artillery may pour tons of projectiles into hostile positions; the air corps may drench the enemy with cargoes of gas and high explosives; the infantry themselves may deluge their antagonist with torrents of small-arms missiles—but it is only the grimy, sweat-lathered doughboys crashing the last barriers with fourteen inches of sharp, cold steel on the busy ends of empty rifles, who nail down the victory.

The essence of all field artillery tactics is to enable the infantryman to reach this point undamaged, and, when accomplished, the field artillery may lay undisputed claim to the title, KING OF BATTLES.

MAJOR-GENERAL H. G. BISHOP, *Field Artillery, the King of Battles*

COMRADESHIP-IN-ARMS flourished between American and French artillerymen. They served the same pieces, provided by France, and "Frog" crews handled them with Gallic gusto, that was much admired, though "Yanks" preferred to sacrifice a little speed for closer shooting. French gunners, despite years in the emplacements of trench warfare, which in the next conflict would bear fatal fruit in the Maginot Line mentality, quickly adapted themselves to the open fighting of 1918. The massed fire of their cannon, particularly the heavier calibers, ever ready to support American attacks, won the enduring gratitude of the A.E.F. Cannoneers of the two nations traded songs—"Over There" for "Madelon"—or cigarettes for swallows of "red ink" or "van blank." Similar ties held between British gunners and the fewer Americans who fought on their front. All the Allies grimly acknowledged the competence of the enemy artillery: its sharpshooting 77's, the terrifying shrieks of projectiles from high velocity, flat trajectory Austrian 88's, heard simultaneously with the burst of the shells, the thunderous heavies—*furor Teutonicus*—obliterating a strong point or command post or turning a crossroads into a crater.

The German line was thick with guns when in mid-July the enemy resumed an offensive which must be continued or foregone for a defensive doomed to ultimate defeat. Man-power balance was tipping against them. A million Americans were in France by July 4, with the tide of reinforcement rising toward a second million. Most of the newly arrived divisions lacked their artillery; some of it joined later, but some divisions never received their guns. Although these fresh troops were still unseasoned, older divisions stood with the French to meet the formidable German thrusts through Champagne and along the Marne.

A German officer carrying battle plans was captured on the eve of the July 4 attack in the Champagne. Thus forewarned, a heavy Allied barrage anticipated the enemy's by one hour. Artillery of the American 42nd Rainbow Division, holding part of the line, joined in heaping tons of high explosive on assembly points and gun positions. But the German barrage, when it was fired on schedule, was still tremendous. It rolled over the front line, where gallant sacrifice posts held till they were overwhelmed. Then it moved forward, overlaid by machine gun bullets from low-flying planes. Assault waves following it were shredded by the ranked guns of the Rainbow, the 75's almost hub to hub, beating a tattoo of drumfire. Still the Boche came on. Infantry met him with blazing rifles, grenades, and bayonets, fought him off for three hours and flung him back.

The foe struck also on the Marne, attacking east of Château-Thierry. Neither the French nor the 3rd and 28th American Divisions could hold the southern bank of the river under the crushing weight of the German cannon and machine gun bombardment. The 18th Field Artillery of the 3rd suffered the fate every gunner dreads. Shells caught it in column on its way into action, smashing men, horses, and carriages. As the enemy forced the river crossing, the battle split into segments of furious combat. The 38th Infantry, assailed on three sides, beat off repeated onslaughts and with other units helped the 3rd Division earn its title, "Rock of the Marne." Stubborn resistance at last broke enemy momentum and drove him back across the river. He would not be allowed to hold his lines there much longer.

"RIDE 'EM—COWBOY"

Now was the moment for attack. French army orders launched three divisions—the 1st Moroccan (colonial troops and the Foreign Legion) and the 1st and 2nd American—in a surprise thrust toward the broad plateau dominated by the city of Soissons. On the night of July 16 columns totaling sixty-seven thousand men, five thousand animals, and three thousand vehicles groped through the forests of Compiègne and Retz along three roads leading to the front. A furious storm broke over them—rolling thunder, blinding lightning flashes, intensifying the pitch-blackness as they faded, drenching sheets of rain. Providentially it grounded enemy planes that could have spotted the heavy traffic on moonlit roads, but for the marchers it was misery and chaos compounded.

Batteries rolled on, flanked by files of infantry, interspersed with tanks, trucks, staff cars, motorcycles, and mule-drawn machine-gun carts. "Walk 'em out, drivers, Push 'em along." There was urgency in the orders of officers, sergeants, and caisson corporals. The guns must be in position to cover the dawn attack. A jam up ahead, and teams all but telescoped. Strong wheel horses leaned back in their breechings, braking the carriages. Space, unseen but sensed, opened again. "Forward, ho," then "Give way to the right." A couple of big French tanks clattered by. Artillery drivers, helmet brims hunched down to collars in vain attempts to keep the torrential rain from pouring down their necks, patted and steadied their frightened pairs. Guns, caissons, and limbers slithered and slid into the slimy clutches of a drainage ditch. Out of its black depths rose the sound of frantic scrambling and disembodied voices cursing bitterly. "You blasted redlegs! Got the whole damn road. Can't you leave the ditch to the poor bloody infantry?" Through the confusion cut a battery first sergeant's rasping barks, "Man the wheels, you cannoneers. You there, get down in that mud before I throw you in! Ready, drivers. Together now. Forward, ho!" and the guns rolled on.

At last the tortured progress of that dreadful night was past. Soaked to the skin and bone-weary, somehow they had made it. Where battalion commanders with their details waited, positions selected, firing data figured, the guns unlimbered and prepared for action. Yet the pride of artillerymen in coming through was humbled when they watched the exhausted 23rd Infantry covering the last two miles at a stumbling, staggering run to reach the jump-off point in time.

Four thirty-five A.M. Miles of close-laid guns erupted, flaming and crashing like the thunderstorm of the past night. Mud-crusted wheels shuddered, as recoil dug in the trail spades deeper. Chains of cannoneers fused and fed shells into the smoking breeches. Arms of executives and chiefs of section beat the tempo for an uproarious crescendo. "It lasted only five minutes, that barrage, with every French and American gun that could be brought to bear firing at top speed. But they were terrible moments for the unsuspecting Boche." [201] Infantry on the fringes of the forest—Senegalese, legionnaires, doughboys, marines—shed their utter weariness and plunged into battle behind that rolling curtain of fire.

Signal rockets soared from the enemy's front line, calling for help. His artillery's answering barrage was feeble. Assault waves stormed through it. Tanks, heirs to the chariot, the war elephant, and heavy cavalry, lumbered over forward machine-gun nests. Allied planes swooped down to pepper rallying lines in field gray. When the field artillery reached its range limits, it limbered, galloped forward close on the heels of the advancing infantry, and burst again into blazing action. Past the guns charged a full brigade of French cavalry. Soon its shattered remnants reeled back. German machine guns had proved as ruinous as the sunken road at Waterloo to Napoleon's horsemen.

Three days of raging combat—an advance of thirty miles—more than seven thousand prisoners and ninety cannon captured from the enemy. The price was high Allied casualties. Soissons was a victory dearly bought, but a magnificent one, for it marked the turning point of the war. The mighty German machine ground into slow reverse, yet it was as deadly in retrograde as in advance.

American divisions, the 3rd, 4th, 26th, 28th, 32nd, 43rd, and 77th, swept forward with French Army corps, olive drab intermingled with horizon blue. Against the bitterest opposition they fought their way across the Marne, over that blood-dyed little stream, the Ourq, then the Vesle. Now, the crisis past, the time had come for General Pershing to realize his cherished purpose of assembling units scattered along the French and British fronts to form an American army.

East of Verdun the St. Mihiel salient was thrust into the Allied lines, a menacing lance head that might be plunged deeper, a flanking threat to any advance in the area. This four-year-old stronghold, long impregnable to French attacks, severed important railroads and clamped a chancery grip upon mining and industrial areas. Finally the salient had subsided to the status of a quiet sector where both adversaries rested troops, or green American divisions first went into the line.

The time had come when it could no longer be tolerated. Its reduction was prerequisite to the launching of a great offensive to drive the Kaiser's armies back across the Rhine. Bugles, muted to secrecy, blew assembly for the First American Army to assault St. Mihiel—to strike from south and west and pinch off the salient.

Staffs toiled long hours over battle plans of magnitude and complexity unprecedented in American experience. Officers who had handled no more than a division in school exercises struggled with the march orders and logistics of an army. The call for cannon steadily soared upward from a first estimate of 984. General Pershing, on the advice of his artillery chief, Major General E. F. McGlachlin, insisted on a fire preparation that would flatten the formidable defenses of the salient for his infantry—a preparation requiring far more guns than the First Army could provide.[202] The French agreed to fill out his quota. Cannon converged on St. Mihiel in a mighty massing that staggered the imaginations of American artillerymen: 3,010 guns of twenty-six calibers and forty-nine models, using seventy-four types of ammunition. For four hours and forty-five minutes before the attack they would deluge the salient and its supply lines with steel and gas.

In châteaux headquarters near the front weary clerks under hard-driving sergeants major typed off the mission sheets.

> Trench mortars during entire period to cut wire [the orders read]. All other guns, for the first 15 minutes to place an intensive fire on command posts, telephone centrals, trains, billets, and improved roads, to demoralize communications, and prevent the enemy from securing information, or transmitting orders. After the first 15 minutes, this fire to be maintained by a reduced number of guns ... Long distance fire on Metz, Conflans, Mars-la-Tour for psychological effect and to interrupt railroads. Counter-battery. Shelling and gassing trenches and centers of resistance to neutralize occupants, to include towns within the first day's objective, these fires to be continued till the end of the attack. Effective at H hour, a rolling barrage by 75-mm. guns at the rate of ten batteries per kilometer. Observation from the air, requiring 31 squadrons of planes and 34 balloons.

On the black, stormy night of September 11, 1918, the concentration of five hundred thousand assault troops was complete, with the last of the guns in position. In spite of secrecy, German intelli-

gence suspected the coming attack, and a withdrawal had commenced, but ten infantry divisions and their supporting artillery
—180 batteries including some big guns—still held St. Mihiel. At
1 A.M. on the twelfth the cannonade in a full-throated roar crashed
down on the garrison of one hundred thousand. Night turned to
day as the horizon flamed with the flashes of those massed Allied
guns. Tons of high explosive crumbled concrete strong points and
artillery emplacements and paralyzed communications. Where that
vast weight of rending metal did not crush and kill, it stunned and
terrorized. As the hours ticked past, shell fire mounted higher toward
the battle's expenditure of 838,800 rounds.

Twenty minutes before dawn long lines of 75's rolled out a
splendid barrage, smoke and nonpersistent gas mingled with HE.
Behind the fiery curtain, moving forward one hundred meters every
four minutes, the infantry assaulted, cutting rusted barbed wire
where the mortars had not leveled it. Gallant German machine
gunners and riflemen manned their parapets again, but the doughboys drove through on both fronts, the field guns limbering up and
following, plunging ahead through hub-deep mud. With American
planes ruling the air, and the enemy observation post on Mount Sec
finally blinded by smoke shells, the attacking columns closed in.
The 1st and 26th Divisions met, sealing off the salient, and St.
Mihiel was won, with 16,000 prisoners and 443 pieces of artillery
taken. "Seldom in history has a military operation been carried out
more precisely according to program." [203]

Now in a last great offensive the Allies attacked in unison on a
front of 203 miles from the English Channel to Verdun. Between
the Meuse River and the Argonne Forest Pershing flung his First
and Second Armies against the enemy. Battle-proved divisions and
new ones taking their baptism of fire launched a drive that would
continue through forty-seven days of fierce combat. The obstinate
German, that bitter, last-ditch fighter, met them, took his losses, and
exacted a toll that would amount to 120,000 American casualties
before he was willing to acknowledge inevitable defeat.

Again the guns were massed. Three thousand nine hundred and
twenty-eight of them, from trench mortars to 14-inch railroad, thundered in a concentration:

which tore to pieces the concrete and barbed wire of the Hindenburg Line, and in the succeeding six hours upheaved the earth until it was a shambles. Every German battery on the front was smothered in this intense bombardment, which prepared the way for the infantry, who jumped off at 5:30 A.M. September 26, 1918, in the greatest battle thus far of the American Army.

On no other front of similar extent had there been such a terrific bombardment. The aggregate of French and American artillery averaged one gun for each eight meters of front, whereas on July 15 the Germans had in the Champagne one gun for each twenty-five meters of front. In the first day the artillery between the Meuse and the Argonne fired over a quarter of a million rounds on the German forward positions and barbed wire. This so paralyzed the enemy defenders that ... when the eager assaulting waves jumped off behind the cover of their rolling barrage, they met practically no resistance. The infantry and machine gunners swept across the sea of mud, shell holes, shattered wire, and ruined trenches, mopping up the few German dugouts that had weathered that frightful storm of metal.[204]

Once the breach was opened, it was a different story. Infantry, forging rapidly forward, outran their artillery, slowed by mud, tangled in forests, or held up by blown-out bridges. A 4th Division unit, far ahead of its guns, captured a German battery; doughboys, turned cannoneers, swung the pieces around and blasted back the enemy with fifteen thousand rounds of his own ammunition. Pursuit, checked until the artillery caught up, pushed onward through stark woods, over roads pocked with mine craters and lined by the bloated bodies of horses. They fought across old battlefields where the bones of the dead lay so thick it was hard to find clear ground to sink a gun's trail spade. Day followed day of attack and counterattack, of battery and counterbattery. Artillerymen stood to their guns under pounding of 77's, 105's, and heavies, and machine-gunning by low-flying planes. Headquarters, 160th Field Artillery Brigade, developed a novel type of close defense when antiaircraft knocked out a Boche strafer above. Its crew of two bailed out and parachuted down, both ready to fight. The pilot, grasping a machine gun, became fouled in the shrouds and fell to his death, but the sergeant-observer, pistol drawn, descended safely. Before his feet touched ground and he could start shooting, an unarmed captain, John J. McCloy, future Assistant Secretary of War and High Commissioner in Germany, brought him down with a flying tackle.

Blanc Mont, key to the Champagne, barred the Allied advance. French assaults against that almost impregnable ridge had been shattered, companies whittled down to platoons. To storm the height and its angled trenches, affording deadly cross fire, General Pershing lent the 2nd Division. Rushed up into the line, its veteran foot troops poised at the jump-off points while a heavy cannonade raked the route of attack.

> All the French and American guns opened with one world-shaking crash [a marine officer recollected].[205] From the Essen Trench the ground fell away gently, then rose in a long slope, along which could be made out the zigzags of the German trenches. . . . The battalion saw all this ground swept by a hurricane of shell-fire. . . . The heavens seemed roofed over with long, keening noises—sounds like the sharp ripping of silk, magnified, running in swift arcs from horizon to horizon. These were the quick-firing 75's, the clear-cut bark of their discharges merging into a crashing roar. Other sounds came with them, deeper in key, the whine growing to a rumble—these were the heavier shells—105's, 155's, 210's. Almost, one expected to look up and see them, like swift, deadly birds, some small, some enormous, all terrible.

Then the marine witnessed a spectacle prophetic of a mighty weapon in a war to come.

> Far off, Blanc Mont way, a lucky shell found and exploded a great ammunition-dump—the battalion felt the long tremor from the shock of it come to them through the earth and watched, minutes after the high crimson flare of the explosion, a broad column of smoke that shot straight up from it, hundreds of feet, and hung in the air, spreading out at the top like some unearthly tree.

Yet artillery could only blast open the approaches. The storming of the ridge was the infantry's grim and bloody business. "It is only the grimy, sweat-lathered doughboys crashing the last barriers with fourteen inches of sharp, cold steel on the busy ends of empty rifles, who nail down the victory." [206] Such was the manner of the taking of Blanc Mont. The 2nd, ranks pitifully thinned, was relieved except for its artillery, which stayed in the line to support the 36th, whose gunners were still in training. The latter division pushed on, suffering heavy punishment but advancing rapidly.

Toward the end of October, seven fine combat divisions assembled to break the last German line of defense, the redoubtable Kriemhilde Stellung. Again a gathering of the guns, "cannon enough to conquer Hell." Besides the guns of the assault divisions, the artillery brigades of those which had been relieved were retained. Behind the fieldpieces stood the deep-ranged heavies of corps and army. Shells were heaped high around them, brought by broad- and narrow-gauge railroads extended toward the front. Every piece had fired on registration points whence it would shift to its targets at H-hour, targets plotted and pin-pointed on battle maps with the aid of aerial photographs; reconnaissance planes had spotted and snapped nearly every German battery position and machine gun strong point.

It struck "like a million hammers," that last great American barrage of the war, on the night of October 31, 1918, and pounded away savagely for two hours. The reply of the enemy's artillery, many a gun smashed into wreckage of twisted steel, was weak when the infantry surged forward early next morning. In the woods to the east and west fierce resistance was encountered, but center divisions broke through behind a rolling barrage and a vanguard of tanks, overrunning German gunners, and swept ahead for nine kilometers. Flanks pivoted, beating off counterattacks. Then the attack transformed itself from spear into scythe, as the wings swung forward. Here and there the foe rallied for savage rear-guard fights against the hard-driving divisions, far ahead of the massed guns that had opened the way for the break-through and now supported only by their own brigades of fieldpieces but needing no more.

When the Germans made a stand along the southern edge of a thick forest, Bois de Belval, traversed by a single road, orders sent forward a single battalion of the 9th Infantry, accompanied by one battery of the 15th Field Artillery in a daring exploit. On the evening of November 3, as soon as darkness fell, the little command entered the forest. It marched all night, catching enemy machine gunners asleep around their weapons and capturing farmhouse garrisons. By midnight the column had pierced the woods. Dismayed Germans at dawn discovered American infantry and artillery in battle order six kilometers inside their lines, and hastily resumed their retreat.

Assault became pursuit, almost precipitate—a headlong rush on Sedan, divisions striving in rivalry to be first to capture the historic city. It was the famous 1st, the "Big Red 1," directed to cut across divisional boundaries, that held the lead. Sleepless for two days, it marched thirty-eight miles in thirty hours, fighting two engagements. Lieutenant Colonel Theodore Roosevelt, Jr., still limping from a bullet wound received at Soissons, left his car at a blown-out bridge and covered twelve kilometers on foot. But the 1st was halted by orders on the verge of victory, and the trophy of Sedan was fittingly awarded to the French Army.

The eleventh hour of the eleventh day of the eleventh month approached. A cease firing, preliminary to the armistice the Germans had asked in sullen defeat, was about to become effective. Just before the moment struck, shell fire crashed along the line in clamorous valedictory. Then fell that unforgettable silence, more thunderous than the sound of the guns.

After the signing of the armistice, an American army of occupation followed at a distance retreating German forces, quitting the land of France they had so nearly overrun. As a battalion of marines swung through the quiet countryside to take post for the watch on the Rhine, it passed orderly piles of German helmets and a battery of 105 howitzers, abandoned but parked with precision—as if their cannoneers might someday return to man them. Voices were lifted along the marching column in forest green.

"What about the ole Boche?—You think he was licked enough?" "No, I don't. That stuff back there, they laid it down under orders, like they do everything. It's stacked—it ain't just thrown away."—"Remember the other day, when

we was advance-guard, we could see their rear-guard, sometimes—perfect order, and all that—not like a defeated outfit,
at all!" "Sure! I hope to spit in yo' mess-kit, it ain't!—They
ain't licked enough." [207]

The battalion moved on to a town where a towered bridge
spanned the Rhine—Remagen. Americans would march this way
again.

CHAPTER 13

Gunnery: Art to Science

••

Predictors, rockets, and radar—to mention but a few develop-
ments—have made "The Great Art of Artillery" more precise
and less of an art than a Science.

ANONYMOUS, *The Gunner*

For pinpointing accessible targets, the air was normally not
so effective as artillery.

GENERAL DWIGHT D. EISENHOWER, *Crusade in Europe*

Officers should be capable of shooting "the ash of their cigarettes without hurting their faces." ... The infantry have a
blind faith in our shooting, which is very flattering, but it means
that they ask us to do some extraordinary things. For instance,
they think little of surrounding a bunker at about 200 yards
radius, and then ask for a 5.5-inch to bust it, at anything up to
10,000 yards range.

Artillery in Combat [208]

••

ARTILLERY in the first World War had established itself as the
greatest killer on the battlefield, accounting for more than seventy-
five per cent of the casualties. Development of so lethal an arm could
be neglected only in the fatuous belief that the past conflict was "the
war to end wars" it had been declared to be. The War Department
acted with foresight and dispatch. A month after the armistice it
appointed a board of artillery and ordnance officers, headed by
Brigadier General William Westervelt, to make a study of the armament, caliber, type of matériel, kind and proportions of ammuni-

tion, and method of transport to be assigned to a field army. In May, 1919, the board issued a notable report, recommending practical types for immediate development and ideal ones that might be realized if the usual postwar reduction of appropriations was not too drastic.

Most of the board's forward-looking recommendations remained on paper during the seemingly inevitable lean years of the peace interlude, with the surplus equipment of 1918 becoming increasingly obsolescent and ineffective. In allotment of funds, the Army, cast in its perennial role as "the stepchild of the services," fared worse than the Navy, guardian of oceans still regarded as barriers, barriers which the Air Corps, scanted like the ground forces, would override.[209] Yet research and development continued, though the national purse strings were kept so tight that it was a struggle to obtain funds even for pilot models. With the enterprise and ingenuity that would place the Garrand rifle, the light carbine, and other new arms in the hands of the infantry, the artillery maintained the Knox tradition, "the resources of genius," in its search for better weapons, tactics, and techniques.

As horses and caissons bowed out before motor transport, fieldpieces were first carried in trucks (portée artillery), then equipped with balloon-tired carriages and towed, making more room for cannoneers and ammunition. Officers' chargers became jeeps or command cars, the scout's and courier's horse a motorcycle. The gun and the tractor were wedded in self-propelled (SP) artillery, ready to roll into action with the tanks, half-tracks, and armored cars of the fast-moving field artillery battalions of armored divisions. Mortars and the howitzers of cannon companies, assigned to the infantry, gave close support. A new type of flying battery appeared in dive bombers. If bad weather did not ground them, a rapid advance, outrunning its accompanying guns, could still count on the artillery of the air.[210]

Heavy cannon on motorized mounts were no longer road-bound, given bulldozers to pave their way. Disassembled pack howitzers, shifted from the backs of mules to the bellies of planes to be dropped by parachute with their cannoneers, could be assembled and start firing in a few minutes. The 75-mm. gun yielded to the split-trail 105-mm. (4.2-inch) howitzer with a maximum range of 8.2 miles.

Gradually the American arsenal was augmented by improved 155-mm. (6.2-inch) guns, which bore the traditional name of Long Toms; by 8-inch howitzers with a range of 12.3 miles; by 240-mm. (9.6-inch) howitzers and 8-inch guns, the latter capable of hurling projectiles twenty-four miles. Tank destroyers, awaiting combat cues from Rommel panzers in Africa, finally came off production lines as full-tracked and highly mobile, mounting hard-hitting 76's or 90's. The merciless German bombings of London, Coventry, and Rotterdam prompted an extraordinary development in automatically controlled anti-aircraft guns: 75's and later 90's to sweep the skies. Tracking planes by radar at distances up to four miles in clear weather, darkness, or fog, their instruments computed speed, course, drift, and range; they were automatically loaded and similarly fired when on target. AA batteries with their generators and other apparatus looked like small power plants.

Off stage and late to appear was a 90-mm. triple-purpose rifle that would be badly needed to counter the German 88 employed against planes in the Spanish civil war, while its other uses were then craftily concealed. It would subsequently be unveiled as also an efficient and deadly anti-tank and anti-personnel weapon.

Brilliant minds were at work on other improvements and innovations. The rocket was revived as the projectile for the bazooka which, handled by a single soldier, could stop a tank, as ammunition for recoilless cannon as large as 105's, and for batteries of launchers that could drench a target area with the red glare of explosions such as Key watched at Fort McHenry. Magnified a thousandfold, the rocket became Hitler's V-2 bomb, propelled by alcohol and liquid oxygen at three thousand miles per hour, faster than sound, and carrying a twenty-two-hundred-pound war head of TNT. Planes and anti-aircraft fire, which brought down the jet-propelled V-1, could not stop the V-2. The dread age of guided missiles had dawned.

Radar and sonar would give the same sharp perception to the artillery's sound- and flash-ranging sections, spotting enemy guns, as they did the submarine-hunting destroyer. Ammunition kept pace with advances in guns. Cannoneers, when firing was leisurely, chalked shells with Hitler's name, adding sundry uncomplimentary remarks, as they had with the "To Kaiser Bill" missiles of 1918. They were unconsciously carrying on an ancient artillery custom, dating back to the thunderbolt markings and inscriptions on lead pellets cast by Roman slingers.[211] But they no longer loaded shrapnel, which had been outmoded and discarded, though war correspondents persisted in using the term. The artillery of World War II fired high explosive, armor-piercing, smoke, and white phosphorus shells. Gas shells and bombs, held in reserve, were not employed by the adversaries for fear of retaliation in kind on each other's civilian populations. German powder, flashless as well as smokeless, was superior to American and "helped the enemy tremendously in concealing his fire positions." [212] However, it was countered by a notable American invention, the proximity (VT) fuse, which would prove its high worth in the latter part of the war. Requiring no setting—unlike the time fuse—the tiny electronic device it contained exploded the shell when it came into proximity with an objective. It greatly multiplied the effectiveness of antiaircraft fire and delivered deadly air bursts over ground targets. And in the laboratories experiments in atomic fission were creating the appalling aerial bomb that would shatter the last resistance of the Japanese Empire with an explosive that would later load artillery shells and guided missiles.

Artillerymen, struggling with new scientific aspects of their trade, plunged into such refinements as calculating the weight of the paint on various types of ammunition to determine its influence on the flight of projectiles. Gradually simplification cut through complexities to the efficient fulfillment of the artillery's primary mission: support of the other arms. Its age-old basic tactics had not changed. They were still mobility, massing of fires, flexibility of control, and accuracy of delivery.[213] By the perfection of the fire-direction center —the "FDC" of the second World War—devastating concentrations reached a height which must have won a nod of amazed approval from the shade of Henry Hunt of Malvern Hill. Swift and devastating accuracy was achieved by the widespread use of forward observers and of cub planes as spotters. To an infantry colonel, admiring the work of the little planes at Louisiana maneuvers, they had seemed to give heavy and long-range artillery an ability to adjust fire as quickly and accurately as light guns within eyeshot of the target. Their radio reports afforded field commanders "a grasp of the tactical situation—terrain, avenues of movement, concentrations of troops and artillery—almost as complete as in the eighteenth century, when the opposing commanders, from horseback or a hillock, could view all the regiments committed to battle." [214] Later the colonel, promoted general, successfully advocated the adoption of cubs as standard equipment for every division. All the artillery, for invaluable "eyes" given it, would stand in debt to that infantry officer, Dwight D. Eisenhower.

Fateful December 7, 1941, and the surprise attack by Japanese bombers on Pearl Harbor, Hawaii. Another war with a new enemy and shortly on a second front with an old one, who had not "been licked enough." German blitzkriegs in whirlwind operations had crushed Poland, Denmark, Norway, Holland, Belgium, and France. American artillerymen mourned especially the downfall of French comrades-in-arms, who had fought beside them in the open warfare of 1918. The 75's of yore had been abandoned for the big guns of the Maginot Line, outflanked and frustrated when Hitler's swift armored columns cut in behind them through the Ardennes. Once more the death knell of forts had been tolled.

As in the previous conflict, while the United States prepared, the line beyond the Atlantic was held by allies, so soon reduced to valiant Britain, fighting for survival. Renewed hostilities with Germany must wait until we began to deal with the foe in the Far East who was overrunning the Philippines and sweeping across the Pacific from island to island toward our coast.

Again time, tide, and fortune, which proverbially wait for no man, granted grace to the United States of America. The long toil of planning staffs, persistent research and development, blueprints for industrial mobilization—all these sped rearmament and training far faster than the dragging pace of 1917-18. Three large field artillery replacement and training centers—historic Fort Sill, Fort Bragg in North Carolina, and Camp Roberts in California—filled with men who wore the golden crossed cannon and scarlet piping and must learn to merit such insignia, such marks of honor. Ranges rang to the sound of the guns: the boom of 105's, the sharp bark of Long Toms, the thunders of 240's. Ahead lay combat in jungle and desert, on plain and mountain, in scorching heat and bitter cold. Artillerymen would land shipborne guns through surf and knife-edged shoals on scores of islands, repeating the feat of their forefathers at Louisbourg, would man them on snowy fields like Trenton's, fight them through bloody street battles, as at Monterey, and haul them up the heights of other Cerro Gordos; would bring them into action through new Wildernesses, Belleau Woods, Argonnes. And all the great cannonades of history would only faintly echo the volume and fury of their fire.

The vast cyclorama of the second World War limits this chronicle to comparatively few of its artillery actions, selected for their importance, magnitude, or other striking features. Detailed accounts are found in the many-volume *U.S. Army in World War II*,[215] the Historical Division's studies, artillery unit histories,[216] and numerous other sources.[217]

Men of the 1st Marine Division stared from fleet decks at tropical Guadalcanal. The Navy, fighting the first of a series of great Pacific battles, had brought them there, guarding the transports with warships and carrier planes. Now the task of storming this Japanese-held island and the capture of its vital airfield was up to ground forces. Marine and army gunners must somehow jam fieldpieces through those jungles yonder, dense growths which would be tough going even for riflemen and machine gunners. Hemmed in by green walls, they must find fields of fire, must blast back Jap attacks and counterbattery the enemy's artillery.

On August 7, 1942, the six-month battle for Guadalcanal opened as one of the many amphibious operations that would characterize this war. While foot troops clambered down nets into landing craft, guns were hoisted from holds and lowered in their turn into the steel boats. Beached, they were hauled inland, the 75-mm. pack howitzers by jeeps, the 105's by amphibious tractors until their own prime movers—trucks, put ashore from ramp-equipped boats—arrived to take them in tow. The jungle swallowed them and their sweat-drenched crews. Gun by gun at trail sides—there was seldom room for ranked batteries—they joined muffled booms to the rattle of small-arm fire in a desperate combat which would hang in the balance for many days.

It was combat almost as close for artillery as for infantry. In jungle fighting there could be no comparatively safe positions well to the rear for the guns—not if they were to give essential support. Jap riflemen, painted green and hidden up high in trees, let skirmishers pass and held their fire to drop cannoneers or personnel at command posts. One field artillery battalion, moving forward in the wake of the infantry, toppled ten snipers from their perches during its first twenty-four hours in position. Batteries preparing for action dared not risk bellowed commands which might bring fire from infiltrating sharpshooters. Executive and chiefs of section strapped field telephones to their chests, with plenty of wire for freedom of action, and in low voices relayed firing data from observers to the gun layers. Regularly artillery units set up strong defenses around their guns: trenches and foxholes, manned by alert sentries; barbed wire, booby traps, and .30 caliber machine guns.

Muzzles of howitzers rose higher until loaders, bending beneath the breeches, were "literally shoving the shells skyward." Only high-angle fire would serve in jungle warfare. Firing at ranges as short as sixteen hundred yards or even less, they dropped projectiles with reduced charges on enemy lines no farther than two hundred yards from the American front. When such close shooting began, the wily Jap resorted to the ruse of simultaneously bombarding our infantry with mortars, thus persuading the Americans that their own artillery was firing short and landing on them. Calls for cease fire were frequent; it was hard to convince infantrymen that they were not taking hits from their own guns.

In the attack on the Gifu the 105's and 155's were emplaced only two thousand yards from the target: an enemy concentration in ravines behind a hill, held by our infantry. Two thousand, eight hundred yards was the minimum for high-angle fire then listed in firing tables for the heavier caliber. Since some of the 155 shells would probably not clear the hilltop, the infantry was pulled back, and the howitzers opened at twelve hundred. However, infantrymen on an adjacent hill believed the shells were falling short and called for cease fire. "The artillery battalions then adjusted each howitzer individually on the target, a slow task which took over two hours to complete." For ninety minutes, forty-nine howitzers, joined by mortars, placed more than seventeen hundred rounds in an area less than one thousand yards square. "Japanese prisoners, captured during the next few days, were nearly all shell-shocked." [218]

The shooting of the artillery on Guadalcanal was not only close and heavy but fast. During the 25th Division's advance to Kokumbona after the Army had relieved the marines, the 8th Field Artillery Battalion fired at the extremely rapid rate of fourteen and one-half rounds per gun per minute.[219] First-rate gunnery had developed from the use of fire-direction centers and forward observers.

FO's were not new. They had functioned in past wars, sometimes at posts perilously close to targets, deliberately bringing down on themselves the gunfire they guided. Now with advances in communications and techniques, this gallant breed of field artillerymen came into their own. It was one of them, Captain John F. Casey, Jr., of the army artillery reinforcing the marines, who played a key part in the repulse of a formidable and critical night attack.

> Suddenly the whisper came along the line, "Get Captain Casey up to the wall right away," [runs this vivid account.] [220] As I climbed up the hill I stumbled over exhausted forms and muttered the password as sort of an endless chant. Soon I reached the middle line and Lt. Giesal's CP. The situation was not pleasant. The doughboys had withdrawn to the low line of ragged rock which we had used as a CP in the morning, leaving the ridge open above them. A gap had developed between E and F Companies, and Lt. Giesal was begging for more men to fill it. Orders had been given to the grimy, blood-stained, sleep-sodden doughboys that there would be no firing tonight. All charges would be taken on the bayonet or with grenades. There were about 50 rounds per rifle left, and two grenades for every three men. Machine guns also had but a few bursts remaining. Most disturbing of all, the Japs were trying to emplace machine guns on the line which we had just evacuated. From there they would have a complete sweep of our positions, and we would be driven from the hill.
>
> We must pull the artillery on to the hill and forestall the charge. My line had gone out, so I used the infantry line which went through a series of switchboards before it reached Tiger Blue FDC. Everybody was tacked in on the line in a gigantic conference call which, looking back, had its humorous aspects. I called our liaison officer with the Marine FDC,

Capt. Lincoln W. Stoddard, and gave him the story. It was certainly a great mental comfort to be talking to somebody I knew. We would adjust Concentration 941 up onto the hill. The battalion would be firing over the 3rd Battalion, to our north, directly at our positions.

"Give me George Battery, Battery 1 round, Concentration 941."

A voice came on somewhere down the line, "Casey, what is the story? I understood that we are still holding the same positions as this afternoon."

Another voice cut in, "That's right, sir. We are. The observer does not understand infantry tactics; we have just consolidated our lines."

FDC queries, "Is that true, Casey? If so, we can not give you what you asked for."

By this time, we could see the enemy silhouetted on the top of the ridge. Exasperated, I shouted, "Sir, I am sitting in the front lines. I am not on top of the hill. We need fire immediately."

That was good enough for Col. Curry, and the rounds were on the way.

"Left 100. Repeat range."

Someone broke in on the line again, "Cease fire. Those rounds fell too close to the 3rd Battalion."

Another voice cut in, "That's OK, Casey, go ahead."

"Clear the line. FIRE MISSION."

"On the way."

"Left 100, up 50." The rounds echoed through the night, still not quite on the line or in close enough.

"Left 50, up 50." We are creeping now, taking no chances on hitting our own lines. "That sounds better. It's OK for deflection but still got to pull it in more."

One platoon calls in, "Shadows coming down ridge on right."

"Up 50." Wonderful! They are breaking over the wall now, but let's try to get them out on the slope in front.

"Up 25." Cr-r-r-rash! The whole salvo slides over the top

of the hill down toward the Battalion CP. The infantry CO
says, "That's OK, Casey. Nobody hurt. Go ahead."

"Down 25. Battery 10 rounds."

"Concentration 943 on the way."

The doughboys are with us. They love it. Reports come in
from all the companies. "They are landing right in there.
Give them some more. Give them hell."

After that it wasn't so bad. The Japs never got their machine guns in place. A few slipped through the barrage, but
grenades got them. Not only I, but every doughboy on that
hill was an artillery observer that night. Lt. Giesal had wire
communication with each platoon and company in the line.
When the Japs would start an advance word would be whispered in, "They are coming again"—and we would pour old
943 in there.

It was a funny night. We all had that tight feeling in our
throats. Would the Japs withstand the fire and get machine
guns on the ridge? Words from the National Anthem rang
through my head, "Oh, say does that star-spangled banner
still wave,,,,,"; "o'er Hill 27" was substituted for the rest.

Toward dawn the last sustained attack was hurtled back. It
was all right now. It was morning. We were in. . . . It wasn't
such a bad night after all. We had stopped them cold. No
doubt they would be back again, but never would our position be so vulnerable.

Guadalcanal was not wrested from the grip of the Japanese until
March, 1943. They clung to their other Pacific citadels with the
same fanatical tenacity. Meanwhile, as the bloody business of island
hopping proceeded—by sea and air and ground battles—the United
States had taken up the gage on a second front across the Atlantic.
Making good the landings of Operation Torch in North Africa in
November, 1942, American forces joined the British in the drive
through Tunisia against Rommel's *Afrika Korps* and its Italian
allies.

Tank battled tank, and tank destroyers, half-tracks, and armored
cars clashed. Field artillery batteries shot it out with the panzers at
ranges which quickly closed from thousands to hundreds of yards,

then to point-blank blasts. The swift and sudden warfare of the deserts and *djebels* echoed with the clang of armor-piercing shells striking steel "like a sharp blow on a church bell." Overtones were the crescendo shrieks of swooping dive bombers.

Again forward observers played their part, one no less vital than in the jungle but vastly more sweeping and flexible in this open country. Young artillery officers, with battalions of wire—or radio-linked guns at their call and numerous targets in their field of fire, wielded the Jovian power of a fistful of thunderbolts. In an attack east of El Guettar an observer, advancing with an infantry company, found a post on a hill that overlooked the German positions on lower ground as well as their supply and reinforcement routes to the south and east. Spread out under his eyes was a profusion of targets, an FO's dream come true—foot troops, tanks, trucks in column of march or parked, ammunition and supply dumps. On them he adjusted the artillery of his entire division, then of the corps, and opened fire for effect. For eight hours, while he himself was the target of enemy mortars and cannon, he swept the area with high explosive. By the end of the day he had "successfully carried out his mission," runs the dry official report, "and the infantry on his right was able to advance and gain its objective." [221]

February, 1943, brought black days for American arms. Rommel's panzers, supported by dive bombers, smashed through Faid Pass. Green troops, spread thin, hampered by disjointed or inept command, could not halt the onrush. German armor overran them, breaking through Kasserine Pass and taking heavy toll in casualties, prisoners, tanks, and fieldpieces, then thrust on in a three-pronged attack. It threatened to take the British First Army in reverse. As our ally's tanks and infantry strove to bar the way, an urgent call for guns was flashed by radio.

The artillery of the 9th U.S. Division, stationed near Oran, answered. Day and night its column of 2,170 men and 411 vehicles pushed over winding, narrow mountain roads, glazed with ice. A few of its weapons slipped over the edge and crashed down precipitous slopes, but the bulk forged through in an epic march of 735 miles in less than 100 hours. When the guns of the 9th rolled on to the battlefield, a few courageous British platoons and small tanks, shifting from point to point to disguise their weakness, were holding the line against three battalions of German infantry and powerful Mark IV tanks, with artillery and air support. American 105's and 155's opened at twenty-five hundred yards, blasting back the attack. Counterbattery shells burst over them, Stukas bombed, and the Mark IV's came on again. Howitzers met them with point-blank fire, knocked out two, and the tide of attack ebbed in retreat. "Never before in the history of modern warfare had artillery alone stopped the combined assault of tanks, motorized infantry, dive bombers— and dueled enemy artillery as well." [222] That day the 9th's artillery amply earned its citation for conspicuous gallantry and heroism.

With Rommel's drive halted by stiffened American resistance and a strong demonstration by the British Eighth Army, the Allies closed in to win North Africa and take a mighty bag of more than 252,000 German and Italian prisoners.

Sicily, a rough and bloody steppingstone across the Mediterranean. Then the long, heartbreaking campaign of the American Fifth and the British Eighth Army for the mainland of Italy. The Germans never fought more doggedly than in the defense of the peninsula, its mountains, beachheads, and rivers. They mined roads, trails, cross-country routes, even stream beds. Mutually supporting machine guns, "sited to weave a pattern of death," mortars, and fieldpieces covered the approaches. Often they fired from emplacements protected by layers of logs and earth and hewn four or five feet deep in solid rock. Not even intense artillery concentrations could smash such strong points. Big guns must blanket them, stun their occupants, breach the successive defense lines. Cables hummed with emergency demands for the heaviest cannon the United States had produced, and batteries of 240-mm. howitzers and 8-inch guns were rushed across the Atlantic.

Infantry attack waves, machine gunners, and mortar men surged up against the mountain barriers. Behind them rolled the cannon company howitzers, tanks and tank destroyers, the latter two more needed for knocking out enemy pillboxes with direct, flat trajectory fire than for dealing with hostile armor. Field artillery, following, threaded its way through defiles and narrow valleys—105's, 155's, the Long Toms, the 8-inchers, the huge 240's. Ammunition trains achieved feats that were marvelous and almost incredible in such rugged terrain and in view of the vast expenditures of shells they delivered. Pack mules came back out of oblivion to help, flipping long ears in seeming contempt of machines that could not rival them on the ledge trails to dizzy heights.

Massive air strikes augmented the artillery concentrations. At the beachheads warships upheld the high traditions of American naval gunnery. Everywhere the German fought back viciously. During the Salerno landing, when a strong enemy counterattack threatened to split the Fifth Army, artillerymen made a valiant, crucial stand.

> The artillery battalions gathered all available men, stripping their gun crews to a minimum, and posted them on the slope south of the burned bridge to dig in and hold the enemy with rifles and machine guns, supported by 37-mm. guns. Members of the division artillery staff commandeered every soldier they could find. They put Headquarters Battery and even bandsmen into the line and scraped together a reserve of fifteen mechanics and truck drivers to reinforce the most threatened sectors. The sweating gun crews poured artillery fire on the ford by the bridge and on the road leading to it, firing eight rounds per minute per gun at the height of the enemy attack. Altogether the two battalions fired 3,650 rounds. This devastating fire pulverized the roads and fields in the tip of the corridor and, combined with the dogged resistance of the troops at the ford, hurled back every attack. Finally, as darkness fell, the enemy conceded his failure and pulled back his tanks. The artillery had stopped the most serious breakthrough attempted during the entire Salerno beachhead fight.[223]

Lowland, valley, and height reverberated to the sound of the guns. In the assault on Mount Camino, December, 1943, 925 pieces of all calibers deluged enemy positions with tons of high explosive, white phosphorus, and smoke shells—a total of 164,999 rounds or 3,106 tons in a twenty-four hour period. There and often elsewhere our artillery "operated under the most unfavorable conditions. Sunk in the mud, its guns could be shifted only by being winched out; to clear the masks new range tables had to be improvised on the spot." [224]

During attacks on the Anzio beachhead, the Germans unveiled

a secret weapon, a squat miniature tank called "Goliath," crammed with explosives to detonate mine fields and breach barbed wire and concrete walls. Unmanned, it was set in motion toward objectives. American ordnance had developed a huge mortar with a three-foot bore and named it "Little David," but that weapon had not been issued for field use because of its vast weight, nor was it needed against an adversary so appropriately named. With Biblical accuracy gunners of lighter pieces knocked out the "Goliaths."

Enemy assaults to push the Allied forces back into the sea increased in strength and fury. To meet them gun after gun, all calibers up to 240's were landed from the fleet until 432 pieces were blasting out an average of twenty-five thousand rounds per day. Their fire was thickened by salvos from cruisers and destroyers and air bombings. German artillery thundered in reply: field guns, 170-mm. rifles, 210-mm. and 280-mm. railway guns. The roaring onrush of the latter's shells won them a name from the beachhead defenders: "The Anzio Express." But for every shell the enemy artillery fired, the Allied guns hurled back from twenty to thirty. Forward observers directed fire from cave mouths or windows of battered houses. When German tanks blew out a side of a room where they were posted, they shifted to the next one and continued their spotting through gaps in walls or doorways.

> Prisoners taken during the battle almost invariably commented on the "terrific" and "continuous" artillery fire on our part, which caused heavy casualties, shattered nerves, ruined morale, and brought some units to the verge of panic. Often attacking troops were completely cut off from their support; communication between units was dependent almost entirely on radio and on runners, many of whom never lived to deliver their messages; and in some cases, as a result of a breakdown of supply services, units went for days without food.[225]

Anzio, brilliant in conception as an amphibious turning movement, nevertheless ended in stalemate. The Fifth Army was unable to break through the main front to link up with the beachhead forces of the VIth Corps. A long, bitter struggle lay ahead, with the Italian campaign relegated to the status of a secondary theater. Serving to relieve enemy pressure on the Russian front and to draw some of his divisions from France out of the path of forthcoming invasions, the Allied effort in Italy was denied the means of victory on its own ground—at a critical moment it was drained of some of its strength to support other offensives. Yet the names of its battle-fields "are woven into the history of American valor and endur-ance." [226]

Across the Pacific, sea, air, and ground forces fought their way toward the lost Philippines and Japan. One by one the Japanese-held islands fell, but only after desperate resistance. From their airfields and the carriers, planes covered the successive jumps. Boated infantrymen swung over gunwales and fought their way ashore. The maws of landing craft gaped, and truck-drawn guns rolled through the surf onto beaches. Deep-tanned crews, stripped to the waist, brought them into action under fire from enemy machine guns, mortars, and fieldpieces. At the storming of Bougainville in the Northern Solomons, the artillery, including 90-mm. AA guns, used for direct laying counterbattery, "threw everything we had at them" and killed Japs at a ratio of thirty to one. Intense bombardments stripped jungles, so dense that the sun never filtered through, to a desolation of shattered tree trunks, scorched foliage, and yawning craters. Jap prisoners reported whole infantry companies wiped out by the cannonade, and batteries reduced from 130 to 30 men, with all their guns smashed.

General Marshall, the Army's chief of staff, saw to it that gunners were provided with weapons and equipment needed for jungle fighting. On recommendation of ordnance officers sent to the front, big mortars, 105's and 155's, and skid pans for towing heavy artillery in the mud were rushed into production and shipped to the Pacific theater.[227]

Artillerymen learned a lesson in the bloody taking of Tarawa atoll, strongly fortified and held by tough Japanese marines. In November, 1943, American marines stormed ashore on the little island of Betio, less than one square mile in area, site of the main airfield, and clung desperately to the fringe of a beachhead. Not until night were the guns and their seasick cannoneers, hovering offshore in tossing craft, able to land. Under heavy fire they began to deal with the four hundred pillboxes and bunkers, which must be knocked out by direct hits, and followed the assault waves inland. When that fierce conflict concluded, only two hundred of Betio's forty-seven hundred die-hard defenders survived, but its cost was high: 985 marine dead and 2,193 wounded. To save our troops such heavy casualties, artillery, in addition to being moved ashore as rapidly as possible, must be emplaced on adjoining islands to cover landings and support the infantry during the critical time of securing the beachhead.

Kwajalein proved the worth of such tactics. After an intense naval bombardment, battalions of 105's and 155's were put ashore on adjacent unfortified islands and registered on Kwajalein. Next morning, firing at maximum rate, they plastered defenses in the small areas where landings were to be made with high explosive. Two minutes before the infantry hit the beach, the fire of the howitzers lifted, moving inland. As a result, neither the army nor marine landings were opposed, and only slight resistance was met after advances of three hundred yards. Six days later all the islands of Kwajalein atoll were in American hands.

The 81st Division artillery faced a different problem at Angaur Island, needed as a bomber base. There were no near-by islets, and if the 105's were landed on narrow Angaur itself, they would have to fire at targets at less than minimum effective support ranges, or from positions from which proper angles of fall could not be obtained. Yet there was no other practicable landing place except the Angaur beach the infantry was to secure. Gunners ingeniously found a way out of the dilemma. Each of two artillery battalions followed its own infantry regiment ashore but fired diagonally across the front into the other regiment's zone, thus gaining sufficient range and clearance. Their shells, crisscrossing, demolished defenses, and in five days the 81st succeeded in overruning organized opposition and proceeded to clear out isolated patches of the enemy.[228]

It was at Peleliu, also in the Palau Island group, that the Third 155-mm. Howitzer Battalion, U.S. Marine Corps, "combining the Civil War tactics of front line artillery and World War I method of massing artillery fire with guns hub to hub," won a unique nickname—"Infantillery."[229]

In an awe-inspiring preparation for the landing the battle fleet and carrier planes deluged a ten-mile-square area of Peleliu with the heaviest bombardment per yard of ground inflicted on any island in the war. "It appeared impossible that any human could remain alive through such terrific destruction. Much to the dismay of the entire command, there were plenty of the enemy very much alive and waiting for the assault waves. The Japs could really take it." They exacted a heavy toll, and the beach was strewn with American dead when the howitzers came ashore. Only as riflemen won space for them could the firing batteries go into action. Crammed together, firing in three directions, they blazed away, one battery using direct fire at ranges from two to six hundred yards. Forward observers crawled to vantage points and brought down a hail of shells on every type of target. Many pillboxes were destroyed, along with dugouts, caves, buildings, bridges, and ammunition dumps.

The deadly accurate fire of the 155's wrecked the enemy's coastal guns, fieldpieces, and mortars, shifted to rake his infantry and smash reinforcements, and rushed forward in trucks or barges. Shooting at caves in the sheer coral cliffs with direct laying, the howitzers threw shells into their mouths to burst among their garrisons, or crumbled the hillsides to close the caves with rubble.

But Peleliu was a natural fortress, and the Japanese fought fanatically for every foot of ground, counterattacking and infiltrating. On the seventeenth day of the struggle the marine gunners received an order: "Take off your artillery dungarees and don infantry uniform. You are to go to the front lines acting as infantry to hold a defensive sector." Thus was born the term, "Infantillery."

Cannoneers hastily armed themselves with infantry weapons— machine guns, grenades, carbines, and Tommy guns—and 485 of the men of the artillery battalions went into the line. For fifteen days they held it against Jap attacks. Finally a renewed offensive—the 81st Division relieving the depleted 1st Marine—drove enemy remnants into the northern part of the island, mopped up, and completed the operation.

American guns were thundering now around the world—in China, Burma, India, the mountains of Italy, farther westward across the Pacific. And on the British Isles under the eye of General Eisenhower, Supreme Commander, Allied Expeditionary Forces, many-calibered cannon were being mustered by the thousands for a mighty effort.

CHAPTER 14

TOT (Time on Target)

We believe that our use of massed heavy artillery fire was far more effective than the German techniques and clearly out-classed the Japanese. Though our heavy artillery from the 105-mm. up was generally matched by the Germans, our method of employment of these weapons has been one of the decisive factors of our ground campaigns throughout the world.

GENERAL OF THE ARMY GEORGE C. MARSHALL, *Biennial Report of the Chief of Staff of the United States Army, July 1, 1943, to June 30, 1945, to the Secretary of War.*

XII Corps artillery's "TOT's"—where huge tonnages of shells from guns of different calibres and at widely different ranges all burst at the same instant in the same spot—created utter demoralization among German troops.

LIEUTENANT COLONEL GEORGE DYER, *XII Corps, Spearhead of Patton's Third Army*

The fact that all U.S. artillery is motorized is good. It is the most mobile artillery of all first-rate powers ... In tech-nology, the American excels. The standardization of pieces, the quality of the ammunition, the quality of the communication equipment, and the adjustment of fires on battery and division artillery level are superior. Self-propelled weapons such as the 155-mm. gun are indications of what the future will bring. Use of the proximity fuse before any other nation brought it into action needs no further praise. The only visible weak point in U.S. technology is the slight use of rocket-propelled or -fired projectiles.

GENERAL DER ARTILLERIE KARL THOHOLTE, German Army [230]

A Japanese prisoner of war, asked if the American artillery had had any effect on his surrender, replied: "It influenced me considerably because it doesn't make any difference whether you move forward, to the rear, or remain stationary, the artillery always follows. Day or night you have no rest or escape from it. The only way to avoid it is to surrender." [231]

Field Artillery Journal

•••

Rehearsal for conflict. In England and Scotland American artillerymen sweated and swore through months of intensive training for the cross-Channel invasion of France, a daily grind from dawn to dark. They built "mock-ups," fencing in areas on the moors in dimensions of an LCT (Landing Craft, Tank). By day and night battalion drivers practiced backing trucks, pushing a gun or a trailer into the cramped space allotted. Dog-tired backers promised each other that after the war they would buy cars with forward speeds only—no reverse. Often they picked jeeps up by hand and bounced them into place to save backing and filling. Dispatched to waterproofing school, they learned to seal seams, vents, and electrical connections on vehicles with a special grease. It worked, as drivers joyfully discovered when they plunged trucks into the sea up to their fenders and steered out unstalled.

Not only vehicles went swimming. Soldiers must be able to stay afloat and swim fifty yards in helmet, dungarees, and GI boots. They learned how, teeth chattering, in icy winter water. The tough schedule demanded constant calisthenics, a three-hundred-yard run within forty-five seconds, a fifty-yard crawl under barbed wire, a four-mile hike in not more than forty-five minutes. Make the grade, ran the order, or be transferred to another outfit (a softer and less prideful one, presumably).

Soon D-Day exercises shifted from "dry runs" to realism. Gunner battalions rolled to an evacuated section of the coast, almost a duplicate of the Normandy beachhead, sorted themselves into components and boarded DUKW's—the amphibious trucks nicknamed "Ducks." While big naval guns boomed, infantry banged away with live ammunition, and engineers cleared mine fields, the artillery landed, went into position, and "started firing furiously at the un-resisting picture-postcard landscape." [232]

That exhaustively thorough training would save many lives and prove insurance for victory. Now the expeditionary forces, "the world's most massive concentration of military power"[233]—a land, sea, and air strength of 2,876,000 men with all their manifold weapons and equipment—were ready and poised. American, British, Canadian, French, Polish, Dutch, Czech, and Belgian contingents assembled at the ports, awaiting the order that would launch them in five thousand ships, with four thousand additional ship-to-shore craft, across the Channel against the enemy's beach citadels in Normandy. Bad weather postponed the invasion one week and was threatening again when General Eisenhower, bearing a weight of dreadful responsibility few men have sustained, gave the word on June 6, 1944. With tremendous impact the Allied might struck a fifty-mile sector of the French coast.

Artillerymen in tossing transports watched the air armada roar overhead: wave after wave of fighters and bombers, the airborne divisions, glider infantry. Broadsides of battleships, cruisers, and destroyers thundered, knocking out German coastal batteries. H-Hour of D-Day, and the infantry sped ashore to bear the brunt. Rocket batteries and guns of tanks and self-propelled artillery, mounted on landing craft, blazed away in support.

British columns, in their sectors, and the Americans assaulting on Utah Beach successfully fought their way ashore without unduly heavy casualties, but the second American landing area, Omaha Beach, was a place of death and destruction. Recently reinforced by a strong German division, the shores and sea walls of Omaha were most formidably defended by mined underwater obstacles, light and heavy artillery in concrete casements, pillboxed machine guns, and fire trenches surrounded by more mine fields and barbed wire.

Seas ran high, in waves of five to six feet, as artillery sought to follow the infantry in through the crimsoned surf. Gun-laden "Ducks" rolled out of the open ends of LST's to toss in the billows. Waiting vainly for the guns, some of the small advance group of artillerymen of the 111th Battalion who had landed died fighting by the side of the infantry. "Ducks," attempting to rendezvous and chug into the beach, began to ship water. Five of them were swamped and lost before they could close the circle. Another's motor failed, its bilge filled, and it went under. Six more foundered. Naval craft dashed in to pick up swimming cannoneers whose gas masks had helped keep them afloat. One DUKW made it to within five hundred yards of the beach when its motor stopped. Spatting machine gun bullets opened up its side, and it sank. Only two of the battalion's craft were left now. Captains Jack R. Wilson and Louis A. Shuford, battery commanders, ordered them lashed together. They looked shoreward and saw that the infantry was pinned down. There was no base for them.

> "If we can get one gun in, we might be able to destroy one pillbox," Wilson said. At that moment a machine-gun burst cut through the lashings holding the DUKW's together. Shuford said, "I think we better get the hell out of here." Shuford got his motor started and shoved off, but Wilson had gotten a bullet through his motor and couldn't follow; he figured he'd drift in. Then an artillery shell hit the breech-block of his gun, destroyed it, and killed one man. Another shell came in, and the DUKW started to burn and sink. Wilson told his men to jump and start swimming for an LST. A log floated by. They grabbed it. A machine-gun burst shot it out of their hands. Three swam to the LST. Wilson and four others swam to the shore. Three others drowned.[234]

Shuford managed to save his gun by transferring it to another craft as his own started to sink, and at length brought it to shore with the fieldpieces of another battalion. Besides the 111th's loss of all of its guns but one in the hotly contested Omaha landing, six of the 7th FA Battalion's sank along with five out of six of an infantry cannon company's howitzers, plus three of an armored battalion's, mounted on LST's which struck mines. Others took their places, pounding the defenses.

By the end of D-Day the Allies had breached the Atlantic Wall all along the invasion coast, and all assaulting divisions were ashore. Reinforcements in men and guns streamed across the Channel for the drive through the hedgerows of Normandy and onward against the German armies of the West.

Slowly but inexorably the jaws of a vise began to close on the foe. The Russians, following their indomitable defense of Stalingrad, continued their relentless drive westward. The Seventh U.S. Army was soon to land in southern France and assail the enemy in another quarter. Yet almost a year of bitter battling must pass and many men must die before Germany under the evil Swastika of the Nazis would acknowledge defeat.

Breaking out of the beachheads and breaking through fierce resistance, the Allies drove toward the Meuse River. Big planes from bases in Britain roared overhead to drop 3,390 tons of bombs on enemy lines, but one of the strikes fell short. Its missiles thundered down on battalions of the 9th and 30th U.S. Divisions, causing heavy casualties. Lieutenant General Lesley J. McNair, a great artilleryman and training and organizing genius, had just come to the front as an observer. He had survived combat in the first World War, torpedoing by a submarine, a swim of six hours in icy water, and a wound in Tunisia. His number up now, a direct bomb hit on his foxhole killed him.[235]

While the Allied columns thrust deeper to free France, Belgium, and Luxembourg from the German yoke, actions stamped the European campaign from the viewpoint of the gunners' arm as predominantly a corps artillery war—as definitely so as the more confined areas of the Pacific theater limited its actions to divisional guns. Cannon of the corps, backed by the heavy ordnance of army artillery and in turn backing and sometimes embracing the lighter pieces of the divisions, set a classic example of fire power, concentrated and co-ordinated on a vast scale.[236]

In the November, 1944, attack by the XIIth Corps on Delme Ridge in Lorraine, its artillery had carefully registered before torrential rains and low-lying clouds grounded its cub planes and blinded observation posts. The order to fire drenched German forward positions with a deluge of high explosive as thorough as the downpour from the skies. Cannoneers, using time fuses because impact ones would not detonate in the mud, jammed shell after shell into the breeches. For three and one-half hours the crews of seventeen battalions of corps artillery plied their hot pieces, their fire thickened during the first thirty minutes by twenty battalions of divisional guns. They flattened the enemy with 380 concentrations, one every three minutes on the most important targets. Even that tremendous bombardment was heightened when the 90-mm. AA guns, tank destroyers, and howitzers of regimental cannon companies, pushed forward close behind the infantry's jump-off line, let fly with everything they had. Doughboys stormed in from the flanks over enemy dead and wrecked cannon, churned into a muddy mass. They ploughed on through to capture antiaircraft pieces and their gunners. Among the one thousand prisoners they took was one with a glass eye, one with a wooden leg, and two men with self-inflicted wounds. The Reich was scraping the bottom of its man-power barrel.[237]

"ALL RIGHT, ALL RIGHT! ONE AT A TIME!!"

By Lieutenant J. Hagan in *History and Battle Record of the 179th FA Battalion.*

German armies drew back in dogged retreat, fighting for time to reorganize and stand again. More than their determined rear guards, it was mud, Napoleon's "fifth element of war," that slowed the pursuit. When the swift armored columns freed themselves from its clutches and sped ahead, they outran their supplies and clanked to a halt. Trucks, replenishing gasoline and ammunition for the guns, must often make round trips of five hundred or more miles.

Waging the battle of Germany, American troops fought their way through six miles of West Wall fortifications and closed in on Aachen. When surrender of that city was refused, the air command pounded it with 172 tons of bombs, while twelve battalions of artillery of the XIXth and VIIth Corps saturated it with 169 tons of ammunition. Aachen's strong garrison still refused to yield. Elements of twelve enemy divisions repeatedly attacked enveloping lines to raise the siege, but were repulsed. At last American infantry forced their way into the city. As fierce house-to-house fighting raged, tank destroyers and 155-mm. howitzers rolled through the streets and went into action. At point-blank range they battered strong points to bits. Only then did the German commander order the white flag hoisted. "When the Americans start using 155's as sniper weapons," he ruefully remarked, "it is time to give up!"

During the drive through Central Germany, American soldiers hit the dirt or crouched in dugouts at the terrifying sound of the onrush and detonation of huge shells. They were fired by the world's biggest guns, railway-mounted monsters manufactured by the Krupp works at Essen and christened "Gustav Geschütz" or "Dora." [238] Designed for use against the Maginot Line, they were subsequently moved to the Russian front where they effectively bombarded Sevastopol in the Crimea. Some delivered cross-Channel harassing fire on the English coast. Retreating through France into Germany, the "Gustavs" were wrecked and abandoned by their crews before the advancing U.S. Third Army. American artillerymen, coming upon two of them amid shattered railroad cars, gasped at their size. The diameter of their bores was 31.5 inches; the weight of a gun and carriage 1,344 tons. They hurled a projectile of 16,540 pounds 51,000 yards. [239]

American arms in Europe were destined to suffer a setback to victory, a break-through more menacing than that at Kasserine Pass. On December 16, 1944, German panzers pierced the Ardennes on an eighty-mile front, rolled over and routed green divisions, and forged onward in an overwhelming surprise assault intended to split the Allied armies and take Liége and Antwerp. SS troopers, English-speaking and wearing American uniforms, infiltrated the broken lines. In the chaotic confusion, knots of desperate defenders sought to sift foe from friend as they fought the oncoming tanks and mopped up parachutists who had been dropped behind them. The Battle of the Bulge was combat in icy cold and deep snows. Sheets were commandeered to camouflage soldiers whose dark uniforms stood out as targets against the white background. Artillerymen hastily coated guns and trucks with white paint. As vehicles stalled in the drifts, twenty-three picked teams of sledge dogs and drivers were emplaned in Greenland, Labrador, and Newfoundland and flown to France to help move heavy machine guns, mortars, ammunition, and supplies.[240]

Now resistance stiffened. When the SS panzers attempted to smash through in the Monschau sector, a thin screen of mechanized cavalry with artillery support blocked them. Twice more the tanks launched heavy assaults, but by then battalion after battalion of guns had rallied to the defense. Volleys blasted back the panzers—massed fire from four battalions of 105 howitzers and six of 155's, one of 4.5-inch guns, and two of Long Toms. Still heavier pieces—two battalions of 240 howitzers and a battery of 8-inch guns—added their thunders to the din of conflict. Smitten by that steel tempest, the SS reeled back. A third time, now strongly reinforced, they came on. An SS attack was as relentlessly sacrificial as a Japanese banzai charge, less headlong and hysteric, but more resolute and implacable. This one, even with the momentum of the sweeping drive of the German army behind it, could not prevail. It was rent and shattered by a tremendous cannonade, termed one of the finest demonstrations in the war of the decisive effect of massed artillery. So decimated were the assault columns that only one battalion of infantry succeeded in breaching the American line, and that remnant was quickly crushed.[241]

The 101st Airborne Division at Bastogne, the 7th Armored at St. Vith, made their gallant stands and held. Near Malmédy, Belgium, tanks of the 1st SS Panzer Division trapped Battery B of the 285th FA Observation Battalion. As the prisoners were herded into a snowy field, a Nazi trooper fired into them. Machine guns on the tanks rattled, cutting down the helpless men. Noncoms strode among the fallen, pistoling all who showed signs of life; if in any doubt a man was dead, they kicked him in the face to see if he winced. Out of some two hundred captured, thirty-six, four of whom later died of wounds, escaped. Such wanton Nazi savagery as the Malmédy massacre and the horrors of the prison camps planted seeds of vengeance.

The German thrust was contained, blunted, halted. In and around the Bulge, American troops hit back at an enemy resolved not to be dislodged or denied the iniative that had carried him so far.

The splendid part played by the guns in the battles of early January has been described by a gunner officer who fought through them, Lieutenant Colonel William R. Jesse of the 6th Armored Division Artillery: [242]

Moving to positions on the outer fringe of the bulge into the southern flank of the German spearhead, with headquarters of both groups in Bastogne, the artillery fought ceaselessly day and night, without rest or respite, in bitterly cold weather. Biting cold winds, blinding snow and sleet, and ice-covered supply roads drifted high with snow, created tremendous difficulties of supply and ammunition. Observation was difficult; liaison air activity was restricted to a minimum. Despite these almost unsurmountable difficulties in the face of the most determined efforts on the part of the best troops in the German army to crack the Bastogne defense, the artillery time after time inflicted extremely heavy casualties on enemy personnel and equipment. Artillery fire repeatedly broke up counter-attacks as they were being formed. Prisoners of war complained of the accurate and devastating nature of the artillery fire, singling it out as the most damaging factor in their inability to press any attack to a successful breach of our defense.

Every artillery battalion was shelled repeatedly, so the habitually selected and surveyed alternate positions were occupied many times under the most trying conditions of enemy shellfire from all calibers of German artillery, weather, and terrain restrictions. It was bombed by planes of the Luftwaffe, as were the positions of the battalions. In battle vernacular, the whole area was "red hot" during this entire period, but not once did supported units find the artillery, for any reason at all, unable to give them the fires they wanted, whether of a planned or emergency nature—and of the latter there were many instances of extreme emergency...

While the "Battle of the Bulge" could never have been won by artillery alone, it was the superhuman effort of the artillery that prevented it from being lost on repeated occasions.

By the intensity and accuracy of its fire the way was paved for the final breakthrough and rout of the cream of the German army.

Once more the advance surged forward, often checked for a time but smashing through. In the Rhineland campaign was presented "one of those rare and fleeting opportunities which occasionally occur in war and which, if grasped, have incalculable effects in determining future successes." [243] Elements of the 9th Armored Division dashed to seize the towered railroad bridge across the Rhine at Remagen. Reckless infantrymen rushed over it, with demolition charges exploding beneath them. Engineers, with equal gallantry, cut wires and main cables to remaining charges that would have destroyed the span. It was the only bridge throughout the entire length of the Rhine captured intact. Infantry, armor, and field artillery streamed over it, crossed at other points, drove deeper into Germany.

American gunners had begun using the new proximity fuse. Shells that burst over the enemy's ground troops or beneath his planes with such uncanny timeliness struck terror into his heart. The accuracy of our artillery fire on targets across the Rhine became increasingly lethal. Every method of directing it was skillfully used: photographs taken by air reconnaissance; observers in cub planes or on the ground, forward with the infantry; flash and sound ranging; "shell reps." The last, a highly valuable source of information, consisted of reports on enemy shells fired on our positions. Measurement of fragments by special instruments, furnished the shell-rep teams, could identify the caliber of the gun from which the projectile came. Troops in combat, urged to co-operate,[244] responded remarkably well in spite of the natural reaction of men being shelled.

At last German resistance, prolonged beyond reason or hope, crumbled and collapsed. American and Russian troops met at the Elbe River. The Red Army stormed Berlin, sowing its dragon's teeth. Germany's surrender on May 7, 1945, ended the war in Europe.

A tank destroyer unit, the 8th TD Group, carried home a memory which would linger longer than some grimmer aspects of its service. When the group, moving up to establish a new command post, rolled into the little village of Lullange in Luxembourg in January, 1945, it found the enemy had retreated. Incessant bombing

of roads and railways had cut off his supplies. A few yards away
bulked the steel skeletons of Tiger tanks, blown up by their crews
when they ran out of gasoline. The group, without orders to advance
further, halted and camped. The commanding officer, Lieutenant
Colonel Harry C. Larter, Jr., led some of his men into Lullange's
chapel, built in 1789. They stood there, uncovered, before a small
statue of St. Barbara, patron saint of the artillery and equally ven-
erated by the villagers, lead miners of the Ardennes who wore her
image on their caps as protection against premature explosions.

The colonel, steeped in the lore of the artillery, stood with bowed
head before the statue. Wonderingly the village curé at his side
listened to the words of the officer he knew to be a Protestant. "Because of St. Barbara's intercession," the colonel said reverently, "the
Germans did not stay to fight, and your village and the lives of many
of your people were spared by their guns and ours."

Willing artillerymen of Headquarters and Headquarters Company set to work to repair and refurbish the chapel. The colonel
himself, a clever artist, repainted St. Barbara's statue. Before the
edifice a French field gun, captured by the Germans and used against
the Americans, who had retaken it and turned it back against the
enemy, was placed as a votive offering.

> There [the curé wrote down in his archives] the cannon now
> stands peacefully in front of the little St. Barbara Chapel next
> to the Lullange pond. It bears, inscribed by American hands,
> the White Star of the United States and the Red Lion of
> Luxembourg. Next to the silent gun three Germans, killed in
> action, rest tranquilly in graves, overshadowed by mighty
> trees: one SS, one Wehrmacht, and one Volkssturm soldier.
> And above the chapel rises the Cross of Our Saviour.[245]

Not until more than four months after the German surrender
would final victory be won in the war in the Pacific. Dying echoes
of the guns in Europe were caught up and reamplified on the islands
of the Western ocean.

Japanese prisoners declared that:

> the artillery was the most feared and deadly weapon of the
> American army and that it accounted for a great proportion

of the enemy dead. Every effort was made by the enemy to destroy our artillery. The assignment of forces [to do so] was prevalent in captured enemy orders, although in almost all cases the personnel assigned to this mission was pitifully insufficient to accomplish the mission. Natives and prisoners reported that harassing fires were extremely effective and in many instances drove the enemy from defensive installations before the arrival of our troops. In addition to the killing effect, harassing fires reduced the efficiency and morale of the enemy forces. Artillery barrages broke up counterattacks occurring where artillery was available. Time fire proved very effective in killing the enemy in open foxholes and forced them to dig their foxholes down and then back, forming an "L." [246]

The Navy and the Air Force achieved their smashing triumph over the Japanese fleet at the Battle of Leyte Gulf, fending it off from our transports, sinking ship after ship with gunfire, torpedoes, and bombs. Landing craft, laden with infantry and artillery, beached on that southernmost island of the Philippines. General MacArthur had kept his promise, "I will return." Much hard fighting over mountain and through jungle, along with other landings, remained before the Stars and Stripes would wave again over Manila and Corregidor.

As the Sixth Army on Luzon fought its way toward the capital, artillerymen turned captured arms and equipment against the enemy. Manning overrun howitzers, crews from the 33rd Division Artillery and Philippine Scouts formed what they called Battery "J," the J standing for Jap. They substituted seized German sights, forehandedly shipped from the States, for inferior Japanese ones, and fired thousands of rounds of the foe's ammunition back at him. Abandoned small arms were served out for close defense, while Jap radios supplemented communication.

Closing in on Manila, "Pearl of the Orient," they stormed it in bitter battling, house by house, street by street. Desperately the Mikado's men defended the thick-walled buildings and individual fortresses, some of them requiring more than a day of continuous fighting to reduce. The guns, from 75's to 155's, hammered them with point-blank fire, using concrete-piercing shells. Riflemen, grenadiers, and flame throwers assaulted the breaches, blowing them wider with drums of gasoline ignited by thermite. Only after a fierce seven-day struggle were the stout structures of the University of the Philippines carried. Manila was another Monterey, Mexico City, Peking, Aachen. There was slaughter in the cellars where garrison remnants, refusing to surrender, fought to annihilation. When tank and tank destroyer guns and the lighter fieldpieces failed to batter gaps, medium artillery moved in. Ringing one building after another, semicircles of 155's poured in hundreds of rounds, punching great holes with unfused shells. Eight-inch howitzers blasted down the walls of Intramuros, sixteen feet high and forty feet thick at the base. On March 4, 1945, the last building was cleared, and the city, strewn with 16,665 counted Japanese dead, was won. Best of trophies were American prisoners, wan and emaciated from long captivity—survivors of the Bataan death march and Corregidor, freed at long last.

Soon afterward the flag was hoisted over Iwo Jima, an historic scene commemorated by photograph and in bronze. The cost of the small island, which could be stormed only by frontal assault, was high—more than twenty thousand marine and naval casualties—but it supplied a base of utmost importance for heavy bombers.

Okinawa, the last battle and one of the toughest. It is an island of limestone hills, honeycombed by caves connected by tunnels. Each hill was a large-scale, almost indestructible natural stronghold. Defenses were thoroughly concealed by camouflage, which had to be burned off by napalm fire bombs before the positions stood revealed. A strong garrison, well armed and supplied, defended Okinawa to the death, nor did it fight alone. The Japanese war lords, as if aware this was a crucial and perhaps a last stand, dispatched waves of Kamikaze suicide planes, manned guided missiles, to be crashed by pilots with their bomb loads on the decks of the invader's warships.

The American fleet, notwithstanding severe losses in beating off the Kamikazes, gave the assault on Okinawa magnificent backing. Naval gunfire was there employed longer and in greater quantity than in any other battle in history.[247] It supported ground troops and supplemented field guns from the first day of the landing until action advanced to the extreme southern tip of the island where combat was so close and confined that bombardment would have endangered our infantry. Ships and their batteries were assigned to support missions like artillery battalions: one vessel to back up each front-line regiment, one to each division, a number for corps concentrations. Battleships, cruisers, and destroyers also constantly fired star shells and flares until nights were as bright as day, and no counterattack of any size could be launched without being spotted. With bombers and field artillery joining in—

> literally, the Japanese were enveloped by fire power, from the ground in front, from the air above them, and from the water on their flanks—fire power and explosives the like of which had never been seen in such concentrated form in so restricted an area. Surely, all this fire power must have pulverized the Japanese positions and rendered the enemy incapable of prolonged resistance. But it had not.[248]

The troops of Nippon, holed up in their caves, defied it. Long-range bombardment could not blast them out. Breaking through those redoubtable, close-linked defenses became the bloody business of the infantry-tank team, including the new armored flame thrower —of hand-to-hand combat—of point-blank fire by the fieldpieces, the 75-mm. pack howitzers, the 105's and 155's.

Cannon met cannon as never before in the war with Japan. Nowhere else had the enemy's artillery appeared in such strength nor been better served. Some five hundred weapons, from 75's to heavy calibers, pounded our infantry and counterbatteried our guns. Powerful 150-mm. rifles with a range of twenty-seven hundred yards threw shells at our airfields. Projectiles from ponderous 320- and 250-mm. mortars burst over the American lines, swept simultaneously by a hail of large-sized rockets.

Painfully, paying a heavy cost, army and marine infantry crawled forward. They rooted out "the mole-like Nip" with satchel charges, spurts of flame, stabbing bayonets. The guns followed, covering advances with repeated barrages, shooting out the Jap's wire lines. Up ahead artillery forward observers directed fire. Not a few died at their posts, picked off by snipers or cut down by machine-gun bursts. Tanks, tank destroyers, and self-propelled 105's blasted away at the pillboxes.

The Jap emerged from his cave or tunnel to man his guns. Sometimes he fought it out with batteries in the open, ringed by AA guns to keep off cub planes, spotting for American counterbattery. He screened his positions and cannon flashes with dense clouds from smoke pots. Shells from a 150 nightly bombarded our Yontan and Kadena airfields, corps and army command posts located near by. A demand for the silencing of "Yontan Pete," as the 150 was dubbed, caused corps artillery to devise a plan.

> One night early in May [a gunner officer relates] [249] we had laid the entire corps artillery on plan Peter Xray to lie in wait for Yontan Pete. About the middle of the evening the officer on duty in the corps artillery fire direction center was galvanized into action by the whistle of the Yontan express passing overhead. He leaped for the phone and yelled: 'Plan Peter Xray,' hearing as he did so, the second section whistling for the crossing. As round number three screamed by and thudded into the airfield, the muffled roar of the entire corps artillery rolled back to the CP, and Yontan Pete never rode again.

Pete had been twins. A captured Japanese artillery lieutenant later told the other side of the story:

> We frequently used to shell the airfields at night, using two 150-mm. guns and firing them alternately. When American artillery fire would come down on one, it would cease firing, and the other would take it up. One night we had set up to shell the airfields. After we had fired only three rounds, all of a sudden a most *terrific* artillery barrage came down. It killed most of the crew and ruined the gun, and we never fired at the airfield again.

For the April 19 assault on the Shuri Line "the greatest concentration of artillery ever employed in the Pacific war sounded the prelude to the attack at dawn." [250] With a deafening roar twenty-seven battalions of corps and division artillery erupted—a total of 324 pieces from 105's to 8-inchers—an average of 75 guns to every mile of front. Their massed fire thundered down on enemy lines, sweeping from east to west for twenty minutes. Then the wall of bursting shells rolled forward five hundred yards. As the infantry feinted an attack, and the Japanese manned parapets to meet it, the barrage was pulled back to inundate enemy front lines. It smote them for forty minutes with nineteen thousand shells before lifting to rear areas again. But the Japs in their caves had scarcely been touched. Corps artillery doubted it had killed as many as 190 of them, or one for every hundred shells fired. The attack failed.

Guns alone could not conquer the coral strongholds. They could only help. It was finally the infantry, reigning always as Queen of Battles, that won Okinawa, its fine fleet anchorage and its airfields close to Japan's homeland. The American toll was high: 39,430 casualties, including 7,374 killed—but thrice that number had been exacted of the enemy: 107,500 counted dead, with probably 20,000 more sealed in the caves, and 7,400 prisoners.

Big bombers took off from Okinawa's airfields and soared north. They dropped two atom bombs, one on Hiroshima, one on Nagasaki. Last resistance crushed by the appalling might of the dreadful new weapon,[251] Japan surrendered on September 2, 1945.

CHAPTER 1 5

Enemy Among the Guns

●━●●●●●●●●●●●●●●●●●●●●●●●●●●●●●●●●●●●●●●●━●

Artillerymen have a love for their guns which is perhaps stronger than the feeling of any soldier for his weapon or any part of his equipment...That guns will never be deserted simply because danger threatens is a point of honor around which the artillery has largely built the solid discipline of its corps.

> COLONEL S. L. A. MARSHALL, *Army Combat Forces Journal* [252]

Artillery to justify its existence must do two things in connection with the accomplishment of its supporting mission to its infantry; it must continue to serve its guns while under counter battery fire without taking cover and it must fight as infantry to prevent its guns falling into enemy hands during close-in ground attack. Twenty-nine times during my service in Korea, battery positions of the 25th Division Artillery were subjected to close-in ground attack. Every battery was involved in one or more attacks and only once did we leave guns permanently in the hands of the enemy. In this case, the batteries of the 90th Field Artillery that were involved, received the Presidential Unit Citation for the action—they did all that was humanly possible. On two other occasions, guns were lost temporarily and recovered by counter attacks.

> GENERAL G. B. BARTH, *Tropic Lightning and Taro Leaf*

●━●●●●●●●●●●●●●●●●●●●●●●●●●●●●●●●●●●●●●●●━●

T HE second World War stands on our annals as a proud and mighty achievement. We trained and fought with our own weapons, splendid ones for all the services. With our allies we waged and won it on ground that often presented almost insuperable difficulties, defeating enemies whose opposition ranged from tenacity to fanaticism.

Unhappily the peace interval proved to be the briefest between all our wars. It was, however, characteristic. The gnawing homesickness every soldier knows and the pressure of public opinion at home brought influence to bear that forced rapid demobilization. The Army swiftly sank to a strength of 592,000, nor would the nation accept universal military training, though training, as the Normandy beachheads and many other battlefields had demonstrated, saves many lives. There would be time enough for it, Americans assumed, if another conflict came. But there would not be time enough.

As war clouds gathered over Korea, American troops stationed in Japan suffered the inevitable lowering of combat efficiency resulting from prolonged occupation duty. Artillerymen manned guns whose tubes had been worn from firing thousands of rounds in the past conflict. Although a vast surplus of arms and equipment existed, there were shortages of essential parts. Most serious would be the lack of the will to fight in the early days of the war ahead. With no Pearl Harbor to make them fighting mad, American soldiers were abruptly thrown into desperate combat. They were aware that they were woefully under strength and under-powered, "due to the Administration's adoption of 'Economy' divisions that lacked many fighting units and much heavy armament." Deeper factors were the failure of the recruiting service to stress the obligations of a soldier; the fact that he might have to enter battle was neglected in favor of painting a rosy picture that filled quotas. And military leaders admittedly failed to prepare their men psychologically for combat.

Fortunately it would come—that all-important will to fight—while the war was still at an early stage. In a counterattack the bodies of six American infantrymen were recovered. Their hands had been tied behind their backs, and each had been shot through the head.

This news traveled like wildfire, and our men realized that they were pitted against a ruthless foe who recognized no rules and gave no quarter. Our men now knew what they were up against and that they must fight to survive. The murder of our soldiers was the first and, probably one of the greatest mistakes the Reds ever made.[253]

The Korean peninsula, jutting from the Chinese mainland, was jointly held, south of the Thirty-eighth Parallel by the United States, north of it by the Soviet Union which, belatedly declaring war on Japan, had invaded through Manchuria. In North Korea, as in East Germany, Red Russia sowed dragon's teeth before ostensibly terminating occupation in 1948.

When the United States withdrew all forces but a military advisory group from South Korea in mid-'49, it did not leave the government it had sponsored defenseless. Eight ROK (Republic of Korea) divisions—one hundred thousand men—had been formed and trained. But only six of them possessed artillery: one battalion of 105's apiece, with no mediums or heavies.

Sound of the guns once more. Suddenly and unexpectedly on June 25, 1950, the North Korean army, supplied with Soviet-made tanks and aircraft, struck across the Thirty-eighth Parallel. It smashed back the ROK's, inflicting heavy losses, and rolled southward. Upon the vote of the United Nations to support South Korea against unprovoked aggression, American air, naval, and ground forces were rushed from Japan. Contingents from twenty-one other nations eventually joined them as fighting units or hospital corps, but the United States shouldered the heaviest weight of the conflict.

The manner in which the artillery fought the Korean War, maladroitly termed "a police action," is worthy of the arm's highest traditions. Although it used the same basic weapons as in World War II—the 105 howitzer, the 155 howitzer and gun, the 8-inch and 240 howitzer—there were certain advances in matériel and techniques. Proximity fuses were improved by a timing mechanism, which prevented their radio-actuated tubes from detonating shells until they reached the target. Previously objects being passed during the projectiles' course would explode the rounds; now they could clear a ridge and burst over its reverse slope. VT-fused ammunition, properly used, tripled casualties. Launchers of 4.2 rockets—twenty-four tubes in four banks—were mounted on wheels. Their "ripples" at ranges up to five thousand yards could sweep clean areas where assaults were massing.

Forward observers and cub plane pilots again proved their value and their courage. So heavy was the fire they directed, plus the concentrations called for to support offensives or stop enemy drives, that even the large stock of World War II ammunition ran low. By 1951 it had dropped to minimum levels. Deficiency, coupled with immense difficulties of transportation, forced the adoption of rationing to build up front-line supplies.

Pre-eminently, the story of the American artillery in Korea is an epic tale of close defense of the guns in the midst of support missions, coverage of our infantry assaults, and repulse of the enemy's.[254] In that land of rugged mountains and masking ravines, ideal for infiltration—in combat where lines broke and disintegrated—North Koreans and Red Chinese attacked battery positions from front, flanks, and rear. In the shock of surprise of the first of these infiltration attacks near Taejon, the 63rd Field Artillery Battalion, assailed from three quarters, was driven from its position in confusion. All its guns and most of its transportation were lost. The battalion was reorganized, re-equipped with borrowed guns, and back in action within twenty-four hours, a bitter lesson learned.

There were no front lines, such as we used to know, in this war. Batteries must fight as infantry in defense of their guns—must beat off the enemy with rifle, pistol, and grenade—must blast him out of their positions with machine guns, dug in or mounted on the half-track vehicles called "Quad 50's." A Negro artilleryman summed it up. "Us wears one crossed cannon and one crossed rifle," he said.[255]

As always since the first cannon thundered in battle, it was a point of honor to save the guns, or if lost, to recover them.

Hemmed within the Pusan perimeter, troops of the United Nations fought with their backs to the sea. The situation was desperate that September of 1950. With the North Koreans mounting a powerful assault, and infiltration a constant threat, Captain Leroy Anderson prepared his Battery A, 64th Field Artillery Battalion, for close defense. He grouped his six howitzers as compactly as possible and around the position set up light and heavy machine guns, along with a Quad armed with four .50-caliber MG's.

On the dark, foggy night of September 3 the enemy fell suddenly upon the battery. The first sergeant challenged three shadowy figures pulling a wheeled machine gun. They dropped into a ditch and opened fire. Flame stabbed through the murk from other quarters. A North Korean cut down two signalers with a burp gun, then tossed a grenade into the telephone dugout. Its explosion killed two of the three occupants. The third, Corporal John M. Pitcher, not seriously wounded, bravely stayed by the switchboard and continued to operate it all night, the two bodies beside him.

Bullets raked the gun emplacements. Answering fire from the battery's outlying machine guns ceased, as gunners drew back, realizing the position was being overrun. The traversing mechanism of the Quad jammed. Its crew backed the vehicle into a gully. In the dark gun pits cannoneers fought back with side arms. An enemy grenadier crawled close to one section and threw twice. The first missile killed one artilleryman and wounded several others. The second exploded on the ammunition. Powder charges for more than one hundred rounds flamed luridly. The chief of section ordered his men out. They retreated to the gully, joined by two other hard-pressed crews.

In other pits they stood fast. Two howitzers went into action, sweeping the enemy-held ridge in front, shells bursting at two hundred yards. Officers and noncoms rallied the men in the gully, machine guns covering them as they returned to their posts.

Thanks to Corporal Pitcher, the telephones were still working. The battalion commander, calling in, offered help from other batteries. "A" asked for fire on the ridge to the fore and got it promptly. A 155 shell landed squarely on the target. Lieutenant Kincheon H. Bailey, Jr., "A's" executive observing, yelled through the fire direction center: "Right 50, drop 50. Fire for effect!" It was close shooting, the rounds falling just in front of the battery's position. The enemy began to melt away, leaving twenty-one dead. A tank, rolling up to the rescue, scourged the retreat.

Battery A had lost seven killed and twelve wounded. Four of its trucks had been destroyed, but all its howitzers were undamaged. "Normal support missions," Captain Anderson ordered, and the guns boomed again.

In those hectic early days American guns were spread out thin. No more than three batteries could be massed to support a local attack. As at Okinawa, the Navy helped out, furnishing a destroyer, anchored off the south coast, as a floating battery. An artillery officer, equipped with radio, was put aboard. From maps and charts and with cub planes spotting for him, he directed effective night firing. The destroyer's 5-inch guns, longer-ranged than the light field artillery ashore, used illuminating shells to light up the targets and added greatly to the Army's fire power.

Battering back the enemy from his positions, often with direct fire, the artillery was constantly in heavy action. On one day the 159th Field Artillery Battalion expended fifty-two hundred rounds. Frequently gunners were so exhausted that during a lull in the firing they slumped over their sights, fell asleep, and had to be shaken awake to fire again. Fifteen forward observers and their parties were overrun or surrounded in the first ten days of September. "Some came back; others never did."

More than once disaster threatened at Pusan, but the lines held. Breakout from the perimeter followed General MacArthur's skillfully planned amphibious landing at Inchon. The enemy, caught by surprise, taken in the rear, saw his main supply line severed. UN forces, driving through from Pusan, linked up with the Inchon columns. The North Koreans reeled back in disorganized, demoralized retreat, yielding many prisoners, streaming back across the Thirty-eighth Parallel and on to the Manchurian border. The victors, pressing the pursuit, were soon to exchange roles with the vanquished in a debacle written in dark letters on American military annals.

Chinese Communist forces secretly assembled in Manchuria, which would remain a sanctuary under the protection of a UN order prohibiting offensive operations against them north of the Yalu River. That ruling hamstrung the Allies and brought them close to disaster, as eighteen Chinese divisions of so-called volunteers struck the right wing of our Eighth Army. They split its contact with the Xth Corps, which in its turn was assailed by nine more divisions.

The 2nd U.S. Division was hit hard and smashed back. Its artillery, field and AA, formed the rear guard for a bitter retreat over a single traffic-clogged road. Kanu-ri Pass was a gantlet that must be run, a defile of death. Through it rolled the big howitzers of the 17th Field Artillery Battalion, 8-inchers, their proper post well to the rear in any normal operation but now facing front-line combat. Chinese machine gunners and riflemen blazed from flanking ridges and came howling down for the kill. The 17th fought them off with .50 and .30 caliber MG's, mounted on its prime movers. Over the heads of retreating ROK's, Lieutenant Colonel Elmer Harrelson, battalion commander, opened fire with howitzers on charging Reds, blasting them back. A respite gained, the guns lurched onward. In the darkness heavy wheels lumbered sickeningly over soft bumps in the road, bumps that could have been sleeping bags—or bodies.

Now machine guns sewed a seam of lead along the length of the column. It kept rolling, weapons on its trucks spitting bullets in reply. A sharp turn, and an 8-incher careened over an embankment and crashed down into a forty-foot gully. Then a 40-mm. Bofors, stalled and blocking the road, was pushed over after the howitzer. A gallant volunteer—nobody recognized him in that black night—slid down the slope to destroy the fallen guns with thermite. Headlights, turned on to help him, drew a hail of mortar shells and white phosphorus grenades. The 17th let the two pieces go, forged ahead, cleared the gantlet, and saved the rest of its guns.

Other battalions, following the heavies, fared far worse. The 37th, next in column, lost ten guns. "Some were hit and ruined by enemy fire. Others got hung up behind a block of debris in such a way that they could not turn out and around. A few perhaps were lost in the dark when crews were killed, and there was none to see and report." [256] Battery B of the 503rd battled desperately to save its 155's, as Chinese Reds, bugles blaring discordantly, charged and overran it at a roadblock. "B's" cannoneers, clubbing rifles and carbines, strove vainly to beat them off in a wild melee. Odds were too heavy. The enemy set off explosive charges under the leading and rear tractors. Flame roared through the rent metal. In a last stand around the guns, every man of the battery was either killed, wounded, captured, or driven off. Only two officers and twenty enlisted men survived.

Other batteries of the 503rd, ably supported by a company of infantrymen, fought on gallantly to break free. Lit up by twenty burning vehicles in the column, they dropped howitzer trails in a paddy field and went into action against besetting machine guns. At one of them, spitting lead from a post only seventy yards away, Major John C. Fralish bore-sighted a 155, peering through its barrel. A cannoneer, serving the howitzer with him, slammed the breechblock shut, jerked the lanyard. They got off three rounds. Then Fralish saw the man at his side topple. The major, thinking his Number One had been knocked over by the recoil, reached down a hand to help him up. He touched a limp body, headless. An enemy rocket had pierced the gun shield, disabled the piece, and decapitated the cannoneer at the instant he fired the last shot.[257]

Some of them made it through the gantlet, vehicles heavy-laden with wounded. But the 38th Field Artillery Battalion, last to receive the order to pull out, never reached that perilous pass. Before it could join the end of column, extending for seven miles of chaos, it was engulfed with all its guns. Some of its men, traveling cross-country under cover of the dark, escaped to the Allied lines. Others lived to endure the tortures, physical and mental, of Communist prison pens. Many died where they stood.

Fighting raged on in near-zero temperatures. The tide of retreat still ebbed through the choked channel of the road. Lieutenant Colonel John W. Keith, Jr., of the artillery, consulted with the commander of infantry he was supporting. If guns overturned on that sole route to salvation, all that followed would be blocked and sacrificed. The officers decided to fire off all remaining shells and destroy the guns. The artillery's trucks, picking up infantrymen as they fell back from the ridges, would be sent on through.

Keith's forward observers adjusted on advancing assault columns of four hundred and five hundred Chinese. With the incessant booming of giant kettledrums, amplified a thousandfold, the batteries fired on and on. Clerks and cooks, reinforcing regular crews, shoved shell after shell into the smoking breeches. Paint peeled off the guns, and breech blocks turned black. Red-hot tubes were doubtless ruined, but it did not matter. In twenty-two minutes the battalion fired a phenomenal 3,206 rounds. Forward observers reported that the enemy attacks had been stopped cold.

Colonel Keith ordered firing locks and sights removed in case destruction of the 105's was not complete, but thermite grenades, placed in barrels, did their work. Racking explosions, and the guns perished except for a lone one, spared. It was kept in action by its battery commander, Captain Robert W. Smithson, until the last of the artillery vehicles was on the road.

Let a requiem be spoken for the lost guns of those battalions:

As at Omaha Beach [wrote Colonel S. L. A. Marshall],[258] where one battalion had lost its guns because they were beaten down into the sea, it happened this night that faithful gun crews suffered the same loss because their guns were beaten into earth beyond extrication, snared behind the funeral pyre of some other outfit or forfeited because the mover was riddled, and there was no other source of power. Perhaps not every man kept the trust and did his utmost; under battle's pressure, men are not found equal. But that which needs to be remembered is that hundreds died or became missing in the effort to save machined metal which in the nature of the situation was beyond salvation.

Where the Xth Corps also fought off encircling Chinese hordes in the icy darkness, Battery H, 3rd Battalion, 11th Marine Artillery, could justly boast that its guns never grew cold. At a roadblock artillerymen stood off the enemy with machine guns, then brought their howitzers into action. They smashed attacks with any type of ammunition that came off the trucks—high explosive, white phosphorus, armor-piercing—using Charge 1, the lowest-powdered, at point-blank ranges. There had been no time to dig in trails. Cannoneers, bracing the carriages with their bodies, took up all the recoil they could. They pushed guns back into position and fired on. At one gun, Charge 7, the strongest, was loaded by mistake. The pieces leaped backward twenty feet, rolling over the entire crew. Captain Benjamin S. Read yelled, "Return to your gun!" Battered marines jumped up and manned it again. They broke through the roadblock, leaving eight hundred enemy dead on the battlefield.[259]

Momentum of the Communist offensive diminished, its supplies low. The UN forces, driven many weary, bloody miles, rallied south of the Thirty-eighth Parallel, which they had crossed in triumph only three months previously. By January they were counterattacking, with Turkish, British, and Philippine artillerymen winning special admiration from American gunners. That hard-fighting general, Matthew B. Ridgway, took field command, stiffening backbones. "The issues at stake," he declared, "are enslavement of the body and mind instead of freedom for both . . . collective decency or group brutality." See to it that a soldier understands what he is fighting for, give him morale and *esprit de corps,* and a war that must be waged becomes more than bitter duty of the drafted, and battle rises above a struggle for self-preservation.

The Red venom was far from spent. Twice in the spring of 1951 they staged offensives, which at points made gains of thirty-five miles, but were finally hurled back with heavy casualties. The first year of the war cost the Communists an estimated 1,165,000 killed and wounded, plus huge losses in equipment, as against 250,000 UN casualties, 79,000 of them American. Drawing on the vast reservoir of Asiatic man power, the enemy attacked again. His rank and file exercised a soldier's privilege of griping about incessant night marches, bad treatment from officers, lack of adequate clothing and medical care, lack of air and artillery support to counter the opposition's. Aware they were wasting their breath, they fatalistically fought on. Nor was it the fatalism of despair—not with victories so often won. The Chinese Reds were grim fighters, quick to become battlewise. Though they were short of big guns, their mortar men, as every veteran of Korea will testify, were first-rate. Their artillery forward observers were daring and skillful. One with a two-man detail infiltrated and took post on a mountain behind the American rear. Thence he directed fire by radio on a division headquarters, a hospital, and an air strip for two days before he was spotted and rooted out.

The enemy still took toll of Allied guns. In a furious onslaught near the center of the peninsula toward the end of April, 1951, one ROK artillery battalion and the 2nd Rocket Field Artillery Battalion were completely overrun and lost all their arms and equipment. The 987th Armored FA Battalion, hard hit also but not submerged, lost some of its weapons.

Before the drive Lieutenant Colonel Leon F. Lavoie's 92nd Battalion, self-propelled 155-mm. howitzers, fell back, battery by battery, to new positions. They prepared for action, registering the pieces. Although no one had slept much for thirty-six hours, in that tense situation the colonel permitted no rest until the battalion's perimeter was fortified. Gunners dug in, established telephone and radio networks, put out patrols, rigged trip flares in front of the outposts just beyond grenade range. Quads and machine gunners took their posts. By dark they were as ready as they could be, as time allowed.

That night as the battalion reinforced the fires of the 1st Marine Division, Colonel Lavoie received orders to move at dawn. Men were finishing breakfast in the first glimmer of daylight when a cannoneer spotted three Chinese crawling on their bellies toward his battery. As he yelled, a trip flare blazed up. Machine guns rattled. The chow line scattered. A bullet zipped through the mess tent over the Colonel's head. He ran out and shouted, "Man battle stations!"

All around the perimeter machine guns sputtered. Enemy tracer bullets from Hill 200 flung a red arch over them. Telephone wires were shot out, and the radios took over. The fusillade rose in intensity, as Chinese riflemen and grenadiers bored in on the howitzers. They flooded into two emplacements, driving out crews who ran, grenades bursting a few feet behind them. Machine guns succored them, wiping out pursuers and riddling half a dozen Reds attempting to blow up a howitzer. Sergeant Theral J. Hartley manned a Quad and backed it out of reach of the grenadiers, crushing one hidden beneath it.

Colonel Lavoie covered the battle line, checking the defense. Captain Bernard G. Raftery reported to him: "Sir, Battery C has Chinks all through its area."

"Are they dead or alive?"

"Both," Raftery answered.

"Don't worry about the dead ones. Just take care of the live ones and make every bullet count."

Battery A had been ordered to move and cover a gap in the perimeter. For a moment cannoneers, under a spate of lead, hesitated to venture into the open and crank up trail spades. Sergeant James R. White, blazing away from a Quad, stood up, exposed himself to whistling bullets, and steadied them. They left cover, rushed to the guns. The SP's were ready to roll when the shift was countermanded. Captain John F. Gerrity ran up to direct fire on two machine guns laying down heavy fire on the battalion. Range one thousand yards. The howitzers boomed. A direct hit. Fragments of Chinese gunners and their weapon hurtled high in the air. The crew of the other gun spilled out of their trench. One of "A's" machine guns raked them, cutting some down, harrying the survivors' flight. Then the battery moved and plugged the gap in the circle. Artillery skirmishers mopped up. While some of the batteries swept enemy from the hills with direct fire, others opened in support of the infantry and, with a cub plane observing, scoured out two groups of about thirty Communists each in a valley.

"Artillery," Colonel Lavoie reflected, "if it makes up its mind, will set itself up so that it can defend itself from enemy infantry action." Plainly he and the 92nd had so determined. When the battalion marched in accordance with original orders, it left 179 dead Reds in and around the position it had defended with such stanch valor.

The war ended in stalemate upon the signing of an armistice July 27, 1951. Long-drawn negotiations in the truce tents with an enemy who gave repeated evidence then and later that he would not keep faith, concluded an uneasy peace. What had the war accomplished, Americans asked in bitter disillusionment, beyond the salvation of South Korea and the demonstration that the United Nations, the Soviet Union abstaining, would to a limited extent act together to uphold their principles? It was, many sadly decided, a futile war, a lost cause.

A veteran of Korea, Captain Richard A. McMahon, sat calling up his memories, as veterans will. The bloody storming of Hill 312 came back to him. He remembered comrades-in-arms fallen in its taking, medals won for gallantry over and above the call of duty. They had not died fighting for nothing, because free men will not give up their lives for nothing. "More important than the medals that came out of 312," he told himself with deep assurance, "was the spirit of the men who took it—the teamwork, the sacrifice, and the determination of each man to do his part. So long as men are inspired to do these things, I thought, there is no such thing as a lost cause." [260]

CHAPTER 16

Slingshot to Guided Missile

- -

The artillery accepts with pride its mission as the primary supporting arm to the infantry and armor. It operates zealously to maintain its established reputation as the greatest killer on the battlefield. Whether by conventional shell, atomic projectile, free rocket, or missile, it executes its mission with an esprit that is widely recognized as the spirit of the artillery.

Test of the 280 mm. Gun

The development of a cannon, capable of the battlefield delivery of atomic shell fire, rapidly, accurately and under all weather conditions is a signal landmark in military history.

MAJOR GENERAL A. M. HARPER

The existence of any weapon which fully jeopardizes a whole society necessitates the readiness for defense by the whole society.

COLONEL S. L. A. MARSHALL, *Men Against Fire*

- -

As small arms and hand-carried, crew-served weapons evolved from the bow and arrow, so from the slingshot stemmed artillery arms: the catapult, the cannon, guided missiles from the first crude rockets to the terrible "birds of war" that were ready to fly in the fifty-sixth year of the twentieth century. The slinger's stone had been transmuted into the atom bomb and shell and on into the still more devastating hydrogen bomb.

The first atomic cannon was developed from experiments begun in 1944 to improve heavy field artillery. A powerful 280-mm. gun, it was ready for test in 1952. On its two transporters it looked like earth-moving machinery, which in a sense it was. Old-time gunners pictured a section of horse-drawn artillery beside it, teams, limbers, gun, and caisson shrunken to toylike dimensions. The weight of the complete unit had been kept down to eighty-five tons by extensive use of high-tensile, high-carbon steels and aluminum, and it was not much more ponderous than other heavy pieces in service. It could cross bridges capable of carrying them, travel cross-country as well as on highways at thirty-five miles per hour, fit into a landing ship designed for amphibious operations. Despite its length of twenty-four feet, two inches, it could negotiate corners of streets only twenty-eight feet wide.

A battery of five officers, one warrant officer, and ninety-five enlisted men manned the great guns on their turntables powered by hydraulic jacks. Their shells, regular or atomic, were loaded by a hydraulic rammer. Cannoneers stepped up the rate of fire to one round every six minutes at ranges of twenty or more miles. March order for a move was achieved in from eight to twenty-five minutes, depending upon the terrain.

Gunnery experts reduced time required for computing firing data from one hour to as low as four minutes by inventing a device called a "whizz wheel." Since concealment was all-important—the cannon must be able to fire its awesomely destructive atomic shells without being spotted and counterbatteried—a one-round, "silent" adjustment was employed. The fuse for that round was set so that it would not detonate but fall inert in enemy territory. Radars tracked it and provided data from which corrections were made for fire for effect.

They gave the first big 280 a name, following the old artillery custom—"Atomic Annie." A later piece was dubbed "Up and Atom." Battery A, 867th Field Artillery Battalion, 52nd FA Group, manned Atomic Annie for her test with conventional shells on the range at Fort Sill. Shifted to the Nevada proving grounds, on a historic occasion, May 25, 1953, she fired the first atomic shell. Seven miles away it burst on target. A vivid, blinding flash. Thunderous roar of a vast explosion. The sands upheaved. A broad column of dense, billowing smoke soared high and hung in the air, "spreading out at the top like some unearthly tree"—such a sight as a marine officer in the first World War had witnessed in preview when a huge ammunition dump exploded—the dread spectacle made familiar by the air-dropped atomic bomb.

Now the artillery had harnessed the atom. A-cannon battalions were ordered to Europe to help hold lines against sudden assault on that troubled continent under the threatening shadow of the Soviet Union, possessed also of the atom's secret.

Heavy pieces were taking to the air. In 1956 a new airborne division was organized, its planes to carry not only 105-mm. mortars and 90-mm. self-propelled guns but, eventually, atomic artillery as well. Helicopter-lifted 4.2-inch mortars previously had passed tests. A 155 (12,800 pounds) had been successfully dropped by parachute. Artillerymen predicted atomic-energy-powered self-propelled guns and tanks. Great advances were being made in troop carriers and other vehicles, capable of traversing almost any type of terrain. Development of burnable case ammunition, which would eliminate shell-case salvage, was reported. So was automation artillery with devices reducing a gun crew from thirteen to three men and making it possible for even heavy guns to fire a shell a second.[261]

"The rocket's red glare," streaking through history to sear a scarlet line on the score of our national anthem, had slowly faded for more than a century. In the German V-2 of the second World War it flamed again with ominous incandescence. As a grim commentary on Allied victory, some of the German scientists who had devised that weapon helped American laboratories develop its successors, while others of them served the Soviet Union. A race in guided missiles, with potential cataclysmic consequences to civilization, began. How it would end, no man could foretell.[262]

Guided missiles had become "the army artilleryman's long thrust." [263] In the surface-to-surface category (air-to-air and sea-to-sea missiles are the provinces of the other services), these weapons are high-level, ground-based artillery with ranges rising from several hundred miles toward a thousand and more.

Defending key cities, American artillerymen manned batteries armed with "Nike," named after the Greek goddess of victory. Nike, mighty heiress to antiaircraft guns, is a liquid-fuel rocket launched by a solid-fuel booster and steered toward invading bombers by radio. Twenty-five feet long and carrying three hundred pounds of explosive, the rocket can soar to a height of fifty thousand feet, with a range of more than twenty miles. In flight at fifteen hundred miles per hour, the rocket itself falls away, and its war head continues, guided by the same radio beam that is tracking the bomber until, finding the target, it explodes. Also in the Army's arsenal are "Little John" and "Honest John," free, unguided rockets that can be transported in trucks. These are missile-age divisional artillery. Mightiest of all is the developing intermediate range intercontinental ballistic missile for which ranges of one thousand miles, fifteen hundred, and more are contemplated.

For the army of the Atomic Age, Major Nels A. Parson, Jr., an artilleryman and guided missiles expert, foresaw the need of missile weapons with extended ranges, permitting gunners to fire from deep in friendly territory.

> A modern enemy force will have the capability of attacking with airborne units or long-range weapons only hours or minutes after launching from distant points [he wrote in *Guided Missiles in War and Peace*]. The army commander must have the means under his direct control to attack these very real and immediate threats to his command.
>
> Long-range SSM's [surface-to-surface missiles] are also needed because the army will attack over great distances. Not only are enemy airfields, supply centers, strategic reserves, and other targets moving deeper into hostile territory, but also one's own troops. A modern army will no longer be forced to accomplish an important mission at a location hundreds of miles away by painfully fighting overland to the objective. Airborne units can now move directly to that objective. Within the next ten years airborne movement will become a normal operation for almost all combat units. SSM support of such maneuvers from distant launching sites will be essential.[264]

Methods and means of warfare have changed radically; none of its means more markedly than the one-time art of artillery. Yet the old maxim in regulations for gunners stands unaltered: The reason for the existence of artillery is its ability to assist the other arms, especially the infantry, upon the field of battle. It must fulfill that mission both with long-range guided missiles and with free rockets, field artillery, and demolition employing both atomic and conventional explosives.

> To sum it all up, a modern military force must be capable of fighting either a nuclear or nonnuclear war. And whether the weapons used are nuclear or not, their use must be accompanied by the ability to follow with physical occupation. Otherwise war will be indecisive or will be made decisive only by senseless and total destruction and the defeat of the very aim we seek, lasting peace.[265]

Slingshot—ballista and catapult—bombard and culverin—smooth-bore—rifled piece. The evolution of artillery through past ages cannot match its amazing development within the memory of living men. Concentrated in a single gun, the A-cannon, is the massed fire of fifty batteries. The atom bomb, dwarfing the TOT's of the second World War, yields to the stupendous power of the guided missile with nuclear war head.

Mighty weapons, appallingly destructive ones. Yet for centuries before and since Virgil sang of arms and the man, a truth still holds. If armies march again to the sound of the guns, it will be proven once more that "the national strength lies only in *the hearts and spirits of men.*" [266]

Notes and References

CHAPTER 1

1. Sparks, *Works of Franklin*, VII, 16.
2. Pargellis, ed., *Military Affairs in North America*.
3. Originally the Military Company of Massachusetts, the Ancient and Honorable Artillery was organized after the civil authorities' fears of promoting militarism had been allayed. Its charter provided: "Now as many of that Company of officers which desire to learn the art of gunnery, so needful for every captain and officer of a Company to be experienced in, they may enter their names as Scholars of the Great Artillery." Captain Robert Keayne, its first commander, willed funds to mount cannon and targets. It early carried the pine tree flag, which was repeated as an emblem on a later standard and shown flying unfurled behind the figure of General Washington, standing beside a fieldpiece; its obverse depicts an Indian warrior with bows and arrows. On both sides appeared crossed cannon, adopted as the insignia of American artillery.
4. Parkman, *A Half Century of Conflict*, Vol. II.
5. Drake, *The Taking of Louisbourg*, p. 104.
6. Manucy, *Artillery through the Ages*, p. 5.
7. Sermon to the Company, June 1, 1691. *Military Duties Recommended to an Artillery Company*.
8. Letter to Colonel Robert Hale, Essex Regiment, from John Payne.
9. Private George Mygate, 9th Massachusetts Regiment. *Louisbourg Journals*, p. 102.
10. "This day I was ordered & had a Commission From ye General To over See Twenty odd Smiths in Clearing ye Cannon Tutch holes yt ye French had stopt up." Pomeroy's *Journal*, May 5, 1745.
11. Matross = cannoneer. French *matelot*, Dutch *matroos*, meaning seaman; hence from naval gunnery.
12. Washington Irving, *Chronicles of the Conquest of Granada*. Siege of Zahara.
13. Parkman, II, 153 and n. 1892 edition.
14. Diary of a soldier, anonymous. *Louisbourg Journals*.
15. However, Colonel Gridley was again present and distinguished himself.

CHAPTER 2

16. Pargellis, ed., *Military Affairs in North America.*

17. *Ibid.*, Appendix II, 479-487, lists more than two hundred items under "A Proportion of Brass Ordnance, Howitzers and Stores for the Intended Expedition of North America. By Order of the Board dated the 12th October 1754." Royal artillery headquarters in Boston computed that "for fifty rounds of regimental practice with a single six-pounder there were required, in addition to round shot, 400 tin tubes, 30 portfires and matches, flannel cartridges, fine paper, corned powder, sheepskins and sponge tacks (both for rammer staffs), and worsted in Proportion."—Pargellis, *Lord Loudon in North America.*

18. Joseph Thaxter, letter, Edgartown, Massachusetts, November 3, 1824.

19. This two-gun action by the Royal Artillery deserves high rating in gunner annals.

20. Gridley's record at Crown Point, both Louisbourg sieges, and Quebec won him a British commission, the grant of a seal and cod fishery, and three thousand New Hampshire acres. He forfeited half pay, for which Congress promised to reimburse him, when he accepted an American commission, dated May 19, 1775, as chief engineer and colonel of artillery.

21. Philadelphia's company was founded 1755, Charleston's 1757.

22. Robins' work (London, 1747) is notable for its advanced thinking such as his suggestion of rifling cannon. His experiments determined that atmospheric conditions affect the flight of projectiles, factors which became increasingly important as ranges lengthened. From his findings derive the meteorological sections of modern artillery, essential to the accurate computation of firing data, especially for antiaircraft guns and guided missiles. Müller's first edition (London, 1757) was dedicated to the Duke of Gloucester. In its pirated Philadelphia reprint, 1779, that inscription was patriotically transferred to Generals Washington and Knox, Colonel Proctor, and the officers of the Continental Army.

23. Bishop, *Field Artillery, the King of Battles,* p. 4.

24. The Palma Vecchio painting hangs in the Church of Santa Maria Formosa, Venice. In Rafael's Sistine Madonna, Barbara kneels at the left of Mary.

25. "Gridley is grown old, is much governed by a son of his who vainly supposed he had a right to the second place in the regiment...." *Warren-Adams Letters,* I, 101.

26. Private Peter Brown, of Prescott's regiment. Letter to his mother (Cambridge, June 25, 1775).

27. "The wretched blunder of the over-sized balls sprung from the dotage of an officer of rank in that Corps, who spends his whole time in dallying with the schoolmaster's daughters [*sic*]. God knows he is old enough—he is no Sampson [*sic*]—yet he must have his Delilah." From a letter in *Detail*

and Conduct of the American War, reprinted in *Historical Magazine,* June, 1868, p. 368.

28. Quoted in Drake, *Bunker Hill,* pp. 60 f.

29. "Prior to 1808 the artillery teams were rarely driven by enlisted men. The wagoner, the teamster, the carter, and the driver—all were civilians following their normal trade, or farmers offering themselves and their draft animals for hire during the off season to eke out meager incomes. As with the Crown troops, since before the days of the Braddock campaign, the normal practice in the Army was to hire these men, with or without their animals, vehicles, and harness. Hire was on contractual basis for short periods to cover a single movement or operation, or for a campaign, or even by the year. Both oxen and horses were used for artillery draft. Terms of hire varied according to the work to be performed and equipment provided." Larter, *Military Collector and Historian,* Vol. V, No. 3, September, 1952, p. 57. See also Flenley, "A History of Artillery" in *Journal of the Royal Artillery,* XLVII, 441 f.

30. Greenwood in *Captain John Manley,* pp. 22 ff., declares that the *Nancy* also carried 2 brass 24's, 2 18's, 10 fieldpieces, 30 8-inch howitzers and 10 5½'s "according to various accounts" (unspecified). Other sources —French, Frothingham, etc.—do not mention any such respectable addition to the American artillery. In any event Washington's siege ordnance was insufficient, as evidenced by his eagerness to obtain guns from Quebec. Force, IV, 494, states that the American army by October 20, 1775, had 5 24's, 6 18's, 7 mortars, 8 howitzers, and 25 light pieces.

31. *New England Chronicle, or Essex Gazette,* December 14, 1775. "A Song Composed by a Soldier of the Continental Army" (to the tune of "The Black Sloven").

32. Leake, *Memoir of the Life and Times of General John Lamb,* and Roberts, *March to Quebec.*

33. Colonel Sydney E. Hammersley, "History of a Wandering Cannon," in *Bulletin of the Fort Ticonderoga Museum,* Vol. 1, No. 1, 1952.

34. The inscription on the plaques reads: "Through this place passed General Henry Knox in the winter of 1775-1776 to deliver to General George Washington at Cambridge the train of artillery from Fort Ticonderoga used to force the British army to evacuate Boston."

35. The best account of this "remarkable achievement," as Freeman terms it in his biography of Washington, is Alexander C. Flicks's "General Henry Knox's Ticonderoga Expedition" in New York State Historical Association *Proceedings,* Vol. XXVI, and *Quarterly Journal,* IX (1928), 119-135.

CHAPTER 3

36. American artillery in the Revolution used cannon of thirteen calibers. The largest, 32-pounders, were iron. Smaller pieces were usually bronze.

37. Firing commands, later standardized by William Stevens, a captain

in Lamb's regiment, in his *A System for the Discipline of the Artillery of the United States of America,* comprised fourteen evolutions: 1. Attention. 2. Unlimber piece. 3. Secure side boxes. 4. Man out the piece (attaching dragropes to axles and holding them to check the gun's recoil). 5. From right to left, dress. 6. Advance sponge. 7. Tend vent. 8. Sponge piece. 9. Handle cartridge. 10. Charge piece. 11. Ram down cartridge. 12. Prime. 13. Take aim. 14. Fire. Commands were given by voice or drum taps.

38. "The officers and men of the artillery, who fought the *six pieces* [author's italics] we had in the action, covered themselves with honor. They were 'the flower' of Knox's regiment, picked for a field fight." Long Island Historical Society, *Memoirs,* III, 197 f. Adams' *Studies Military and Diplomatic,* p. 56, specifies the fieldpieces as one 5½-in. howitzer, four 6-pounders and one 3. Knox seems to have kept most of his field guns on Manhattan as a mobile defense against landings from British warships.

39. "Company" was then and until the close of the Napoleonic wars the term for an artillery unit. "Battery" was originally applied only to guns emplaced for the siege or defense of a fortified place. However, the terms are used interchangeably in the text.

40. Azoy, *They Were Not Afraid to Die,* p. 138.

41. In *Our Lusty Forefathers* (Downey), pp. 153-160, the Battle of Trenton is reconstructed as told in modern language by an American artillery sergeant in combat against German troops.

42. Even before the German attack on Poland in World War II, War Department planners foresaw American involvement and made preparations against an invasion of the United States by way of the old Champlain Valley warpath. Captain Harry C. Larter, Jr., an artilleryman with a thorough knowledge of history, was detailed in top secret orders to pick battery positions along the route of an enemy drive that would threaten the New England industrial section. Among the sites he chose was Mount Defiance whose neglect had cost St. Clair Fort Ticonderoga.

43. Ranges from Adye, *The Bombardier and Pocket Gunner.*

44. *Autobiography: Reminiscences and Letters of John Trumbull,* pp. 30-39.

45. Nickerson, *The Turning Point of the Revolution,* pp. 143-144.

46. *Ibid.,* p. 165.

47. Smith, autobiography. *Historical Magazine,* second series, Vol. VII.

48. Fitzpatrick, *The Spirit of the Revolution.*

49. Stryker, *Battle of Monmouth,* p. 207.

50. *Ibid.,* p. 237.

51. Azoy, *op. cit.,* p. 287.

52. "One of the few remaining Colonial buildings, the Nelson House, still has cannon-balls embedded in the walls." *New York Herald Tribune,* November 28, 1954.

53. Johann Conrad Dohla, *Tagebuch.*

54. The fine reconstruction of Knox's Mansion, "Montpelier," Thomas-

ton, Maine, contains many mementos of the great Chief of Artillery of the Revolution.

CHAPTER 4

55. The history of Hamilton's battery following the Revolution was traced in 1923 by officers of the 5th Field Artillery. Gen. G. B. Barth, then regimental adjutant, states in a letter to the author: "The coat of arms of the 5th Field Artillery was based on the family crest of Alexander Hamilton, since Battery 'D' traces an unbroken history to the original Hamilton Battery. We were well along in this project when, much to our chagrin, the *Coast Artillery Journal* came out with the coat of arms of the 62nd Coast Artillery on its cover and the statement that this organization was the descendant of the old Hamilton Battery and, therefore, the only unit of the active Army with continuous service since the Revolution. We knew that wasn't so, but felt that the 62nd must have a pretty good case based on records. Our commander therefore sent an officer on special duty to Washington to search the archives and try to substantiate our claim. The result was very interesting. This officer found that the original Hamilton Battery had been moved west to the vicinity of Vincennes, Indiana, to fight Indians and was under the command of a Captain Maylen Ford. In those days, of course, there was no numerical designation for units, but each bore the name of its commander. Also, there was apparently no replacement system, and the unit fought until it became decimated to the point where it was no longer effective. At that time a new unit was recruited in the east and sent to take over the remnants of the old unit. This had been done, a new Battery having been formed in Boston, Massachusetts, and sent west overland. I don't remember the name of the Battery Commander of the new unit, but we unearthed an order stating that Captain So-and-So and his Battery, having reached Vincennes, would absorb the remnants of Captain Maylen Ford's Battery, and that the said Maylen Ford would 'consider himself deranged.' Our researcher was able to trace the history of this Battery down to the present time where it is Battery 'D,' 5th Field Artillery. The controversy arose due to the fact that Captain Ford refused to stay 'deranged.' The record showed that he returned east, organized a new Battery, which, of course, was also called Ford's Battery and took it to the Seminole Indian War. This second Ford Battery later became the 62nd Coast Artillery."

A postscript is added by Colonel Edward L. Austin, Artillery, in a letter to the author, May 23, 1956. In 1941 at Fort Devens, Massachusetts, the 1st Provisional Anti Tank Battalion was organized from the antitank elements of the 1st Infantry Division Artillery. It comprised all the thirty-seven platoons of the battalions plus D Battery of the 5th Field Artillery Battalion. Despite the 5th's protests, D's guidon was transferred to the new unit, subsequently designated Company C, 601st Tank Destroyer Battalion. That company served with distinction in the European Theater,

World War II. However, tradition prevailed, and by order of the Secretary
of the Army the guidon was finally restored with appropriate ceremonies
to Battery D, 5th Field Artillery Battalion.

56. Birkhimer, *Historical Sketch of the Artillery, United States Army*,
pp. 34 f.; Jacobs, *The Beginning of the U.S. Army*, pp. 274 ff.; Larter,
Military Collector and Historian Journal, September, 1952, pp. 53-60; Niles'
Register, LXXII, 176.

57. Tousard adopted a coat of arms showing crossed American and
French flags, the British gun he captured, and above it his severed arm.

58. Jacobs, *op. cit.*, p. 386.

59. Babcock, *The War of 1812 on the Niagara Frontier*, p. 155.

60. Tucker, *Poltroons and Patriots*, p. 613.

61. *Ibid.*, p. 617.

62. Swanson, *The Perilous Fight*, p. 102.

63. Scharf, *History of Maryland*, III, 101. Probably the 42's came from
a French warship which had taken refuge in Baltimore harbor from the
British fleet.

64. Swanson, *op. cit.*, p. 442.

65. Johnson, *Andrew Jackson*, p. 9.

66. Adams, *The War of 1812* (DeWeerd, ed.), p. 311.

67. Gleig, *A Narrative of the British Campaigns*.

68. James, *Andrew Jackson*, I, 261.

69. *Ibid.*, p. 264.

70. Buell, *History of Andrew Jackson*, II, 200.

71. Parton, *Life of Andrew Jackson*, II, 208.

72. Tucker, *op. cit.*, p. 704.

CHAPTER 5

73. Rodenbough, *The Army of the United States*, contains histories of
the first five artillery regiments (the 5th was organized in 1861) by officers,
including Birkhimer, who served with them.

74. Birkhimer, *op. cit.*, p. 200 n.

75. Spaulding, *The United States Army in War and Peace*, p. 154. "Ten
companies of artillery, representing all four regiments, were assembled
there. By detail from these batteries and from the artillery at large, an administrative and instructional staff was formed, including departments of
mathematics, engineering, drawing and chemistry. Cadets assigned to the
artillery upon graduation from the Military Academy were sent here for a
year's practical and theoretical training before joining their regiments."

76. Split trails, permitting greater elevation of the barrel, would reappear
in the post-World War I design of metal gun carriages.

77. Birkhimer, *op. cit.*, p. 248.

78. Ganoe, *The History of the United States Army*, p. 176.

79. *Ibid.*, pp. 167, 171.

80. Ringgold designed a saddle tree, later improved by and named for George B. McClellan. This saddle would remain standard for artillery and cavalry through World War I.

81. Larter, *Military Collector and Historian Journal*, March, 1938, p. 18. Todd and Kredel, *Soldiers of the American Army*, 2nd ed., Plate No. 13.

82. Alfred Hoyt Bill, *Rehearsal for Conflict: the War with Mexico, 1846-1848*.

83. *Two Wars, Mexican and Confederate*.

84. DeVoto, *The Year of Decision*, p. 194.

85. Alcaraz, *The Other Side*.

86. Then spelled with one *r*.

87. Bill, *Rehearsal for Conflict*, p. 144.

88. French, *Two Wars*, p. 62.

89. Bill, *op. cit.*, p. 152.

90. French, *op. cit.*, p. 66.

91. Not to be confused with William Tecumseh Sherman, whom fate had shunted to a California garrison. He was one of the few top Civil War leaders who took no active part in the Mexican conflict.

92. An excellent account of the San Patricio Battalion will be found in Blanche Marie McEniry's *American Catholics in the War with Mexico*.

93. Among the drastic punishments causing desertions from the U.S. Army was bucking and gagging; in bucking, a man was trussed up like a fowl with a stick thrust under his knees and over arms bound in front of them. The practice drew a bitter jibe in a song written by an English-born corporal of Company I, 1st Artillery. (Anonymous, *Autobiography of an English Soldier in the United States Army*. New York, 1953, pp. 247, 282). One stanza runs:

> "Sergeant, buck him and gag him," our officers cry,
> For each trifling offence which they happen to spy;
> Till with bucking and gagging of Tom, Dick, and Bill,
> Faith, the Mexican ranks they have helped to fill.

94. Johnston, *Marching with the Army of the West*, p. 78.

95. Hughes, *Doniphan's Expedition*, p. 395 n.

96. Heymann in *John Zizka and the Hussite Revolution*, p. 100 f., describes the war wagons' armament. They carried a large number of cross-bows, some small firearms, and stone-barreled cannon on special gun carriages. That remarkable field artillery of the early fifteenth century was used not only to breach enemy ranks but in offensive action that won battles.

97. Smith, *The War with Mexico*, Vol. I.

98. Carleton, *Battle of Buena Vista*, p. 103, pays a tribute to the San Patricios. "It was a fine battery, and the havoc it made in our ranks was a melancholy evidence of the skill with which it was served."

99. Private S. E. Chamberlain, 1st Dragoons, later a Union brigadier.

His then unpublished diary is cited by Smith, *op. cit.*, I, 554. A second refutation of the "a little more grape, Captain Bragg," legend is found in Birkhimer, p. 337, who states that Bragg, who carried no grapeshot in his ammunition chests, declared that Taylor simply ordered him, "Captain, give them hell!" Buell in *The Cannoneer*, p. 15, quotes a story told him personally by Alfred Pleasanton, Civil War Union cavalry commander, who as a dragoon lieutenant acted as aide to Taylor at Buena Vista. Pleasanton's version of the interchange ran as follows. Taylor: "What are you firing, Captain?" Bragg: "Canister, sir." "Double or single?" "Single, sir." "Then double it, and give 'em h - - l!"

100. *Lew Wallace: An Autobiography*, I, 174 n.

101. Quoted by William L. Haskin, present as a young lieutenant, in his *The History of the First Regiment of Artillery*, p. 98.

102. Smith, *op. cit.*, II, 109.

103. Bill, *op. cit.*, p. 278.

104. Smith, *op. cit.*, II, 115.

105. *Ibid.*, p. 117.

106. Wilcox, *History of the Mexican War*, p. 395.

CHAPTER 6

107. The mule-back episode is related in a memoir by James Stewart, who subsequently commanded the battery, in Buell, *The Cannoneer*, pp. 389 f.

108. For an excellent technical study of Civil War artillery matériel, illustrated with plates and photographs, the reader is referred to Jac Weller, *Military Collector and Historian Journal*, June, September, and December, 1953. Mr. Weller adds in "British Cannon in the Confederacy," Ms.: "As the war wore on, everyone began to realize that long range artillery fire didn't cause many casualties and could be practically disregarded by seasoned troops. The reason for this is startlingly apparent from a study of projectile fragments from any one of the battlefields ... [They] show positive evidence of having been fired but not exploding ... By 1864 field rifles of all types had lost much of their popularity on both sides. The muzzle-loading, smooth-bore, bronze 12-pounder Napoleon, when used like a monster shotgun with double charges of canister at close range, was the real casualty producer. No rifle could equal it for use right in the trenches with the infantry."

109. Catton, *A Stillness at Appomattox*, pp. 47 f.

110. Wilkeson, *Recollections of a Private Soldier in the Army of the Potomac*, pp. 23 f.

111. Gen. James B. Fry in *Battles and Leaders of the Civil War*, I, 189.

112. Tidball, Ms., p. 15.

113. Wilkeson, *op. cit.*, pp. 32 ff.

114. Wise, *The Long Arm of Lee*, I, 195 f.

115. Stiles, *Four Years Under Marse Robert*, p. 81.

116. Steele, *American Campaigns*, p. 189.

117. Wise, *op. cit.*, I, 197, 216.

118. Stiles, *op. cit.*, 104.

119. Freeman, *Lee's Lieutenants*, I, 602.

120. Lee, Jr., *Recollections and Letters of General Robert E. Lee*, pp. 76 f. Lee had permitted his son to leave the University of Virginia and enlist in the artillery the previous spring. In the fall young Lee was commissioned and served through the rest of the war on the staff of his brother, W. H. F. Lee, cavalry commander.

CHAPTER 7

121. Colonel Wise's two volumes on the gunners and guns of the Army of Northern Virginia are the finest work on the artillery of the Civil War in detail, vivid action, and color. They give full credit to able and gallant opponents of the Union arm. Nothing comparable on the artillery of the Army of the Potomac has yet appeared.

122. "The number of fired but unexploded Confederate shells recovered from the battlefield bears out the estimates of Confederate artillery officers as to the extremely high percentage of their shells that were defective. A shell with a two-second fuze often went further before exploding than one cut for twice that time, if they both went off at all." Jac Weller, *Military Collector and Historian Journal*, June, 1953, p. 32 f.

123. See Chapter 10. Also Ramsdell, "General Lee's Horse Supply," on the crippling losses of the Confederate artillery and cavalry.

124. Wise, I, 111. *Rebellion Records*, Series 4, II, 194.

125. Wise, II, 546.

126. *Ibid.*, p. 547.

127. Wise, *Field Artillery Journal*, Vol. XIII, 1923.

128. *Ibid.* Colonel Wise's comments in his article, "Field Artillery in Rearguard Actions," deserve full quotation:

"As an example of almost superhuman courage and energy, Dilger's exploits at Chancellorsville are interesting. His gallantry like that of little Ackley is above praise. But the numerous lessons which the incident carries with it are more than praiseworthy. They are of the utmost value to the student of artillery tactics.

"First, there was a perfect reconnaissance on his part; second the instant appreciation of the significance of his observations, and third, the soundest judgment on his part as to the value of military intelligence, which in the emergency carried him direct to the various headquarters where the information in his possession instantly acquired the greatest value, whether properly estimated or not. He saw at a glance that not merely a brigade, or division, or corps, or even the entire right wing of the army were in jeopardy, but that the whole army was in imminent peril; that nothing which could now be done by Von Gilsa or Devens would save the situation, and that Hooker alone could prevent a disaster by an immediate realignment in force behind the right wing of the army. The High Command refusing to act, he still endeavored to accomplish the necessary shift of front by warning the commander of the endangered wing, and having done all that was in his power as a subordinate to warn his superiors of the danger of which he was aware, forthwith he prepared himself to delay the execution of the obvious plan of the enemy momentarily, at least, while it was disclosing itself to his incredulous superiors.

"The manner in which he posted his guns illustrates the best manner in which to cover a vital approach. He might have inflicted as many casualties with his fire from other positions but his primary aim was to delay the movement of the enemy, not merely to inflict casualties upon him. So long as the free use of the turnpike was denied the enemy, there was bound to be an interruption of his movements and a consequent dislocation of his plans, for it was by this road alone that the artillery could move forward in support of the attacking infantry. It must be remembered that light artillery moved with the infantry in 1863. Furthermore, the maximum effect of canister was not to be had by oblique fire through the woods upon the roadway from a position on its flanks, canister being effective only in the open. Again, under the circumstances of so restricted a field of fire he exercised the best judgment in retaining one gun only instead of trying to handle a full battery on the narrow pike, since one gun was more readily handled and firing constantly gave the maximum fire effect obtainable in so limited a field of fire with far less risk of loss."

129. "On taking command of the army, General Hooker had transferred the military command of the artillery to his own headquarters, to be resumed by the chief of artillery only under specific orders and for special occasions, which resulted in such mismanagement and confusion at Chancellorsville that he consented to organize the artillery into brigades. This was a decided improvement, which would have been greater if the brigade commanders had held adequate rank. As it was, there was no artillery commandant in chief for months before the battle of Gettysburg, and of the 14 brigades 4 were commanded by field-officers, 9 by captains, and 1 by a lieutenant, taken from their batteries for the purpose." Hunt in *Battles and Leaders of the Civil War*, III, 259.

130. The author had the privilege of visiting Gettysburg with his grandfather, George Mason Downey, who as a lieutenant of Union infantry was twice brevetted for gallantry in the Peach Orchard.

131. Hunt's report on Gettysburg, Artillery Headquarters, September 27, 1863.

132. Colonel Allen J. Greer, "The Roaring Guns from the Seven Days to Cold Harbor," *Field Artillery Journal*, XXVI, 1936.

133. *The Cannoneer*, p. 70.

134. Bigelow, *The Peach Orchard*, p. 57 f.

135. II, 647 f.

136. Major General E. M. Law, C.S.A., *Battles and Leaders*, III, 327.

137. Colonel Wise in a letter to the author, Nov. 29, 1955, emphasizes that the detailed study in his book of Confederate artillery dispositions at Gettysburg shows that "never were the Corps artillery commands brought into cooperation, and, that with the large Reserve almost completely inactive, like the battalions of the three Corps, it was not concentrated on Culps Hill or Cemetery Ridge at any time; that the only artillery fire delivered upon the latter was direct during successive corps attacks and even during the crucial charge of Pickett's Division, so that the Federal artillery and infantry always had the maximum protection and remained intact at the crisis of the final action involving the assault. Indeed the mishandling of the artillery was so patently gross that the Union Chief of Artillery actually scolded General Long of Lee's army on a later occasion for this appalling blunder that bared the breast of the infantry assault to the guns of the defenders.

"The reason for all this is plain. On no other battlefield had the problem of dislodging defenders from a single position presented itself to those who found themselves assailants instead of defenders, since Malvern Hill where the [Confederate] artillery was still unorganized for joint action. Thus the Reserve and the Corps artillery not only had no liaison but no experience in the mass action, as in the case of Napoleon's artillery which ordinarily decided the issue by overwhelming the defenders before his infantry bared its breast.

"Manifestly to blame Longstreet for the result of July 3 is absurd.

"Look at your map and see that while the three corps separately could only deliver direct fire, when operating individually, the Reserve at all times could have been moved up on the left of Hill behind Ewell to cross fire with the corps battalions, making the Union position untenable."

138. *The Battle of Gettysburg*, pp. 50 ff.

139. Bishop, *Field Artillery, the King of Battles*, 137 f.

140. Whitelaw Reid, war correspondent for the *Cincinnati Gazette*.

CHAPTER 8

141. "Our Experience in Artillery Administration." Vol. XII, March, 1891.

142. Buell, *op. cit.*, p. 163.

143. Fort Popham was garrisoned in 1865, during the Spanish War in '98 and in World War I. Today, made obsolete by bomber planes, it is maintained as a historic site. Dunnack, *A History of Fort Popham Memorial*.

144. "Whistling Dick," now a trophy at West Point, is a 7.5-inch Blakely (English-made) rifle, which seems to have fired an expanding copper-

sabotted shell. The fast pitch of its rachet-type rifling gave its shells, weighing probably from 120 to 140 pounds, a rapid spin. Hence their unusual sound in flight. Jac Weller, "British Cannon in the Confederacy," Ms.

145. Buell, *op. cit.*, pp. 165 f., 169 f., quoting Private F. O. Talbot. Wilkeson, *op. cit.*, pp. 83-86. Casualties of 1st Maine at Petersburg: Fox, *Regimental Losses in the American Civil War.*

146. *Memoirs*, II, 241.

147. Wise, *op. cit.*, II, 833.

148. Buell, *op. cit.*, 179 f.

149. Stiles, *op. cit.*, 272 f.

150. Du Pont's superb rear-guard fight, given scant notice in most accounts of New Market, is related in detail by Colonel Wise in *Field Artillery Journal*, Vol. XII (1922), 502-510.

151. Buell, *op. cit.*, pp. 209 ff.

152. General William J. Snow, "The Functions and Training of Field Artillery." Ms. in Fort Sill Library.

153. Quoted in Wise, *op. cit.*, II, 863 f.

154. Major Robert Stiles.

155. In "The Roaring Guns from the Seven Days to Cold Harbor" (*Field Artillery Journal*, January-February, 1936) Col. Allen J. Greer, FA, sums up the methods of employment of the artilleries of the Army of the Potomac and that of Northern Virginia as follows:

"1. At all times the Army of the Potomac had a decisive superiority in numbers of guns, in their calibers, and in quantity and quality of ammunition. This superiority tended to produce a result that Napoleon mentions, namely, that infantry having to fight long with superior artillery against them would be disorganized.

"2. Superiority in numbers and calibers had a direct effect upon the tactical employment of the two artilleries.

"3. Wherever there was sufficient space to put their batteries in position and there was a good field of fire, the Union artillery's fire was massed and dominated that of the Confederates.

"4. On those occasions when the artilleries of both sides could be employed in large masses, the great superiority of Hunt, the Union chief of Artillery, over the Confederate chief, in leadership, tactical ability, and skill in coordination of fire, was an important element in deciding the battle.

"5. Probably the most effective employment of the Confederate artillery was at Fredericksburg, where the great majority of the guns made no attempt to engage the Union artillery, but remained under cover until the opposing infantry launched its assault, then came into position and at close ranges poured withering fire on the attackers.

"6. While both artilleries had more or less the same doctrines and tactical methods, still the conditions of the two forces brought out two distinct phases in the employment of artillery, quite different in character, although not always so considered.

"The Union artillery with its greater proportion of rifles, outnumbering and outranging its opponents, illustrates primarily the massing of batteries under common control, furnishing the army commander with a great reserve of fire power, with which he can neutralize the opposing guns and place destructive fire on his infantry. Such use of massed artillery practically decided the day at Malvern Hill, and at Antietam and Gettysburg was one of the most important factors."

156. Brevet Major General Joshua Lawrence Chamberlain, U.S.V., who as Colonel of the 20th Maine won a Medal of Honor in the defense of Little Round Top. *The Passing of the Armies*, p. 350.

CHAPTER 9

157. *Field Artillery Journal*, Vols. XXIX, XXX.

158. "The Caissons," whose story is told later in this chapter, is the artillery's most beloved song. Others include: "Keep Them Rolling," "The Red Guidon," "The Mountain Battery," "O'Reilly's Gone to Hell," all by Colonel Gerald E. Griffin; "Crash On! Artillery" (Coast Artillery Marching Song) by J. F. Hewitt and A. H. Osborn; "Song of the Two-Forty" (240-mm. howitzers, GHQ Reserve) by Major R. A. Kimble; "We'll be Comin' Through the Mountains" (2nd Batt., 13th FA); "We Don't Know Where We're Going, but We're on Our Way" (12th FA); Motorized Version of "The Caissons" by Fairfax Downey; "Field Artillery Guns," music by Murray Cohen, words by Downey; "The Battery Rolls On," music by Channing Lefebvre, words by Downey; "938th Field Artillery Battalion March" by Melville B. Coburn; "Song of the Eighty-Second" by John M. Jenkins; "Seventy-Sixth Field Artillery Song" by Edith H. Ward. Scores of some of the songs listed are in *Field Artillery Journal, Army Song Book, Field Artillery Song Book* and *Famous Artillery Songs* (Fort Sill, Oklahoma, 1937 and 1950), *The Bearcat Hymn Book—Songs of the Field Artillery* (Monterey, California, 1927).

159. Downey, *Indian-Fighting Army*, p. 229.

160. The Medal of Honor, except for the brevetting of officers, was then the only award for gallantry in action. Lesser decorations—Distinguished Service Cross, Silver Star, etc.—had not yet been authorized.

161. Frederick P. Todd in *Military Collector and Historian Journal*, Vol. VII, No. 2 (summer, 1955), p. 50, quoting Rufus F. Zogbaum in *Harper's Weekly*, May 4, 1895.

162. Todd, *ibid.*, p. 51.

163. Bishop, *Field Artillery, the King of Battles*, p. 8.

164. Alger, *The Spanish-American War*, Chapters II and III.

165. Dunne, *Mr. Dooley in Peace and War*, p. 6.

166. *Field Artillery Journal*, XVI, 443 f.

167. Capt. Michael V. Gannon, FA.

168. Downey, *Field Artillery Journal*, XXXI (1941), 485.

169. The story of Reilly's Battery is adapted from an article by the author in *The American Legion Magazine* (July, 1927), based on the first-hand accounts of one of Reilly's lieutenants and his first sergeant: General Charles P. Summerall and Master Sergeant B. S. Follinsby. The author served as a battery officer and regimental adjutant in World War I under another of Reilly's lieutenants, Colonel Manus McCloskey, 12th FA.

CHAPTER 10

170. *Field Artillery Journal*, XXIX (January, 1939), 26.

171. *Army Song Book*, pp. 62 f.

172. Stiles, *Four Years Under Marse Robert*, p. 234 f.

173. Buell, *The Cannoneer*, p. 30 f.

174. *Saturday Evening Post*, January 21, 1933.

175. "Jeanne d'Arc's" story was told in fiction form by Fairfax Downey in *War Horse*.

176. Hal Burton, "The Army's Orneriest Heroes," in *Saturday Evening Post*, July 11, 1953.

177. Wyman, *The Wild Horses of the West*. American horse exports to Europe between 1933 and 1938, in preparation for World War II, totaled 11,434.

178. Galtrey, *The Horse and the War*.

179. *Barrack-Room Ballads*. "Snarleyow" belonged to the Bengal Horse Artillery of the East India Company's army.

180. Snow, *Signposts of Experience*, p. 187 n.

181. During the attack on Monte Cassino in the Italian campaign, World War II, a spotter plane caught a column of German horse-drawn artillery on the march and directed fire that destroyed it. After a glimpse of the carnage the pilot "radioed that he could stomach no more and that fire must be continued unobserved. Few sights shake a man so much as that of dying horses in their helpless agony, and consideration for horses, according to several British horse-drawn artillerymen, allowed the Germans to bring their artillery well forward in 1940." *Field Artillery Journal*, XXXV, 113.

182. Downey, *Army Song Book*, p. 22.

183. Downey, *War Horse*, p. 230.

184. See chapter heading.

CHAPTER 11

185. Hagedorn, *The Bugle that Woke America*, p. 37.

186. Robert M. Danford, first commanding officer of the Yale Batteries

and future chief of field artillery. Foreword to Snow's *Signposts of Experience.*

187. Farrow, *American Guns in the War with Germany,* Chapter VII.

188. *Ibid.,* p. 3.

189. Snow, *op. cit.,* pp. 57 f.

190. Farrow, *op. cit.,* pp. xiv f.

191. Leriwell, *The History of Military Mobilization in the United States,* Part II, Chapter IX.

192. Capt. George D. Wahl's excellent account of the progress of Battery B, 12th FA, from training in the U.S. into action in France. *Field Artillery Journal,* xiv (January, March, and May, 1924).

193. "Because of its cost, and the limited effect of its projectile, the Paris Gun did not pay for itself in material effect upon the enemy. Nevertheless, it had unquestioned moral effect in the early bombardments, causing frequent general alarms and virtually stopping all normal business activity for many hours. Had the Germans been able to hold their territorial gains of the spring offensive of 1918, these guns could have been emplaced at shorter ranges where the life of the tubes would have been much longer." Field Artillery School, *History of the Development of Field Artillery Matériel,* p. 66.

194. *Ibid.,* p. 62. "In the year ending November 10, 1918, the Allies expended 160,615,000 rounds of ammunition. In the American Civil War, the Union army expended in the year ending June 30, 1864, only 1,950,000 rounds. American artillery at St. Mihiel fired 1,000,000 rounds in a single four-hour preparation. During the World War the average field gun fired 33 rounds per day, as compared with a Civil War average of four rounds. The cost of ammunition in the Civil was $10,000,000; in the World War it amounted to $30,000,000."

195. In this officer's honor, "F" of the 7th FA was named Feigl Battery, reviving an Old Army custom. The battery's four guns were christened Feigl, Flaherty, Fluff, and Fox. Its guidon staff was a steel lance, presented by a French dragoon, rescued by men of the battery when he was severely wounded near its position. Larter, *Military Collector and Historian Journal,* VII, No. 4 (1956), pp. 109 f.

196. Following the surprise introduction of poison gas by the Germans at Ypres, "both sides employed it freely in the rest of the war, particularly in artillery shells. It put large numbers out of action, but killed relatively few. Although even more effective gases were prepared for World War II, they were not used by either side; fear of reprisal in view of the development of aerial bombing of cities kept gas out of the war. There had been, to be sure, an international agreement to forego the use of gas; the United States and Japan had not signed this. Chemical warfare (in World War II) was restricted largely to smoke shells for screening movements and phosphorous shells which produced burns." U.S. Dept. of the Army. *Senior ROTC Manual,* 1947, Chapter 10.

197. Butler's amusing cartoons, collected in *"Happy Days!,"* are artillery history in sketches, often more vivid than words. Humor, drawn, written, or verbal, played an important part in keeping World War I morale high. See also files of the A.E.F. newspaper, *The Stars and Stripes,* and lighthearted chronicles by Charles MacArthur (*War Bugs*) and William Hazlett Upson (*Me and Henry and the Artillery*).

198. Van Every, *The A.E.F. in Battle,* p. 54.

199. *Ibid.,* p. 73.

200. *Ibid.,* p. 79.

CHAPTER 12

201. Thomason, *Fix Bayonets!,* p. 94.

202. "It was the insistence of General Pershing to have this artillery, and to wait until he got it, and to his decision, on the advice of his chief of artillery, Major Gen. E. F. McGlachlin, to use it in a suitable artillery preparation, that is due the substantial result obtained at St. Mihiel." Colonel Conrad H. Lanza, FA, *Field Artillery Journal,* XXII (1932), 609.

203. Thomas, *The History of the A.E.F.,* p. 211.

204. *Ibid.,* pp. 243 f.

205. Thomason, *Fix Bayonets!,* pp. 157 f.

206. See chapter foreword.

207. Thomason, *op. cit.,* p. 235.

CHAPTER 13

208. Under this title the Artillery School, Fort Sill, published several booklets on World War II artillery at the front.

209. "During the postwar period, continuous paring of appropriations had reduced the Army virtually to the status of that of a third-rate power." Gen. Marshall, *Biennial Report.*

210. Accompanying guns and dive bombers, as developed by the Germans, were prime features of the blitzkrieg that crushed Poland.

211. Tunis, *Weapons.*

212. "German ammunition was charged with smokeless, flashless powder which in both night and day fighting helped the enemy tremendously in concealing his fire positions. United States riflemen, machine gunners, and gunners of all types had to expose their positions with telltale muzzle flashes or puffs of powder smoke. German preparations had given them time to develop this high-grade powder and manufacture tremendous quantities of it. They had it there and they used it." Marshall, *op cit.*

213. "The mission of surface-to-surface artillery is twofold: (1) To support the other arms by fire, neutralizing or destroying those targets which are most dangerous to the supported arms; and (2) to give depth to combat and to isolate the battlefield by counterfire, by fire on hostile reserves, by restricting movement in rear areas, and by disrupting hostile command

facilities and other installations. The efficient exploitation of field artillery provides a powerful means of influencing the course of combat. These capabilities include the ability to: maneuver massed fire rapidly within a large area and on a wide front without change of position; displace quickly; regroup units to bring greater fire power on important sectors; deliver accurate fire with the appropriate calibre and type of ammunition on targets encountered under all conditions of visibility, weather, and terrain; deliver effective fires with or without adjustment." General Edward T. Williams, *Army Combat Forces Journal*, July, 1955.

214. Eisenhower, *Crusade in Europe*, p. 12.

215. Twenty-eight volumes had appeared by 1955 out of a total of some ninety projected.

216. An extensive listing, *Artillery Unit Histories*, Special Bibliography No. 6, was prepared by the Editorial Division, Department of Publications and Nonresident Training and published in mimeograph (1955) by the Library, Artillery and Guided Missile Center, Fort Sill, Okla. See also *Artillery in Combat*, FA School, 1944-45.

217. The U.S. Military Academy texts, *A Military History of World War II with Atlas*, 2 vols., admirably afford a compact yet comprehensive treatment.

218. Miller, *The United States Army in World War II: Guadalcanal,* pp. 299 f.

219. *Ibid.*, quoting 25th Div. G-2 Journal, 20 January, 1943.

220. *Field Artillery Journal*, XXXIII, 563-568.

221. *Artillery in Combat*, No. 1.

222. Mittelman, *Eight Stars to Victory*, pp. 91 f.

223. *A Military History of World War II*, II, 125.

224. Starr, *From Salerno to the Alps*, p. 62.

225. *Ibid.*, p. 159.

226. *Ibid.*, p. 452.

227. ". . . In the late spring of 1943 I selected an expert ordnance officer, Colonel William A. Borden, and directed him to work under me independently of normal War Department channels in the development and manufacture of weapons and improved techniques. His first efforts were directed to increase the effectiveness of our weapons against the Japanese in jungle fighting. As a result, the 105-mm. and 155-mm. mortars, flame throwers, ground rockets, improved launching devices, skid pans for towing heavy artillery in mud, improved bazooka ammunition, and colored smoke grenades were developed and produced and shipments to the theaters were expedited." Marshall, *op. cit.*, 256 f.

228. Smith, *The United States Army in World War II: Approach to the Philippines*, p. 470.

229. Lieutenant Colonel R. A. Evans, USMC, "Artillery on 'Nothing Atoll,' " *Field Artillery Journal*, XXXV (1945), 6-10.

CHAPTER 14

230. *Field Artillery Journal,* XXXV, 715.

231. *Ibid.,* XXXVI, 211.

232. *Ibid.,* XXXV, 11 ff. Lieutenant Bruce Bliven, Jr., FA, "How We Trained for D-Day." Republished from *The New Republic.*

233. *A Military History of World War II,* I, 361.

234. Lieutenant Colonel S. L. A. Marshall in *Field Artillery Journal,* XXXV, 13 ff.

235. "Eisenhower declared he would no longer employ heavy bombers against tactical targets. 'I don't believe they can be used in support of ground forces,' he explained. 'That's a job for artillery. I gave them a green light this time. But I promise you it's the last.' It was to be the last until we required another in the winter battles." Bradley, *A Soldier's Story,* p. 349.

236. See chapter opening.

237. Cole, *U.S. Army in World War II: Lorraine Campaign,* p. 367 f.; Dyer, *XII Corps,* p. 252.

238. *Cf.* "Big Bertha," long-range gun of World War I, named for Bertha Krupp, then principal owner of the arms works at Essen.

239. Colonel F. B. Porter, FA, in *Field Artillery Journal,* XXXV (1945), 545 ff.

240. Downey, *History of Dogs for Defense,* pp. 67 f.

241. *A Military History, op. cit.,* p. 510 n.

242. "Bastogne—an Artillery Classic." *Field Artillery Journal,* XXXV (1945), 718 ff.

243. Eisenhower report.

244. Eye-catching posters, urging troops to supply data on shell fire falling in their vicinity, were distributed. Decorated by a drawing of a bosomy beauty, the posters enjoined: "Check these points! If a German shell falls near you—determine the following: 1. The direction it came from. 2. The time of shelling. 3. The number of rounds. 4. The location (co-ordinates). Then report it!"

245. Maertz, *Luxembourg during the Rundstedt Offensive,* pp. 394 ff.

246. *Artillery in Combat,* pp. 109 f.

247. *U.S. Army in World War II: Okinawa,* p. 353.

248. *Ibid.,* p. 355.

249. Colonel Bernard S. Waterman, "The Battle of Okinawa, an Artillery Angle," in *Field Artillery Journal,* XXXV (1945), 526.

250. *U.S. Army in World War II, op. cit.,* p. 194.

251. "The first atom bomb, dropped on Hiroshima, caused an estimated 135,000 casualties, of whom 66,000 were killed, out of a population of 255,000. The second one, dropped on Nagasaki, caused 64,000 casualties, with 39,000 killed, out of a population of 195,000. The central portions of both cities were completely destroyed. Whole buildings were engulfed as

though a giant hand had pushed them. This destruction was on a scale that dwarfed the German air attack on Britain and even the Anglo-American saturation attacks on enemy cities such as Hamburg in 1943, and Tokio in 1945. More people were killed in Hiroshima alone than the total of civilians who were victims of air power during the whole war in England. Not only was the slaughter appalling, but terror caused the panic flight of the survivors. And all this was the result of but two bombs, one on each city, dropped in each case from a single airplane." U.S. Department of the Army. *Senior ROTC Manual,* 1947, Chapters 8 and 9.

CHAPTER 15

252. May, 1953, p. 11.

253. Barth, *Tropic Lightning and Taro Leaf,* p. 91.

254. Service of the combat arms in Korea was given battlefield coverage by able officers of the Historical Division, U.S. Army. Particularly vivid and detailed are accounts of artillery action in Colonel S. L. A. Marshall's *The River and the Gauntlet* and a book by Captain Russell A. Gugeler, Artillery, *Combat Actions in Korea,* in which he assembled his own and his colleagues' reports.

255. Barth, *op. cit.,* p. 60.

256. Marshall, "They Fought to Save Their Guns." *Army Combat Forces Journal,* May, 1953.

257. *Ibid.,* p. 15.

258. *Ibid.,* p. 11.

259. Read, "Our Guns Never Got Cold," *Saturday Evening Post,* April 7, 1951, p. 148.

260. McMahon, "The Day We Took 312," *Army Combat Forces Journal,* July, 1955, p. 49.

CHAPTER 16

261. Joseph and Stewart Alsop, *New York Herald Tribune,* 1955.

262. "But missilemen also have a hope that supports them: The ultimate weapon may produce the ultimate stalemate, a world in which all factions are afraid to start a war, and will take measures to keep it from starting accidentally." *Time,* January 30, 1956. See also *Reader's Digest,* March, 1956: Francis Vivian Drake, "Guided Missiles: Key to Peace."

263. Parson, *Guided Missiles in War and Peace.*

264. Parson, *op. cit.*

265. Parson, *Army,* March, 1956, p. 53.

266. Marshall, *Men Against Fire.*

Bibliography

Abbot, Brevet-Brigadier General Henry L. *Siege Artillery in the Campaigns against Richmond, with notes on the 15-inch gun.* New York: 1868.

Adams, Charles Francis. *Studies, Military and Diplomatic, 1775–1794.* New York: 1911.

Adams, Henry. *The War of 1812.* Maj. H. A. DeWeerd, ed. Washington: Infantry Journal Press, 1944.

Adams, John. *Warren-Adams Letters.* 2 vols. Boston: Massachusetts Historical Society, 1917, 1925.

Adye, Ralph Willett. *The Bombardier and Pocket Gunner.* First American edition. Boston: 1804.

Alcaraz, Ramon, ed. *The Other Side; or Notes for the History of the War between Mexico and the United States.* Albert C. Ramsey, translator. New York: 1850.

Aldrich, Thomas M. *The History of Battery A, First Regiment Rhode Island Light Artillery.* Providence: Snow & Farnham, 1904.

Alexander, General Edward Porter. *Military Memoirs of a Confederate.* New York: Charles Scribner's Sons, 1907.

Alger, Russell Alexander. *The Spanish-American War.* New York: Harper & Brothers, 1901.

American Historical Association. *Annual Reports.* Washington: 1885–1954.

Anderson, Captain Robert. *An Artillery Officer in the Mexican War, 1846–7.* New York: G. P. Putnam's Sons, 1911.

———. *Instruction for Field Artillery, Horse and Foot.* Translated from the French. Philadelphia: 1839.

———. *Evolutions of Field Batteries of Artillery.* New York: 1860.

Army, Army Combat Forces Journal.

Azoy, A. C. M. *They Were Not Afraid to Die.* Harrisburg, Pennsylvania: Military Service Publishing Company, 1939.

Babcock, Louis L. *The War of 1812 on the Niagara Frontier.* Buffalo: 1927.

Baker, Henry Moore. "Defense of American Commerce and the Spirit of American Unity," *Journal of American History,* V (1911), 17–32.

BALCH, THOMAS. *The French in America during the War of Independence of the United States, 1777–1783.* 2 vols. Philadelphia: 1895.

BARNEY, MARY CHASE. *A Biographical Memoir of the Late Commodore Joshua Barney.* Boston: 1832.

BARTH, GENERAL G. B. "Tropic Lightning and Taro Leaf in Korea, July 1950–May 1951." Mimeographed. 2nd ed. Athens, Greece: 1955.

Battles and Leaders of the Civil War. Robert Underwood Johnson, ed. 4 vols. New York: 1884–1887.

BEECHAM, CAPTAIN R. K. *Gettysburg: the Pivotal Battle of the Civil War.* Chicago: A. C. McClurg & Co., 1911.

BEIRNE, FRANCIS F. *The War of 1812.* New York: E. P. Dutton & Co., Inc., 1949.

BELCHER, HENRY. *The First American Civil War.* 2 vols. London: The Macmillan Co., 1911.

BELLAH, JAMES WARNER. *The Valiant Virginians.* New York: Ballantine Books, Inc., 1953.

BIGELOW, JOHN. *The Peach Orchard, Gettysburg, July 2, 1863.* Minneapolis: Kimball-Storer Co., 1910.

BIGELOW, MAJOR JOHN, JR. *The Campaign of Chancellorsville.* New Haven: Yale University Press, 1910.

———. *Reminiscences of the Santiago Campaign.* New York: Harper & Brothers, 1899.

BILL, ALFRED HOYT. *Rehearsal for Conflict: The War with Mexico, 1846–1848.* New York: Alfred A. Knopf, 1947.

———. *The Campaign of Princeton, 1776–1777.* Princeton, New Jersey: Princeton University Press, 1948.

BILLINGS, JOHN D. *Hard Tack and Coffee.* Boston: 1888.

———. *The History of the Tenth Massachusetts Battery of Light Artillery in the War of the Rebellion.* Boston: J. D. Billings, 1881.

BLACKFORD, LIEUTENANT COLONEL WILLIAM WILLIS. *War Years with Jeb Stuart.* New York: Charles Scribner's Sons, 1945.

BIRKHIMER, WILLIAM E. *Historical Sketch of the Organization, Administration, Matériel, and Tactics of the Artillery, United States Army.* Washington: 1884.

BISHOP, MAJOR GENERAL HARRY G. *Elements of Modern Field Artillery, U. S. Service.* Menasha, Wisconsin: G. Banta Publishing Co., 1914.

———. *Field Artillery, the King of Battles.* Boston: Houghton Mifflin Company, 1935.

BOATNER, MAJOR MARK M., III. *Army Lore.* Tokyo, Japan: 1954.

———. *Military Customs and Traditions.* New York: David McKay Company, Inc., 1956.

BOLTON, CHARLES K. *The Private Soldier under Washington.* New York: Charles Scribner's Sons, 1902.

BONSAL, STEPHEN. *When the French Were Here.* New York: Doubleday & Company, Inc., 1945.

BOURKE, CAPTAIN JOHN GREGORY. *On the Border with Crook.* New York: Charles Scribner's Sons, 1892.

BOWMAN, ALLEN. *The Morale of the American Revolutionary Army.* Washington: American Council on Public Affairs, 1943.

BRADLEY, GENERAL OMAR N. *A Soldier's Story.* New York: Henry Holt & Co., Inc., 1951.

BRADY, CYRUS TOWNSEND. *Northwestern Fights and Fighters.* New York: The McClure Company, 1907.

BROGAN, EVELYN. *Famous Horses of American History.* San Antonio, Texas: 1923.

BROOKS, NOAH. *Henry Knox, a Soldier of the Revolution.* New York: G. P. Putnam's Sons, 1899.

BRUSH, LIEUTENANT JAMES P. *A Short History of the Fifth Regiment, U. S. Artillery.* New York: 1895.

BUELL, AUGUSTUS C. *The Cannoneer; Recollections of Service in the Army of the Potomac.* Washington: 1890.

————. *History of Andrew Jackson, Pioneer, Patriot, Soldier, Politician, President.* 2 vols. New York: Charles Scribner's Sons, 1904.

BULLARD, LIEUTENANT GENERAL ROBERT L. *Personalities and Reminiscences.* New York: Doubleday, Doran & Company, Inc., 1925.

BURCHARD, JOHN ELY, ed. *Rockets, Guns and Targets.* Boston: Little, Brown & Company, 1948.

BURGOYNE, GENERAL JOHN. *A State of the Expedition from Canada as Laid before the House of Commons.* London: 1780.

BUTLER, CAPTAIN ALBAN B., JR. *"Happy Days!" A Humorous Narrative in Drawing of the Progress of American Arms, 1917–1919.* Washington: 1928.

CANADA ROYAL SOCIETY. *Procedures and Transactions,* vol. 5. Toronto: 1887.

CARLETON, CAPTAIN JAMES HENRY. *The Battle of Buena Vista.* New York: 1848.

CARRINGTON, GENERAL HENRY BEEBE. *Battles of the American Revolution.* New York: A. S. Barnes & Co., 1876.

CASTLE, HENRY A. *The Army Mule.* Indianapolis: Bobbs-Merrill Co., 1897.

CATTON, BRUCE. *Mr. Lincoln's Army.* New York: Doubleday & Company, Inc., 1951.

————. *The Glory Road.* New York: Doubleday & Company, Inc., 1952.

————. *A Stillness at Appomattox.* New York: Doubleday & Company, Inc., 1953.

CHADWICK, FRENCH ENSOR. *The Relations of the United States and Spain: the Spanish-American War.* New York: Charles Scribner's Sons, 1911.

CHAMBERLAIN, BREVET MAJOR-GENERAL JOSHUA LAWRENCE. *Five Forks.* Portland, Maine: 1902.

————. *The Passing of the Armies.* New York: G. P. Putnam's Sons, 1915.

CHAMBRUN, COLONEL J. A. DE. *The American Army in the European Conflict.* New York: 1919.

CHURCHILL, WINSTON S. *The Second World War.* 6 vols. Boston: Houghton Mifflin Company, 1948–1953.

CLARK, GENERAL MARK WAYNE. *Calculated Risk.* New York: Harper & Brothers, 1950.

CLEAVES, FREEMAN. *Rock of Chickamauga: the Life of General George H. Thomas.* Norman, Oklahoma: University of Oklahoma Press, 1948.

COFFIN, JOSHUA. *A Sketch of the History of Newburg, Newbury, Newburyport, and West Newbury.* Boston: 1845.

COMMAGER, HENRY STEELE, ed. *The Blue and the Gray.* 2 vols. Indianapolis: Bobbs-Merrill Company, 1950.

Confererate Veteran, The. 40 vols. Nashville, Tennessee: 1893–1932.

CONNELLEY, WILLIAM ELSEY. *Doniphan's Expedition.* Topeka, Kansas: Bryant & Douglas Bk. & Stationery Co., 1907.

COOKE, OLIVER D. *The Artillerist.* Hartford: 1821.

CRANE, STEPHEN. *Great Battles of the World.* Philadelphia: J. B. Lippincott Co., 1900.

CRUIKSHANK, ERNEST. *The Battle of Lundy's Lane.* Welland, Canada: 1943.

CULLUM, GEORGE W. *Biographical Register of the Officers and Graduates of the U. S. Military Academy.* 7 vols. Boston: 1891–1930.

CURTIS, EDWARD E. *The Organization of the British Army in the American Revolution.* New Haven: Yale University Press, 1926.

DAVIS, RICHARD HARDING. *The Cuban and Porto Rican Campaigns.* New York: Charles Scribner's Sons, 1898.

DEAN, GENERAL WILLIAM F. *General Dean's Story.* New York: The Viking Press, Inc., 1954.

DE SCHEEL, HEINRICH OTTO VON. Jonathan Williams, translator. *Tables and Plates Referred to in a New System of Artillery.* Copenhagen, Denmark: 1777.

DE VOTO, BERNARD. *The Year of Decision, 1846.* Boston: Little, Brown & Company, 1943.

Dictionary of American Biography. James T. Adams, ed. 21 vols. New York: 1928–1944.

Dictionary of American History. James T. Adams, ed. 5 vols. New York: 1940.

DOHLA, JOHANN CONRAD. *Tagebuch eines Bayreuther soldaten ... aus dem nordamerikanischen freiheitskrieg von 1777 bis 1783.* Bayreuth, Germany: 1913.

DOUBLEDAY, GENERAL ABNER. *Chancellorsville and Gettysburg.* New York: Charles Scribner's Sons, 1882.

DOUGLAS, MARJORY STONEMAN. *The Everglades.* New York: Rinehart & Co., Inc., 1947.

DOWNEY, FAIRFAX. "Reilly's Battery," *American Legion Magazine* (July, 1927).

————. "The Christening of the Guns," *Mentor* (January, 1930).

————. *Indian-Fighting Army.* New York: Charles Scribner's Sons, 1941.

DOWNEY, FAIRFAX. *War Horse*. New York: Dodd, Mead & Company, Inc., 1942.

————. *Dog of War*. New York: Dodd, Mead & Company, Inc., 1943.

————. *Jezebel the Jeep*. New York: Dodd, Mead & Company, Inc., 1944.

————. *Our Lusty Forefathers*. New York: Charles Scribner's Sons, 1947.

————. *History of Dogs for Defense*. New York: 1955.

DRAKE, SAMUEL ADAMS. *The Taking of Louisbourg, 1745*. Boston: Lothrop, Lee & Shepard Co., 1890.

————. *Bunker Hill: the Story Told in Letters from the Battle Field by British Officers Engaged*. Boston: 1875.

————. *The Campaign of Trenton, 1776–1777*. Boston: Lothrop, Lee & Shepard Co., 1895.

DUANE, WILLIAM. *A Military Dictionary*. Philadelphia: 1810.

DUNNE, FINLEY PETER. *Mr. Dooley in Peace and War*. Boston: Small, Maynard & Co., 1905.

DYER, ALEXANDER BRYDIE. *Handbook of Light Artillery*. New York: John Wiley & Sons, 1896.

EISENHOWER, DWIGHT D. *Crusade in Europe*. New York: Doubleday & Company, Inc., 1948.

ELIOT, ELLSWORTH. *Yale in the Civil War*. New Haven: Yale University Press, 1932.

ELLIOTT, MAJOR CHARLES WINSLOW. *Winfield Scott, the Soldier and the Man*. New York: The Macmillan Co., 1937.

ELLIS, GEORGE E. *History of the Battle of Bunker's (Breed's) Hill*. Boston: Lothrop, Lee & Shepard Co., 1875.

EVERHART, W. C. *Vicksburg National Military Park*. Washington: 1954.

FARROW, EDWARD S. *American Guns in the War with Germany*. New York: 1920.

FIEBEGER, COLONEL GUSTAVE JOSEPH. *The Campaign and Battle of Gettysburg*. West Point, New York: n.d.

Field Artillery; Basic. Harrisburg, Pennsylvania: Military Service Publishing Company, 1943.

Field Artillery Guide. Washington: Field Artillery Journal, 1942.

Field Artillery Journal.

FISKE, JOHN. *The Mississippi Valley in the Civil War*. Boston: Houghton, Mifflin Company, 1900.

FITZGERALD, DAVID. *In Memoriam. Gen. Henry J. Hunt, 1819–1889*. N.d.

FITZPATRICK, JOHN C. *The Spirit of the Revolution*. Boston: Houghton, Mifflin Company, 1923.

FLENLEY, RALPH. "A History of Artillery," *Journal of the Royal Artillery*, Vol. XLVII (1920–21.)

FLICK, ALEXANDER C. "General Henry Knox's Ticonderoga Expedition," *New York State Historical Association Proceedings*, Vol. XXVI, and *Quarterly Journal*, IX (1928), 119–135.

Florida Historical Quarterly. St. Augustine: 1908–1951.

FOOTNER, HULBERT. *Sailor of Fortune: the Life and Adventures of Commodore Barney, U. S. N.* New York: Harper & Brothers, 1940.

FORBES, EDWIN. *Life Studies of the Great Army.* New York: 1899.

FORCE, PETER. *American Archives,* 9 vols. Washington: 1837–1853.

FORTESCUE, HONORABLE JOHN WILLIAM. *A History of the British Army.* 13 vols. New York: The Macmillan Co., 1911–1935.

FOSTER, CAPTAIN PELL W., JR. *A Short History of Battery "B", 12th Field Artillery, Second Division, in the World War.* New York: 1921.

FOX, WILLIAM F. *Regimental Losses in the American Civil War.* Albany: 1889.

FREEMAN, DOUGLAS SOUTHALL. *George Washington, a Biography.* 6 vols. New York: Charles Scribner's Sons, 1948–1954.

———. *Lee's Lieutenants, a Study in Command.* 3 vols. New York: Charles Scribner's Sons, 1942–1944.

———. *R. E. Lee, a Biography.* 4 vols. New York: Charles Scribner's Sons, 1934–1935.

FRENCH, ALLEN. *The Day of Concord and Lexington.* Boston: Little, Brown & Company, 1925.

———. *The First Year of the American Revolution.* Boston: Houghton, Mifflin Company, 1934.

———. *The Siege of Boston.* New York: The Macmillan Co., 1911.

FRENCH, GENERAL SAMUEL G. *Two Wars.* Nashville, Tennessee: 1901.

FROTHINGHAM, RICHARD. *History of the Siege of Boston and of the Battles of Lexington, Concord and Bunker Hill.* Boston: Little, Brown & Co., 1851.

FROTHINGHAM, THOMAS G. *Guide to the Military History of the World War.* Boston: Little, Brown & Company, 1920.

FULLER, J. F. C. *Decisive Battles of the U.S.A.* New York: Harper & Brothers, 1942.

FURSE, COLONEL GEORGE ARMAND. *The Art of Marching.* London: 1901.

FYE, JOHN HARVEY, II. *History of the Sixth Field Artillery, 1798–1932.* Harrisburg, Pennsylvania: 1933.

GALTRY, CAPTAIN SIDNEY. *The Horse and the War.* London: 1918.

GANOE, WILLIAM ADDLEMAN. *The History of the United States Army.* New York: D. Appleton-Century Company, Inc., 1942.

GIBBON, BRIGADIER-GENERAL JOHN. *The Artillerist's Manual.* Washington: 1863.

GIBSON, GEORGE RUTLEDGE. *Journal of a Soldier under Kearny and Doniphan, 1846–1847.* Glendale, California: Arthur H. Clark Company, 1935.

GLEIG, GEORGE ROBERT. *A Narrative of the British Campaigns against Washington, Baltimore and New Orleans.* London: 1821.

GRANT, GENERAL ULYSSES S. *Personal Memoirs of U. S. Grant.* New York: Century Co., 1885–1886.

GREENE, FRANCIS VINTON. *The Revolutionary War and the Military Policy of the United States.* New York: Charles Scribner's Sons, 1911.

GREENWOOD, ISAAC J. *Captain John Manley.* Boston: Goodspeed's Book Shop, 1915.

GREER, ALLEN J. "The Roaring Guns from the Seven Days to Cold Harbor," *Field Artillery Journal,* XXVI (1935), 5–26.

GRINNELL, GEORGE BIRD. *The Fighting Cheyennes.* 2 vols. New York: Charles Scribner's Sons, 1915.

GUGELER, MAJOR RUSSELL A. *Combat Actions in Korea.* Washington: Combat Forces Press, 1954.

HAGEDORN, HERMAN. *The Bugle that Woke America.* New York: John Day Co., Inc., 1940.

HAMMERSLEY, COLONEL SYDNEY E. *History of a Wandering Cannon, Bulletin of the Fort Ticonderoga Museum.* Vol. I, No. 1 (1952).

HANSON, JOSEPH MILLS. *Bull Run Remembers.* Washington: National Capitol Publications, Inc., 1953.

HARBORD, MAJOR GENERAL JAMES G. *The American Army in France, 1917–1919.* Boston: Little, Brown & Company, 1936.

HART, ALBERT BUSHNELL, ed. *Commonwealth History of Massachusetts.* 5 vols. New York: The State History Company, 1930.

HASKELL, COLONEL FRANKLIN ARETAS. *The Battle of Gettysburg.* Madison, Wisconsin: Wisconsin State Historical Society, 1908.

HASKIN, BREVET MAJOR W. L. *History of the First Regiment of Artillery.* Portland, Maine: 1879.

HATCH, CHARLES E., JR. *Yorktown and the Siege of 1781.* National Park Service Historical Handbook, Series No. 14. Washington: 1952.

HEITMAN, FRANCIS B. *Historical Register of Officers of the Continental Army.* Washington: Rare Book Shop Publishing Company, 1914.

———. *Historical Register and Dictionary of the United States Army.* 2 vols. Washington: Superintendent of Documents, 1903.

HENDERSON, GEORGE F. R. *Stonewall Jackson and the American Civil War.* 2 vols. London and New York: Longmans, Green & Co., 1911.

HENRY, ROBERT SELPH. *The Story of the Mexican War.* Indianapolis: Bobbs-Merrill Company, 1950.

———. *The Story of the Confederacy.* Indianapolis: Bobbs-Merrill Company, 1931.

HENRY, CAPTAIN W. S. *Campaign Sketches of the War with Mexico.* New York: 1847.

HERR, MAJOR GENERAL JOHN K., and WALLACE, EDWARD S. *The Story of the U.S. Cavalry, 1775–1942.* Boston: Little, Brown & Co., 1953.

HEYMANN, FREDERICK G. *John Zizka and the Hussite Revolution.* Princeton, New Jersey: Princeton University Press, 1955.

History of the First Troop, Philadelphia City Cavalry, 1774–1874.

HITCHCOCK, MAJOR GENERAL ETHAN ALLEN. *Fifty Years in Camp and Field.* New York: G. P. Putnam's Sons, 1909.

HUGHES, JOHN T. *Doniphan's Expedition.* Cincinnati: 1847.

HUIDEKOPER, FREDERIC LOUIS. *Some Important Colonial Military Operations,* Historical Papers, No. 8. Washington: Society of Colonial Wars in the District of Columbia, 1914.

————. *The Military Unpreparedness of the United States.* New York: The Macmillan Co., 1915.

JACOBS, JAMES RIPLEY. *The Beginning of the U.S. Army, 1783–1812.* Princeton, New Jersey: Princeton University Press, 1947.

JAMES, MARQUIS. *Andrew Jackson, The Border Captain.* Indianapolis: Bobbs-Merrill Company, 1933.

JOHNSON, GERALD W. *Andrew Jackson, an Epic in Homespun.* New York: Minton, Balch & Company, 1927.

JOHNSON, BRIGADIER GENERAL RICHARD W. *A Soldier's Reminiscences in Peace and War.* Philadelphia: 1886.

JOHNSON, ROSSITER. *A History of the French War, Ending in the Conquest of Canada.* New York: 1882.

JOHNSTON, ABRAHAM R. *Marching with the Army of the West.* Ralph Paul Bieber, ed. Glendale, California: Arthur H. Clark Company, 1936.

JOHNSTON, HENRY P. *Yale and Her Honor Roll in the American Revolution.* 2 vols. New Haven: 1888.

————. *The Yorktown Campaign, 1781.* New York: 1881.

JOHNSTON, ROBERT MATTESON. *Bull Run: its Strategy and Tactics.* Boston: Houghton, Mifflin Company, 1913.

JOMINI, HENRI. *The Art of War.* Philadelphia: 1862.

JONES, JENKIN L. *An Artilleryman's Diary.* Madison, Wisconsin: Wisconsin History Commission, 1914.

Journal of the Military Service Institution of the United States. Vols. 1–61. New York: 1880–1917.

Journal of the Royal Artillery. Woolwich, England: 1858–1905.

Journal of the U. S. Artillery and Coast Artillery Journal, Vols. 1–90. Fortress Monroe, Virginia, 1892–1942.

KENDALL, GEORGE WILKINS, and NEBEL, CARL. *The War between the United States and Mexico.* New York: 1851.

KIP, LAWRENCE. *Army Life on the Pacific.* New York: William Abbatt, 1859, 1914.

KIRK, HYLAND C. *Heavy Guns and Light: a History of the 4th New York Heavy Artillery.* New York: 1890.

KNOLLENBERG, BERNHARD. *Washington and the Revolution: a Reappraisal.* New York: The Macmillan Co., 1940.

KOSIUSZKO, GENERAL TADEUSZ. *Manual* (with notes by Jonathan Williams). New York: 1808.

KREDEL, FRITZ, and TODD, FREDERICK P. *Soldiers of the American Army, 1775–1954.* Chicago: Henry Regnery Co., 1954.

LALLEMAND, H. *A Complete Treatise upon Artillery.* New York: 1829.

LAMB, ROGER. *An Original and Authentic Journal of Occurrences During the Late American War.* Dublin, Ireland: 1809.

LANDERS, COLONEL H. L. *The Virginia Campaign and the Blockade and Siege of Yorktown, 1781.* Senate Document No 273. Washington: 1931.

LANDOR, ARNOLD HENRY SAVAGE. *China and the Allies.* 2 vols. New York: Charles Scribner's Sons, 1901.

LEAKE, ISAAC Q. *Memoir of the Life and Times of General John Lamb.* Albany: 1857.

LEE, ROBERT E., JR. *Recollections and Letters of General Robert E. Lee.* New York: Doubleday, Doran & Company, Inc., 1924.

LEECH, MARGARET. *Reveille in Washington.* New York: Harper & Brothers, 1941.

LEFFERTS, CHARLES M. *Uniforms of the American, British, French and German Armies in the War of the American Revolution, 1775–1783.* New York: New York Historical Society, 1926.

LEWIS, LLOYD. *Captain Sam Grant.* Boston: Little, Brown & Co., 1950.

———. *Sherman, Fighting Prophet.* New York: Harcourt, Brace & Company, Inc., 1832.

Life.

LIGGETT, LIEUTENANT GENERAL HUNTER. *Commanding an American Army; Recollections of the World War.* Boston: Houghton, Mifflin Company, 1925.

LONG ISLAND HISTORICAL SOCIETY. *Memoirs.* Vols. 2 and 3. Brooklyn: 1869 and 1878.

LOSSING, BENSON JOHN. *The American Revolution and the War of 1812.* 3 vols. New York: 1875.

———. *The Pictorial Field-Book of the War of 1812.* New York: Harper & Brothers, 1869.

Louisbourg Journals, 1745. Louis Effingham de Forest, ed. New York: Society of Colonial Wars of the State of New York, 1932.

LOXLEY, BENJAMIN. "Account of His Ancestors, of His Parents, and of Himself and Family." Typescript from original (now lost) in possession of Charles Morris Loxley. Philadelphia: 1789.

LYKES, R. W. *Petersburg National Military Park, Virginia.* Washington: 1951.

MACARTHUR, CHARLES. *War Bugs.* Garden City, New York: Doubleday, Doran & Company, Inc., 1929.

MCENIRY, BLANCHE MARIE. *American Catholics in the War with Mexico.* Washington: 1937.

MAERTZ, JOSEF. *Luxemburg in der Rundstedt-Offensive.* Luxembourg: 1948.

MANUCY, ALBERT. *Artillery through the Ages.* National Park Service Interpretive Series, History No. 3. Washington: 1949.

MARCH, GENERAL PEYTON C. *The Nation at War.* Garden City, New York: Doubleday, Doran & Company, Inc., 1932.

MARSHALL, GENERAL GEORGE CATLETT. *General Marshall's Report: The Winning of the War in Europe and the Pacific*. New York: Simon & Schuster, Inc., 1945.

MARSHALL, COLONEL SAMUEL LYMAN ATWOOD. *Bastogne*. Washington: Infantry Journal Press, 1946.

———. *Blitzkrieg*. New York: William Morrow & Co., Inc., 1940.

———. *Men Against Fire*. Washington: Infantry Journal Press, 1947.

———. *The River and the Gauntlet*. New York: William Morrow & Co., Inc., 1953.

MATHER, REV. COTTON. *Military Duties, Recommended to an Artillery Company*. Boston: 1687.

MAURY, GENERAL DABNEY HERNDON. *Recollections of a Virginian in the Mexican, Indian and Civil Wars*. New York: Charles Scribner's Sons, 1894.

MAY, MAJOR E. S. *Achievements of Field Artillery*. Woolwich, England: 1893.

MERCER, PHILIP. *The Life of the Gallant Pelham*. Macon, Georgia: J. W. Burke Company, 1929.

MERIDITH, ROY. *The American Wars; a Pictorial History from Quebec to Korea, 1755–1953*. Cleveland: The World Publishing Company, 1955.

MERRIAM, ROBERT E. *Dark December*. Chicago: The Ziff-Davis Publishing Company, 1947.

MIDDLEBROOK, LOUIS F. *Salisbury Connecticut Cannon, Revolutionary War*. Salem, Massachusetts: Newcomb & Gauss Co., 1935.

MIERS, EARL SCHENCK, and BROWN, RICHARD A., eds. *Gettysburg*. New Brunswick, New Jersey: Rutgers University Press, 1948.

MILES, GENERAL NELSON A. *Recollections of General Nelson A. Miles*. Chicago: 1896.

Military Affairs. "Guide to the Writing of American Military History." Appendix, Vol. XIV [No. 4].

Military Collector and Historian Journal.

MILLIS, WALTER. *The Martial Spirit*. Boston: Houghton, Mifflin Company, 1931.

———. *The Road to War*. Boston: Houghton, Mifflin Company, 1935.

MITCHELL, LIEUTENANT COLONEL JOSEPH B. *Decisive Battles of the Civil War*. New York: G. P. Putnam's Sons, 1955.

MITTELMAN, CAPTAIN JOSEPH B. *Eight Stars to Victory; a History of the Veteran Ninth U. S. Infantry Division*. Washington: 1948.

MONROE, JOHN ALBERT. *The Rhode Island Artillery at the First Battle of Bull Run*. Providence: 1878.

MONTROSS, LYNN. *Rag, Tag and Bobtail; the Story of the Continental Army, 1775–1783*. New York: Harper & Brothers, 1952.

MOORE, EDWARD A. *The Story of a Cannoneer under Stonewall Jackson*. Lynchburg, Virginia: J. P. Bell Co., 1910.

MOORE, SAMUEL T. *America and the World War*. New York: Greenberg, Publisher, Inc., 1937.

MORDECAI, BREVET MAJOR ALFRED. *Artillery for the United States Land Service*. Washington: 1849.

MORETTI, ONORIO, and DANFORD, ROBERT M. *Notes on Training Field Artillery Details*.

MORRIS, RICHARD B. *Encyclopedia of American History*. New York: Harper & Brothers, 1953.

MORTON, JOHN WATSON. *Forrest's Artillery*. Nashville, Tennessee: 1909.

MÜLLER, JOHN. *Treatise of Artillery*. London: 1756 and New York: 1779.

MURDOCK, HAROLD. *The Nineteenth of April, 1775*. Boston: Houghton Mifflin Company, 1925.

————. *Bunker Hill; Notes and Queries on a Famous Battle*. Boston: 1927.

NEESE, GEORGE M. *Three Years in the Confederate Horse Artillery*. New York: Neale Pub. Co., 1911.

NICKERSON, HOFFMAN. *The Turning Point of the Revolution; or, Burgoyne in America*. Boston: Houghton Mifflin Company, 1928.

Niles Weekly Register. Baltimore: 1811–1849.

NYE, W. S. *Carbine and Lance: The Story of Old Fort Sill*. Norman, Oklahoma: University of Oklahoma Press, 1937.

OBERHOLTZER, ELLIS PAXSON. *A History of the United States Since the Civil War*. 5 vols. New York: The Macmillan Co., 1937.

OSWANDEL, J. JACOB. *Notes on the Mexican War*. Philadelphia: 1885.

OTTOSEN, MAJOR P. H. *Trench Artillery, A.E.F.* Boston: Lothrop, Lee & Shepard Company, 1931.

PAGE, THOMAS NELSON. *The Burial of the Guns*. New York: Charles Scribner's Sons, 1894.

PALFREY, F. W. *Antietam and Fredericksburg (Campaigns of the Civil War)*. New York: Charles Scribner's Sons, 1882.

PALMER, COLONEL FREDERICK. *Our Greatest Battle (the Meuse-Argonne)*. New York: Dodd, Mead & Company, Inc., 1919.

PARGELLIS, STANLEY M. *Lord Loudoun in North America*. New Haven: Yale University Press, 1933.

————. (ed.). *Military Affairs in North America, 1748–1765*. New York: D. Appleton-Century Company, Inc., 1936.

PARIS, LOUIS PHILIPPE ALBERT D'ORLEANS, COMTE DE. *History of the Civil War in America*. 4 vols. Philadelphia: 1875–1888.

PARKER, CAPTAIN JOHN HENRY. *History of the Gatling Gun Detachment, Fifth Army Corps, at Santiago*. Kansas City: Franklin Hudson Publishers, 1898.

PARKMAN, FRANCIS. *A Half-Century of Conflict*. 2 vols. Boston: Little, Brown & Company, 1892.

PARSON, MAJOR NELS A. JR. *Guided Missiles in War and Peace*. Cambridge, Massachusetts: Harvard University Press, 1956.

PARTON, JAMES. *Life of Andrew Jackson.* 3 vols. New York: D. Appleton & Company, 1861.

PAXSON, FREDERICK L. *History of the American Frontier, 1763–1893.* Boston: Houghton Mifflin Company, 1924.

PELL, S. H. P. *Fort Ticonderoga.* Ticonderoga, New York: 1954.

PEMBERTON, JOHN. *General Pemberton, Defender of Vicksburg.* Chapel Hill, North Carolina: University of North Carolina Press, 1942.

PEPPERRELL, SIR WILLIAM. *The Journal of Sir William Pepperrell, Kept during the Expedition against Louisbourg, March 24—August 22, 1745.* Charles Henry Lincoln, ed. Worcester, Massachusetts: American Antiquarian Society, 1910.

PERSHING, GENERAL JOHN J. *My Experiences in the World War.* New York: Frederick A. Stokes Company, 1931.

PHILLIPS, MAJOR THOMAS R., ed. *Roots of Strategy.* Harrisburg, Pennsylvania: Military Service Publishing Company, 1940.

Photographic History of the Civil War, ed. Francis Trevelyan Miller, 10 vols. New York: Review of Reviews Co., 1911.

POMEROY, SETH. *Journals and Papers.* Louis Effingham de Forest, ed. New York: Society of Colonial Wars, 1926.

PRATT, FLETCHER. *Eleven Generals; Studies in American Command.* New York: William Sloane, Associates, Inc., 1949.

———. *Ordeal by Fire.* New York: Harrison Smith & Robert Haas, Inc., 1935.

RAIKES, CAPTAIN G. A. *The History of the Honourable Artillery Company.* 2 vols. London: 1878.

RAMSDELL, CHARLES M. "General Robert E. Lee's Horse Supply, 1862–1865." *American Historical Review.* Vol. 35.

Reader's Digest.

REED, SAMUEL ROCKWELL. *The Vicksburg Campaign.* Cincinnati: 1882.

Revue d'Artillerie, vols. 1–24. Paris, France: 1872–1914.

RHODES, JAMES FORD. *History of the Civil War.* New York: The Macmillan Company, 1917.

ROBERTS, KENNETH (comp.) *March to Quebec.* New York: Doubleday, Doran & Company, Inc., 1938.

ROBINS, BENJAMIN. *New Principles of Gunnery.* London: 1742.

RODENBOUGH, THEOPHILUS F., and HASKINS, WM. L., eds. *The Army of the United States: Historical Sketches of Staff and Line.* New York: Charles E. Merrill Co., 1896.

ROE, ALFRED SEELYE. *The Ninth New York Heavy Artillery.* Worcester, Massachusetts: A. S. Roe, 1899.

ROOSEVELT, THEODORE. *The Rough Riders.* New York: Charles Scribner's Sons, 1899.

ROPES, JOHN CODMAN. *The Story of the Civil War.* 4 vols. New York: 1894-1913.

SAINT-REMY, PIERRE SURIREY DE. *Mémoires d'Artillerie.* Amsterdam, Holland: 1702.

SARGENT, HERBERT H. *The Campaign of Santiago de Cuba.* 3 vols. Chicago: A. C. McClurg & Company, 1907.

SCHARF, J. THOMAS. *History of Maryland from the Earliest Period to the Present Day.* 3 vols. Baltimore: 1879.

SCOTT, BRIGADIER GENERAL ERNEST DARIUS. "Gunner in Luzon." *Field Artillery Journal,* Vols. 29 and 30.

SCOTT, GENERAL WINFIELD. *Memoirs of Lieutenant-General Scott, LL.D.* New York: 1864.

SEMMES, LIEUTENANT RAPHAEL. *Service Afloat and Ashore during the Mexican War.* Cincinnati: 1851.

SHANNON, FRED ALBERT. *The Organization and Administration of the Union Army, 1861–1865.* 2 vols. Glendale, California: Arthur H. Clark Company, 1928.

SHERIDAN, GENERAL PHILIP H. *Personal Memoirs of P. H. Sheridan.* 2 vols. New York: 1888.

SMITH, CAPTAIN E. KIRBY. *To Mexico with Scott.* Cambridge, Massachusetts: 1917.

SMITH, JUSTIN H. ed. *The Historie Booke.* (*Ancient and Honorable Artillery Company.*) Boston: 1903.

——————. *Our Struggle for the Fourteenth Colony: Canada and The American Revolution.* 2 vols. New York: G. P. Putnam's Sons, 1907.

——————. *The War with Mexico.* 2 vols. New York: The Macmillan Company, 1919.

SNOW, MAJOR GENERAL WILLIAM J. *The Functions and Training of Field Artillery.* Manuscript. Washington: 1908.

——————. *Signposts of Experience; World War Memoirs.* Washington: U. S. Field Artillery Association, 1941.

Soldier's Handbook. Harrisburg, Pennsylvania: Military Service Publishing Company, 1941.

Southern Historical Society Papers, Vols. 1–50. Richmond, Virginia: 1914–1953.

SPAULDING, COLONEL OLIVER LYMAN, JR. *The United States Army in War and Peace.* New York: G. P. Putnam's Sons, 1937.

——————. *Notes on Field Artillery for Officers of All Arms.* Leavenworth, Kansas: U. S. Cavalry Association, 1914.

—————— and NICKERSON, HOFFMAN, and WRIGHT, COLONEL J. W. *Warfare.* New York: Harcourt, Brace & Company, 1925.

STARR, LIEUTENANT COLONEL CHESTER G. *From Salerno to the Alps: a History of the Fifth Army, 1943–1945.* Washington: 1948.

STEELE, MAJOR MATTHEW FORNEY. *American Campaigns.* 2 vols. Washington: 1943.

STEVENS, WILLIAM. *System of Discipline for the Artillery.* New York: 1797.

STILES, EZRA. *Literary Diary.* New Haven: Yale University Press, 1928.

STILES, MAJOR ROBERT. *Four Years under Marse Robert*. New York: 1903.

STILWELL, JOSEPH WARREN. *Papers*. New York: William Sloane, Associates, Inc., 1948.

STIMSON, HENRY LEWIS and BUNDY, McGEORGE. *On Active Service in Peace and War*. New York: Harper & Brothers, 1948.

The Story of the Campaign and Siege of Yorktown. Senate Document No. 318. Washington: 1931.

STRYKER, WILLIAM S. *The Battle of Monmouth*. Princeton, New Jersey: Princeton University Press, 1927.

———. *The Battles of Trenton and Princeton*. Boston: 1898.

SWANSON, NEIL. *The Perilous Fight*. New York: Farrar, Strauss & Co., Inc., 1945.

THOMAS, SHIPLEY. *The History of the A.E.F.* New York: George H. Doran Company, 1920.

THOMASON, CAPTAIN JOHN W. *Fix Bayonets!* New York: Charles Scribner's Sons, 1926.

TIDBALL, GENERAL JOHN C. *Manual of Heavy Artillery Service*. Washington: 1891.

———. *Remarks upon the Organization, Command and Employment of Field Artillery during War; Based on Experiences of the Civil War, 1861–5*. Typescript. Library, Artillery and Guided Missile Center, Fort Sill, Oklahoma: 1907.

Time.

TREVELYAN, SIR GEORGE OTTO. *The American Revolution*. 4 vols. London and New York: 1921.

TRUMBULL, JOHN. *Autobiography*. New Haven: Yale University Press, 1953.

TRUSCOTT, GENERAL LUCIAN KING. *Command Missions; a Personal Story*. New York: E. P. Dutton & Co., Inc., 1954.

TUCKER, GLENN. *Poltroons and Patriots*. 2 vols. Indianapolis: Bobbs-Merrill Co., Inc., 1954.

TUNIS, EDWIN. *Weapons; a Pictorial History*. Cleveland: The World Publishing Company, 1954.

TYLER, LIEUTENANT DANIEL, trans. *A System of Exercise and Instruction of Field Artillery*. 1826.

U. S. ARMY, ADJUTANT GENERAL'S OFFICE. *Army Song Book*. Washington: 1941.

U. S. DEPARTMENT OF THE ARMY. *Senior R.O.T.C. Manual*. Washington: 1947.

U. S. DEPARTMENT OF THE ARMY, THE ARTILLERY CENTER, FORT SILL, OKLA. *Test of the 280-mm. Gun*. Fort Sill, Oklahoma: 1953.

U. S. DEPARTMENT OF THE ARMY, THE ARTILLERY AND GUIDED MISSILE CENTER. *Artillery Unit Histories, Special Bibliography No. 6*. Fort Sill, Oklahoma: 1955.

———. *Famous Artillery Quotations*. Fort Sill, Oklahoma. (n.d.)

U. S. DEPARTMENT OF THE ARMY, FIELD ARTILLERY SCHOOL. *Artillery in Combat.* Fort Sill, Oklahoma: 1944–1945.

――――. *Battery Officers' Advanced Course. Theses, 1927–28.*

――――. *Instruction Memorandum; History of the Development of Field Artillery Matériel.* Fort Sill, Oklahoma: 1941.

U. S. DEPARTMENT OF THE ARMY, THE INFANTRY SCHOOL. *Selected Readings in American Military History.* 3 vols. Fort Benning, Georgia: 1953.

U. S. DEPARTMENT OF THE ARMY, OFFICE OF THE CHIEF OF MILITARY HISTORY. *Army Lineage Books.* Washington: 1954.

――――. *The History of Military Mobilization in the United States.* Washington: 1953.

――――. (LERIWILL, LIEUTENANT COLONEL LEONARD L.) *The Personnel Replacement System in the United States Army.* 2 vols. Washington: 1952.

――――. *The United States Army in World War II.* 28 vols. Washington: 1947–1955.

U. S. ORDNANCE DEPARTMENT. *A Report on the Characteristics, Scope of Utility, etc. of Railway Artillery.* 2 vols. Washington: 1922.

U. S. DEPARTMENT OF THE ARMY, PUBLIC INFORMATION DIVISION. *The Medal of Honor of the United States Army.* Washington: 1948.

U. S. DEPARTMENT OF THE ARMY, U. S. MILITARY ACADEMY. *A Military History of World War II.* COLONELS T. DODSON STAMPS and VINCENT J. ESPOSITO, eds. 2 vols. West Point, New York: 1953.

――――. *A Short Military History of World War I.* COLONELS T. DODSON STAMPS and VINCENT J. ESPOSITO, eds. West Point. New York: 1950.

――――. *Summaries of Selected Military Campaigns.* West Point, New York: 1953.

U. S. SHILOH NATIONAL MILITARY PARK COMMISSION. (REED, MAJOR D. W.) *The Battle of Shiloh.* Washington: 1902.

U. S. WAR DEPARTMENT. *The War of the Rebellion: Official Records.* 130 vols. Washington: 1880–1901.

UPSON, WILLIAM HAZLETT. *Me and Henry and the Artillery.* Garden City, New York: Doubleday, Doran & Company, Inc., 1928.

UPTON, GENERAL EMORY. *The Military Policy of the United States.* 64th Cong. 1st sess. S. Doc. No. 379. Washington: Superintendent of Documents, 1917.

VAN DE WATER, FREDERIC F. *Lake Champlain and Lake George.* Indianapolis: Bobbs-Merrill Company, Inc., 1946.

VAN EVERY, DALE. *The A.E.F. in Battle.* New York: D. Appleton-Century Company, Inc., 1928.

WALLACE, EDWARD S. *General William Jenkins Worth; Monterey's Forgotten Hero.* Dallas: Southern Methodist University Press, 1953.

WALLACE, LEWIS. *Lew Wallace; an Autobiography.* 2 vols. New York: 1906.

WALLACE, WILLARD M. *Appeal to Arms; a Military History of the American Revolution.* New York: Harper & Brothers, 1951.

WALTON, WILLIAM. *The Army and Navy of the United States from the Period of the Revolution to the Present Day*. Part 4, Sec. 5. Artillery. Boston: 1889–1896.

WARD, CHRISTOPHER. *The War of the Revolution*. 2 vols. New York: The Macmillan Co., 1952.

WASHINGTON, GEORGE. *The Writings of George Washington from the Original Manuscript Sources, 1745–1799*. John C. Fitzpatrick, ed. 39 vols. Washington: 1931–44.

——. *Writings*. Worthington Chauncey Ford, ed. 14 vols. New York: 1889–1893.

WELLMAN, PAUL I. *Death on Horseback; Seventy Years of War for the American West*. Philadelphia: J. B. Lippincott Company, 1947.

WILCOX, CADMUS M. *History of the Mexican War*. Washington: 1892.

WILDES, HARRY E. *Valley Forge*. New York: The Macmillan Co., 1938.

WILEY, BELL IRWIN. *The Life of Billy Yank*. Indianapolis: Bobbs-Merrill Company, Inc., 1952.

——. *The Life of Johnny Reb*. Indianapolis: Bobbs-Merrill Company, Inc., 1943.

WILKESON, FRANK. *Recollections of a Private Soldier in the Army of the Potomac*. New York: 1887.

WILSON, LIEUTENANT A. W. *The Story of the Gun*. Woolwich, England: 1944.

WILSON, GENERAL JAMES H. *Under the Old Flag: Recollections of Military Operations in the War for the Union, the Spanish War, the Boxer Rebellion, etc.* 2 vols. New York: Daniel Appleton Co., 1912.

WISE, JENNINGS CROPPER. *The Long Arm of Lee*. 2 vols. Lynchburg, Virginia: J. P. Bell Co., 1915.

——. *Gunnery: an Elementary Treatise*. Richmond, Virginia: B. F. Johnson Pub. Co., 1912.

WOOD, WILLIAM. *The Great Fortress: a Chronicle of Louisbourg, 1720–1760*. Toronto: 1922.

WRIGHT, COLONEL JOHN W. "Notes on the Continental Army." *William and Mary Quar.*, 1931–1933.

WYMAN, WALKER D. *The Wild Horse of the West*. Caldwell, Idaho: Caxton Printers, Ltd., 1945.

Yorktown, Climax of the Revolution. CHARLES E. HATCH, JR., and THOMAS M. PITKIN, eds. National Park Service. Washington: 1941.

YOUNG, JESSE BOWMAN. *The Battle of Gettysburg*. New York: Harper & Brothers, 1913.

Index